This is the last page.

In keeping with the original Japanese comic format, this book reads from right to left—so action, sound effects, and word balloons are completely reversed. This preserves the orientation of the original artwork—plus, it's fun! Check out the diagram shown here to get the hang of things, and then turn to the other side of the book to get started!

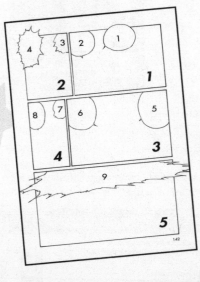

Voice Over!
Seiyu Academy

4

Vol.4
Story & Art by
Maki Minami

TECHNICAL ADVISORS
Yoichi Kato, Kaori Kagami, Ayumi Hashidate,
Ayako Harino and Touko Fujitani

Voice Over! Seiyu Academy

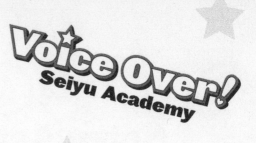

Vol. 4

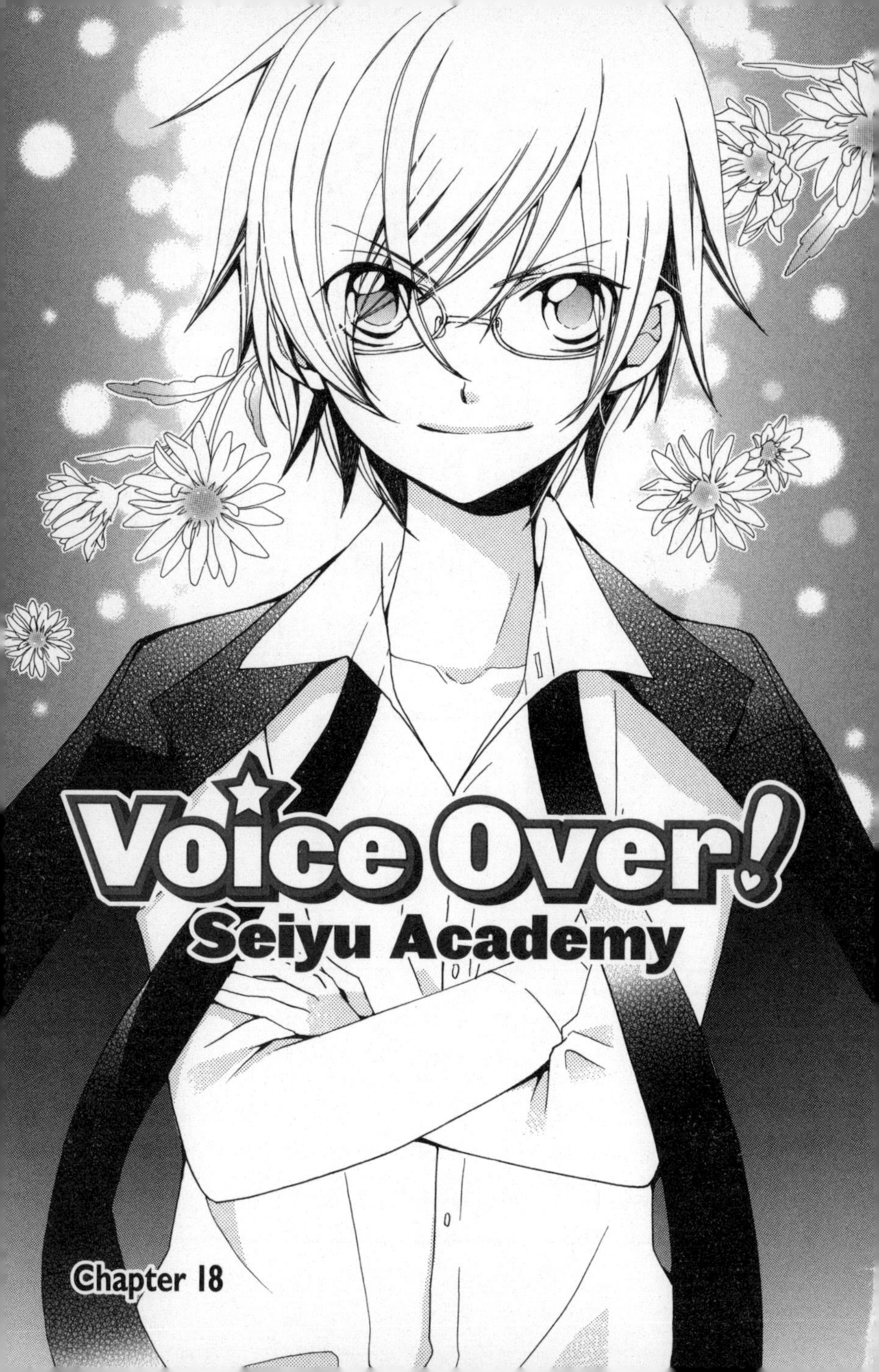
Voice Over!
Seiyu Academy
Chapter 18

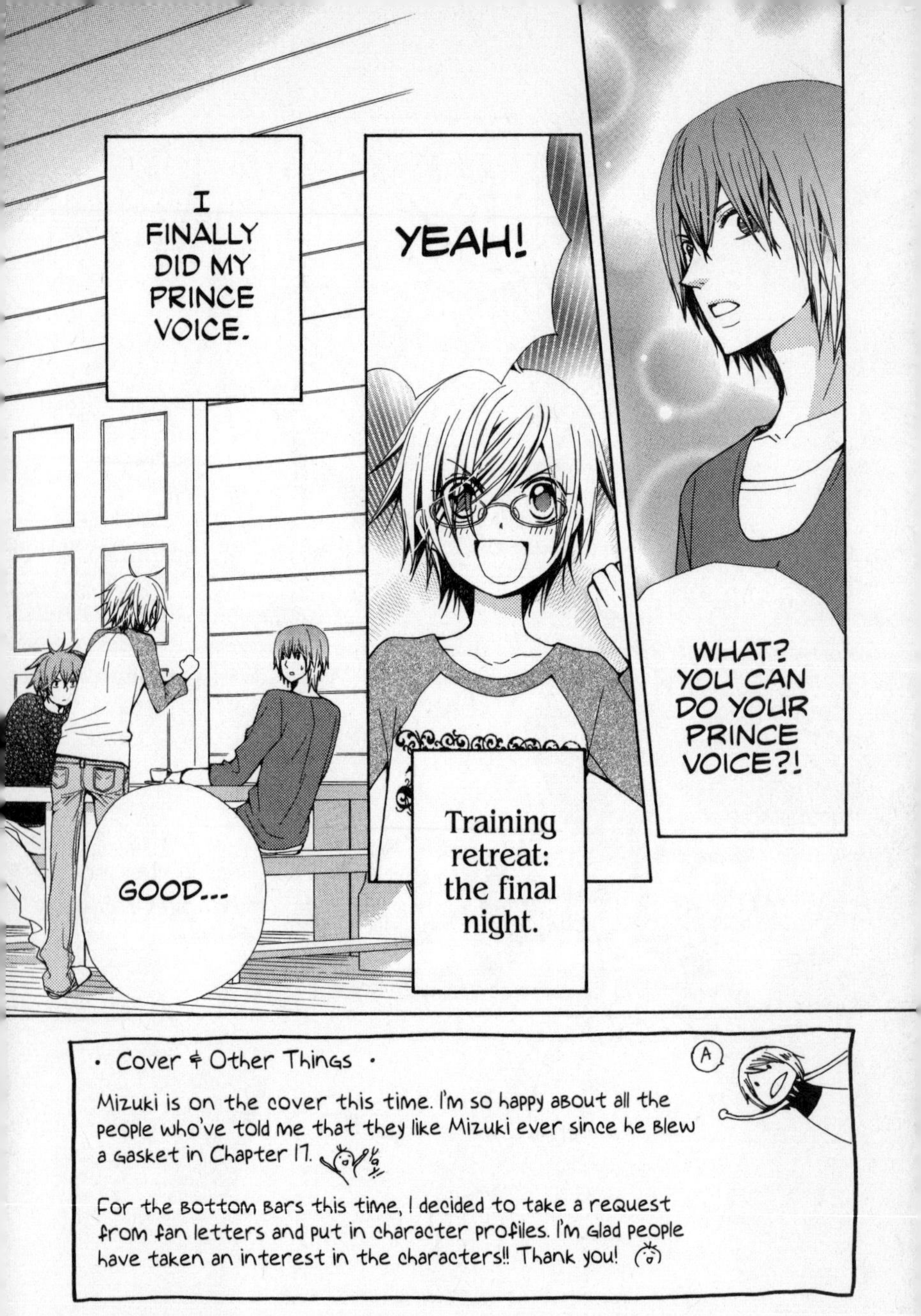
WHAT? YOU CAN DO YOUR PRINCE VOICE?!
YEAH!
Training retreat: the final night.
I FINALLY DID MY PRINCE VOICE.
GOOD...

• Cover & Other Things •

Mizuki is on the cover this time. I'm so happy about all the people who've told me that they like Mizuki ever since he blew a gasket in Chapter 17.

For the bottom bars this time, I decided to take a request from fan letters and put in character profiles. I'm glad people have taken an interest in the characters!! Thank you!

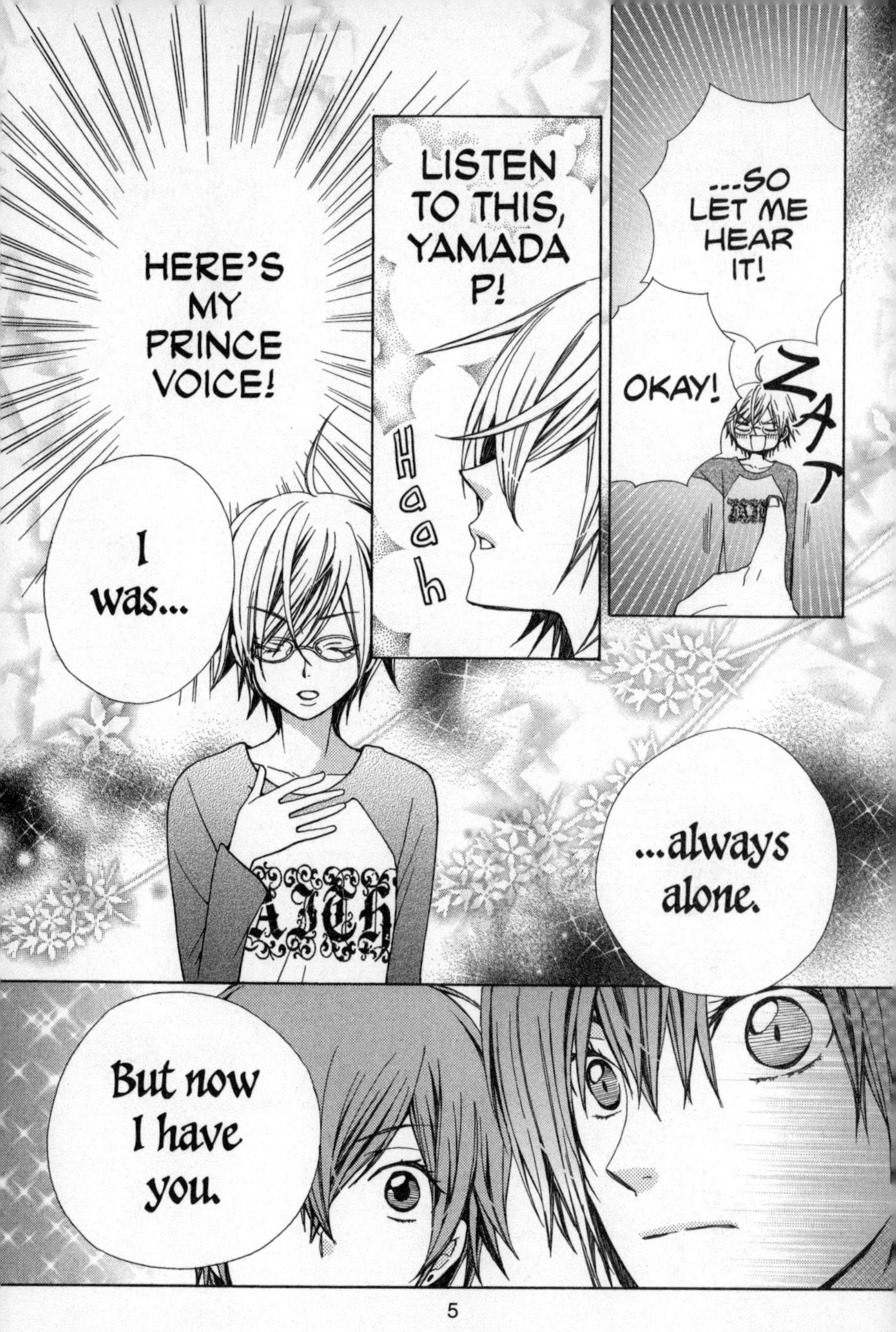
...SO LET ME HEAR IT!
OKAY!
ZAT
LISTEN TO THIS, YAMADA P!
Haah
HERE'S MY PRINCE VOICE!
I was...
...always alone.
But now I have you.

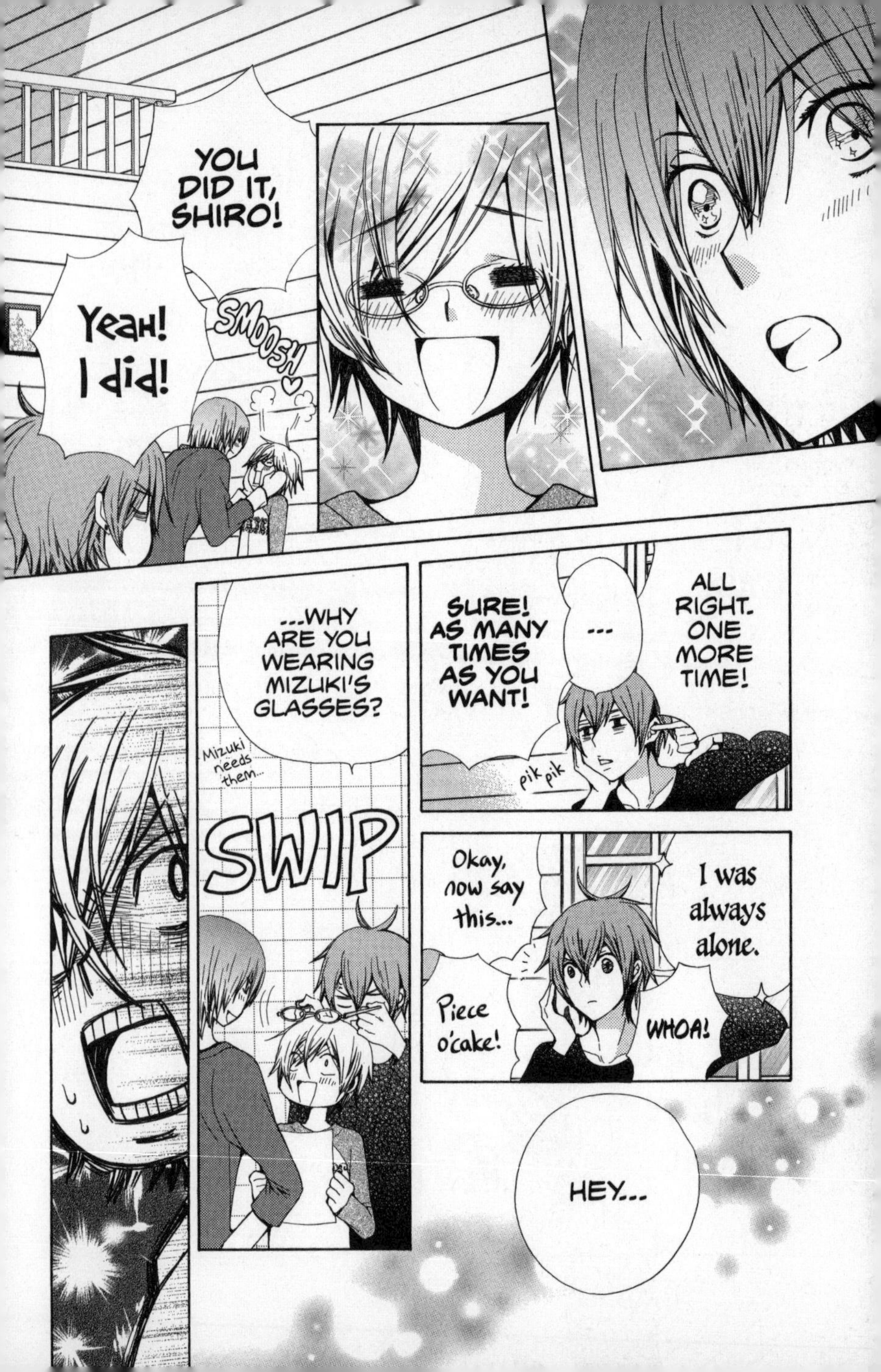
YOU DID IT, SHIRO!
Yeah! I did!
SMOOSH
ALL RIGHT. ONE MORE TIME!
...
SURE! AS MANY TIMES AS YOU WANT!
pik pik
I was always alone.
Okay, now say this...
WHOA!
Piece o'cake!
HEY...
...WHY ARE YOU WEARING MIZUKI'S GLASSES?
Mizuki needs them...
SWIP

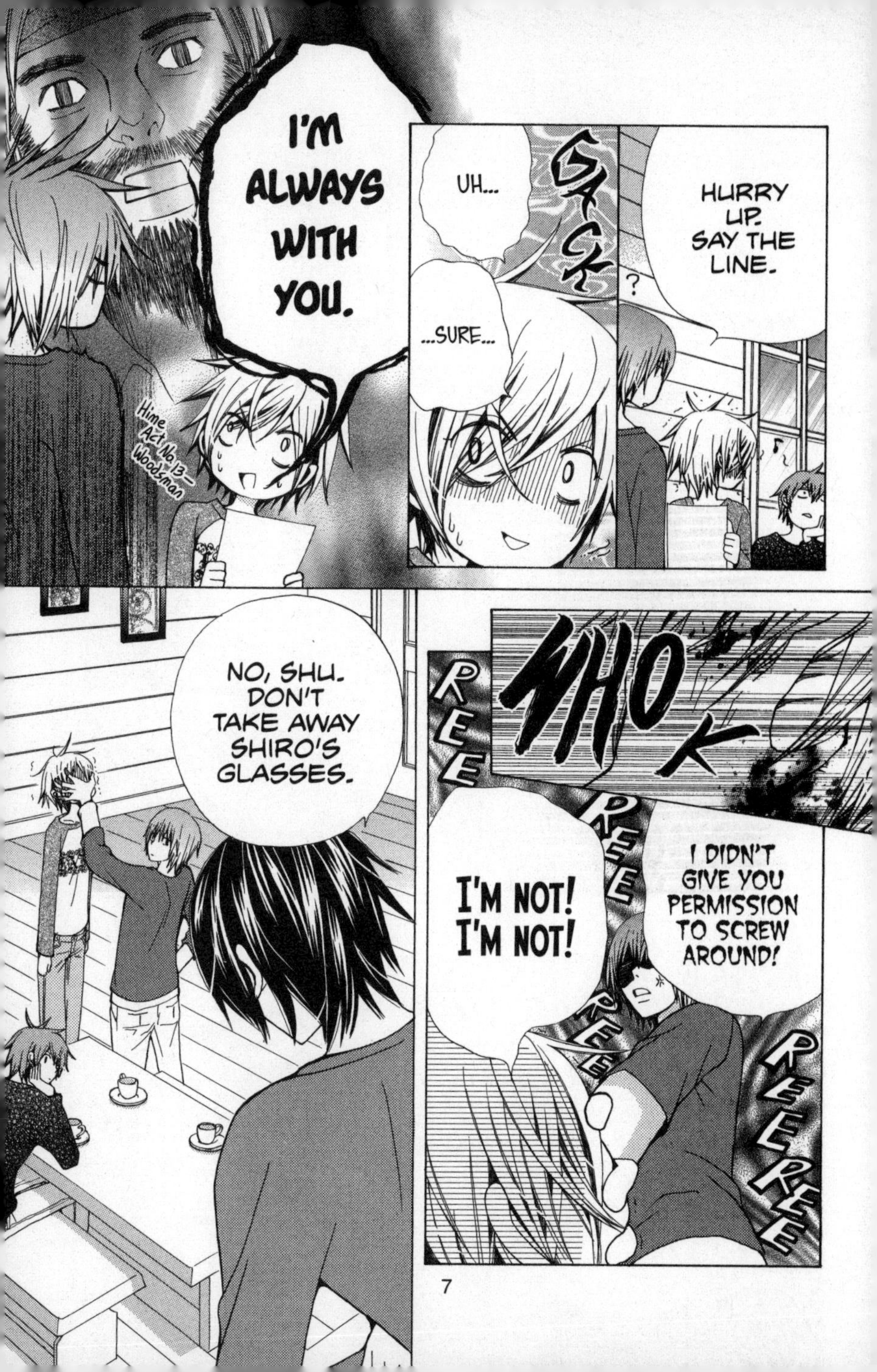
HURRY UP. SAY THE LINE.
?
UH...
GACK
...SURE...
I'M ALWAYS WITH YOU.
Hime Act No. 13—Woodsman
WHOK
REE REE REE
I DIDN'T GIVE YOU PERMISSION TO SCREW AROUND!
REE REE
REE REE REE
I'M NOT! I'M NOT!
NO, SHU. DON'T TAKE AWAY SHIRO'S GLASSES.

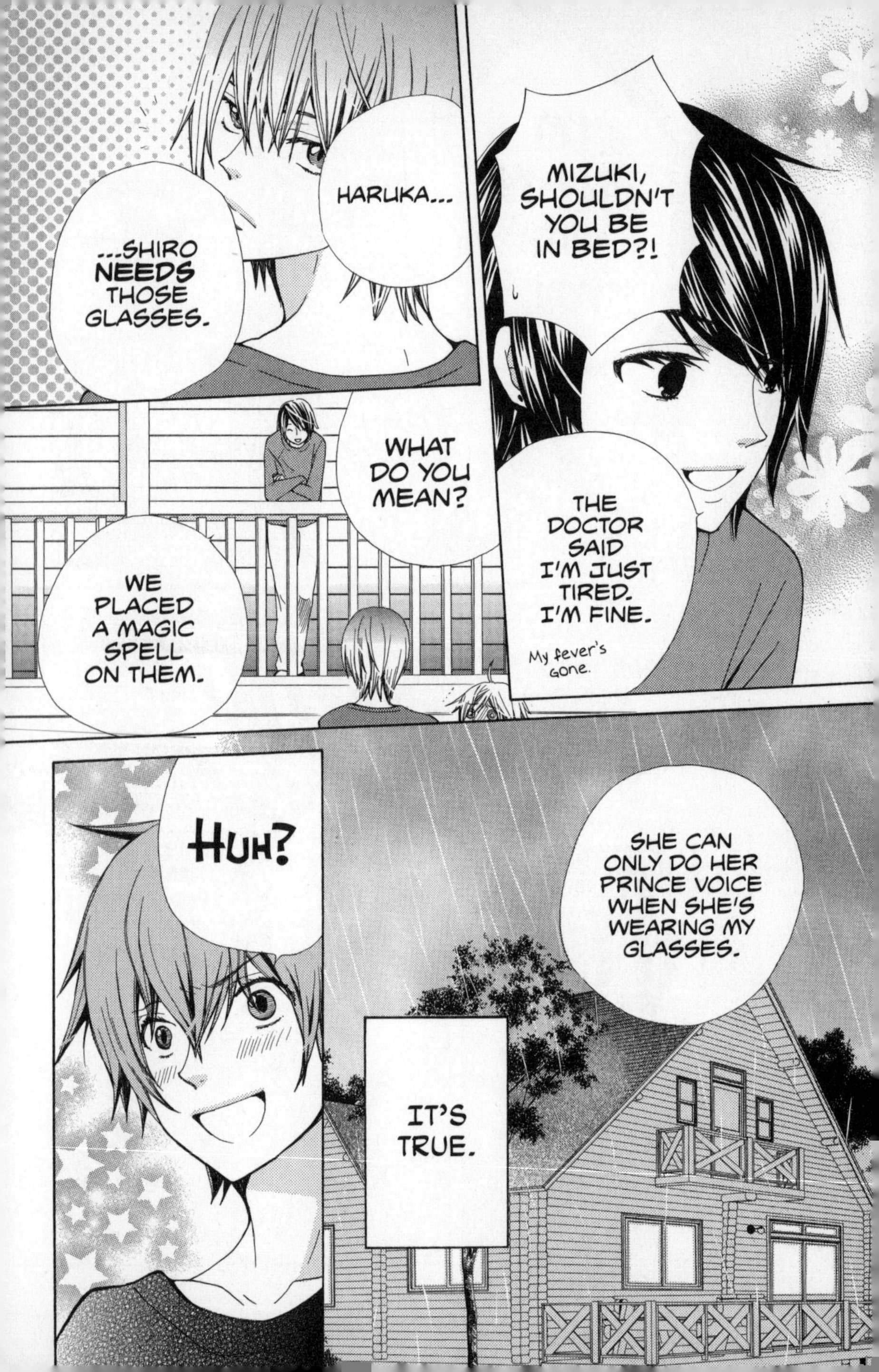
MIZUKI, SHOULDN'T YOU BE IN BED?!
THE DOCTOR SAID I'M JUST TIRED. I'M FINE.
My fever's gone.
HARUKA...
...SHIRO NEEDS THOSE GLASSES.
WHAT DO YOU MEAN?
WE PLACED A MAGIC SPELL ON THEM.
SHE CAN ONLY DO HER PRINCE VOICE WHEN SHE'S WEARING MY GLASSES.
IT'S TRUE.
HUH?

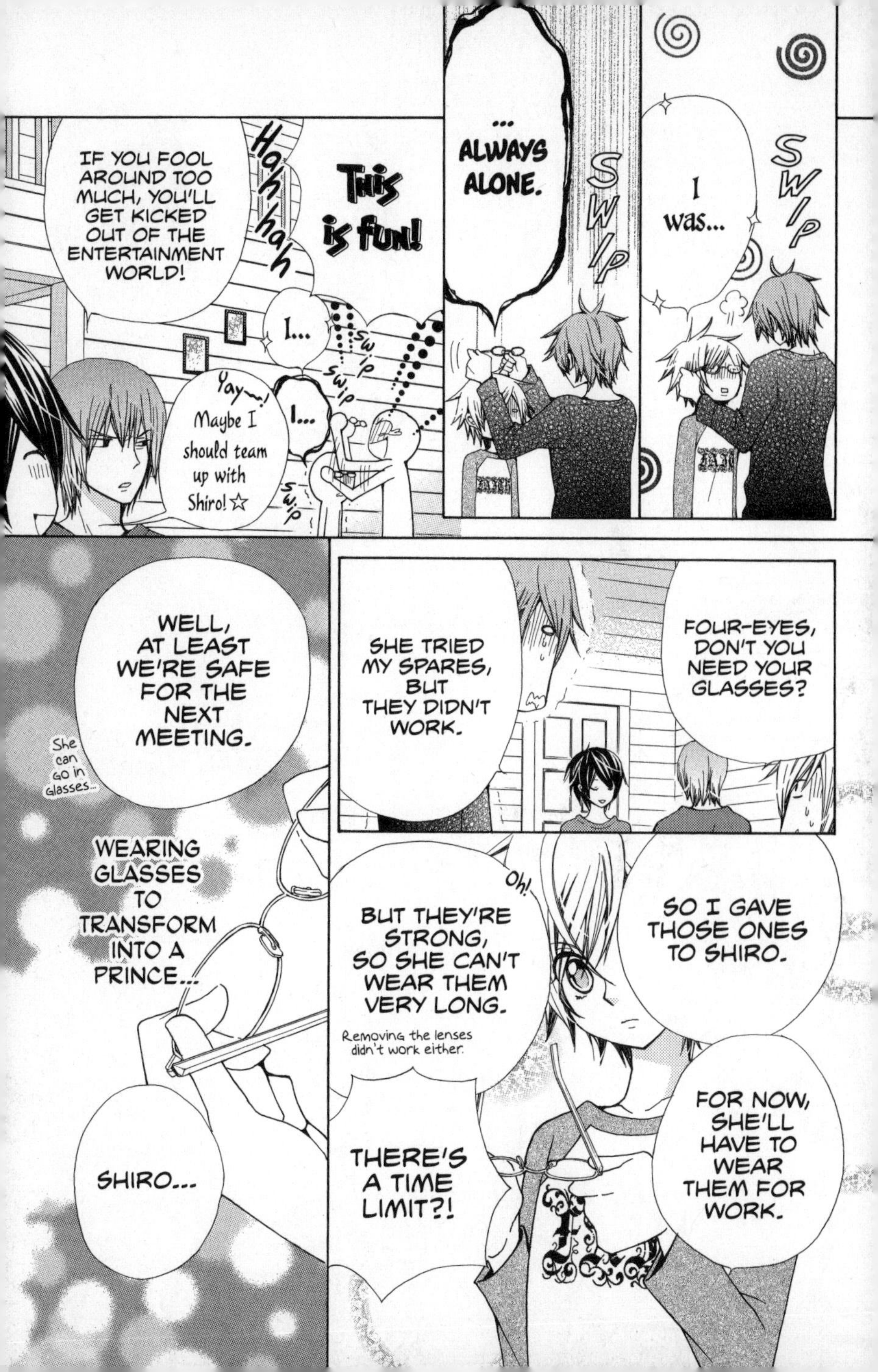
SWIP
I was...
SWIP
...ALWAYS ALONE.
This is fun!
Hah hah hah
IF YOU FOOL AROUND TOO MUCH, YOU'LL GET KICKED OUT OF THE ENTERTAINMENT WORLD!
I...
I...
swip swip swip
Yay~! Maybe I should team up with Shiro! ☆
swip
FOUR-EYES, DON'T YOU NEED YOUR GLASSES?
SHE TRIED MY SPARES, BUT THEY DIDN'T WORK.
SO I GAVE THOSE ONES TO SHIRO.
Oh!
BUT THEY'RE STRONG, SO SHE CAN'T WEAR THEM VERY LONG.
Removing the lenses didn't work either.
FOR NOW, SHE'LL HAVE TO WEAR THEM FOR WORK.
THERE'S A TIME LIMIT?!
WELL, AT LEAST WE'RE SAFE FOR THE NEXT MEETING.
She can go in glasses...
WEARING GLASSES TO TRANSFORM INTO A PRINCE...
SHIRO...

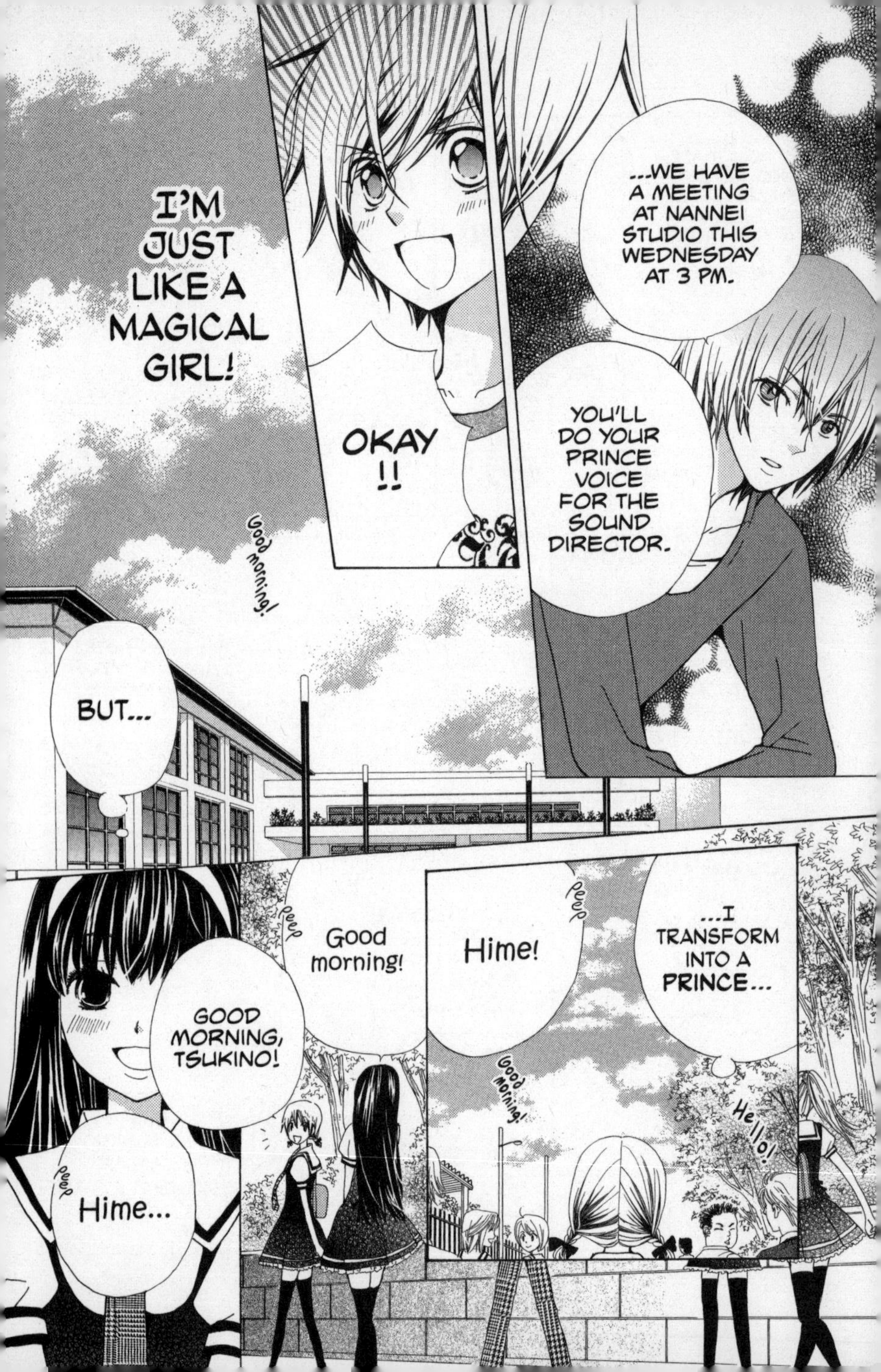
...WE HAVE A MEETING AT NANNEI STUDIO THIS WEDNESDAY AT 3 PM.
YOU'LL DO YOUR PRINCE VOICE FOR THE SOUND DIRECTOR.
OKAY !!
I'M JUST LIKE A MAGICAL GIRL!
Good morning!
BUT...
...I TRANSFORM INTO A PRINCE...
Hello!
peep
Hime!
Good morning!
peep
Good morning!
GOOD MORNING, TSUKINO!
peep
Hime...

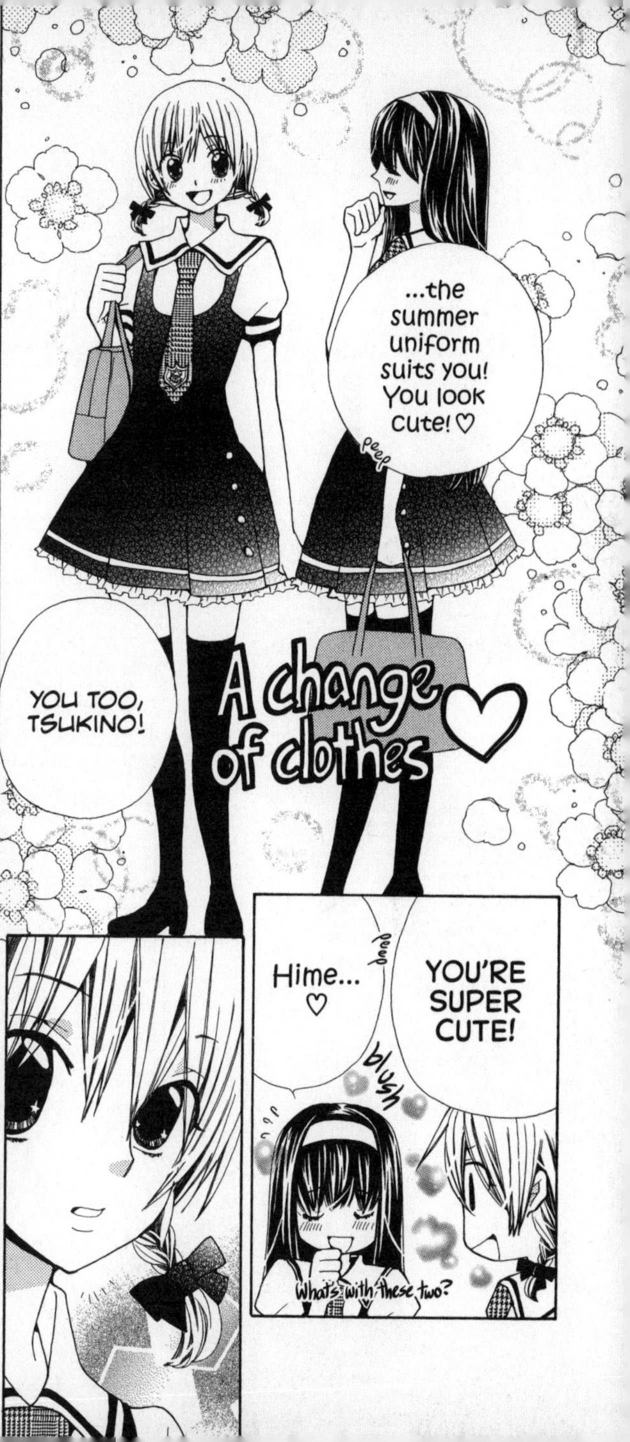
...the summer uniform suits you! You look cute! ♡
peep
A change of clothes ♥
YOU TOO, TSUKINO!
YOU'RE SUPER CUTE!
peep
Hime... ♡
blush
What's with these two?

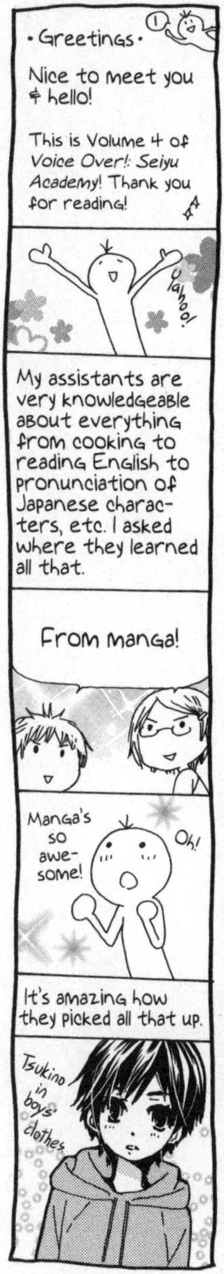
1
• Greetings •
Nice to meet you & hello!
This is Volume 4 of Voice Over!: Seiyu Academy! Thank you for reading!
Yahoo!
My assistants are very knowledgeable about everything from cooking to reading English to pronunciation of Japanese characters, etc. I asked where they learned all that.
From manga!
Manga's so awesome!
Oh!
It's amazing how they picked all that up.
Tsukino in boys' clothes

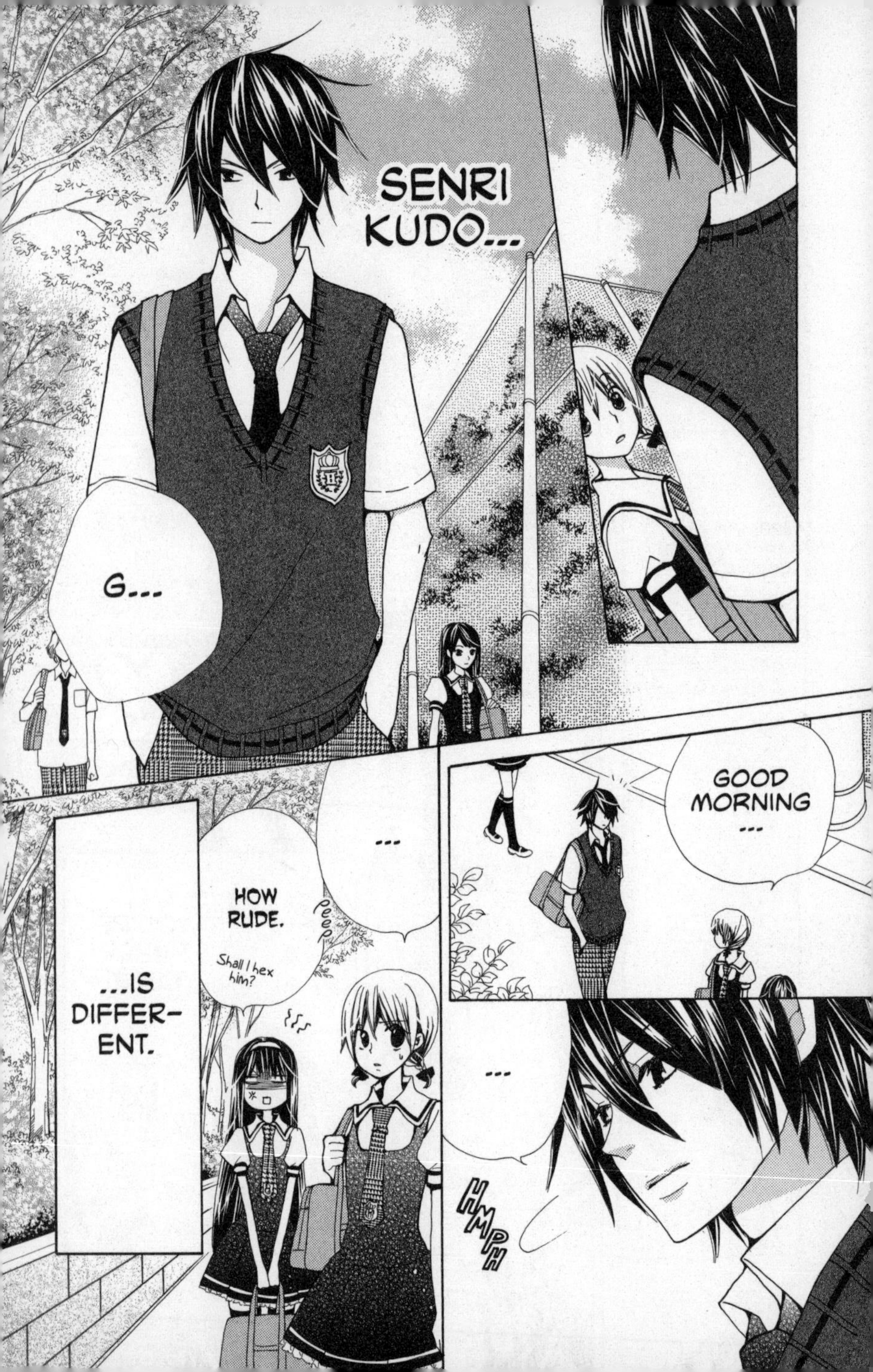
SENRI KUDO...
G...
GOOD MORNING ...
...
HMPH
...
HOW RUDE.
PEEP
Shall I hex him?
...IS DIFFERENT.

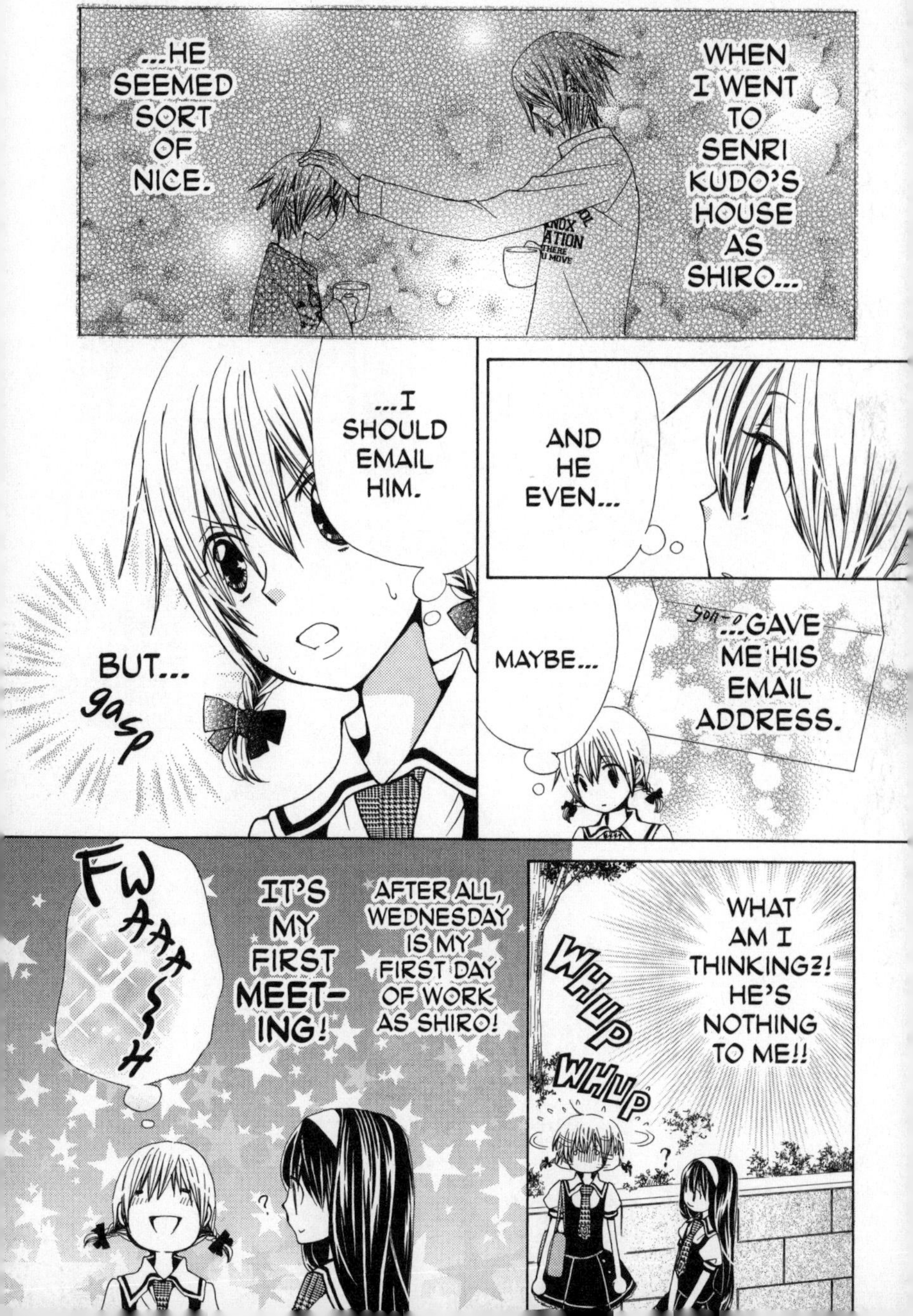
WHEN I WENT TO SENRI KUDO'S HOUSE AS SHIRO...
...HE SEEMED SORT OF NICE.
AND HE EVEN...
...GAVE ME HIS EMAIL ADDRESS.
MAYBE...
...I SHOULD EMAIL HIM.
BUT...
gasp
WHAT AM I THINKING?! HE'S NOTHING TO ME!!
WHUP
WHUP
AFTER ALL, WEDNESDAY IS MY FIRST DAY OF WORK AS SHIRO!
IT'S MY FIRST MEET-ING!
FWAAA~~H

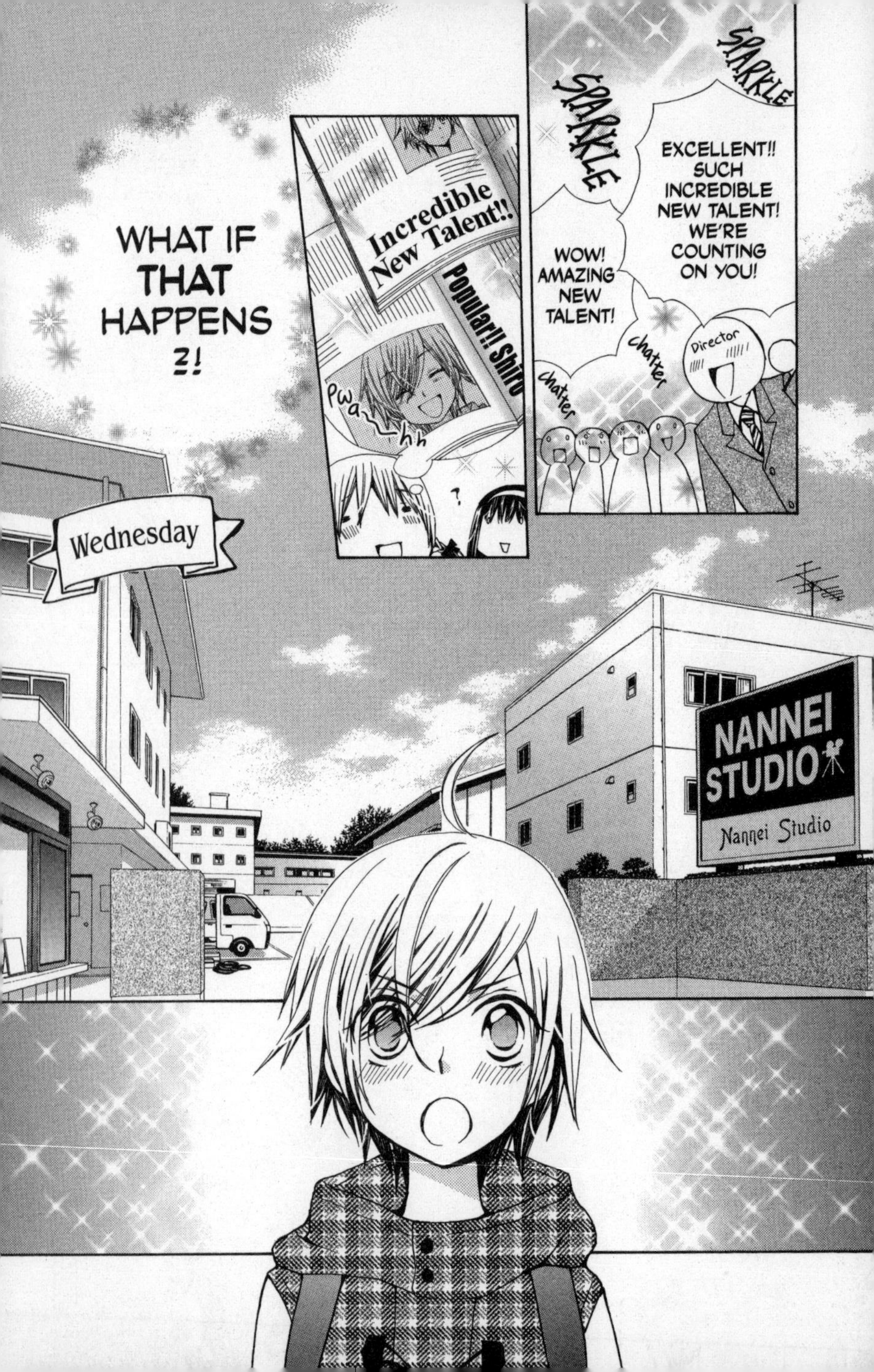
SPARKLE
SPARKLE
EXCELLENT!! SUCH INCREDIBLE NEW TALENT! WE'RE COUNTING ON YOU!
Director
WOW! AMAZING NEW TALENT!
chatter
chatter
Incredible New Talent!!
Popular!! Shiro
Pwa~hh
WHAT IF THAT HAPPENS?!
Wednesday
NANNEI STUDIO
Nannei Studio

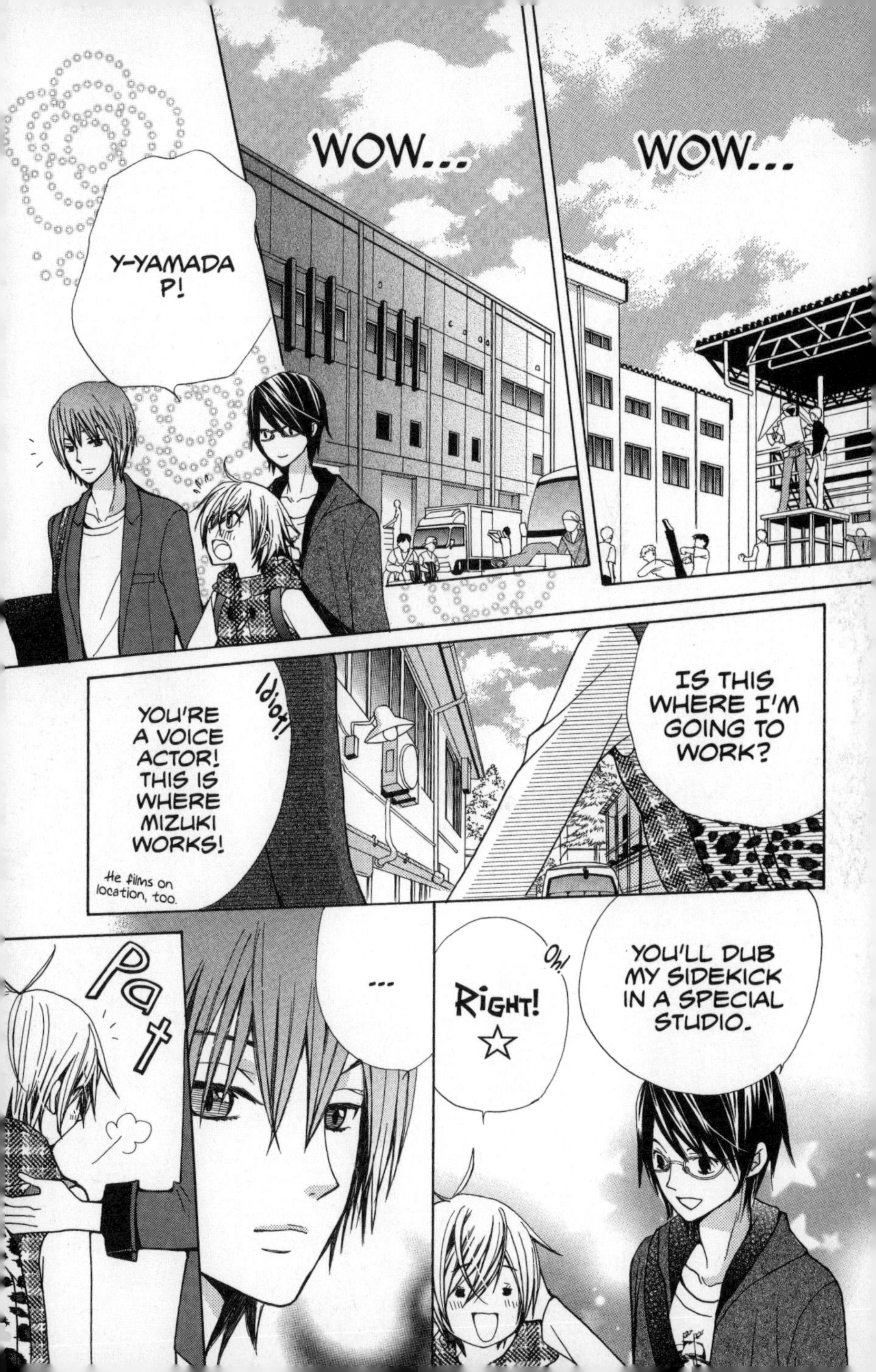
WOW...
WOW...
Y-YAMADA P!
IS THIS WHERE I'M GOING TO WORK?
Idiot!
YOU'RE A VOICE ACTOR! THIS IS WHERE MIZUKI WORKS!
He films on location, too.
YOU'LL DUB MY SIDEKICK IN A SPECIAL STUDIO.
Oh!
RIGHT! ☆
...
Pat

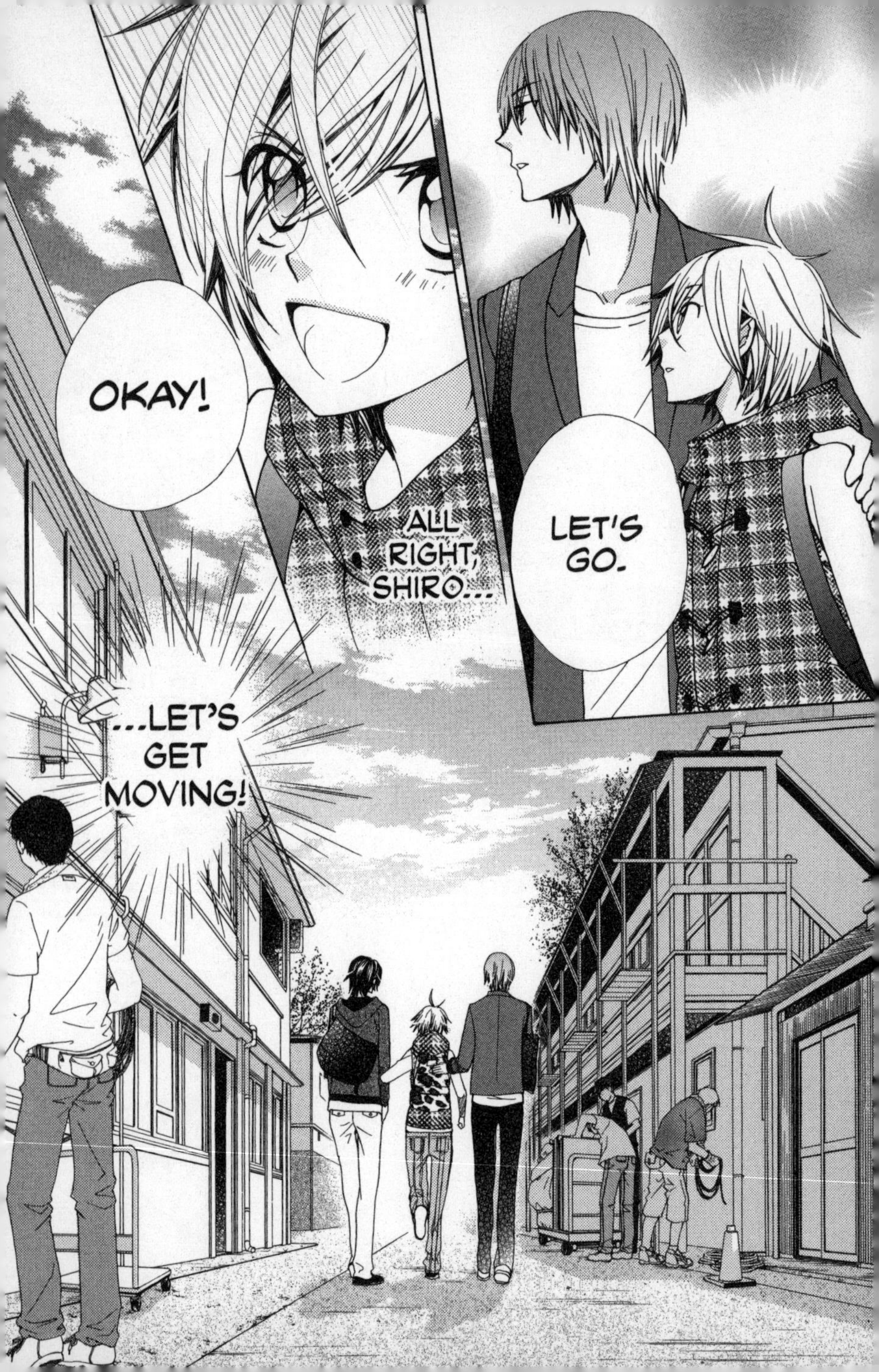
LET'S GO.
OKAY!
ALL RIGHT, SHIRO...
...LET'S GET MOVING!

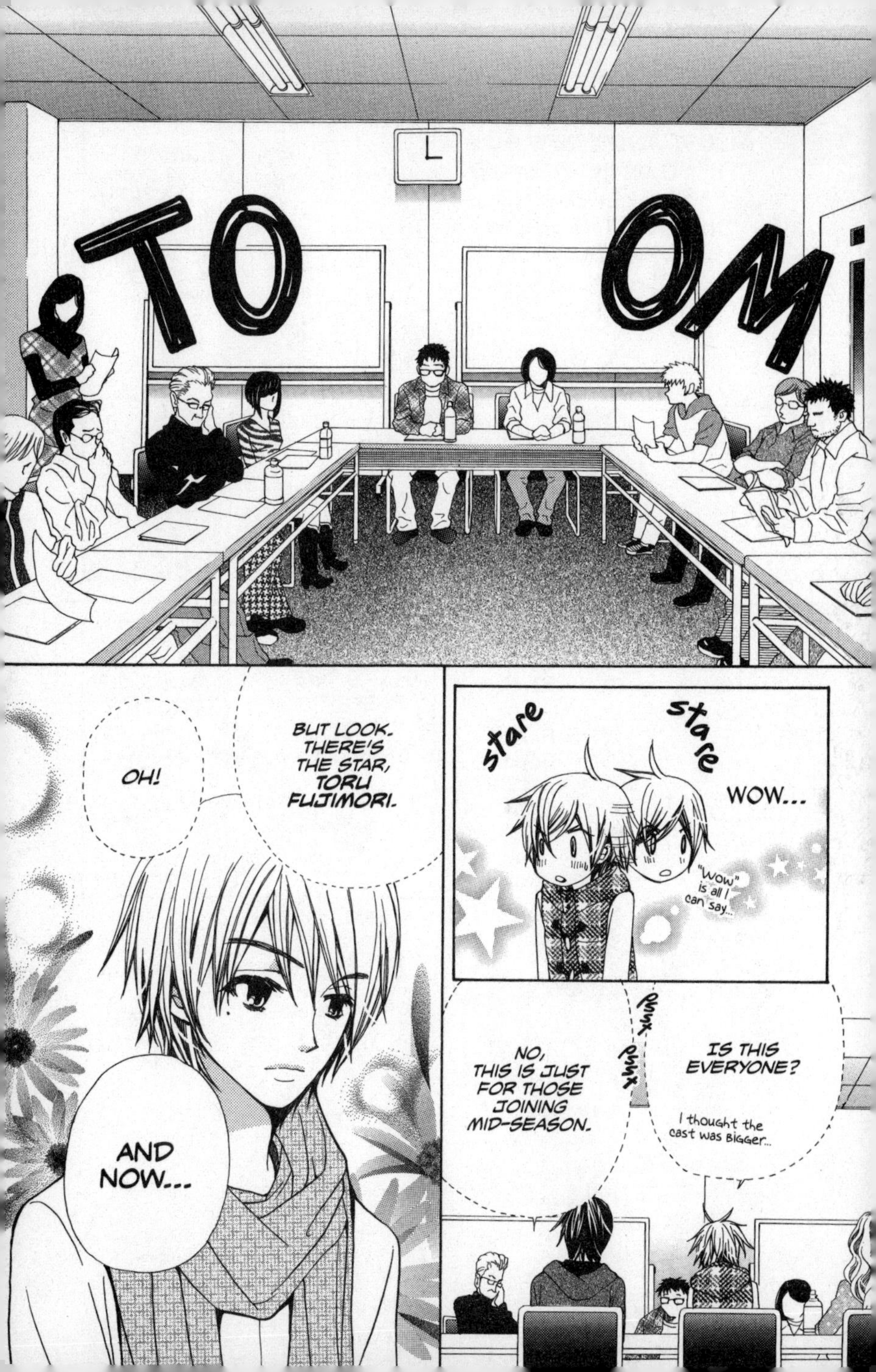
TO OMI
stare
stare
WOW...
"Wow" is all I can say...
IS THIS EVERYONE?
I thought the cast was bigger...
NO, THIS IS JUST FOR THOSE JOINING MID-SEASON.
BUT LOOK. THERE'S THE STAR, TORU FUJIMORI.
OH!
AND NOW...

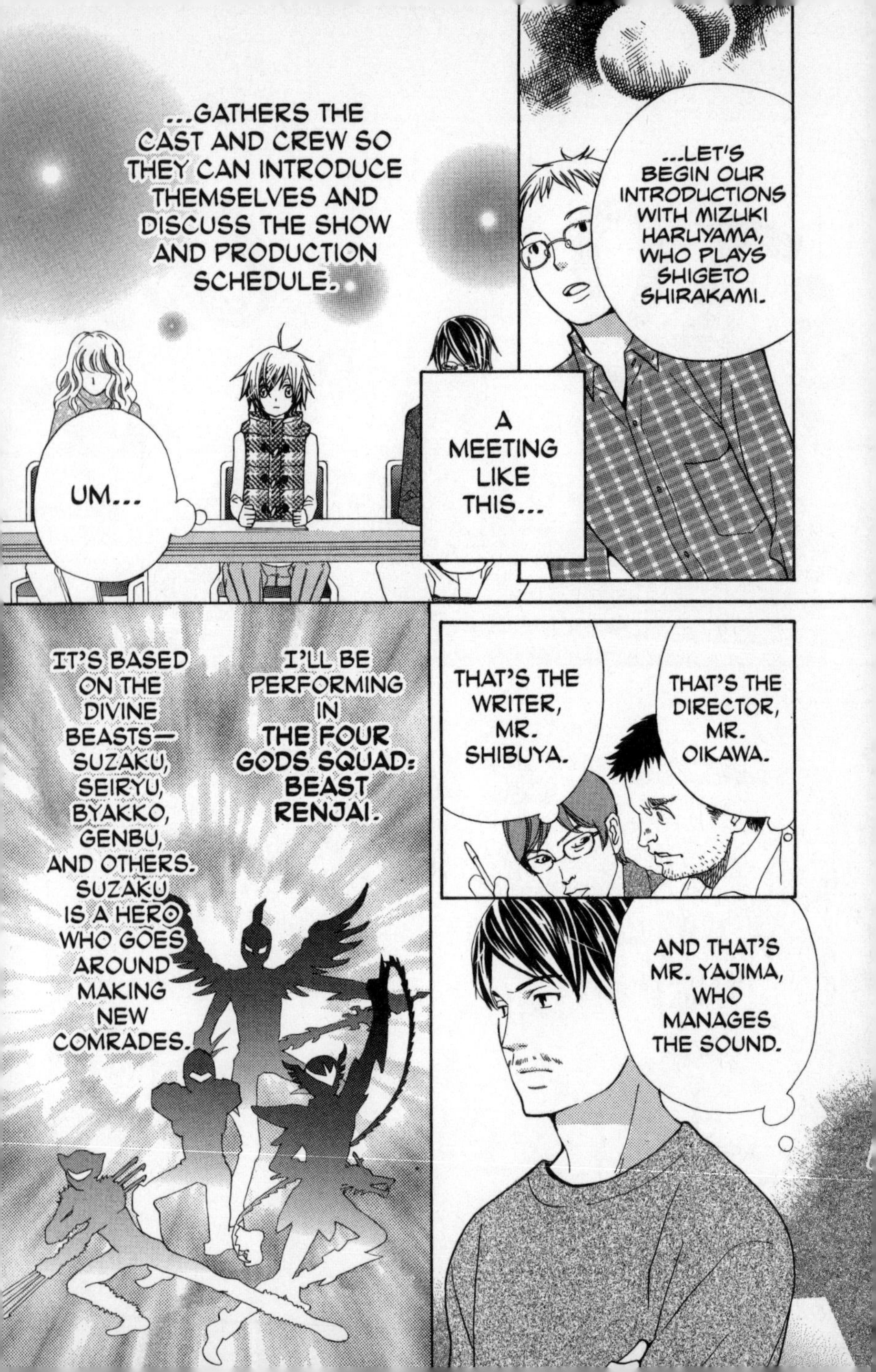
...LET'S BEGIN OUR INTRODUCTIONS WITH MIZUKI HARUYAMA, WHO PLAYS SHIGETO SHIRAKAMI.
A MEETING LIKE THIS...
...GATHERS THE CAST AND CREW SO THEY CAN INTRODUCE THEMSELVES AND DISCUSS THE SHOW AND PRODUCTION SCHEDULE.
UM...
THAT'S THE DIRECTOR, MR. OIKAWA.
THAT'S THE WRITER, MR. SHIBUYA.
AND THAT'S MR. YAJIMA, WHO MANAGES THE SOUND.
I'LL BE PERFORMING IN THE FOUR GODS SQUAD: BEAST RENJAI.
IT'S BASED ON THE DIVINE BEASTS—SUZAKU, SEIRYU, BYAKKO, GENBU, AND OTHERS. SUZAKU IS A HERO WHO GOES AROUND MAKING NEW COMRADES.

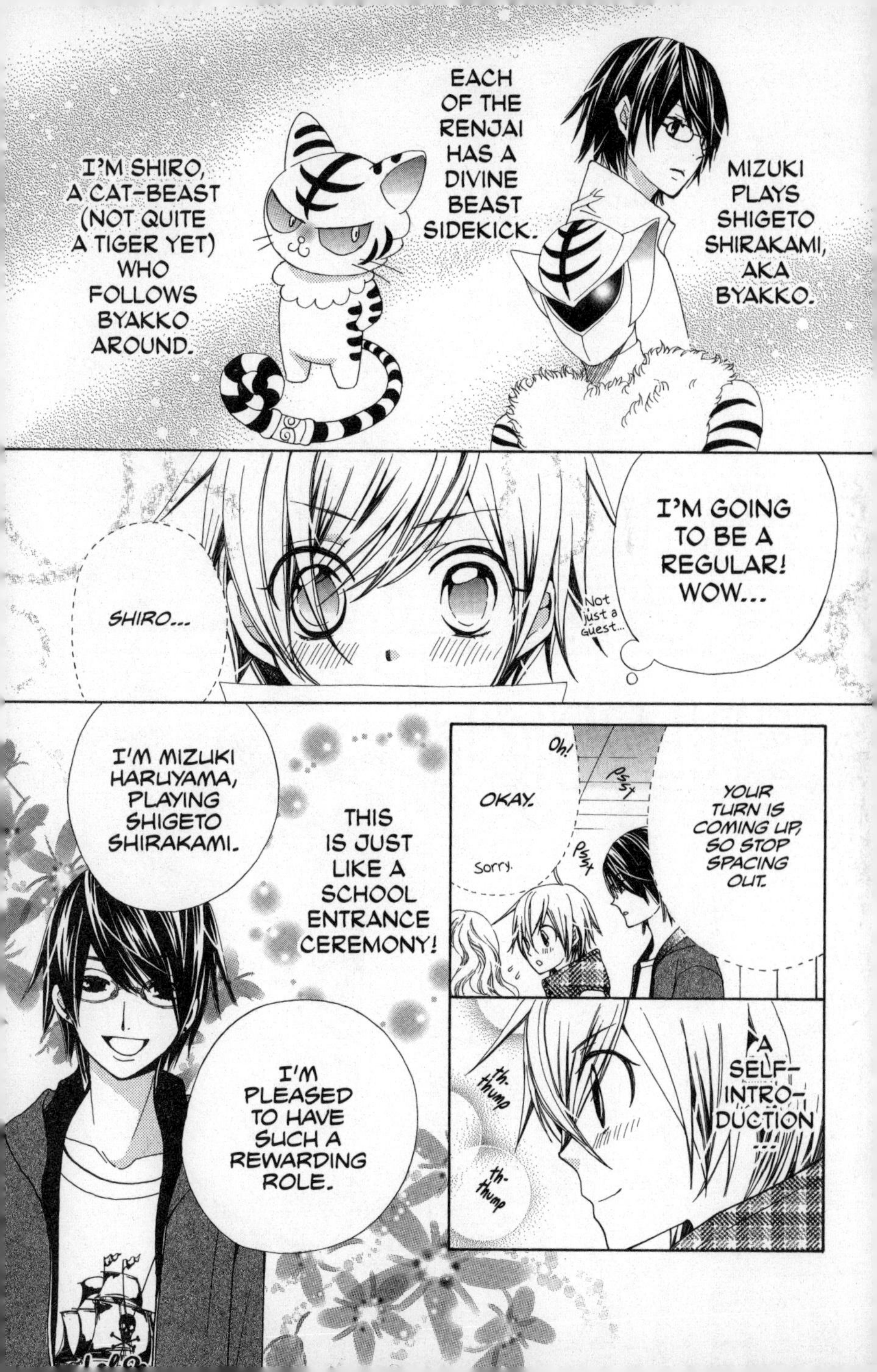
MIZUKI PLAYS SHIGETO SHIRAKAMI, AKA BYAKKO.
EACH OF THE RENJAI HAS A DIVINE BEAST SIDEKICK.
I'M SHIRO, A CAT-BEAST (NOT QUITE A TIGER YET) WHO FOLLOWS BYAKKO AROUND.
I'M GOING TO BE A REGULAR! WOW...
Not just a Guest...
SHIRO...
YOUR TURN IS COMING UP, SO STOP SPACING OUT.
Psst
Psst
Oh!
OKAY.
Sorry.
A SELF-INTRODUCTION...
th-thump
th-thump
I'M MIZUKI HARUYAMA, PLAYING SHIGETO SHIRAKAMI.
THIS IS JUST LIKE A SCHOOL ENTRANCE CEREMONY!
I'M PLEASED TO HAVE SUCH A REWARDING ROLE.

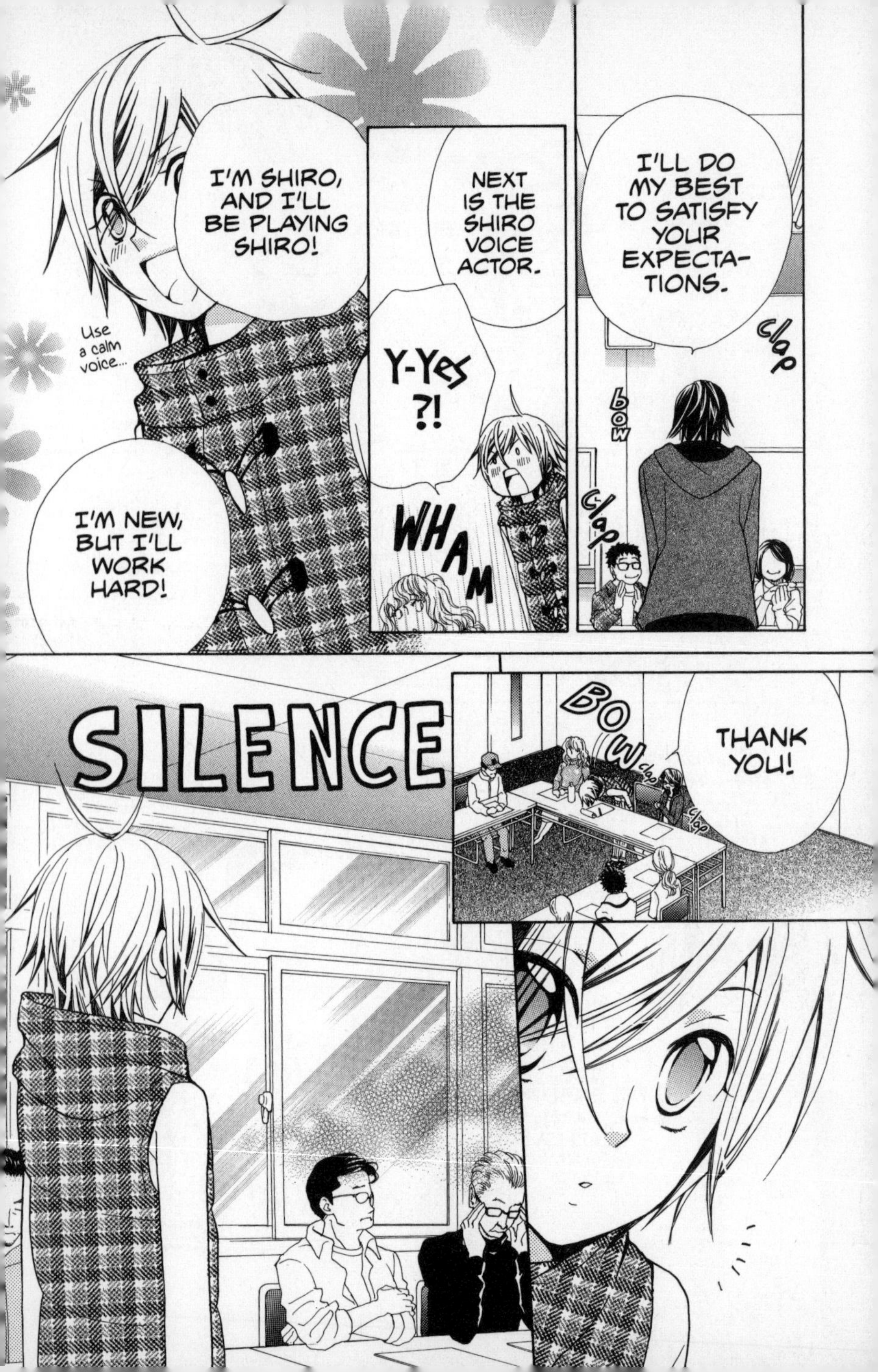
I'LL DO MY BEST TO SATISFY YOUR EXPECTA-TIONS.
clap
bow
clap
NEXT IS THE SHIRO VOICE ACTOR.
Y-Yes ?!
WHAM
I'M SHIRO, AND I'LL BE PLAYING SHIRO!
Use a calm voice...
I'M NEW, BUT I'LL WORK HARD!
THANK YOU!
BOW
clap
clap
SILENCE

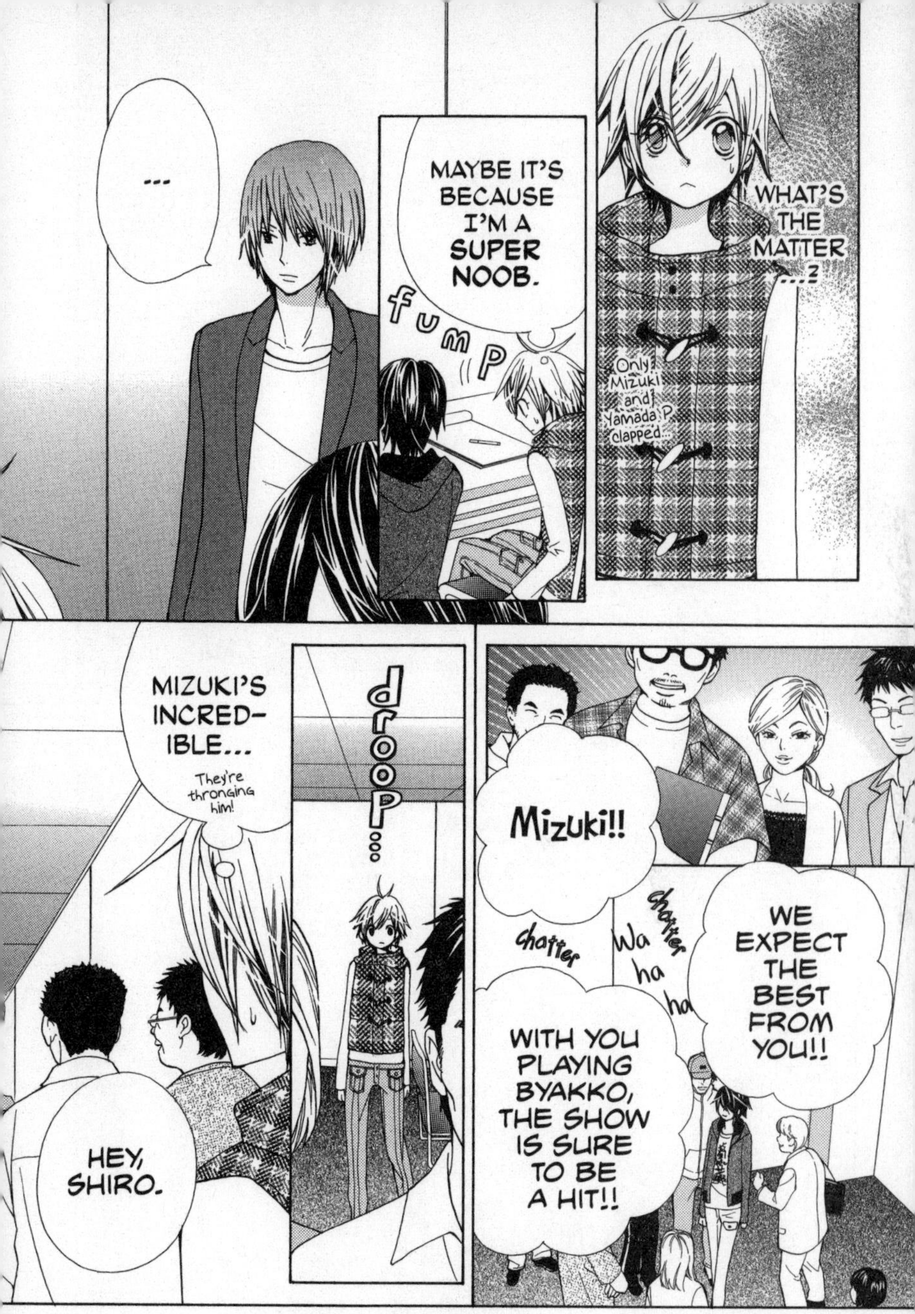
WHAT'S THE MATTER ...?
Only Mizuki and Yamada P clapped...
MAYBE IT'S BECAUSE I'M A SUPER NOOB.
fump
...
Mizuki!!
WE EXPECT THE BEST FROM YOU!!
chatter
Wa ha ha
chatter
WITH YOU PLAYING BYAKKO, THE SHOW IS SURE TO BE A HIT!!
droop...
MIZUKI'S INCREDIBLE...
They're thronging him!
HEY, SHIRO.

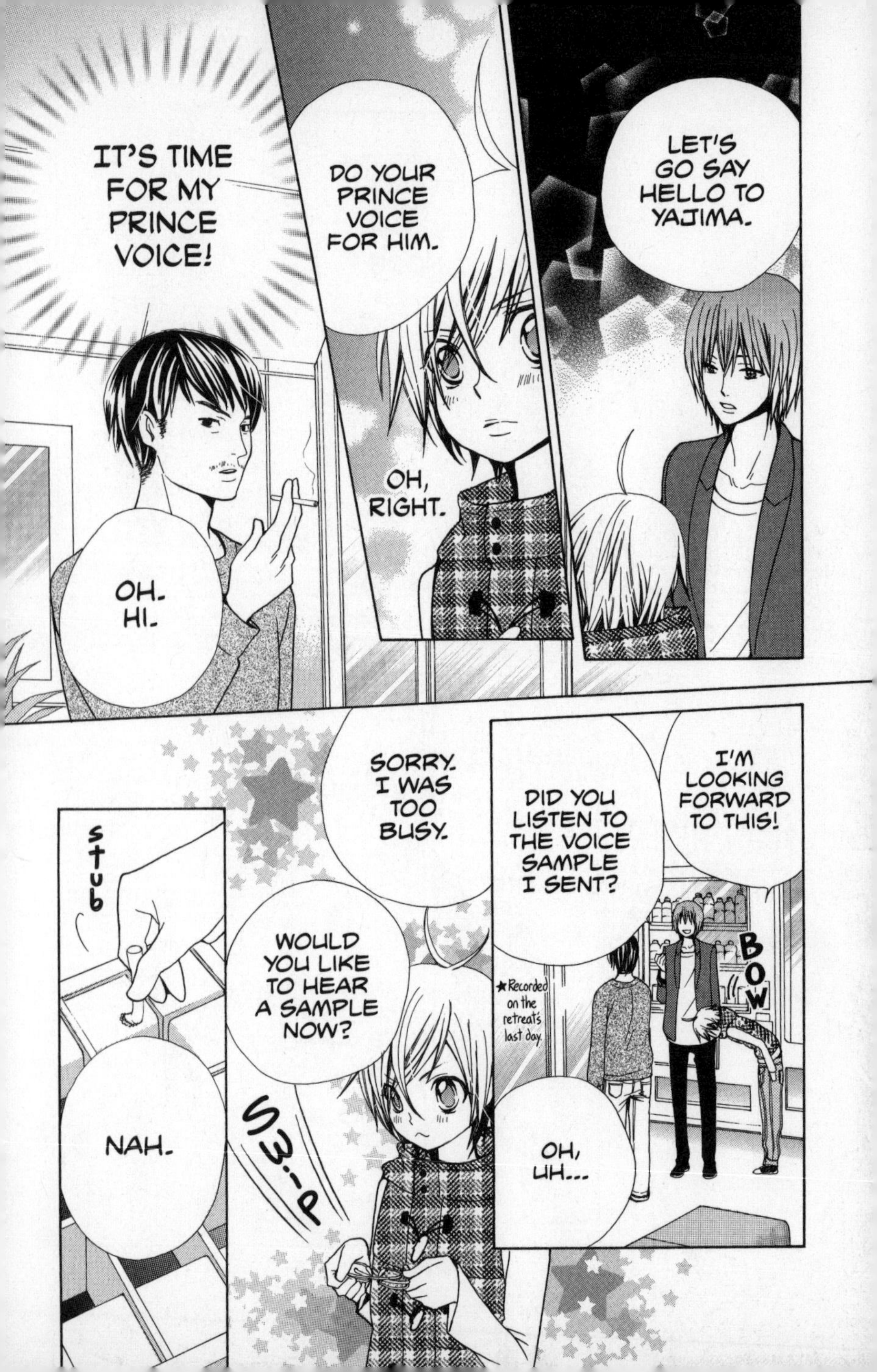
LET'S GO SAY HELLO TO YAJIMA.
DO YOUR PRINCE VOICE FOR HIM.
OH, RIGHT.
IT'S TIME FOR MY PRINCE VOICE!
OH. HI.
I'M LOOKING FORWARD TO THIS!
BOW
DID YOU LISTEN TO THE VOICE SAMPLE I SENT?
★Recorded on the retreat's last day.
OH, UH...
SORRY. I WAS TOO BUSY.
WOULD YOU LIKE TO HEAR A SAMPLE NOW?
stub
NAH.

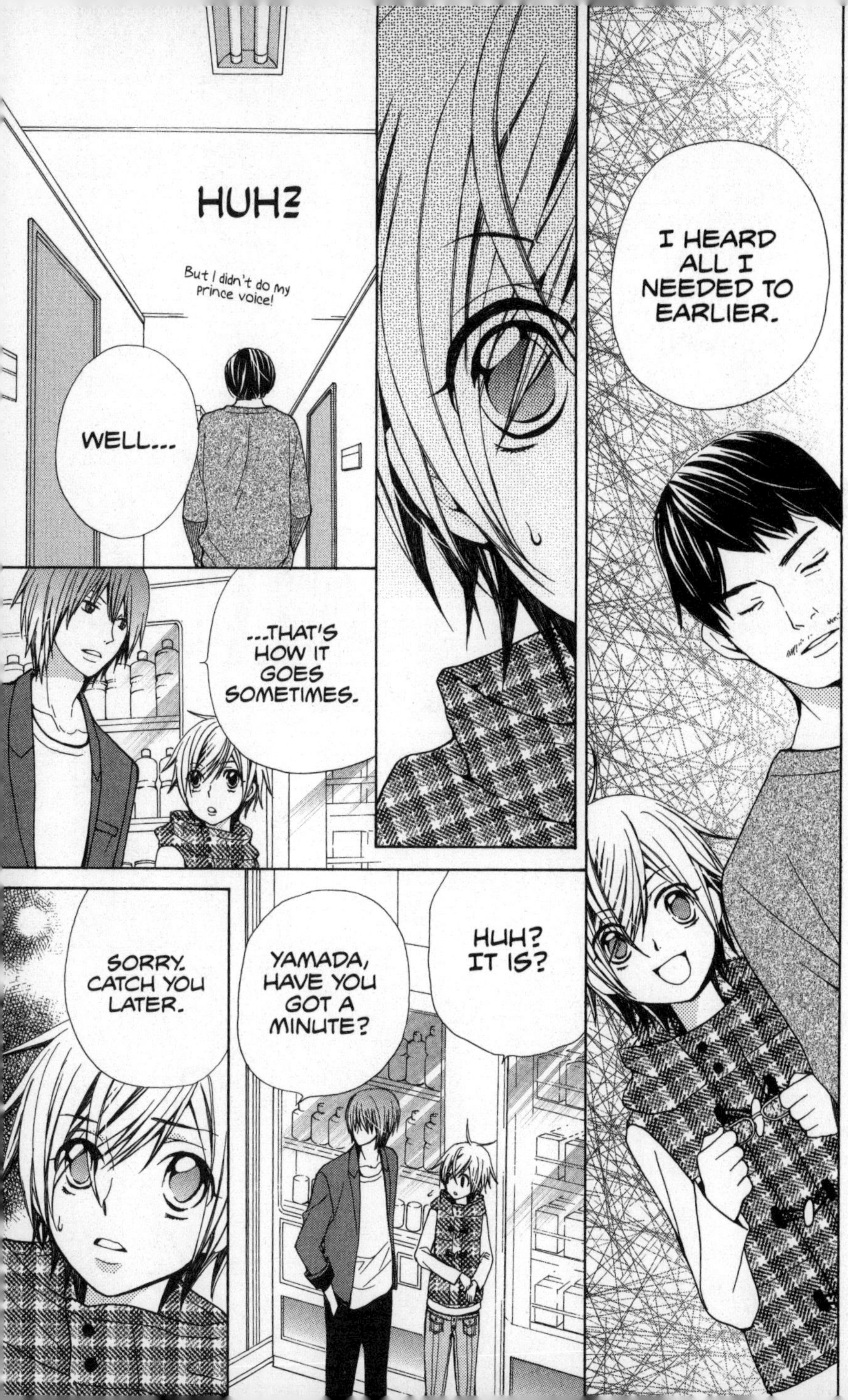
I HEARD ALL I NEEDED TO EARLIER.
HUH?
But I didn't do my prince voice!
WELL...
...THAT'S HOW IT GOES SOMETIMES.
HUH? IT IS?
YAMADA, HAVE YOU GOT A MINUTE?
SORRY. CATCH YOU LATER.

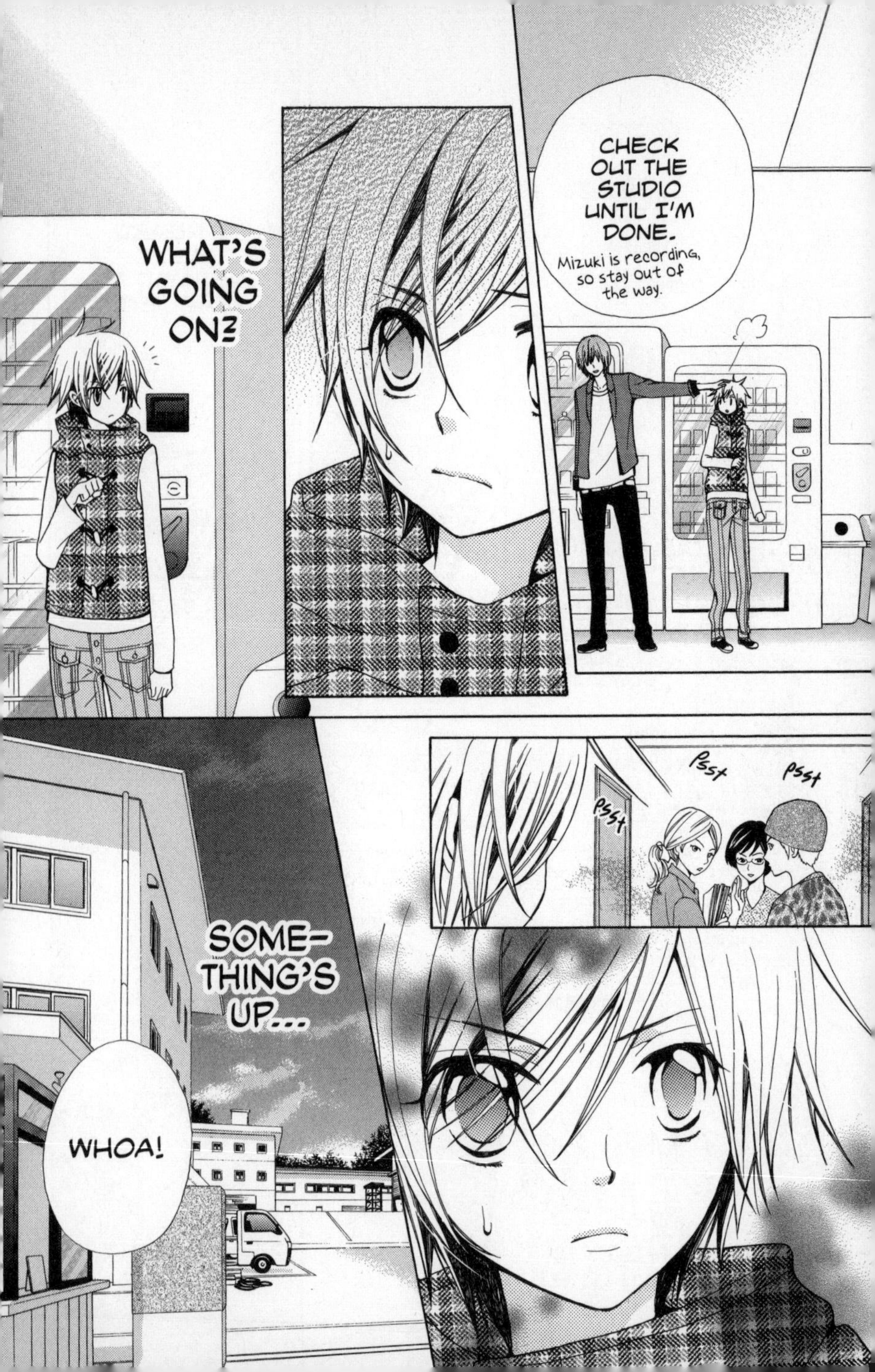
CHECK OUT THE STUDIO UNTIL I'M DONE.
Mizuki is recording, so stay out of the way.
WHAT'S GOING ON?
Psst
Psst
Psst
SOME-THING'S UP...
WHOA!

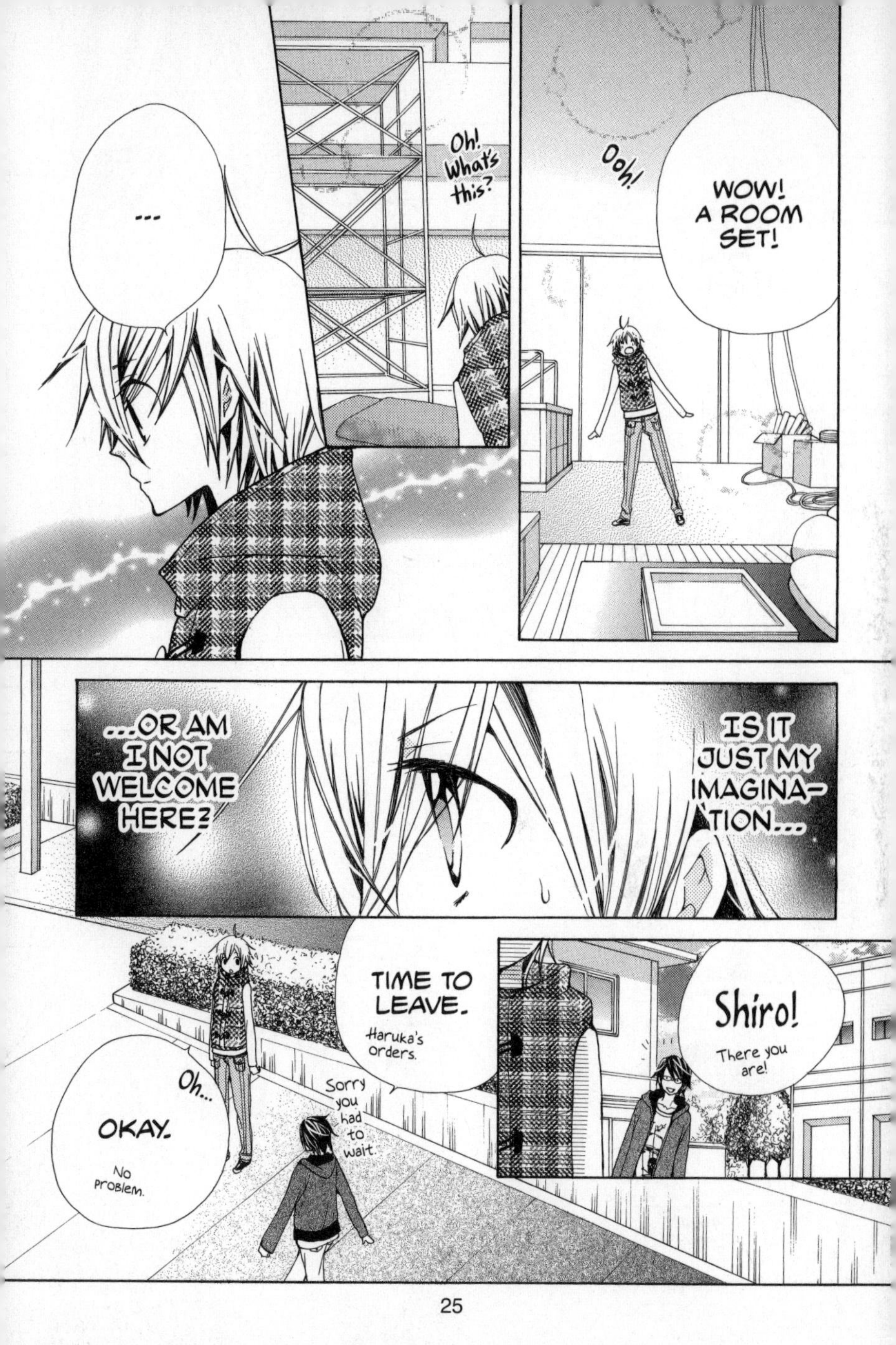
WOW! A ROOM SET!
Ooh!
Oh! What's this?
...
IS IT JUST MY IMAGINA-TION...
...OR AM I NOT WELCOME HERE?
Shiro!
There you are!
TIME TO LEAVE.
Haruka's orders.
Sorry you had to wait.
Oh...
OKAY.
No problem.

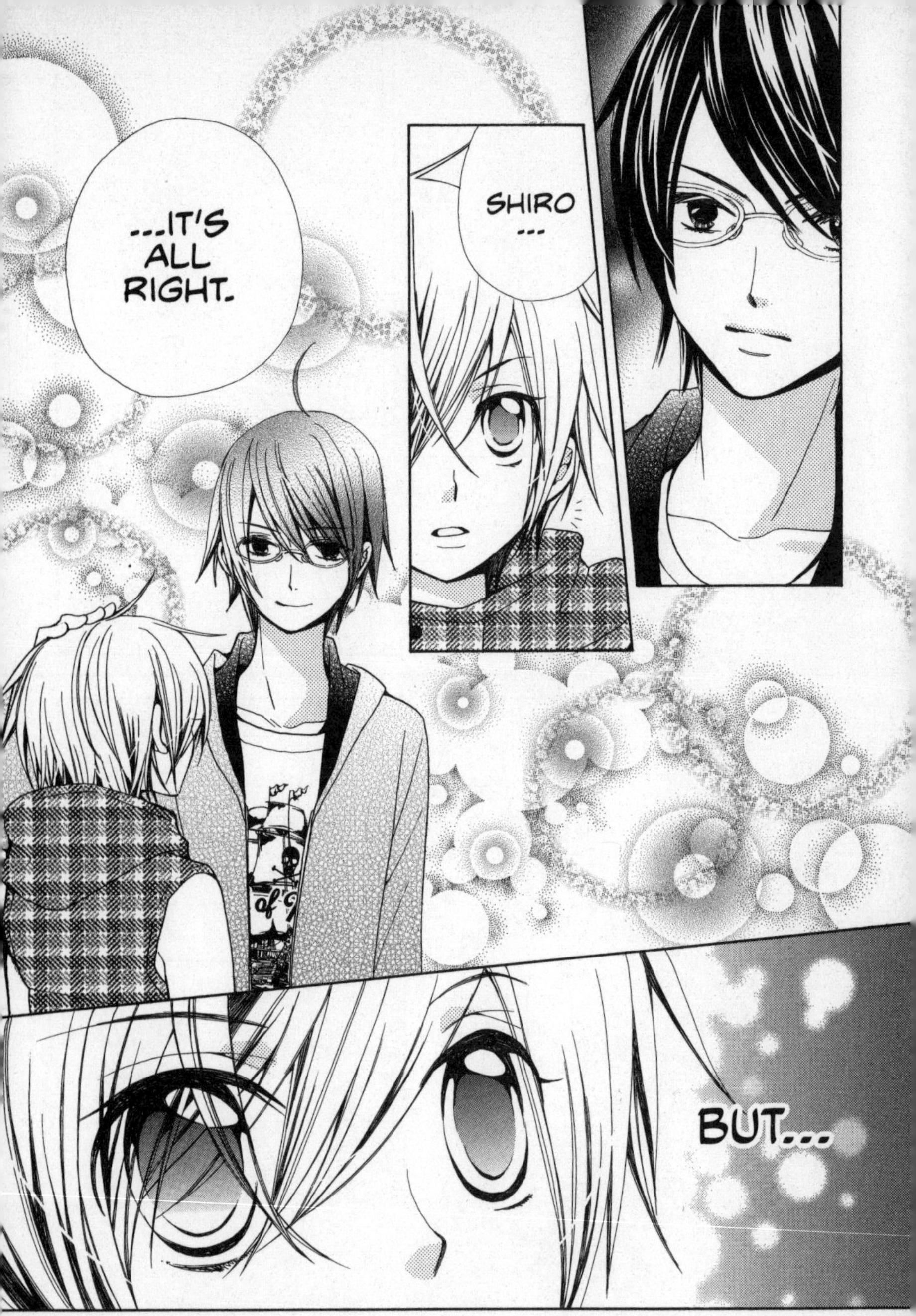
SHIRO...
...IT'S ALL RIGHT.
BUT...

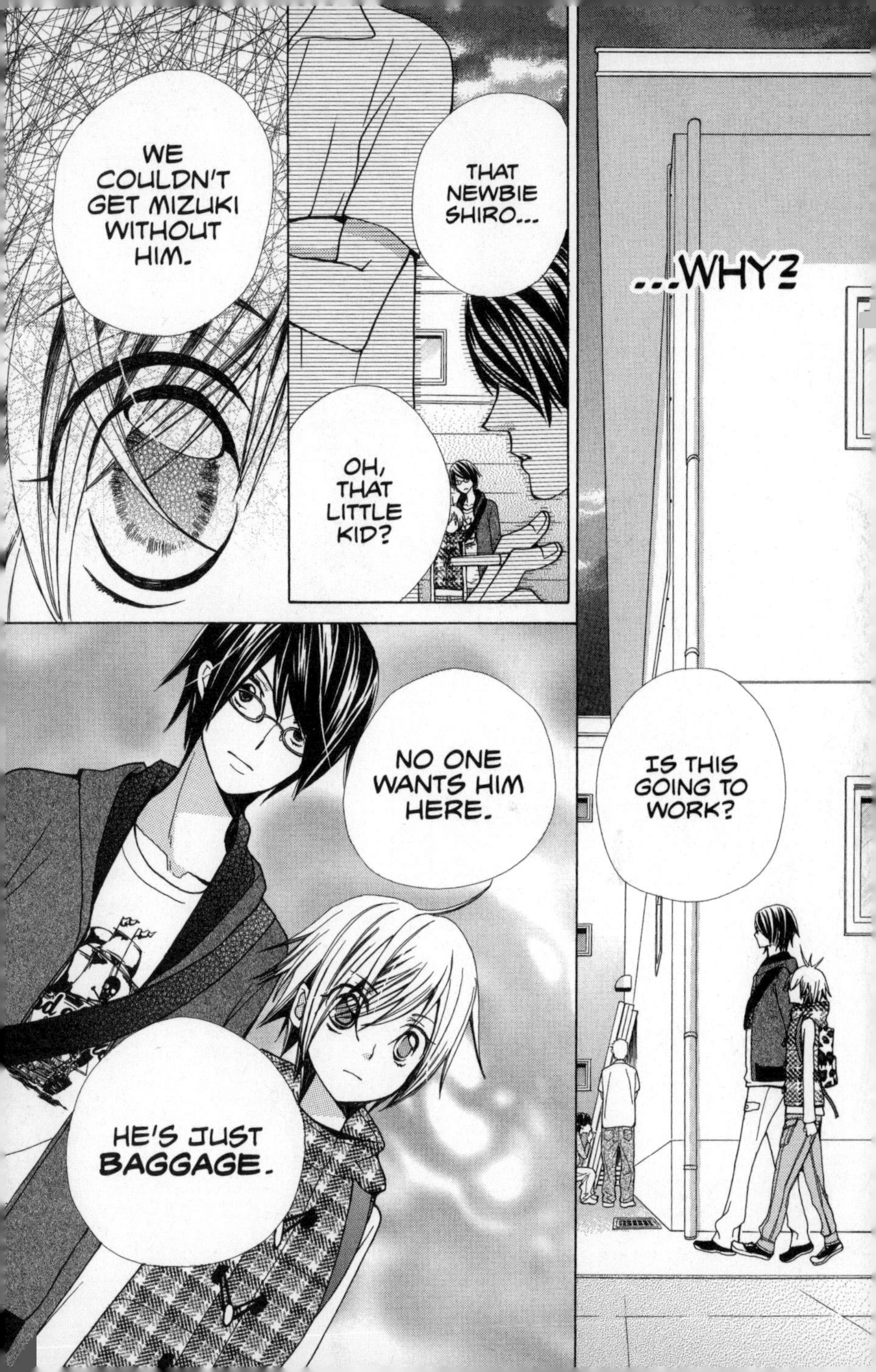
...WHY?
IS THIS GOING TO WORK?
THAT NEWBIE SHIRO...
OH, THAT LITTLE KID?
WE COULDN'T GET MIZUKI WITHOUT HIM.
NO ONE WANTS HIM HERE.
HE'S JUST BAGGAGE.

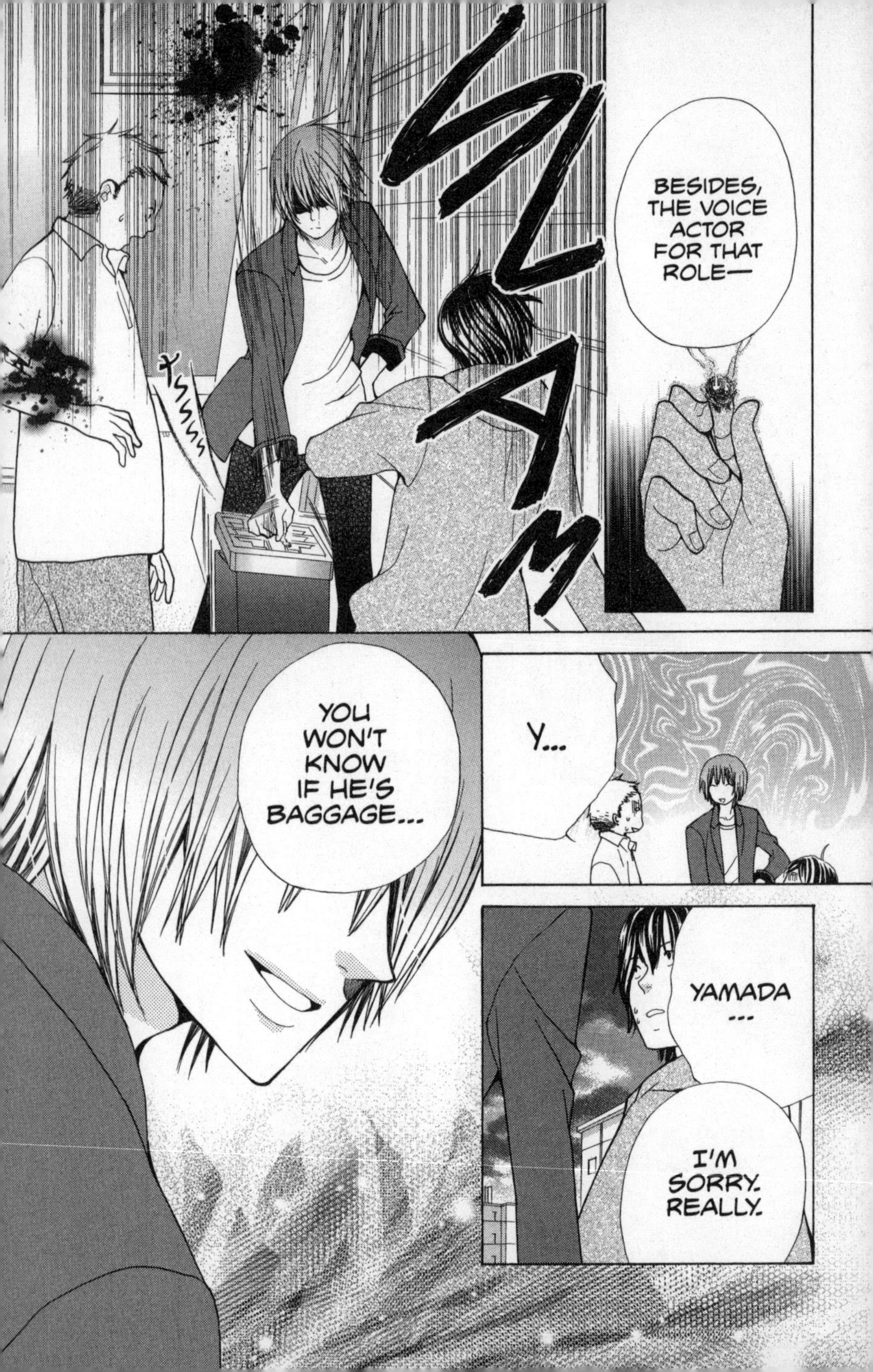
BESIDES, THE VOICE ACTOR FOR THAT ROLE—
SLAM
TSSSS
Y...
YAMADA ...
I'M SORRY. REALLY.
YOU WON'T KNOW IF HE'S BAGGAGE...

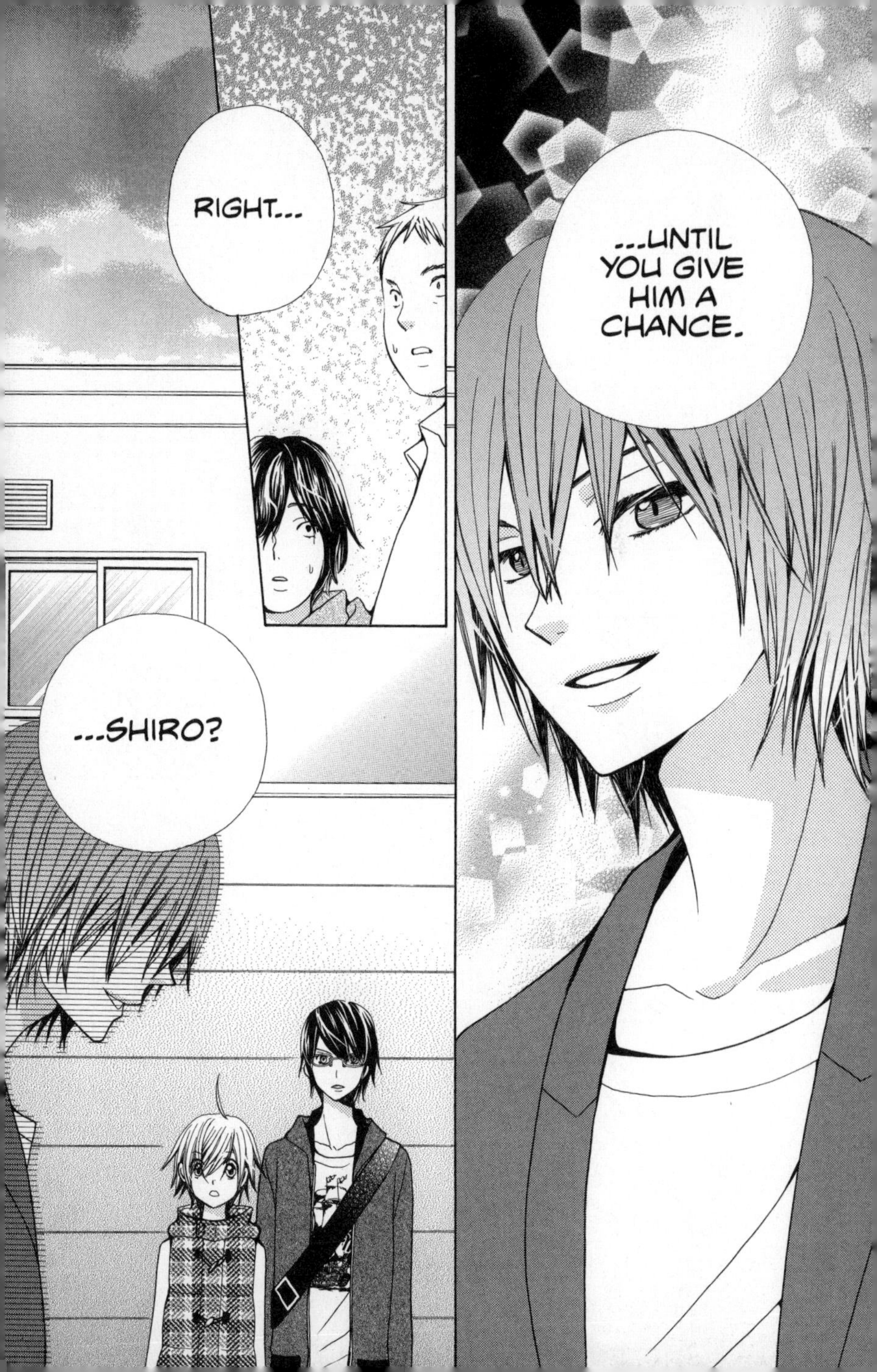
...UNTIL YOU GIVE HIM A CHANCE.
RIGHT...
...SHIRO?

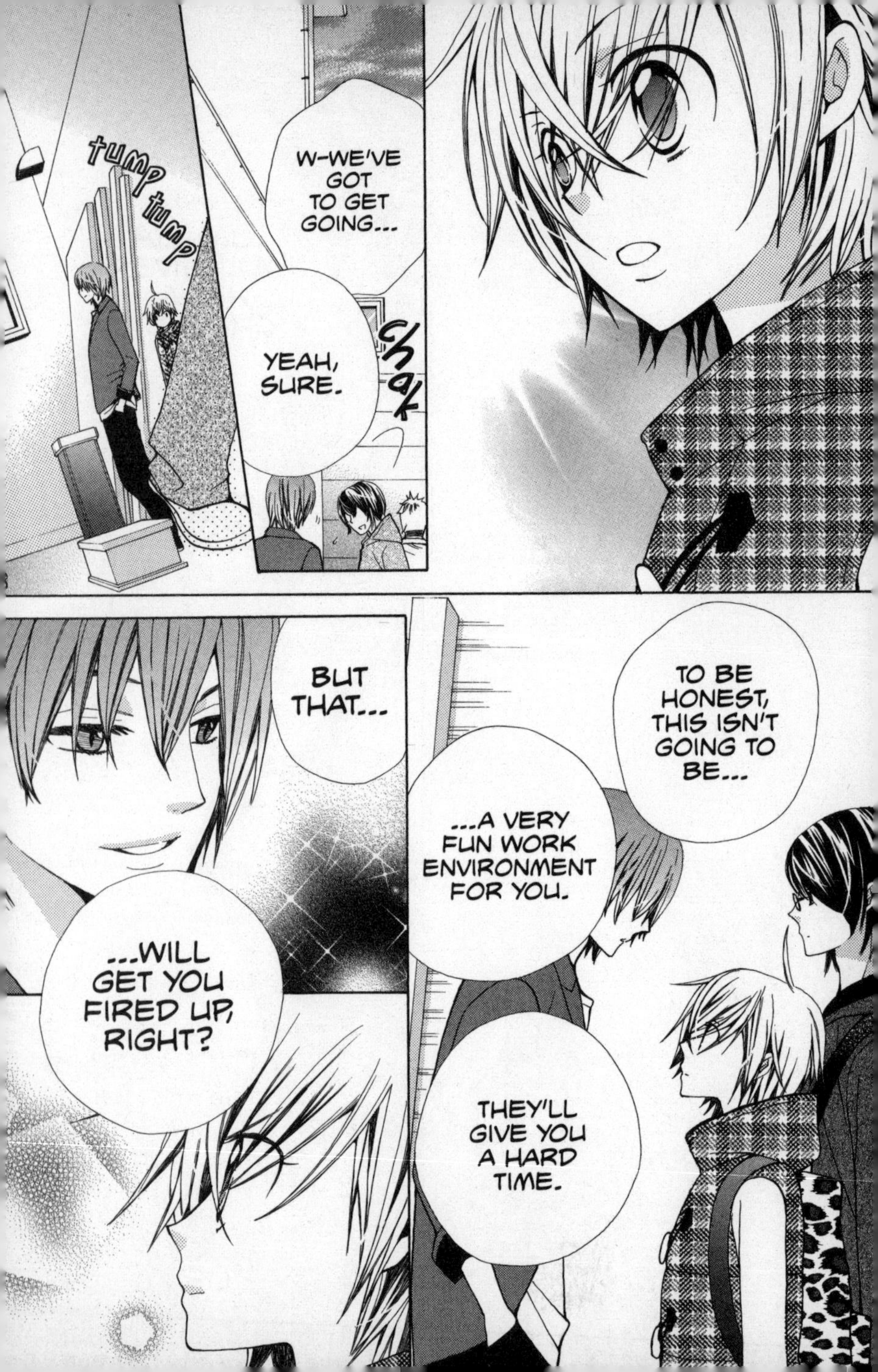
W-WE'VE GOT TO GET GOING...
YEAH, SURE.
CHAK
tump tump tump
TO BE HONEST, THIS ISN'T GOING TO BE...
...A VERY FUN WORK ENVIRONMENT FOR YOU.
THEY'LL GIVE YOU A HARD TIME.
BUT THAT...
...WILL GET YOU FIRED UP, RIGHT?

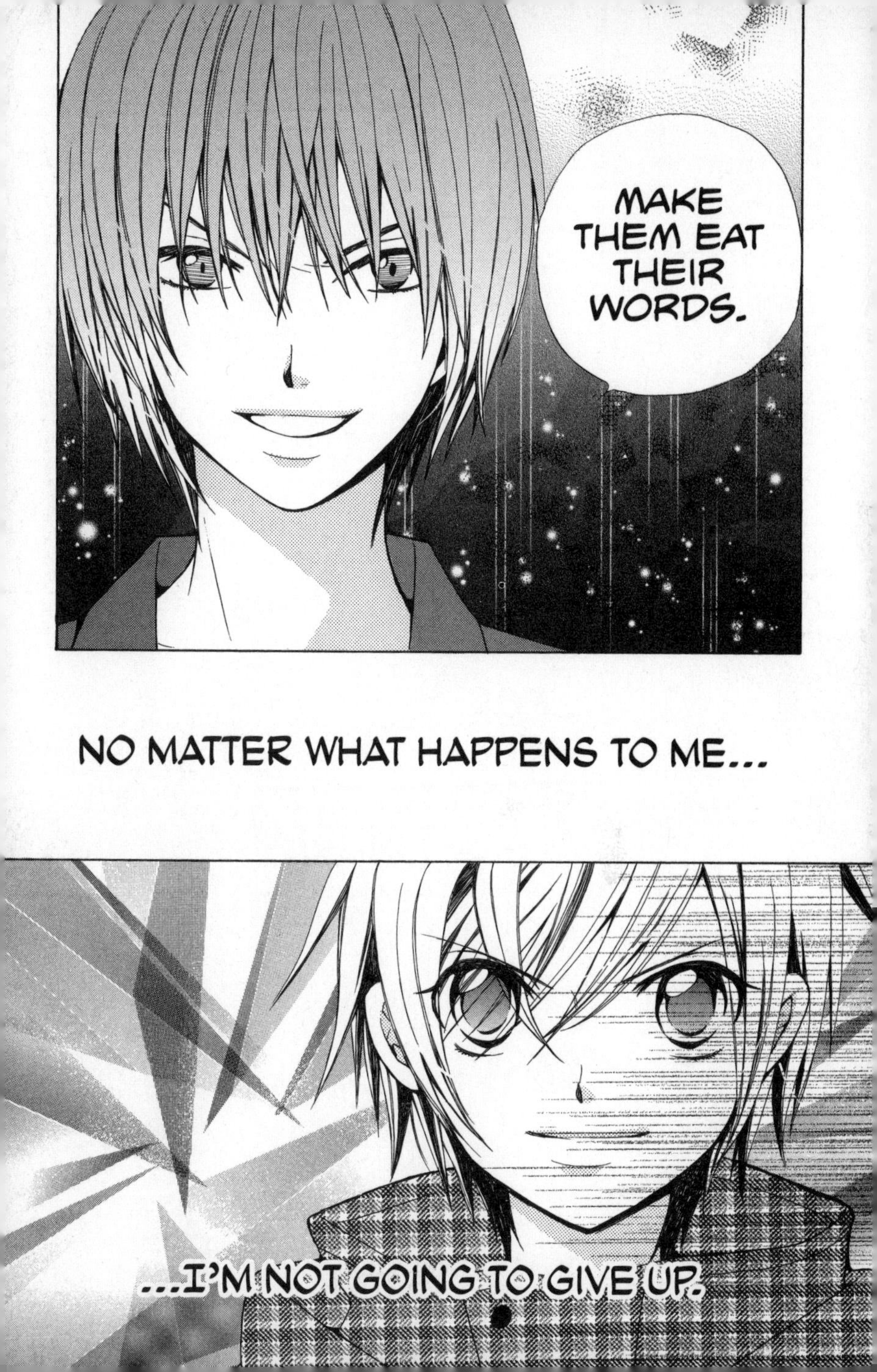
MAKE THEM EAT THEIR WORDS.
NO MATTER WHAT HAPPENS TO ME...
...I'M NOT GOING TO GIVE UP.

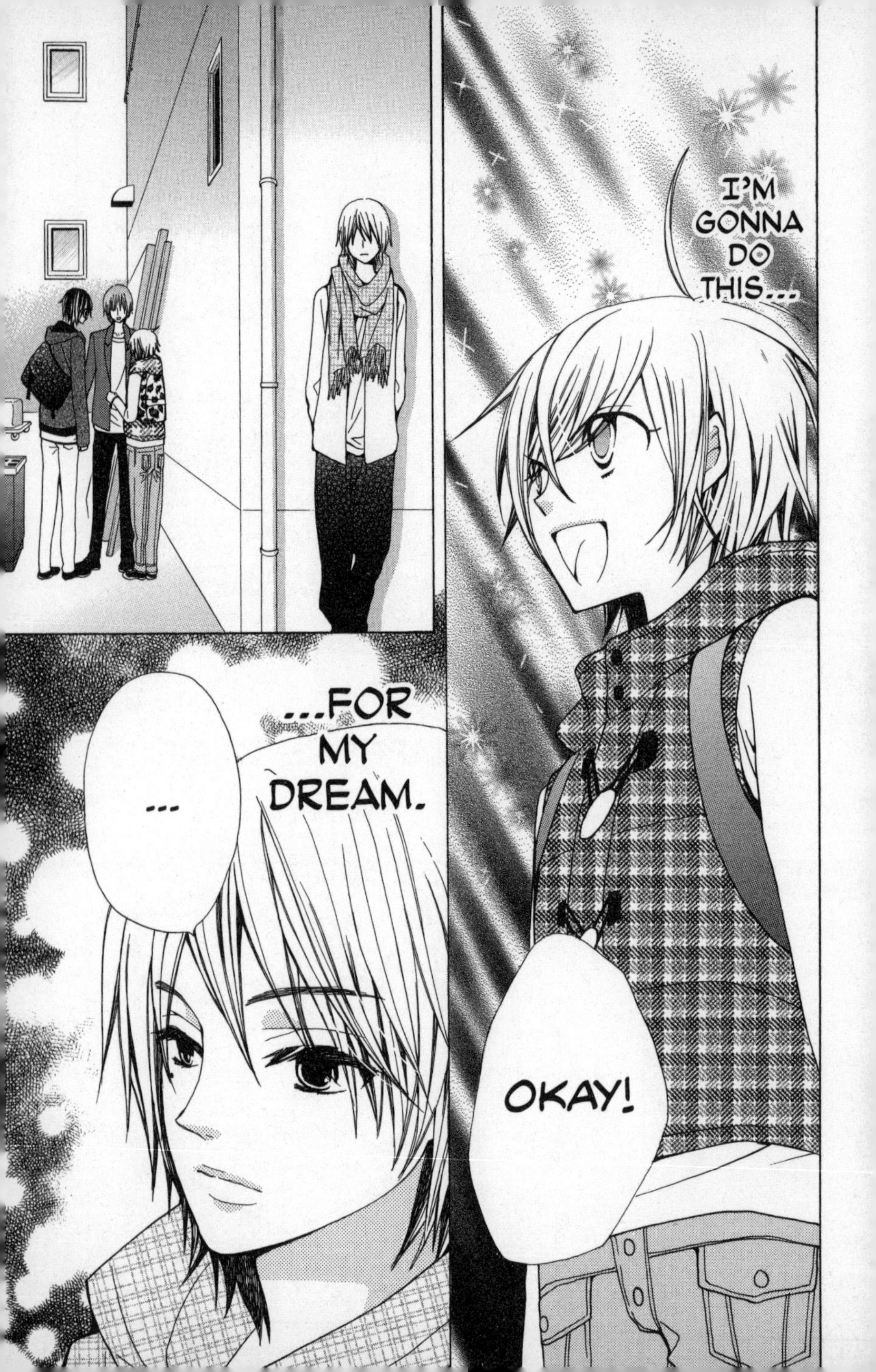
I'M GONNA DO THIS...
OKAY!
...FOR MY DREAM.
...

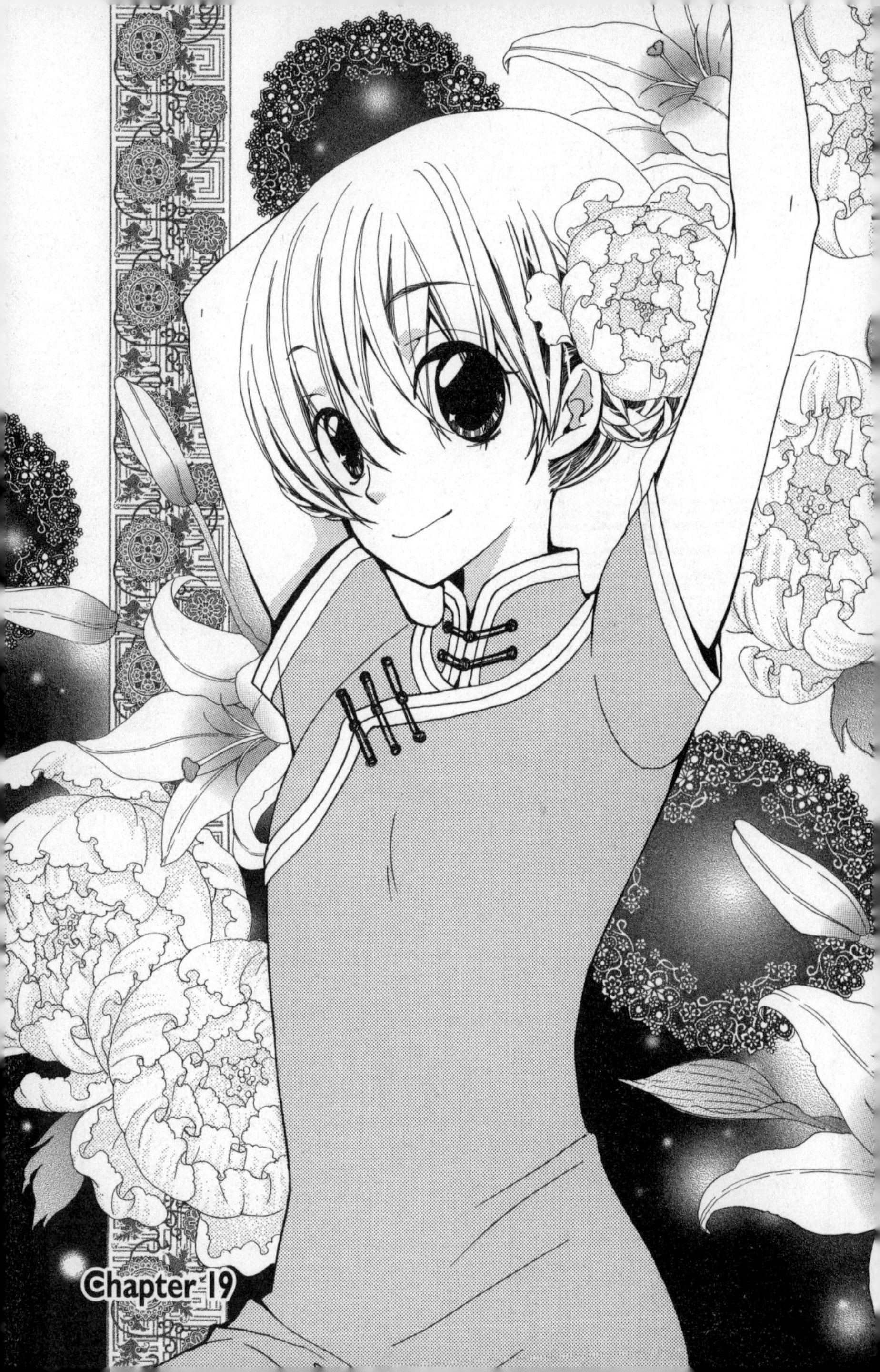
Chapter 19

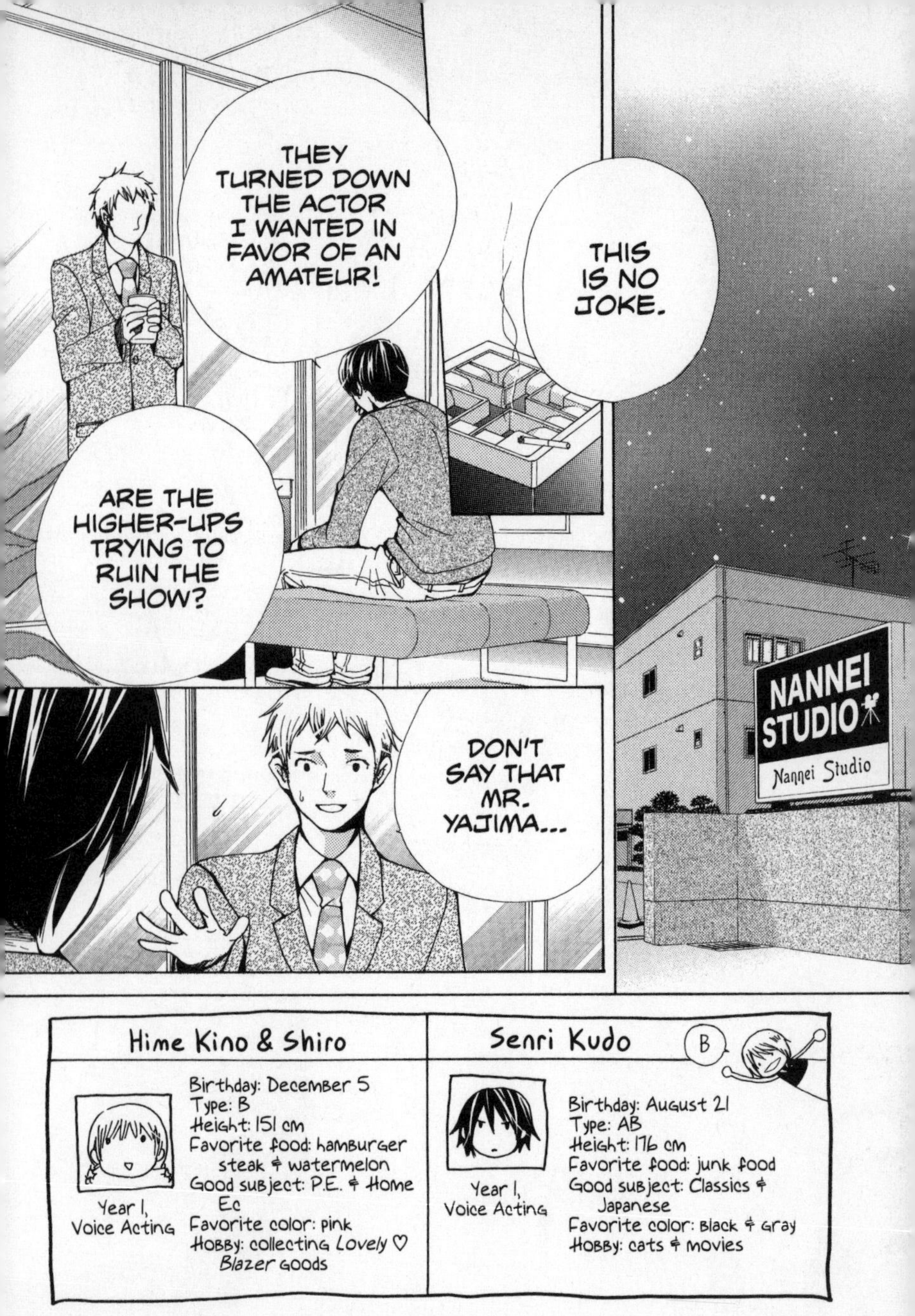
NANNEI STUDIO
Nannei Studio
THIS IS NO JOKE.
THEY TURNED DOWN THE ACTOR I WANTED IN FAVOR OF AN AMATEUR!
ARE THE HIGHER-UPS TRYING TO RUIN THE SHOW?
DON'T SAY THAT MR. YAJIMA...

Hime Kino & Shiro	Senri Kudo
Year 1, Voice Acting Birthday: December 5 Type: B Height: 151 cm Favorite food: hamburger steak & watermelon Good subject: P.E. & Home Ec Favorite color: pink Hobby: collecting *Lovely ♡ Blazer* goods	Year 1, Voice Acting Birthday: August 21 Type: AB Height: 176 cm Favorite food: junk food Good subject: Classics & Japanese Favorite color: black & gray Hobby: cats & movies

B

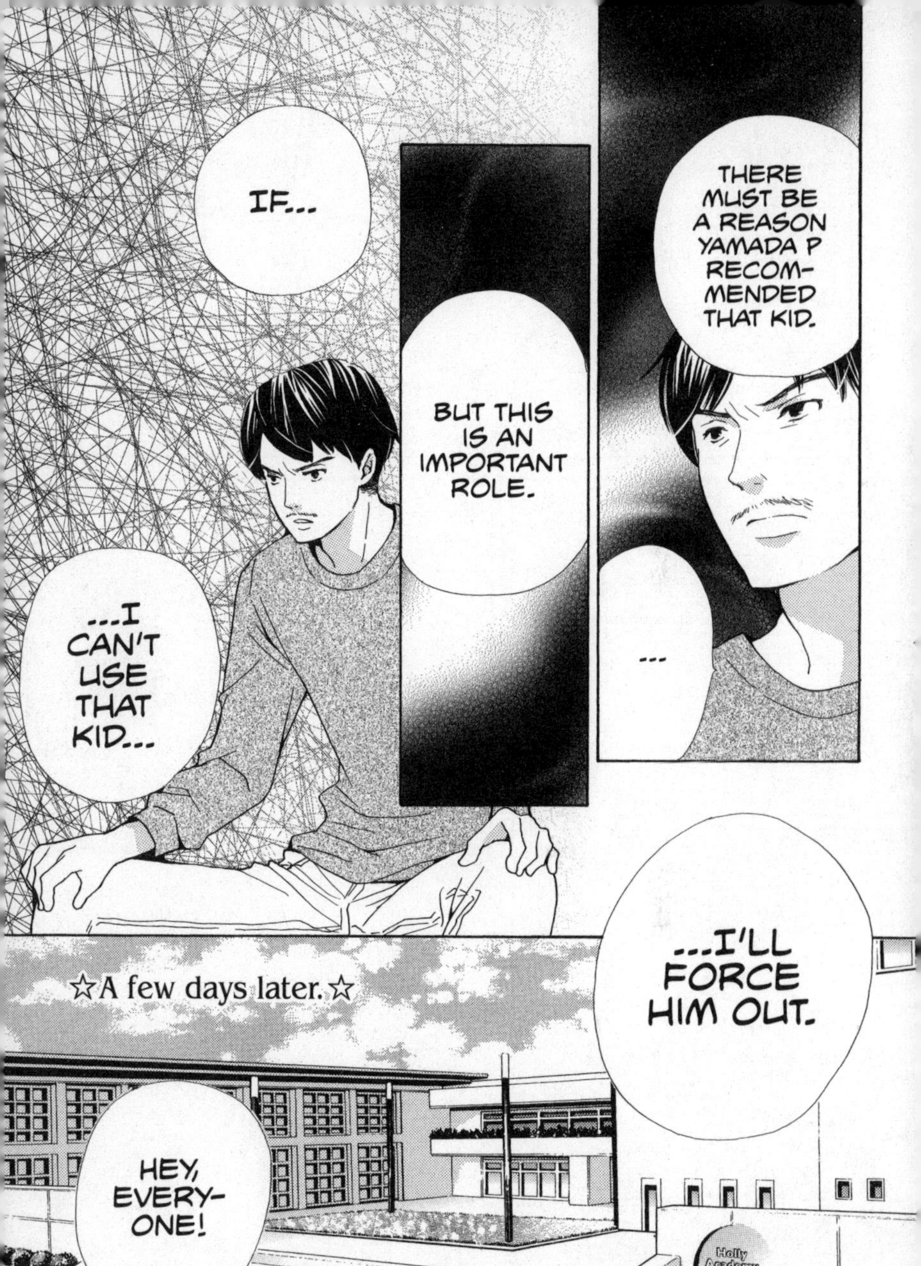
THERE MUST BE A REASON YAMADA P RECOM-MENDED THAT KID.
...
BUT THIS IS AN IMPORTANT ROLE.
IF...
...I CAN'T USE THAT KID...
...I'LL FORCE HIM OUT.
☆A few days later.☆
HEY, EVERY-ONE!
Holly Academy High School

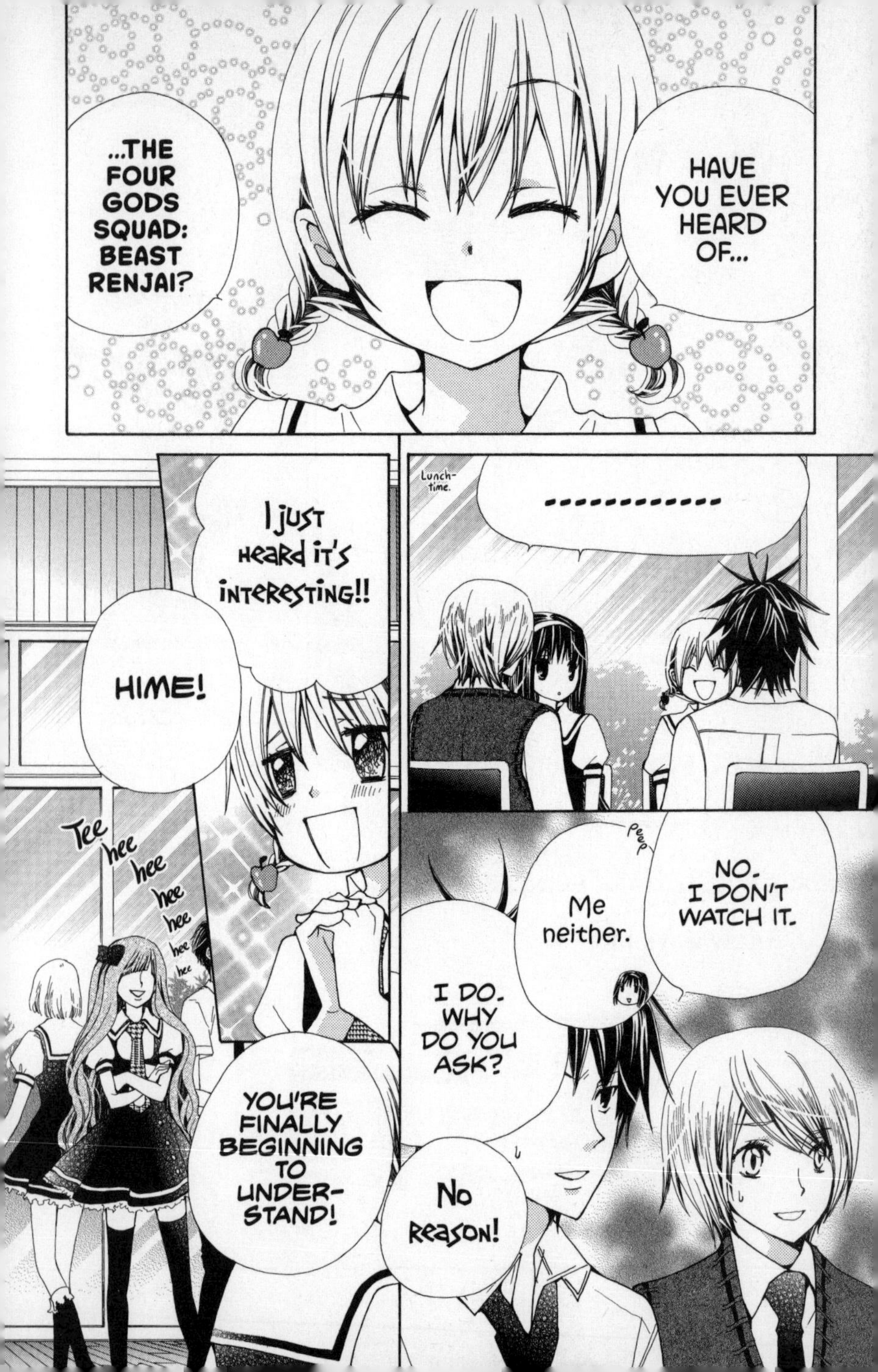
HAVE YOU EVER HEARD OF...
...THE FOUR GODS SQUAD: BEAST RENJAI?
Lunch-time.

NO. I DON'T WATCH IT.
Peep
Me neither.
I DO. WHY DO YOU ASK?
No reason!
I just heard it's interesting!!
HIME!
YOU'RE FINALLY BEGINNING TO UNDER-STAND!
Tee hee hee hee hee hee hee

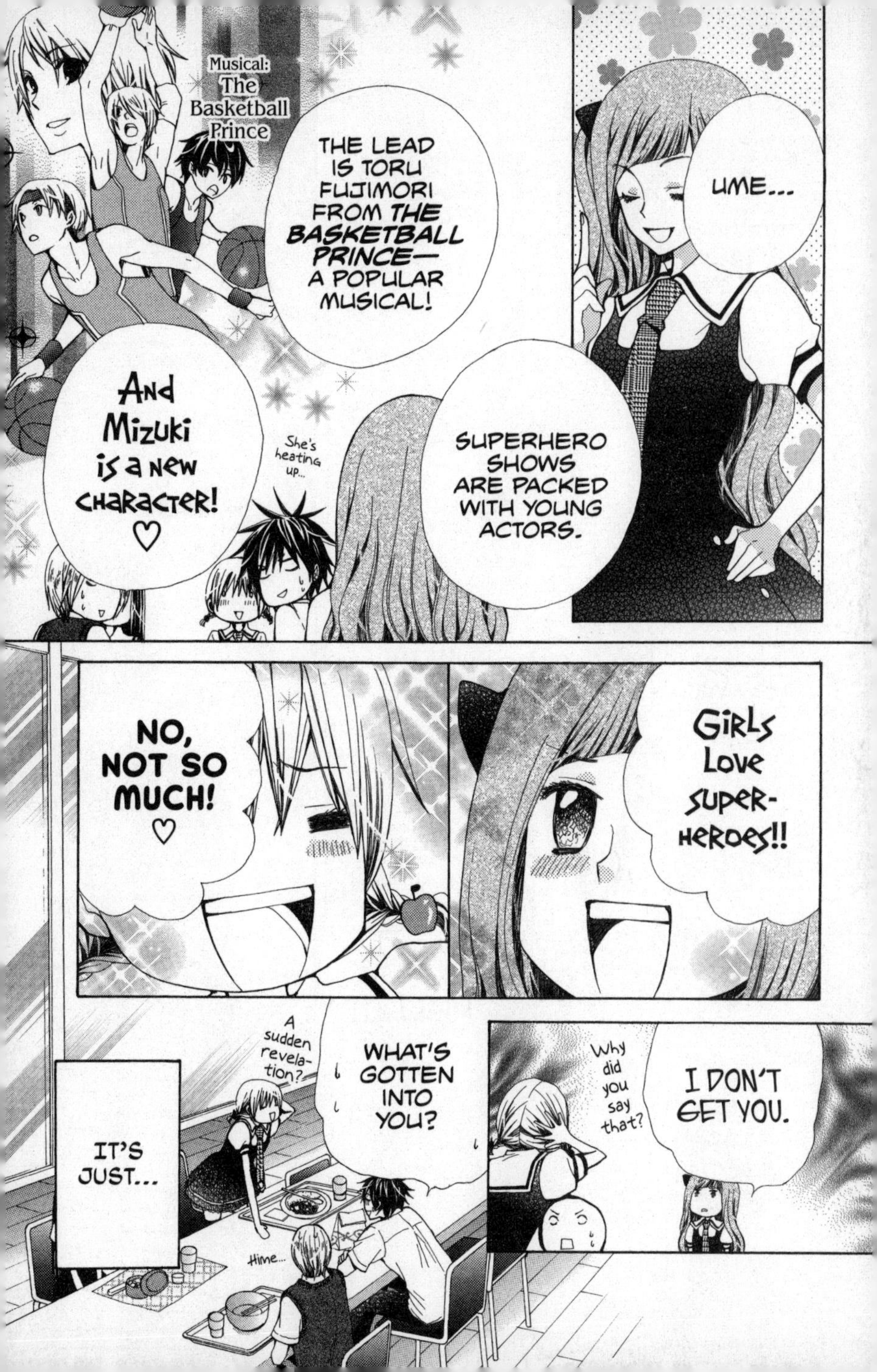
UME...
SUPERHERO SHOWS ARE PACKED WITH YOUNG ACTORS.
Musical: The Basketball Prince
THE LEAD IS TORU FUJIMORI FROM *THE BASKETBALL PRINCE*— A POPULAR MUSICAL!
She's heating up...
And Mizuki is a new character! ♡
Girls Love Super-heroes!!
NO, NOT SO MUCH! ♡
I DON'T GET YOU.
Why did you say that?
WHAT'S GOTTEN INTO YOU?
A sudden revela-tion?
Hime...
IT'S JUST...

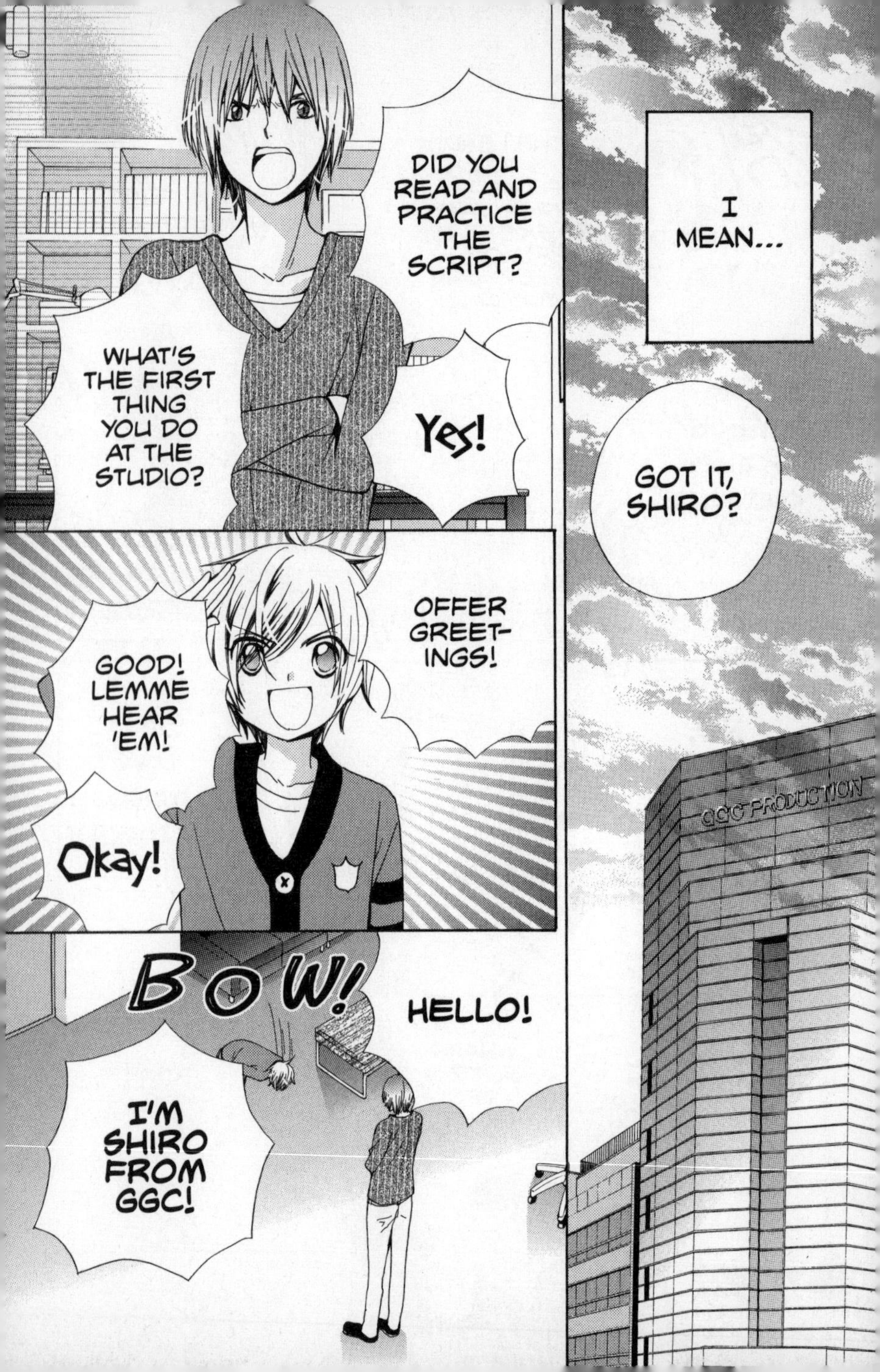
I MEAN...
GOT IT, SHIRO?
GGC PRODUCTION
DID YOU READ AND PRACTICE THE SCRIPT?
Yes!
WHAT'S THE FIRST THING YOU DO AT THE STUDIO?
OFFER GREET-INGS!
GOOD! LEMME HEAR 'EM!
Okay!
BOW!
HELLO!
I'M SHIRO FROM GGC!

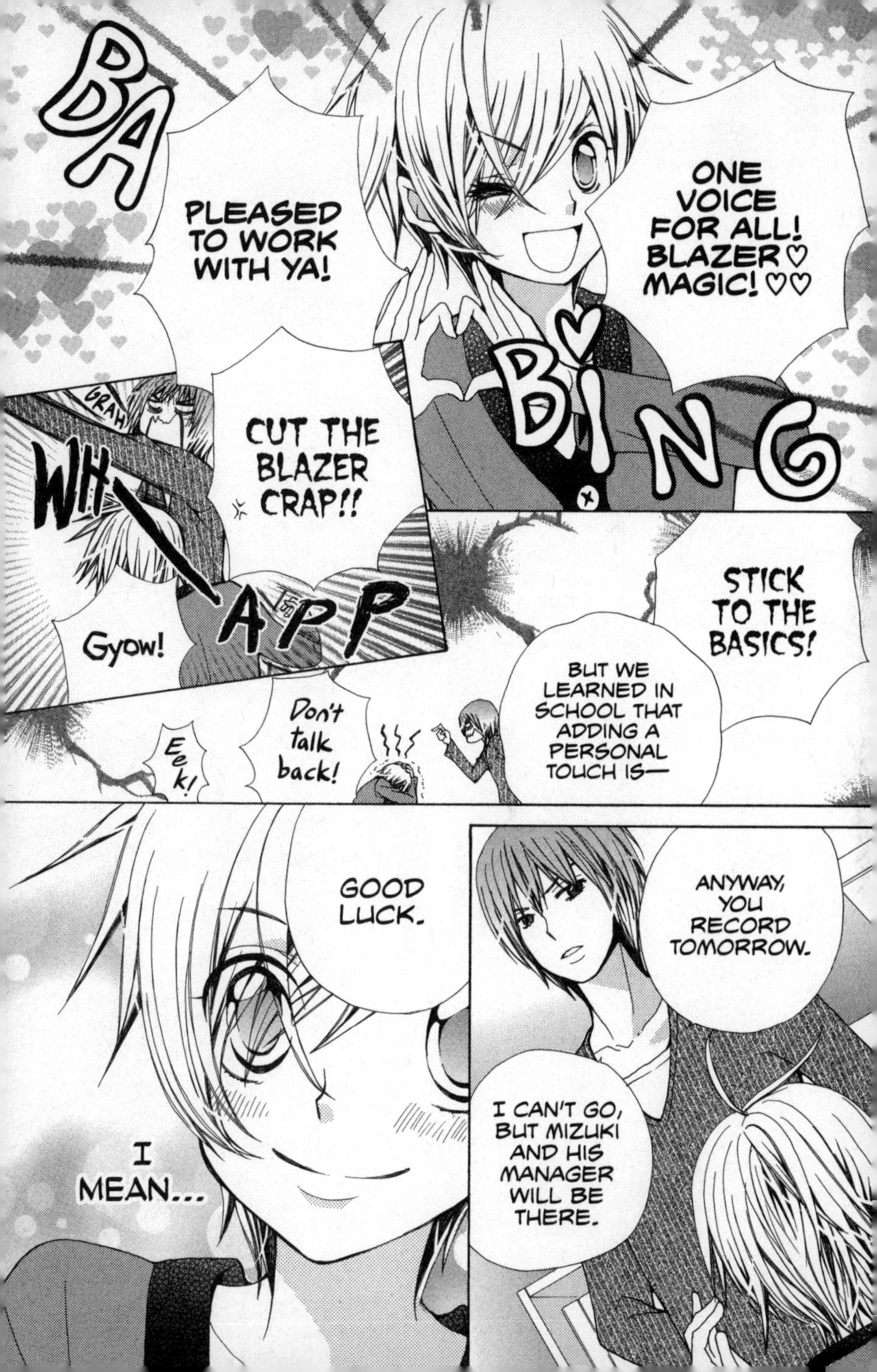
BA
ONE VOICE FOR ALL! BLAZER♡ MAGIC!♡♡
PLEASED TO WORK WITH YA!
BING
GRAH
CUT THE BLAZER CRAP!!
WHAPP
Gyow!
STICK TO THE BASICS!
BUT WE LEARNED IN SCHOOL THAT ADDING A PERSONAL TOUCH IS—
Don't talk back!
Eek!
ANYWAY, YOU RECORD TOMORROW.
I CAN'T GO, BUT MIZUKI AND HIS MANAGER WILL BE THERE.
GOOD LUCK.
I MEAN...

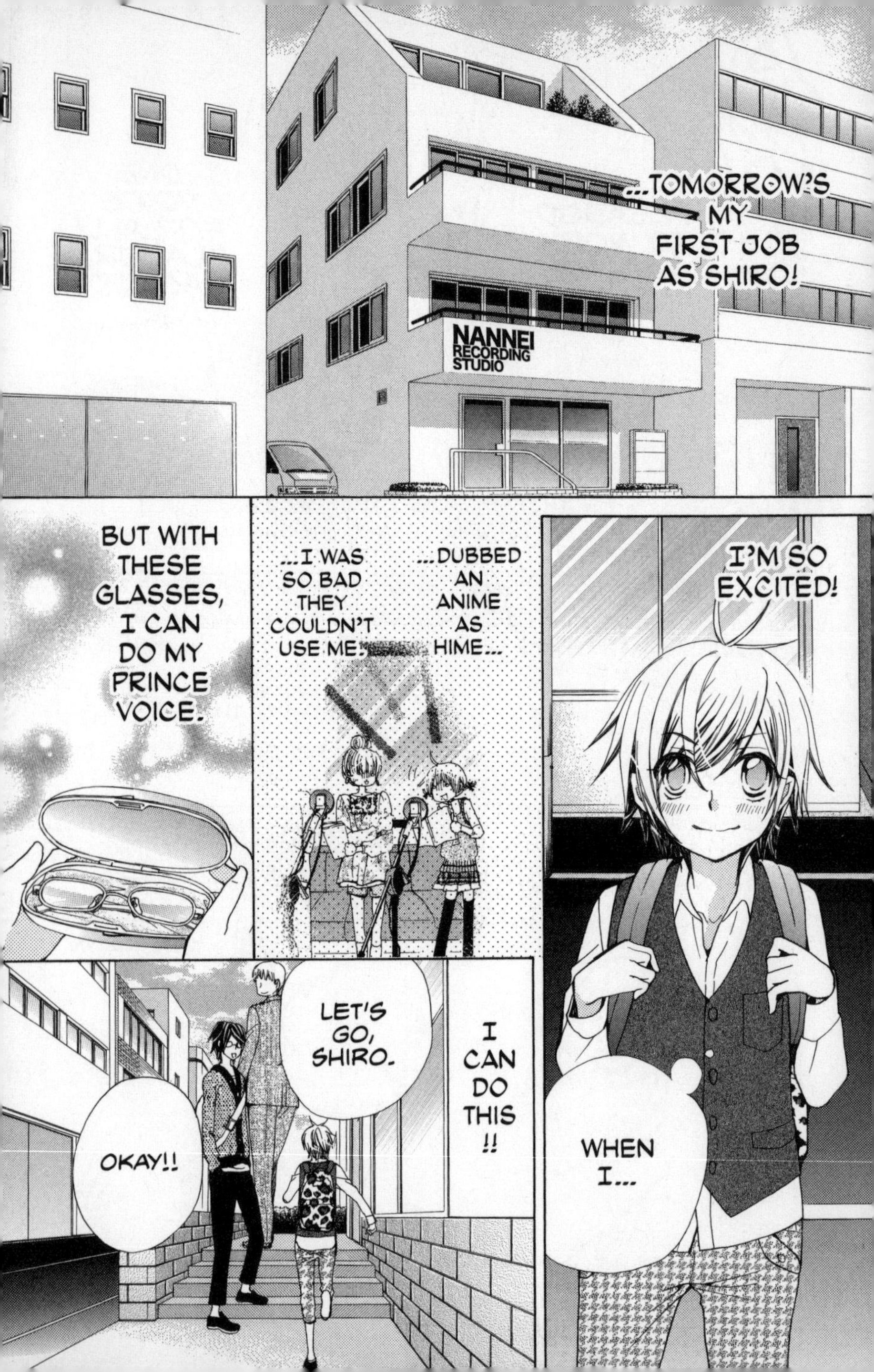
NANNEI RECORDING STUDIO
...TOMORROW'S MY FIRST JOB AS SHIRO!
I'M SO EXCITED!
WHEN I...
...DUBBED AN ANIME AS HIME...
...I WAS SO BAD THEY COULDN'T USE ME.
BUT WITH THESE GLASSES, I CAN DO MY PRINCE VOICE.
I CAN DO THIS!!
LET'S GO, SHIRO.
OKAY!!

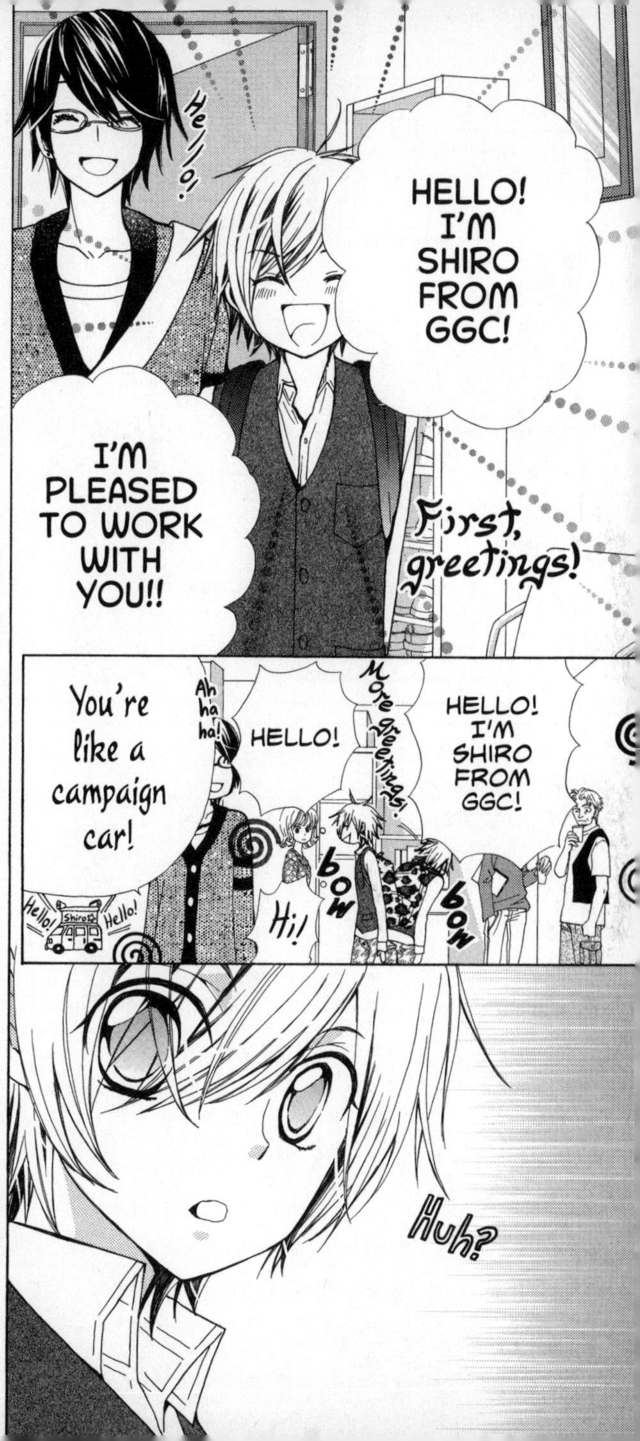
HELLO! I'M SHIRO FROM GGC!
Hello!
First, greetings!
I'M PLEASED TO WORK WITH YOU!!
HELLO! I'M SHIRO FROM GGC!
More greetings!
HELLO!
Ah ha ha!
You're like a campaign car!
bow
bow
Hi!
Hello!
Shiro
Hello!
Huh?

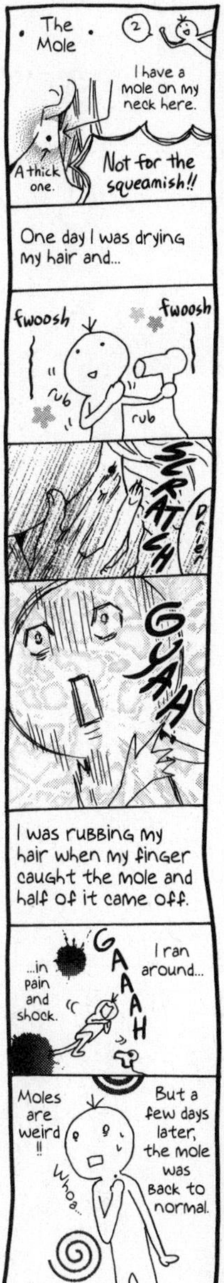
The Mole
2
I have a mole on my neck here.
Not for the squeamish!!
A thick one.
One day I was drying my hair and...
fwoosh
fwoosh
rub
rub
SCRATCH
Drier
GYAH!
I was rubbing my hair when my finger caught the mole and half of it came off.
GAAAAH
I ran around...
...in pain and shock.
But a few days later, the mole was back to normal.
Moles are weird!!
Whoa...

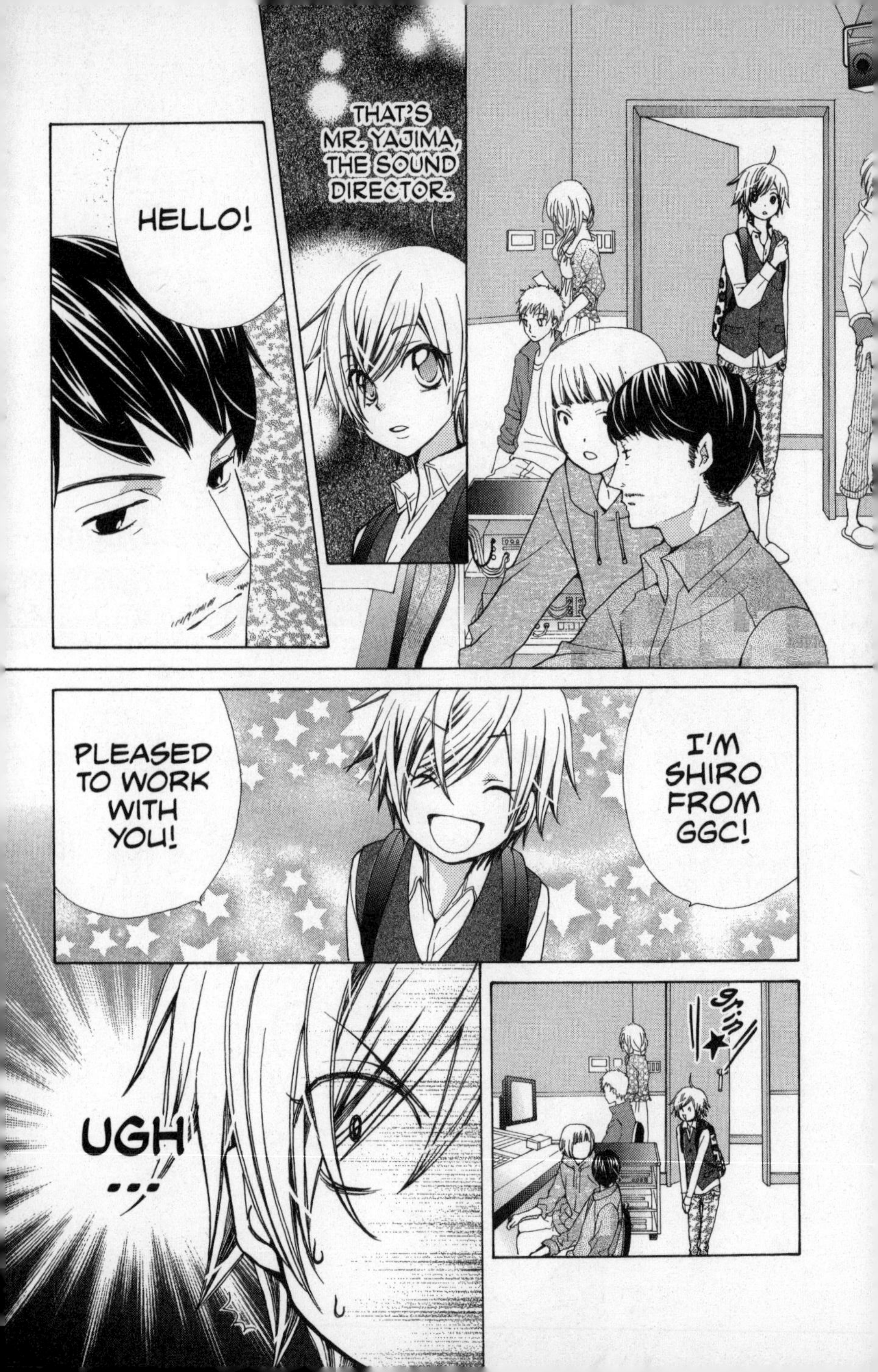
THAT'S MR. YAJIMA, THE SOUND DIRECTOR.
HELLO!
I'M SHIRO FROM GGC!
PLEASED TO WORK WITH YOU!
grin ★
UGH...!

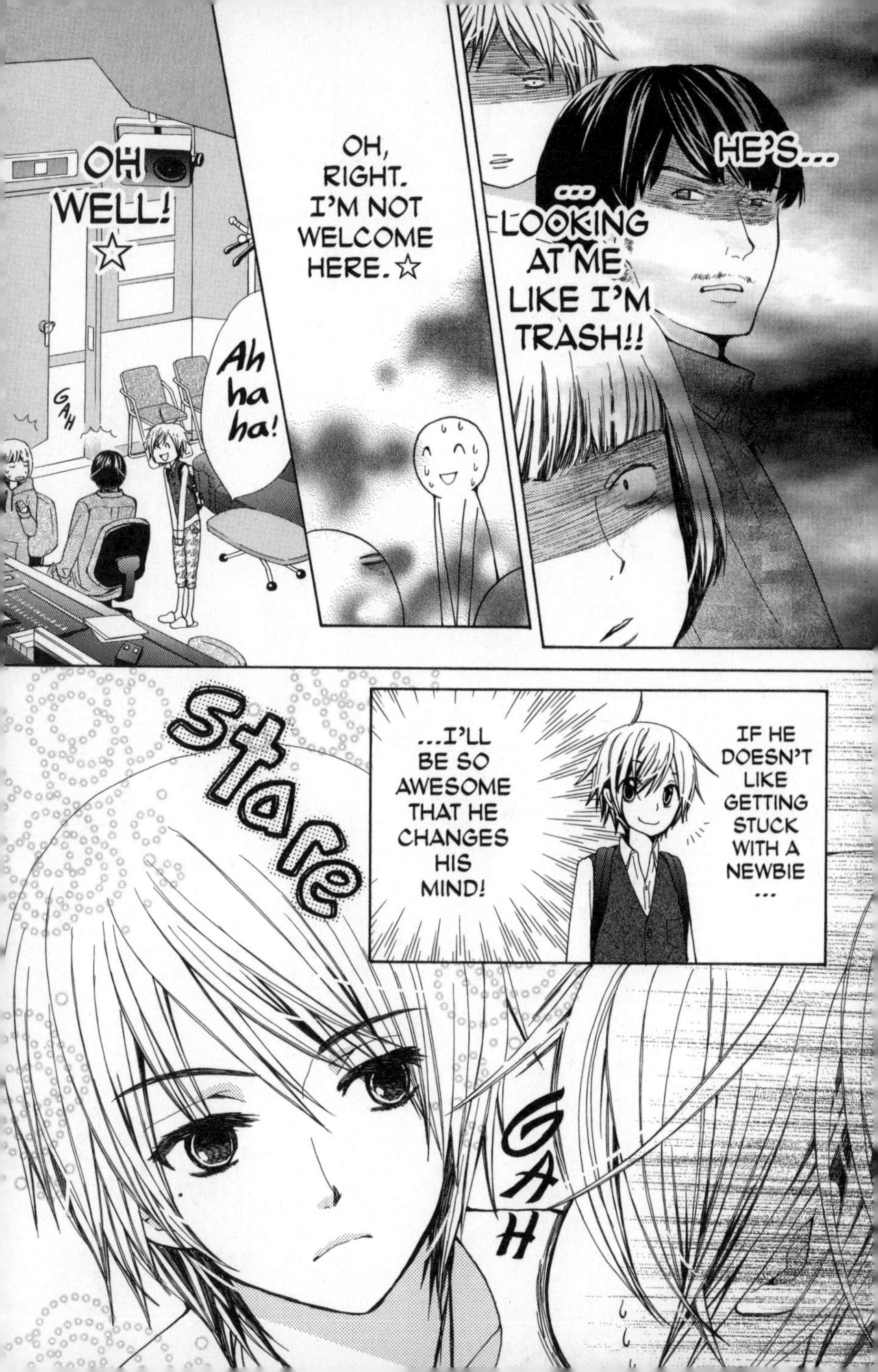
HE'S...
...
LOOKING AT ME LIKE I'M TRASH!!
OH, RIGHT. I'M NOT WELCOME HERE.☆
OH WELL! ☆
Ah ha ha!
GAH
IF HE DOESN'T LIKE GETTING STUCK WITH A NEWBIE...
...I'LL BE SO AWESOME THAT HE CHANGES HIS MIND!
Stare
GAH

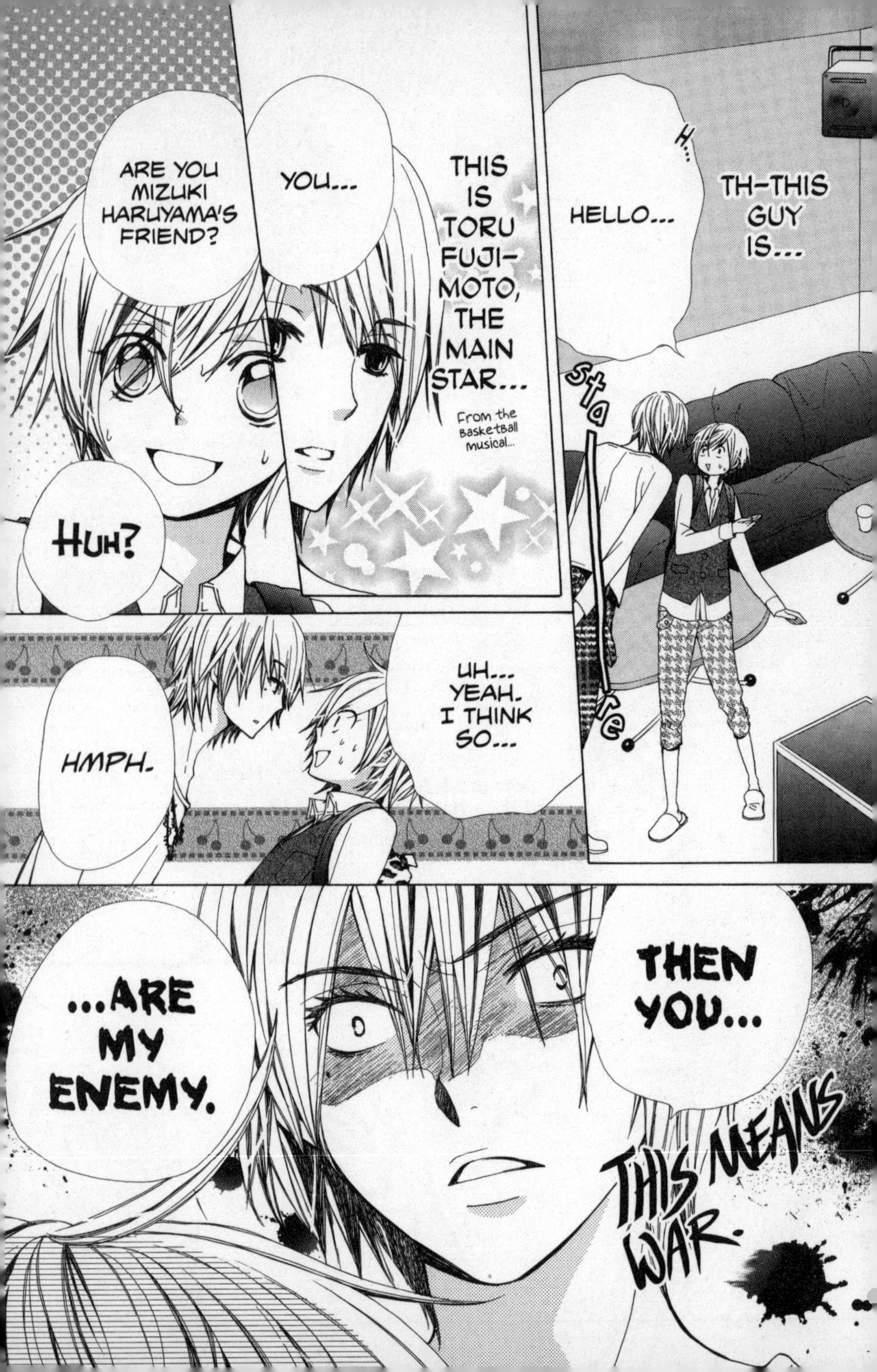
TH-THIS GUY IS...
H...
HELLO...
stare
YOU...
THIS IS TORU FUJI-MOTO, THE MAIN STAR...
From the BasketBall musical...
ARE YOU MIZUKI HARUYAMA'S FRIEND?
HUH?
UH... YEAH. I THINK SO...
HMPH.
THEN YOU...
...ARE MY ENEMY.
THIS MEANS WAR.

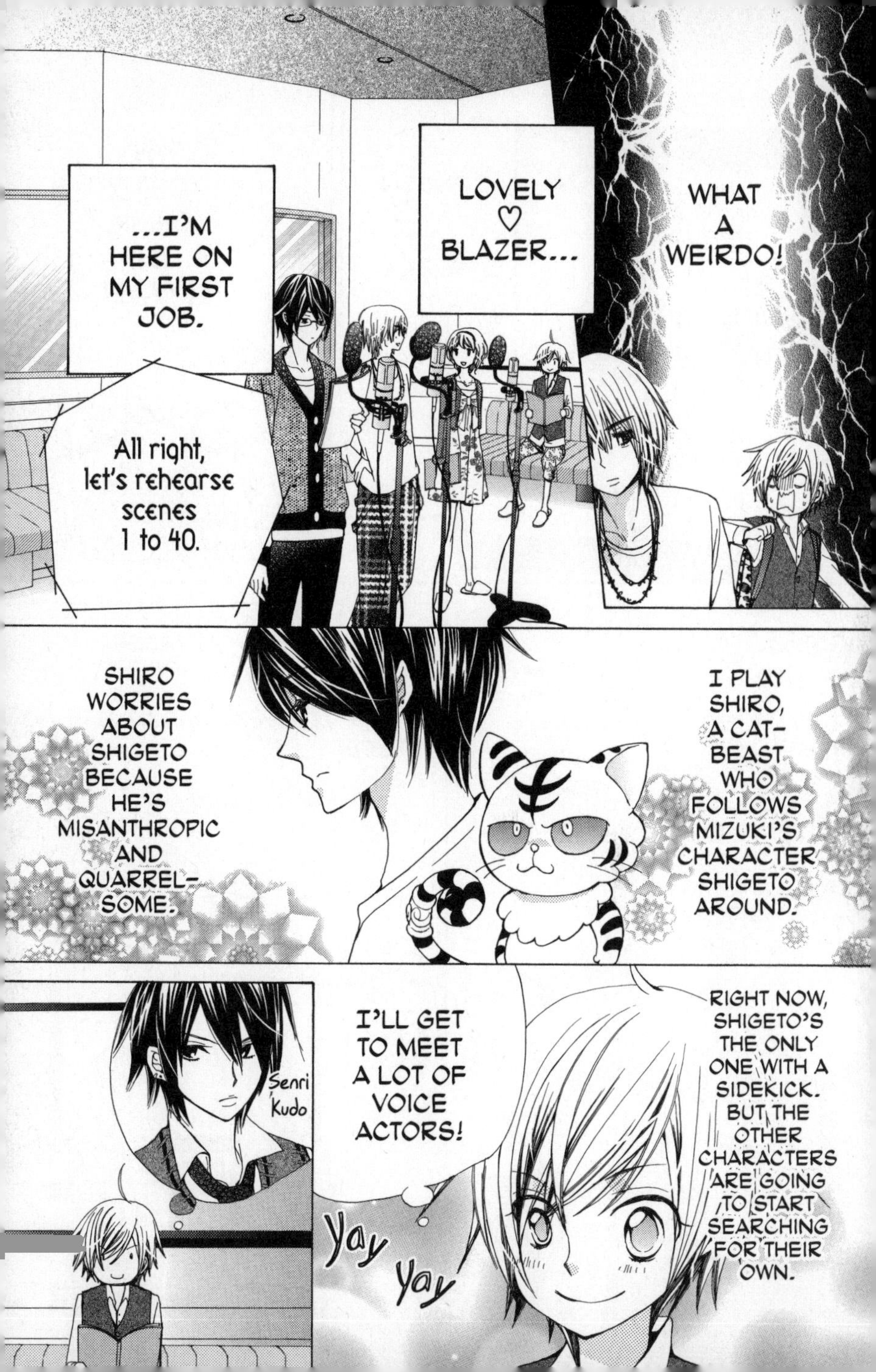
WHAT A WEIRDO!
LOVELY ♡ BLAZER...
...I'M HERE ON MY FIRST JOB.
All right, let's rehearse scenes 1 to 40.
I PLAY SHIRO, A CAT-BEAST WHO FOLLOWS MIZUKI'S CHARACTER SHIGETO AROUND.
SHIRO WORRIES ABOUT SHIGETO BECAUSE HE'S MISANTHROPIC AND QUARREL-SOME.
RIGHT NOW, SHIGETO'S THE ONLY ONE WITH A SIDEKICK. BUT THE OTHER CHARACTERS ARE GOING TO START SEARCHING FOR THEIR OWN.
I'LL GET TO MEET A LOT OF VOICE ACTORS!
Yay Yay
Senri Kudo

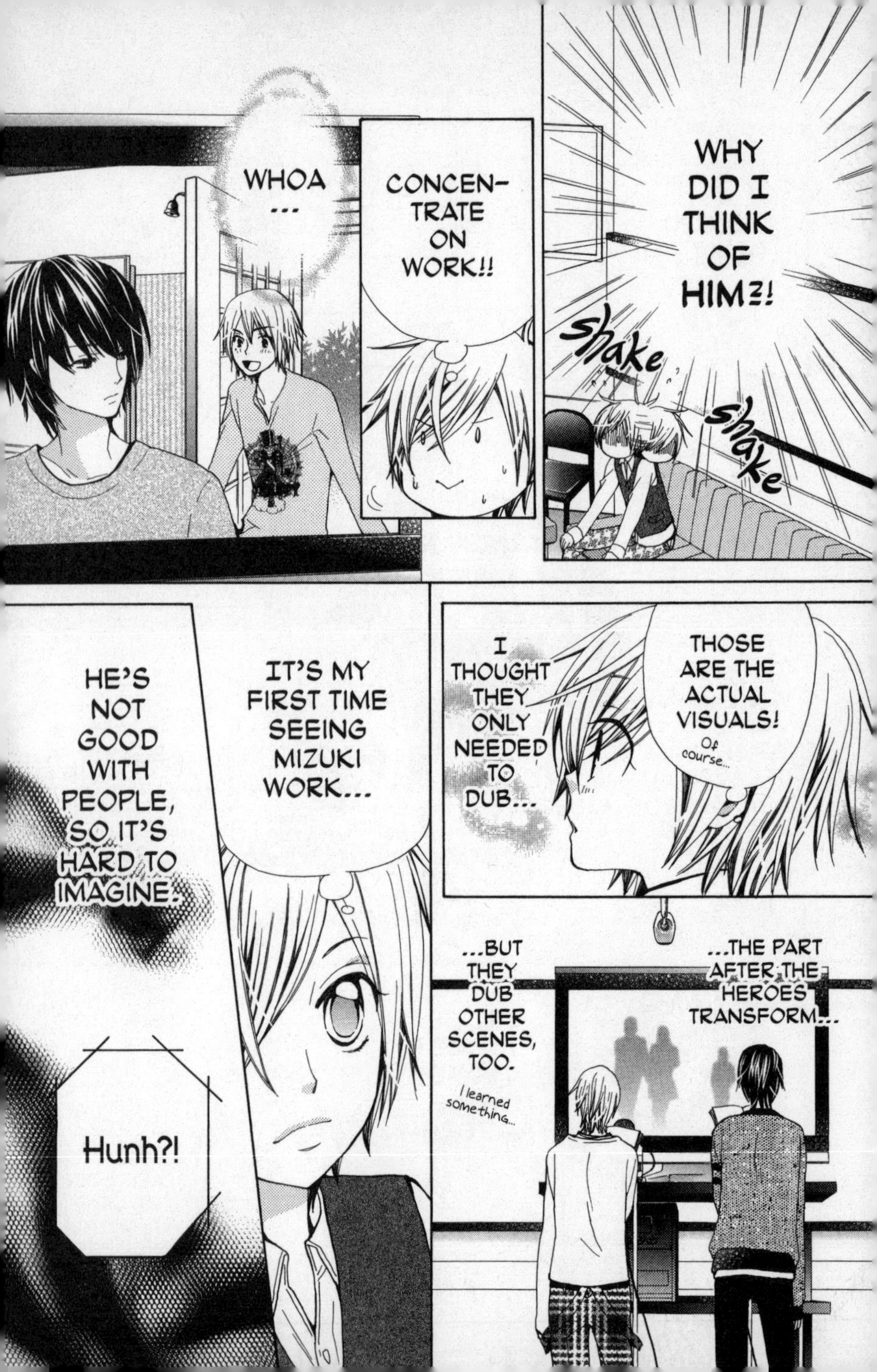
WHY DID I THINK OF HIM?!
shake
shake
CONCEN-TRATE ON WORK!!
WHOA...
THOSE ARE THE ACTUAL VISUALS!
Of course...
I THOUGHT THEY ONLY NEEDED TO DUB...
...THE PART AFTER THE HEROES TRANSFORM...
...BUT THEY DUB OTHER SCENES, TOO.
I learned something...
IT'S MY FIRST TIME SEEING MIZUKI WORK...
HE'S NOT GOOD WITH PEOPLE, SO IT'S HARD TO IMAGINE.
Hunh?!

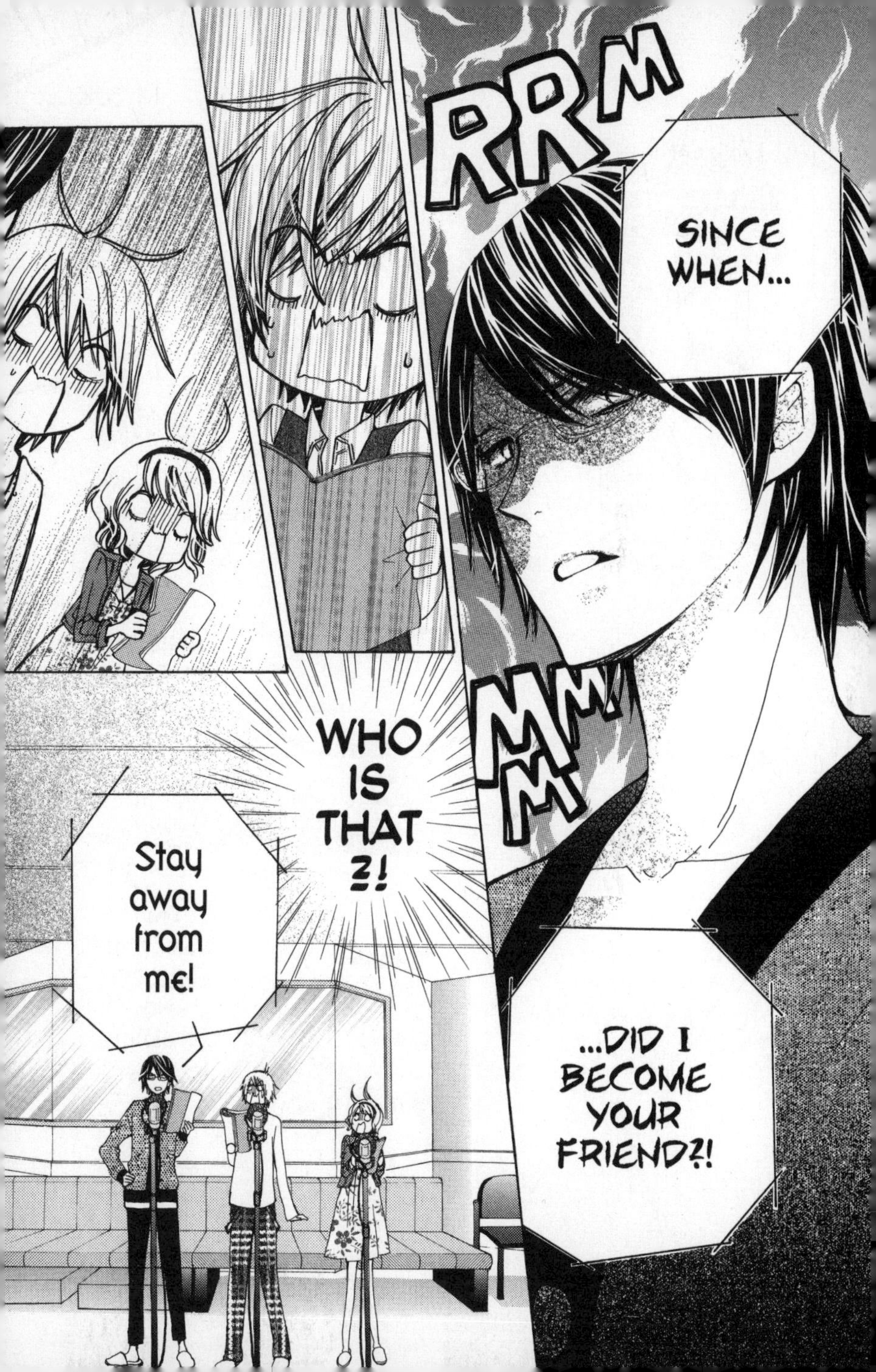
RRM
SINCE WHEN...
MMM
...DID I BECOME YOUR FRIEND?!
WHO IS THAT?!
Stay away from me!

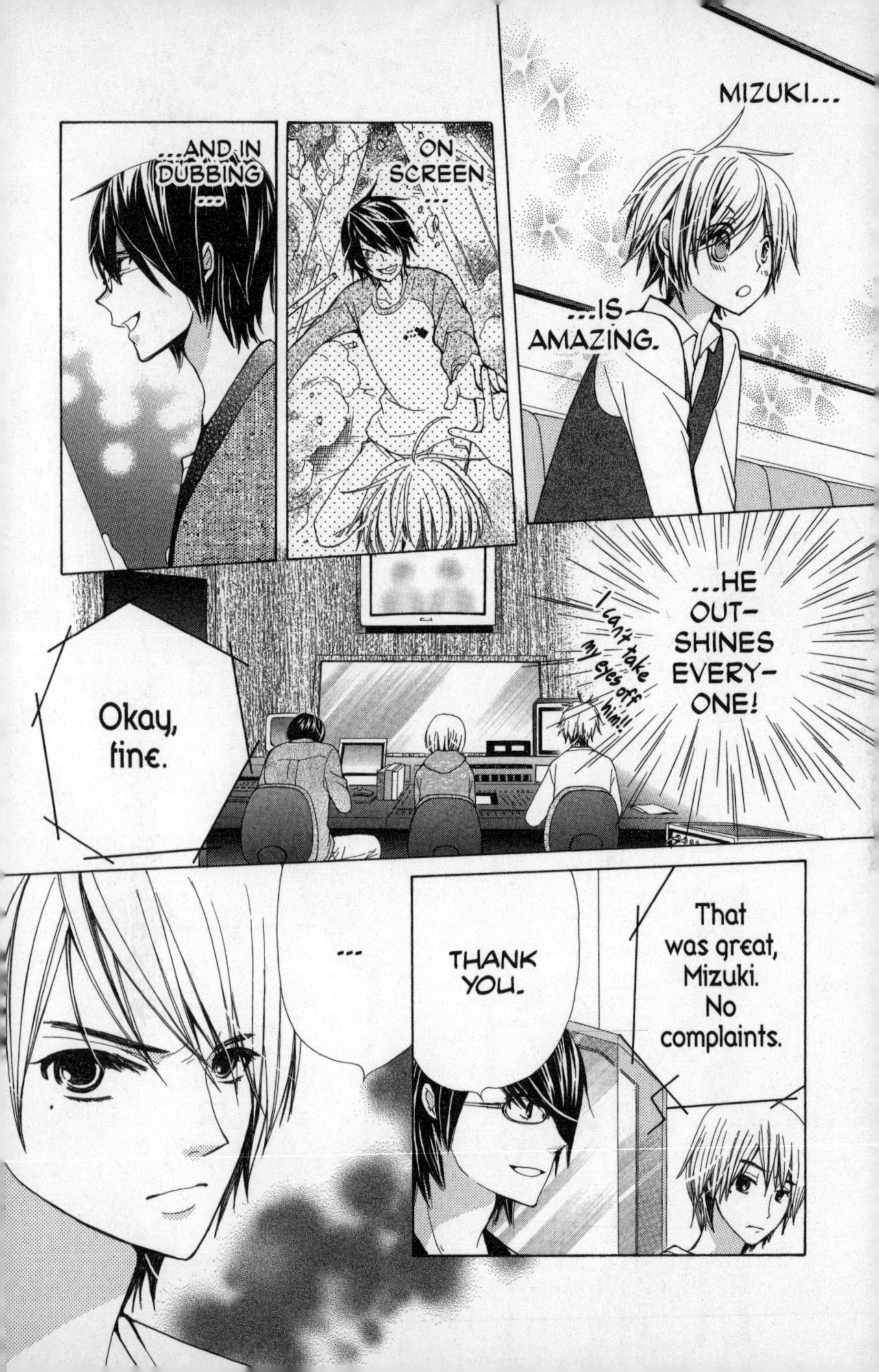
MIZUKI...
...IS AMAZING.
ON SCREEN...
...AND IN DUBBING...
...HE OUT-SHINES EVERY-ONE!
I can't take my eyes off him!!
Okay, fine.
That was great, Mizuki. No complaints.
THANK YOU.
...

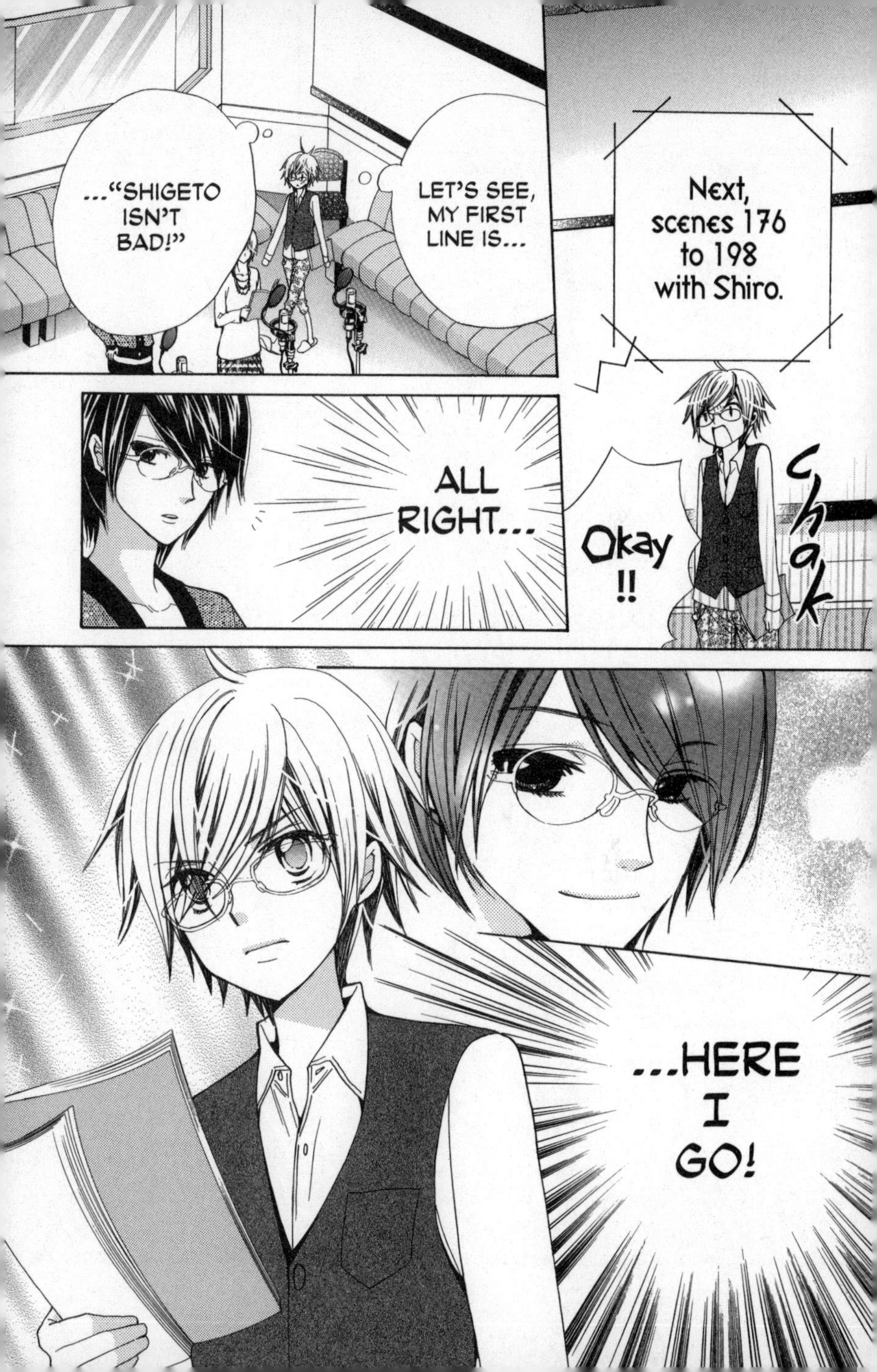
Next, scenes 176 to 198 with Shiro.
LET'S SEE, MY FIRST LINE IS...
..."SHIGETO ISN'T BAD!"
Okay!!
chak
ALL RIGHT...
...HERE I GO!

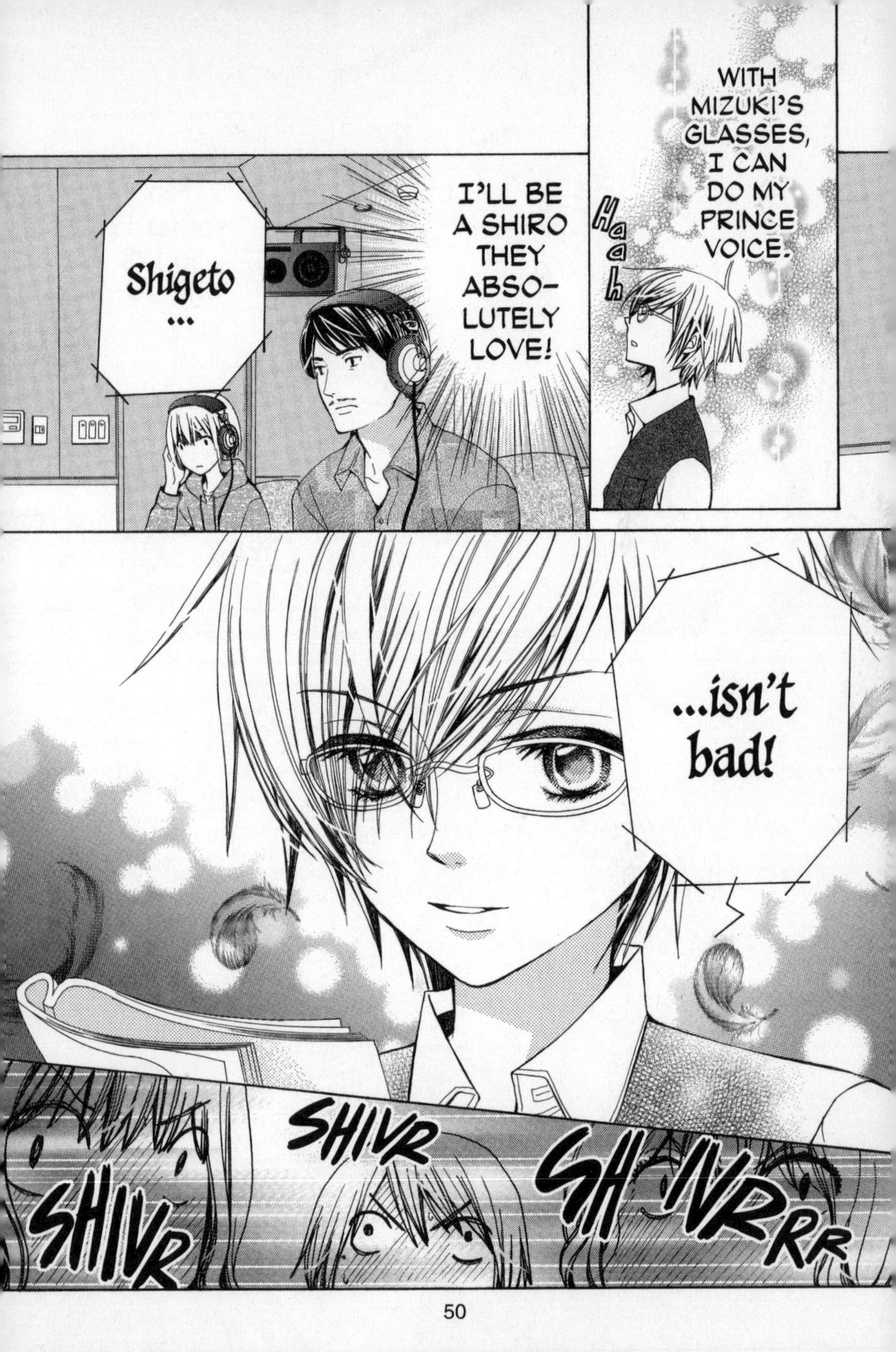
WITH MIZUKI'S GLASSES, I CAN DO MY PRINCE VOICE.
Haah
I'LL BE A SHIRO THEY ABSO-LUTELY LOVE!
Shigeto ...
...isn't bad!
SHIVRRR
SHIVR
SHIVR

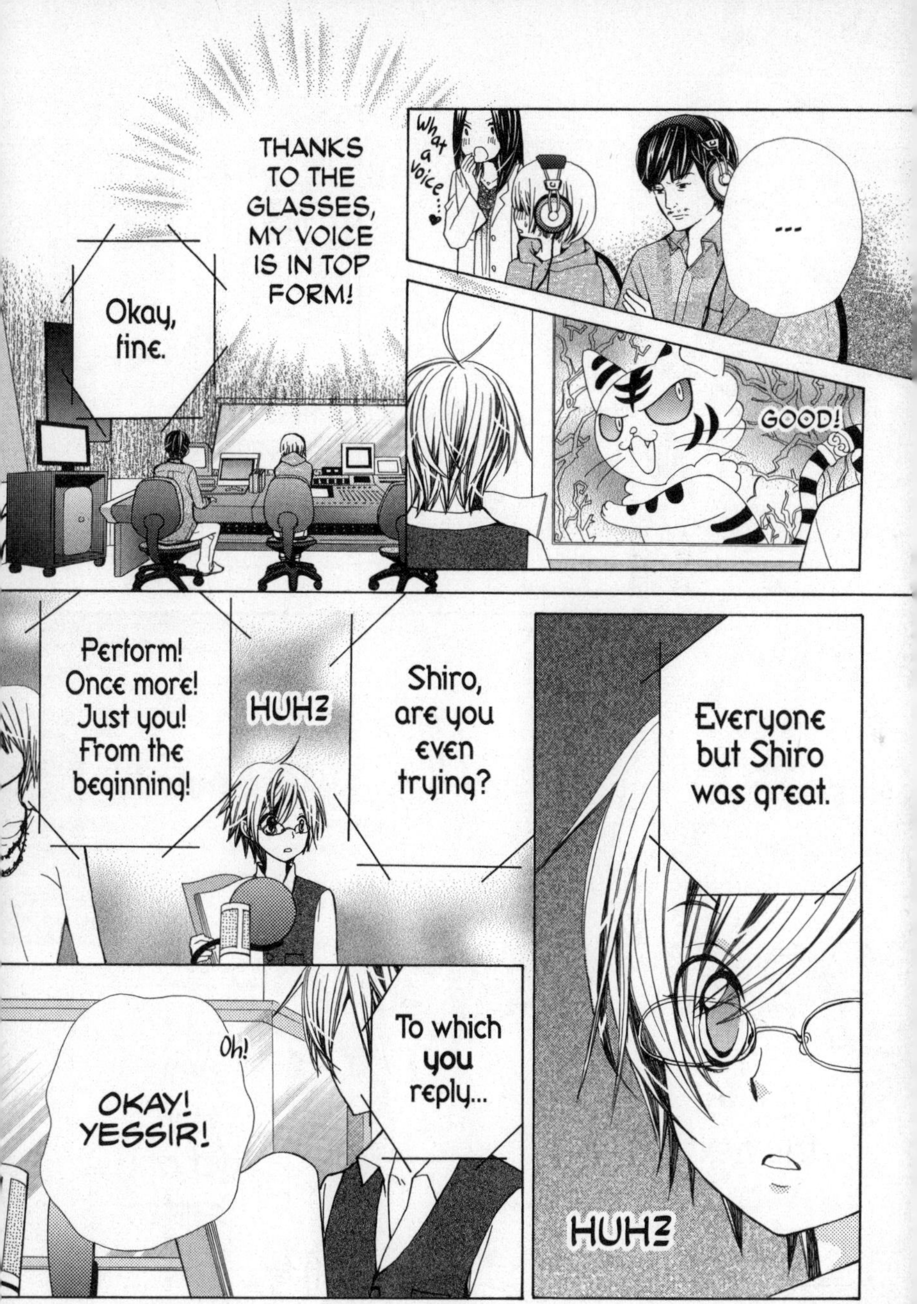
What a voice...♥
...
GOOD!
THANKS TO THE GLASSES, MY VOICE IS IN TOP FORM!
Okay, fine.
Everyone but Shiro was great.
HUH?
Shiro, are you even trying?
HUH?
Perform! Once more! Just you! From the beginning!
To which you reply...
Oh!
OKAY! YESSIR!

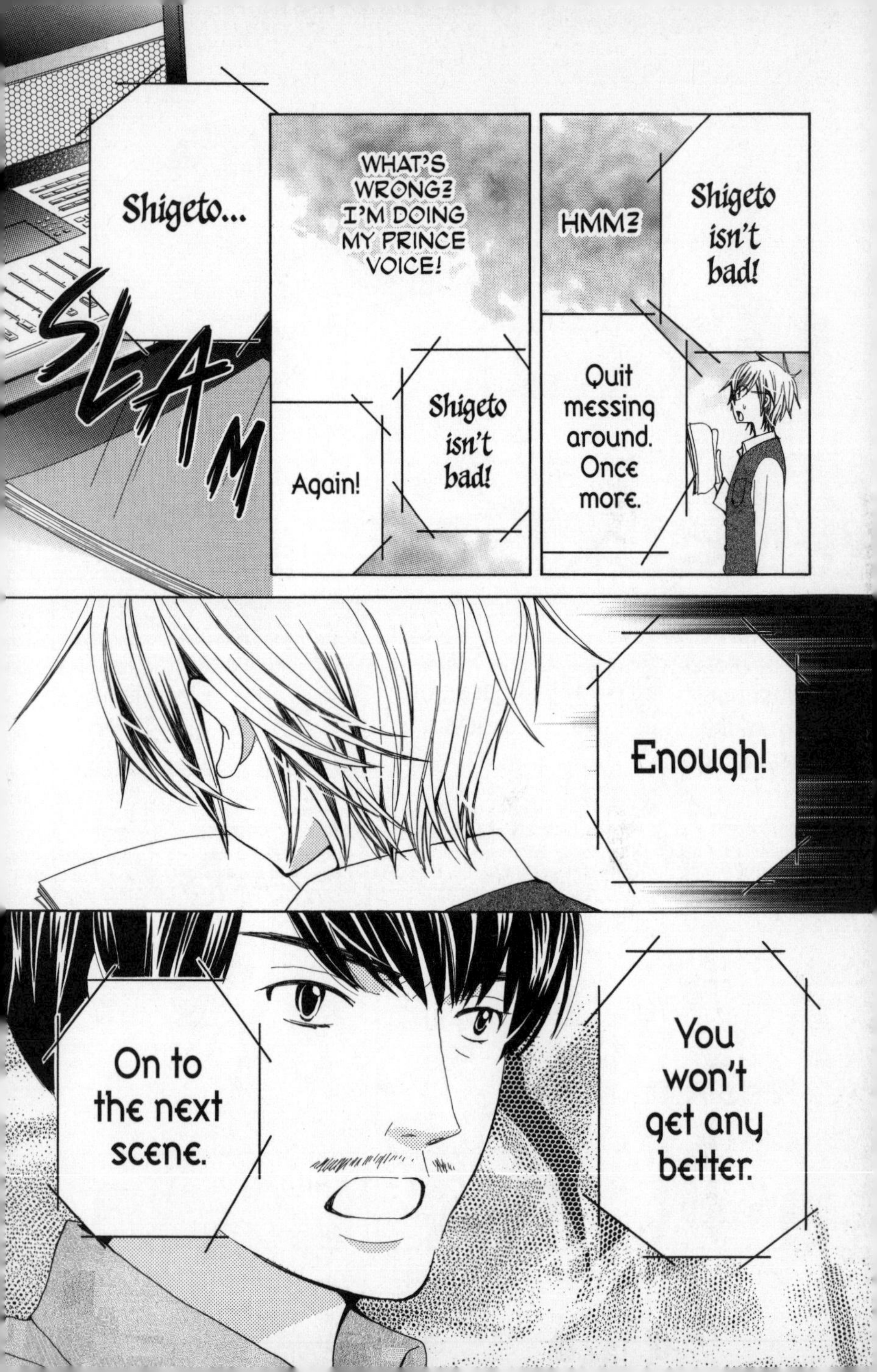
Shigeto isn't bad!
HMM?
Quit messing around. Once more.
WHAT'S WRONG? I'M DOING MY PRINCE VOICE!
Shigeto isn't bad!
Again!
Shigeto...
SLAM
Enough!
You won't get any better.
On to the next scene.

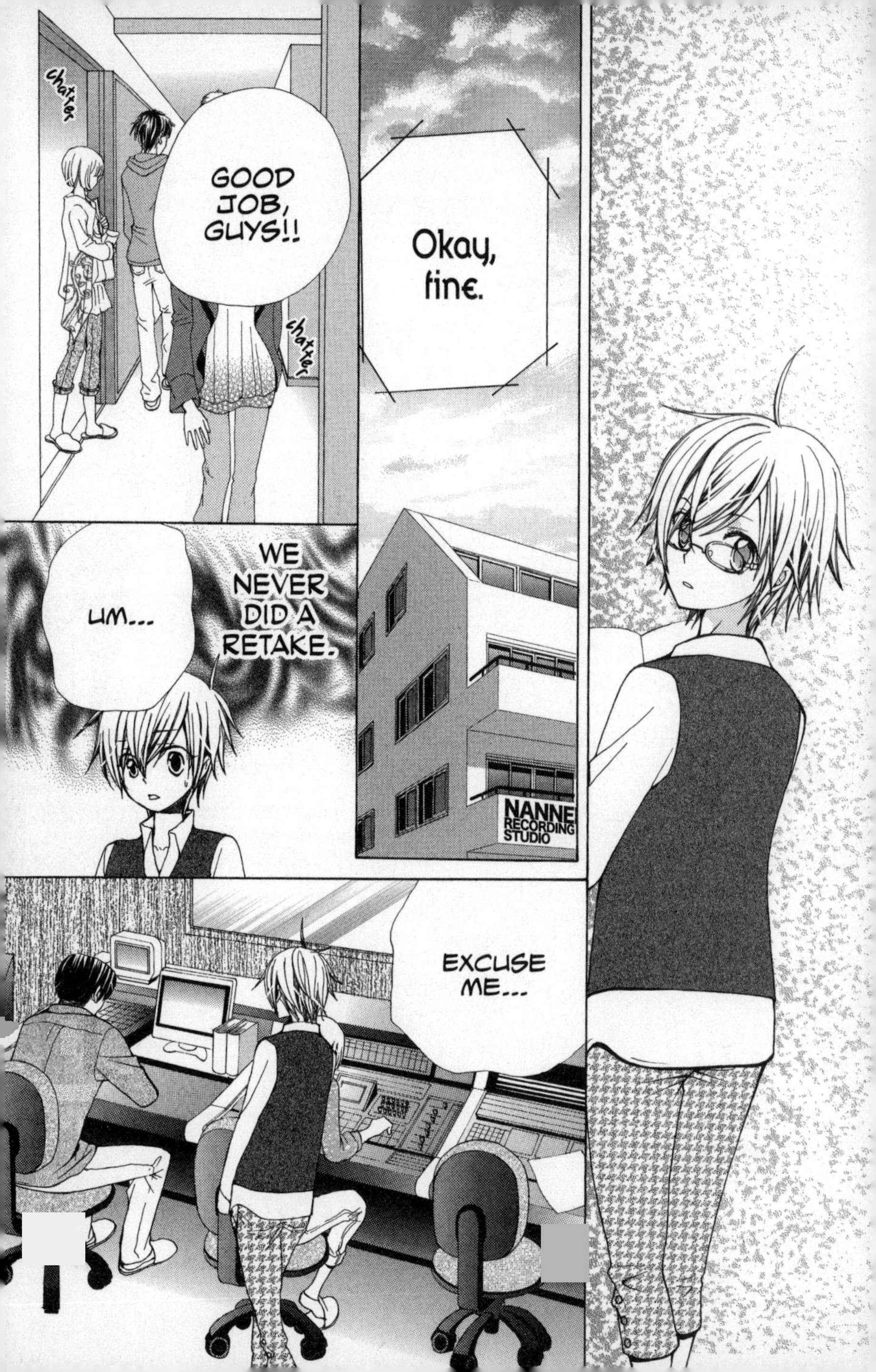
Okay, fine.
chatter
GOOD JOB, GUYS!!
chatter
WE NEVER DID A RETAKE.
UM...
NANNE RECORDING STUDIO
EXCUSE ME...

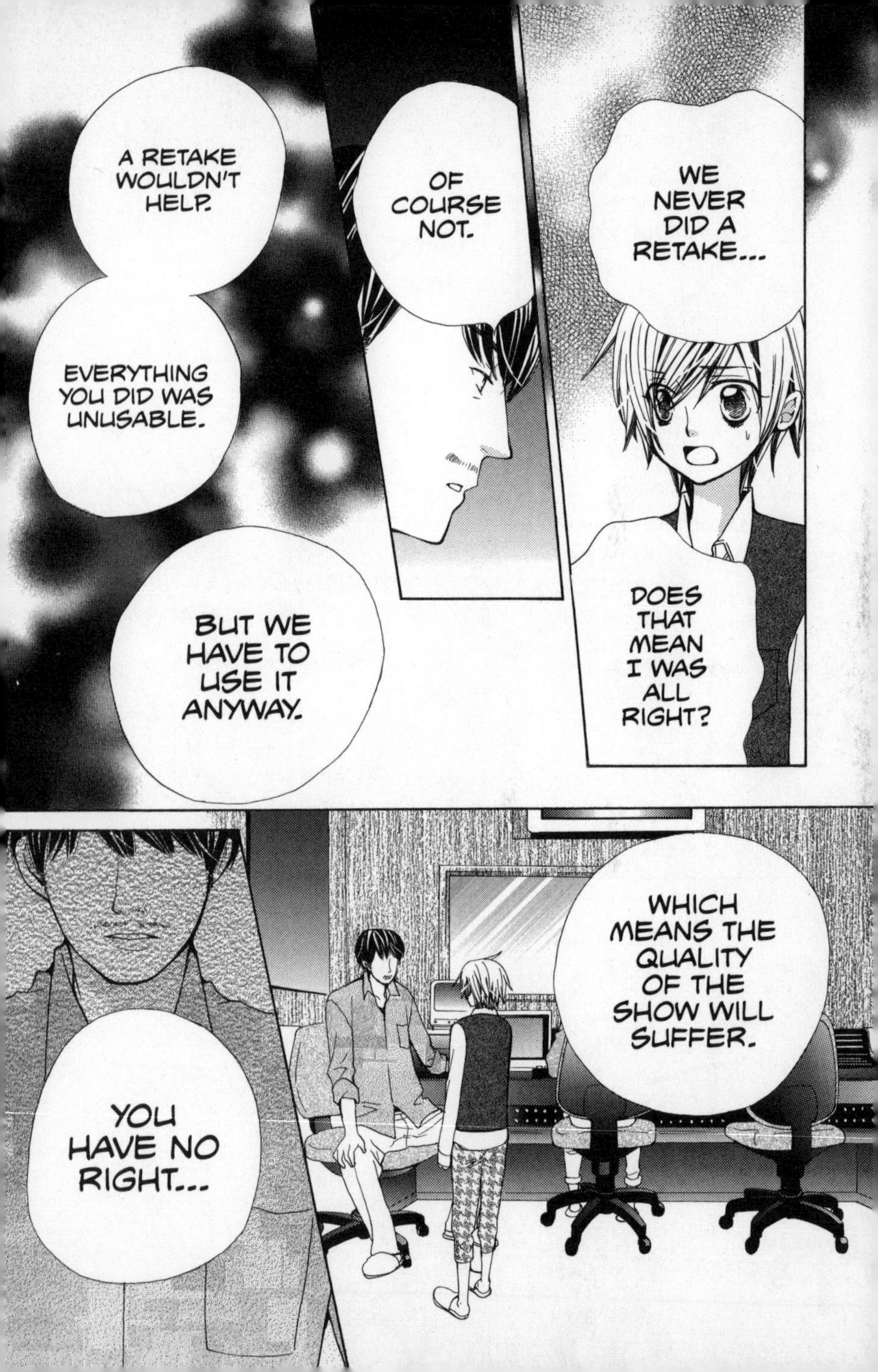
WE NEVER DID A RETAKE...
DOES THAT MEAN I WAS ALL RIGHT?
OF COURSE NOT.
A RETAKE WOULDN'T HELP.
EVERYTHING YOU DID WAS UNUSABLE.
BUT WE HAVE TO USE IT ANYWAY.
WHICH MEANS THE QUALITY OF THE SHOW WILL SUFFER.
YOU HAVE NO RIGHT...

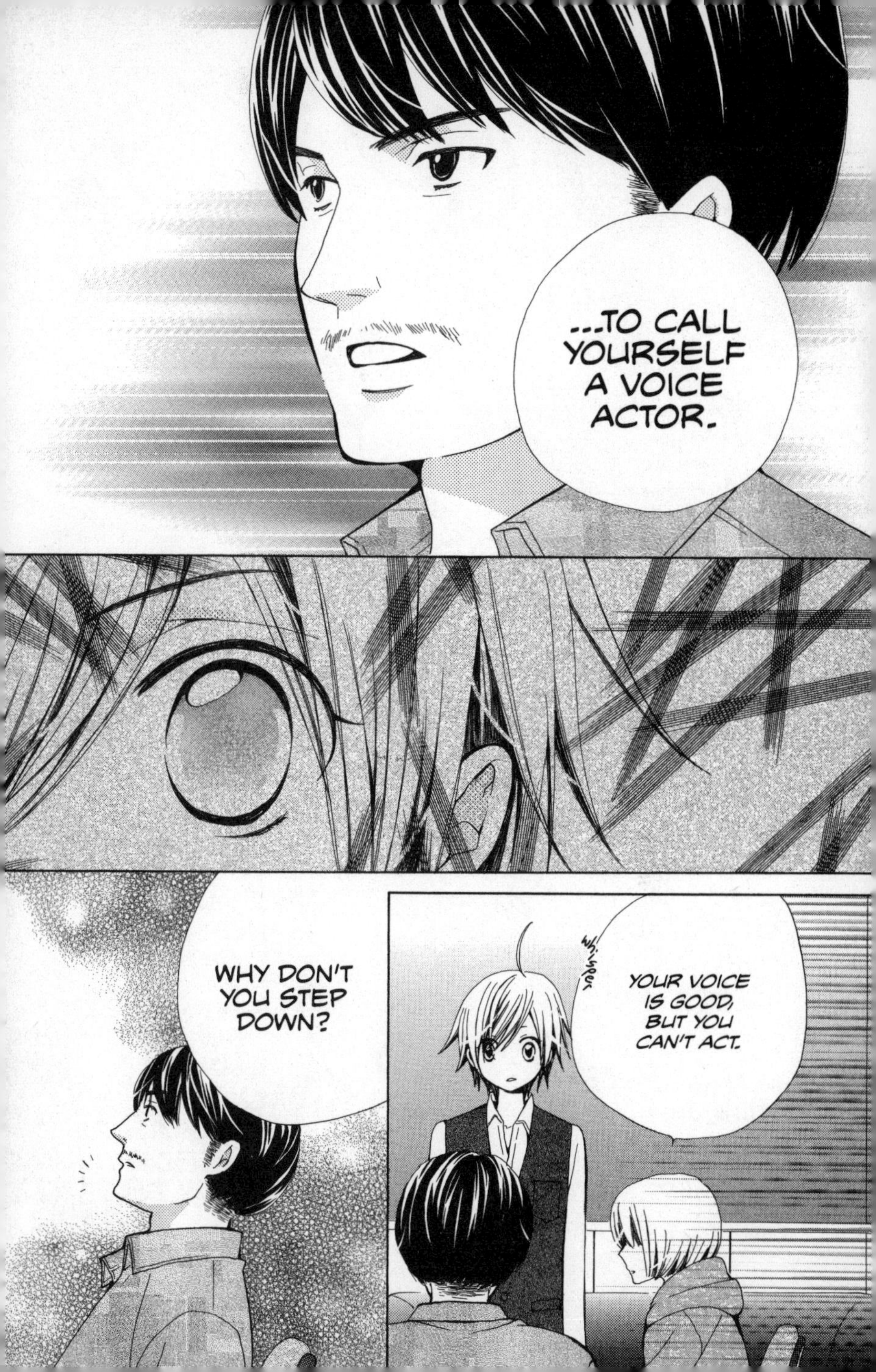
...TO CALL YOURSELF A VOICE ACTOR.
whisper
YOUR VOICE IS GOOD, BUT YOU CAN'T ACT.
WHY DON'T YOU STEP DOWN?

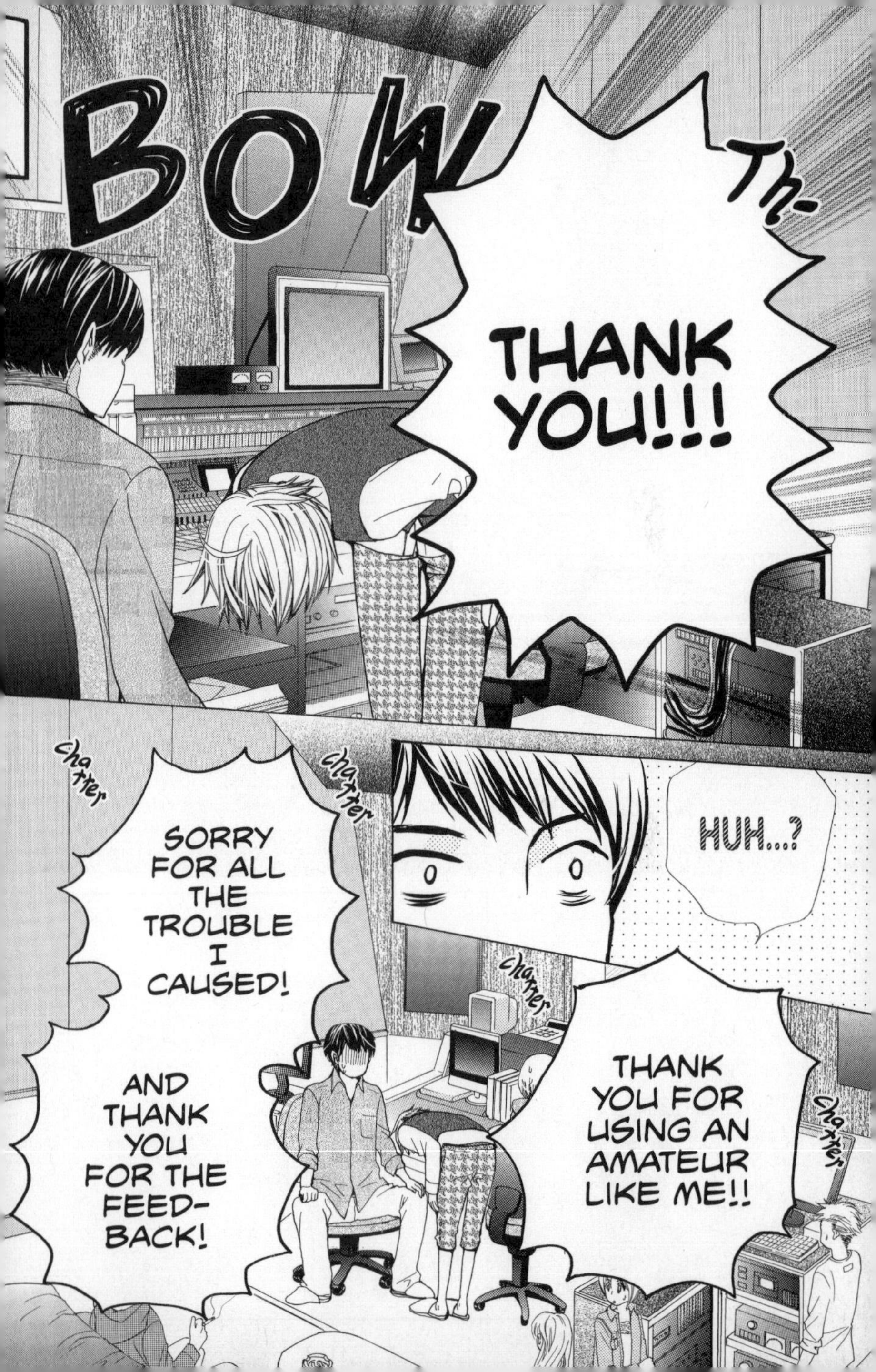
BOW
Th-
THANK YOU!!!
HUH...?
chatter
chatter
SORRY FOR ALL THE TROUBLE I CAUSED!
chatter
THANK YOU FOR USING AN AMATEUR LIKE ME!!
chatter
AND THANK YOU FOR THE FEED-BACK!

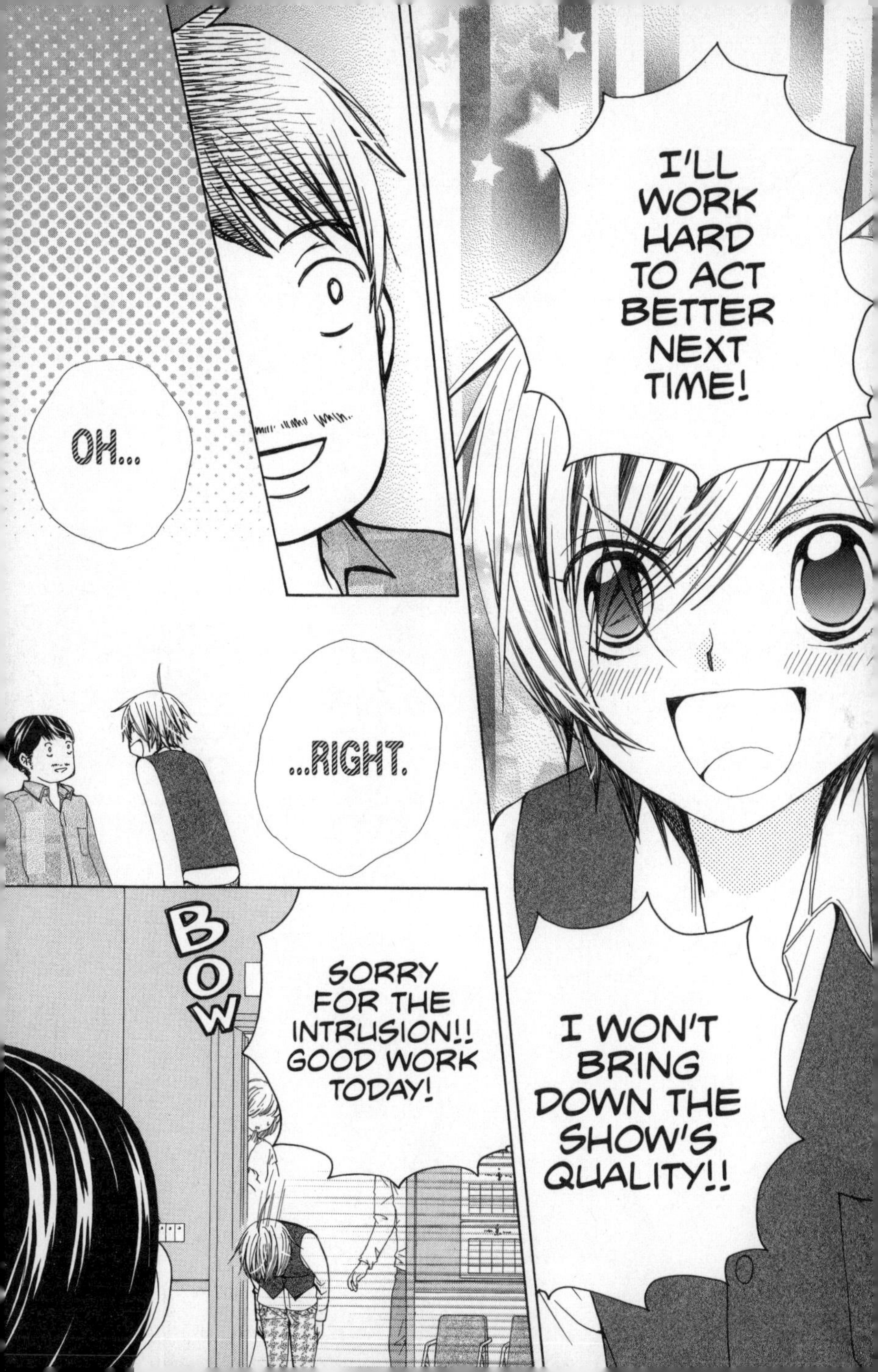
I'LL WORK HARD TO ACT BETTER NEXT TIME!
I WON'T BRING DOWN THE SHOW'S QUALITY!!
OH...
...RIGHT.
SORRY FOR THE INTRUSION!! GOOD WORK TODAY!
BOW

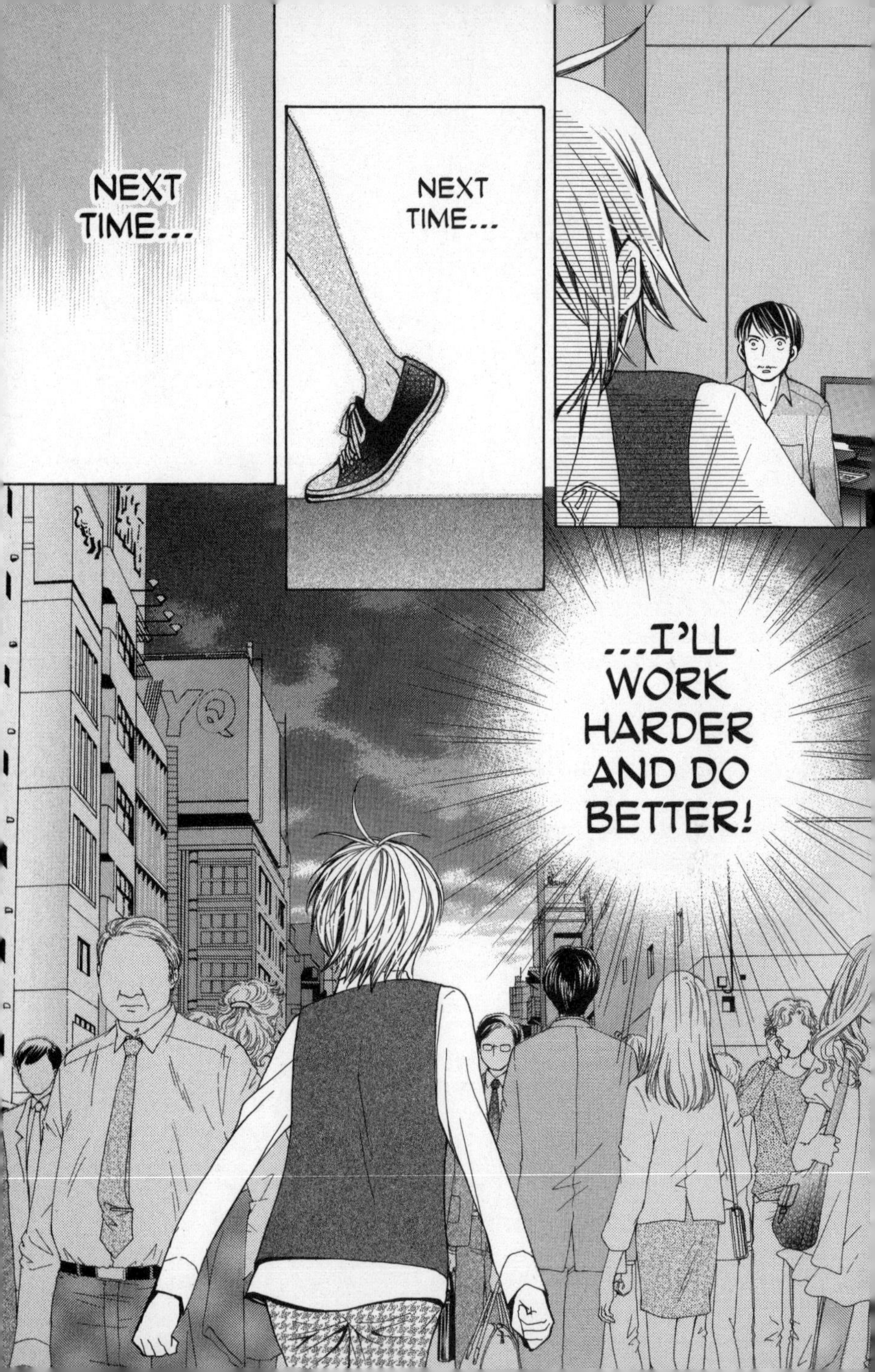
NEXT TIME...
NEXT TIME...
...I'LL WORK HARDER AND DO BETTER!

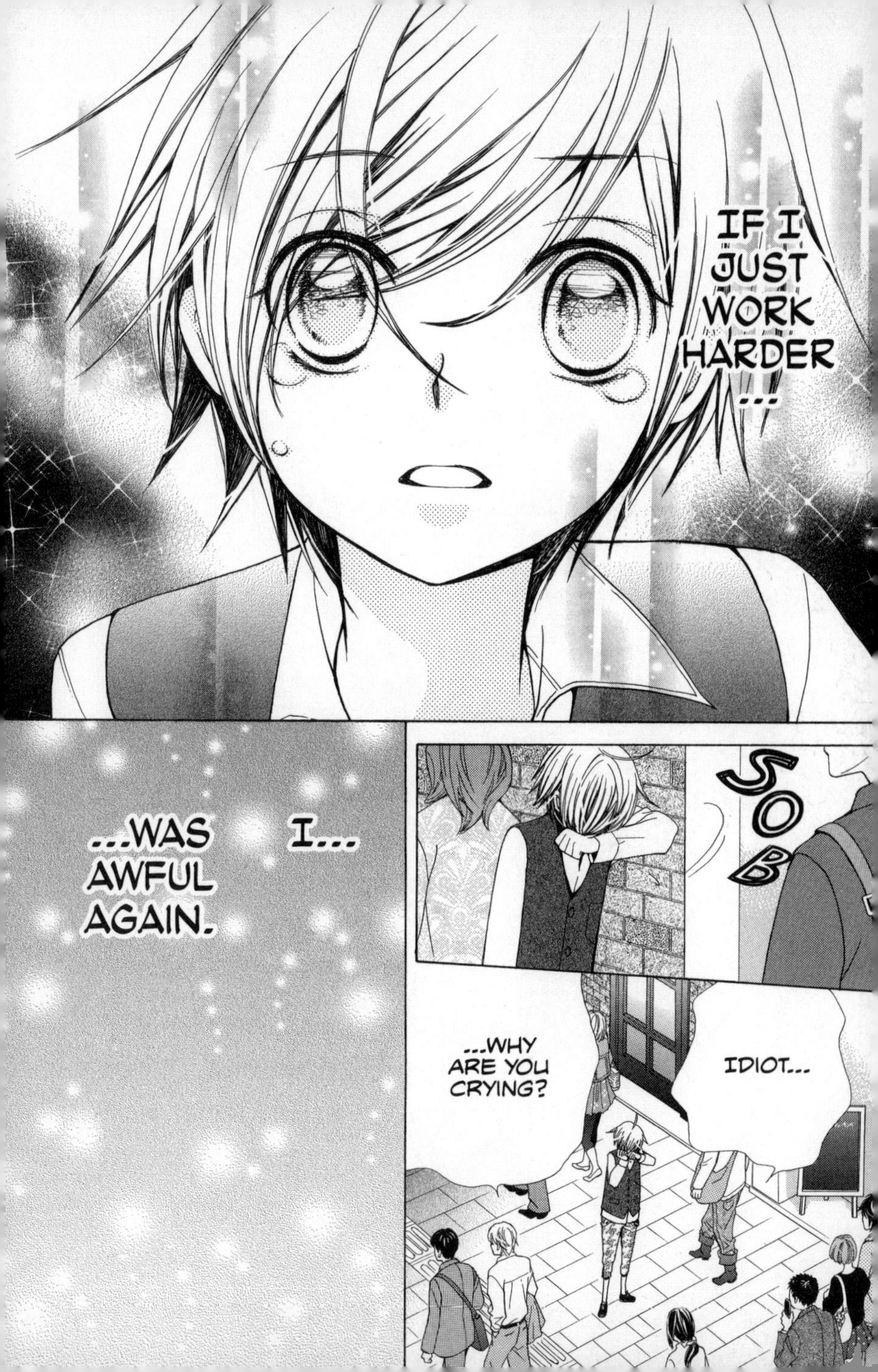
IF I JUST WORK HARDER...
SOB
IDIOT...
...WHY ARE YOU CRYING?
I...
...WAS AWFUL AGAIN.

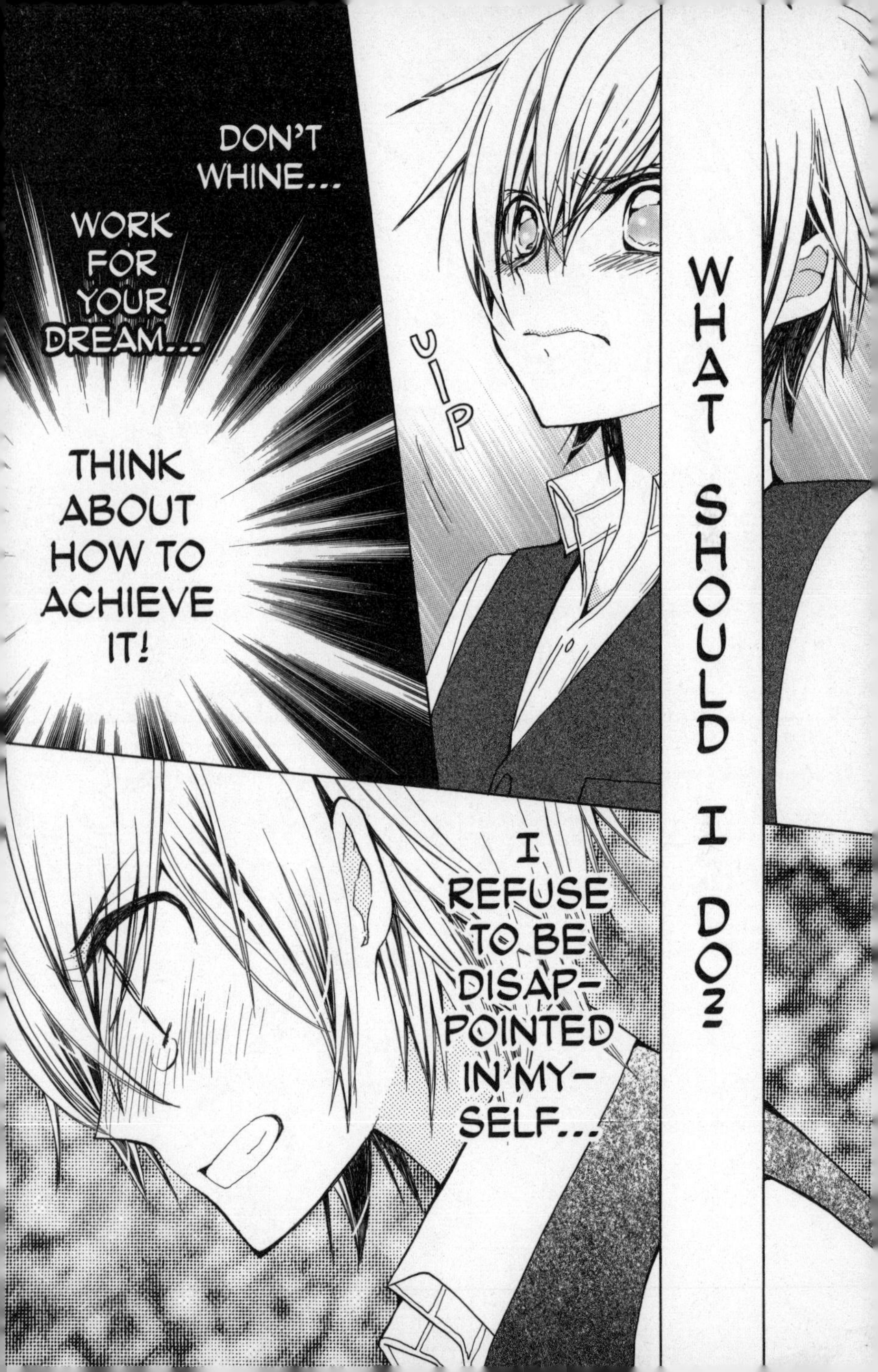
WHAT SHOULD I DO?
DON'T WHINE...
WORK FOR YOUR DREAM...
UIP
THINK ABOUT HOW TO ACHIEVE IT!
I REFUSE TO BE DISAPPOINTED IN MYSELF...

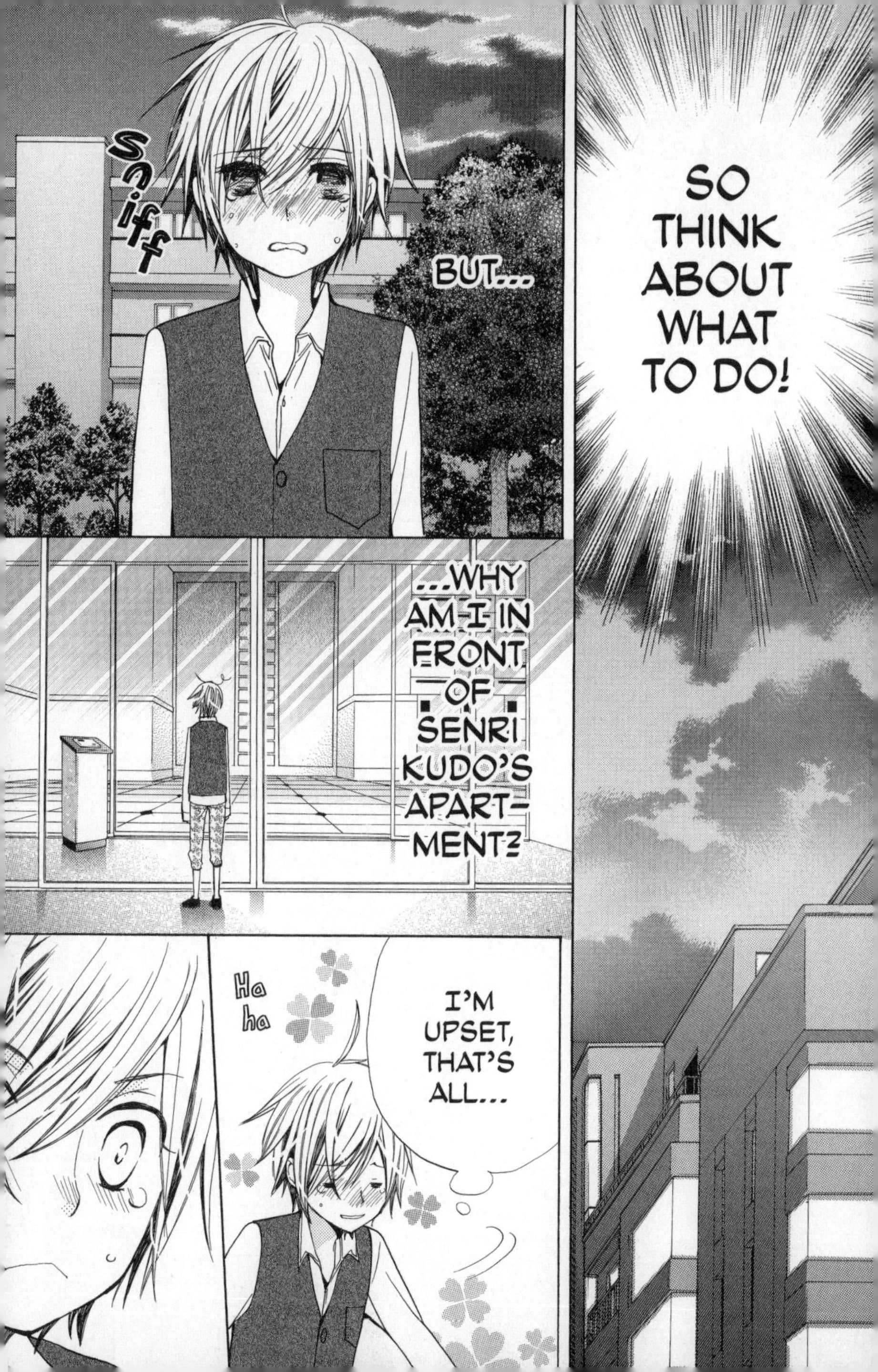
SO THINK ABOUT WHAT TO DO!
BUT...
sniff
...WHY AM I IN FRONT OF SENRI KUDO'S APARTMENT?
I'M UPSET, THAT'S ALL...
Ha ha

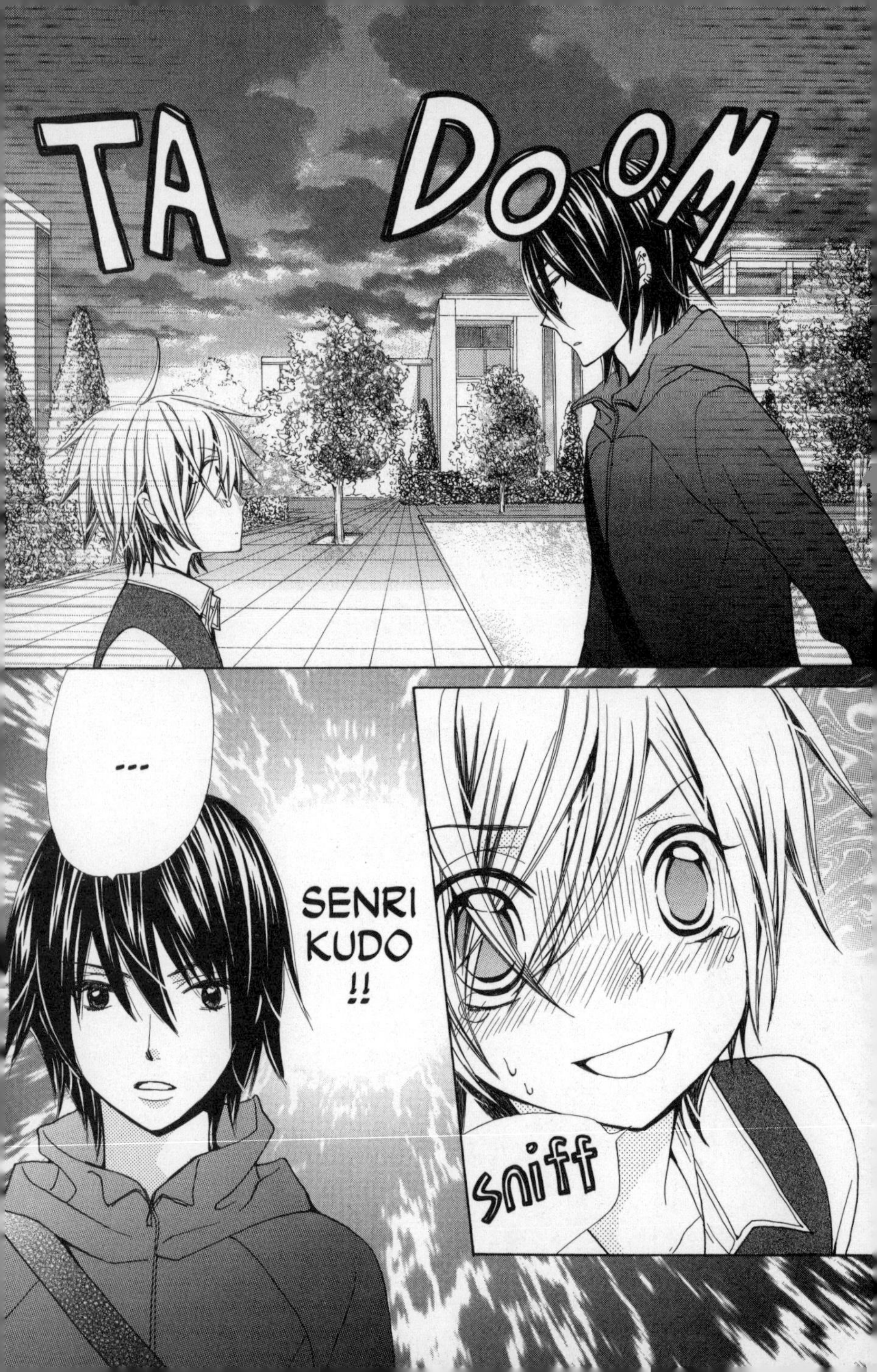
TA DOOM
sniff
...
SENRI KUDO !!

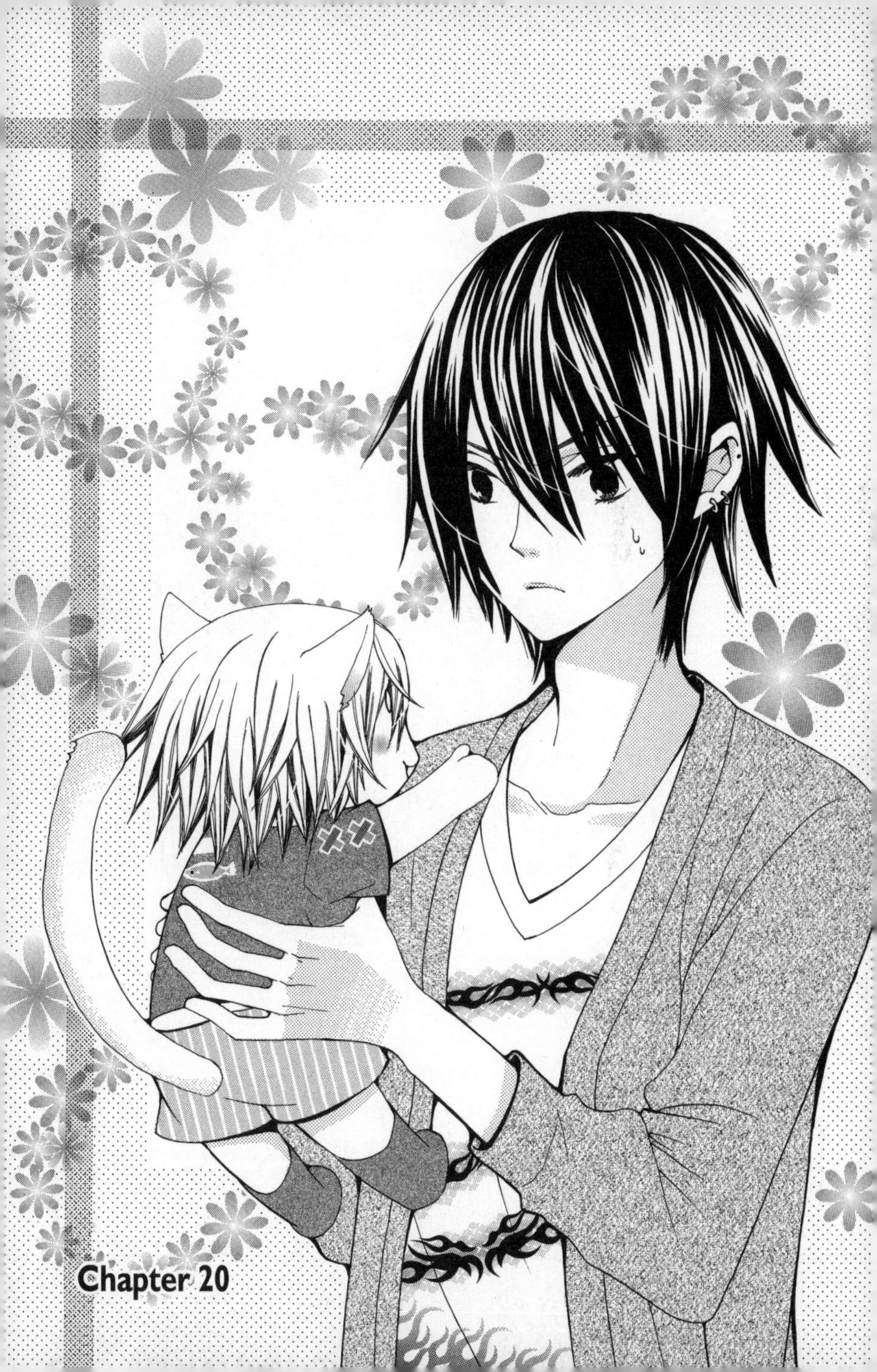

Chapter 20

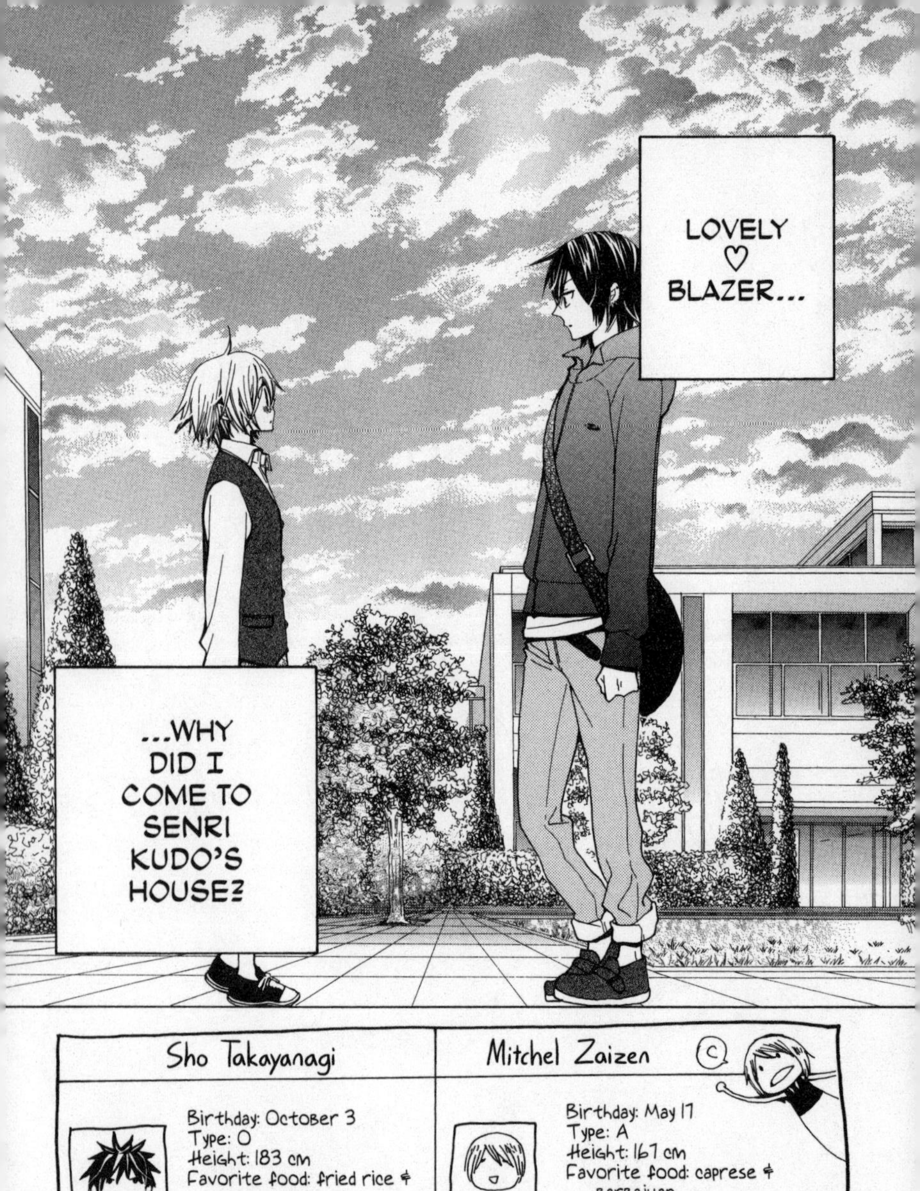
LOVELY ♡ BLAZER...
...WHY DID I COME TO SENRI KUDO'S HOUSE?

Sho Takayanagi

Year 1, Voice Acting

Birthday: October 3
Type: O
Height: 183 cm
Favorite food: fried rice & pork cutlet
Good subject: P.E. & Math
Favorite color: red & black
Hobby: physical training & yakuza movies

Mitchel Zaizen ©

Year 1, Voice Acting

Birthday: May 17
Type: A
Height: 167 cm
Favorite food: caprese & barbajuan
Good subject: English & Physics
Favorite color: white & blue
Hobby: checking under the skirts of figurines

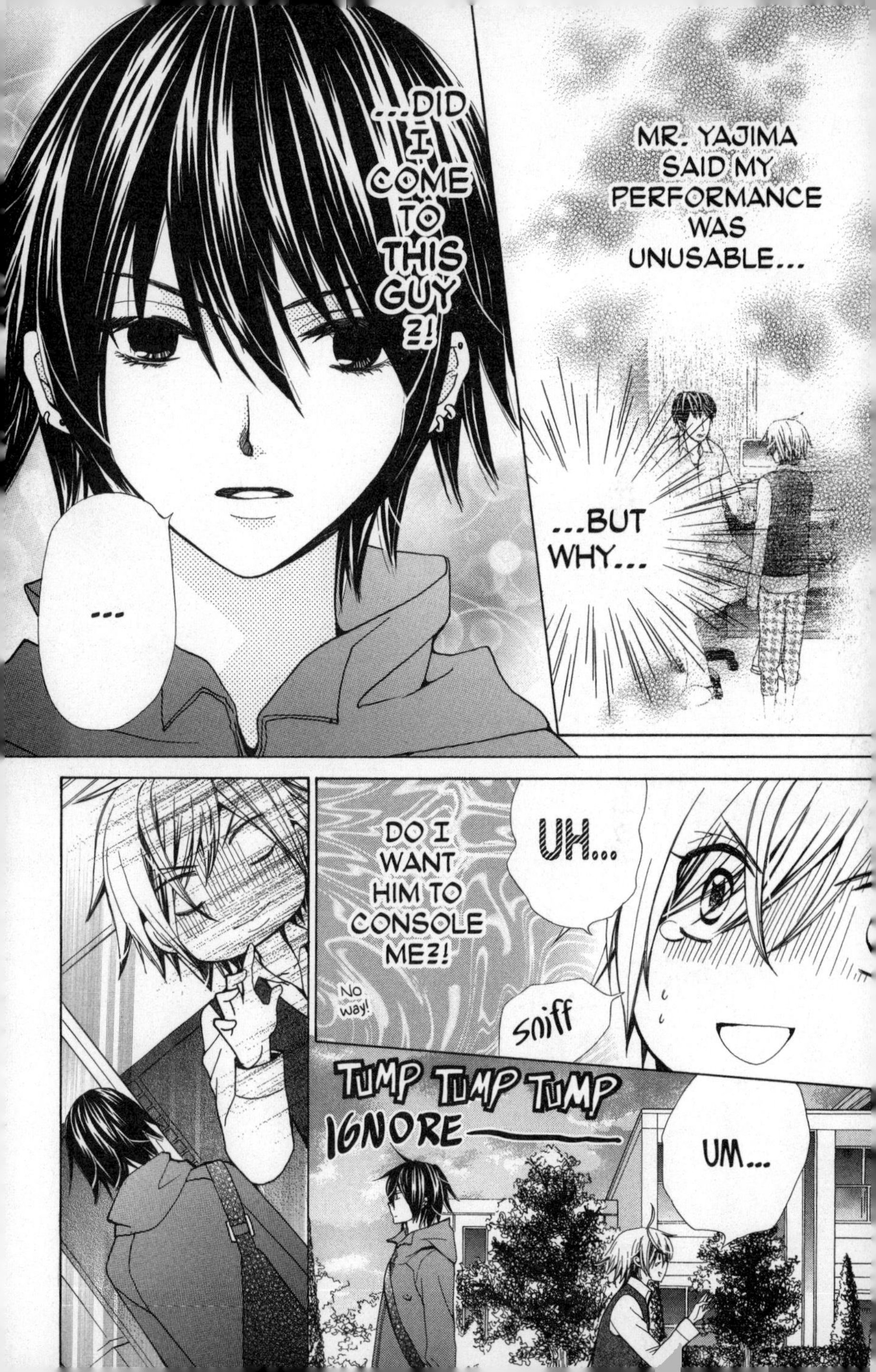
MR. YAJIMA SAID MY PERFORMANCE WAS UNUSABLE...
...BUT WHY...
...DID I COME TO THIS GUY?!
...
UH...
Sniff
DO I WANT HIM TO CONSOLE ME?!
No way!
TUMP TUMP TUMP
IGNORE———
UM...

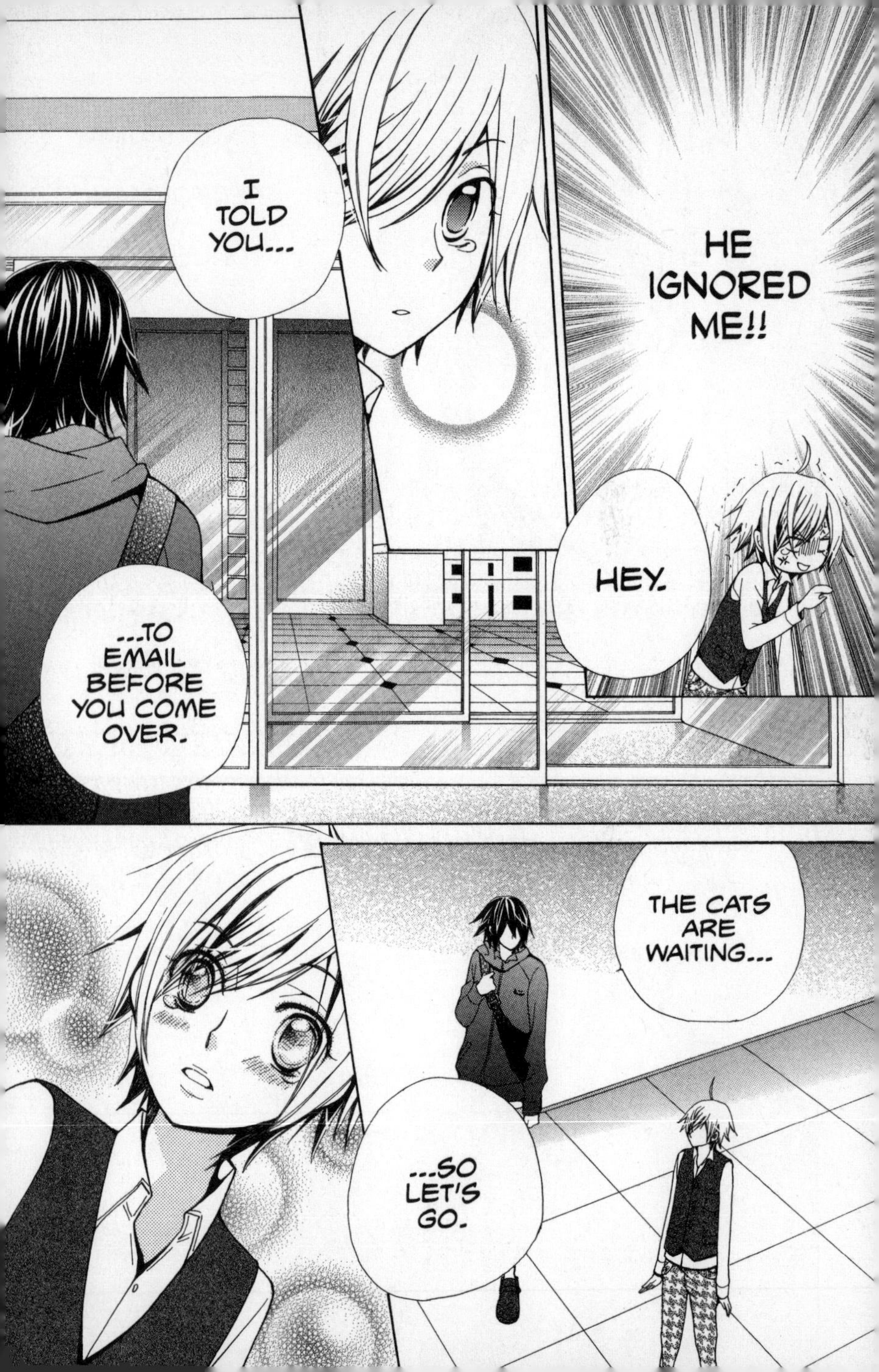
HE IGNORED ME!!
HEY.
I TOLD YOU...
...TO EMAIL BEFORE YOU COME OVER.
THE CATS ARE WAITING...
...SO LET'S GO.

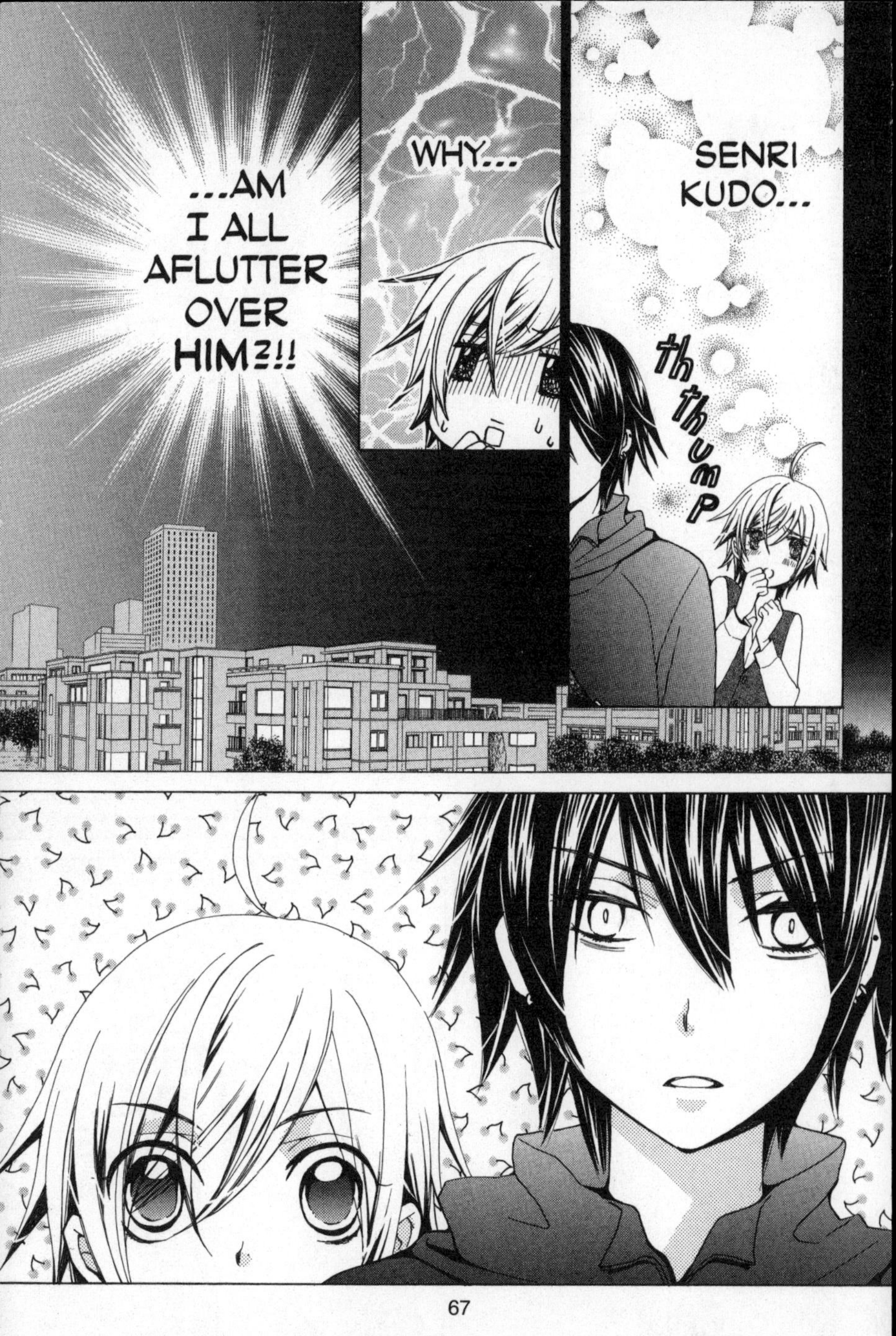
SENRI KUDO...
th thump
WHY...
...AM I ALL AFLUTTER OVER HIM?!!

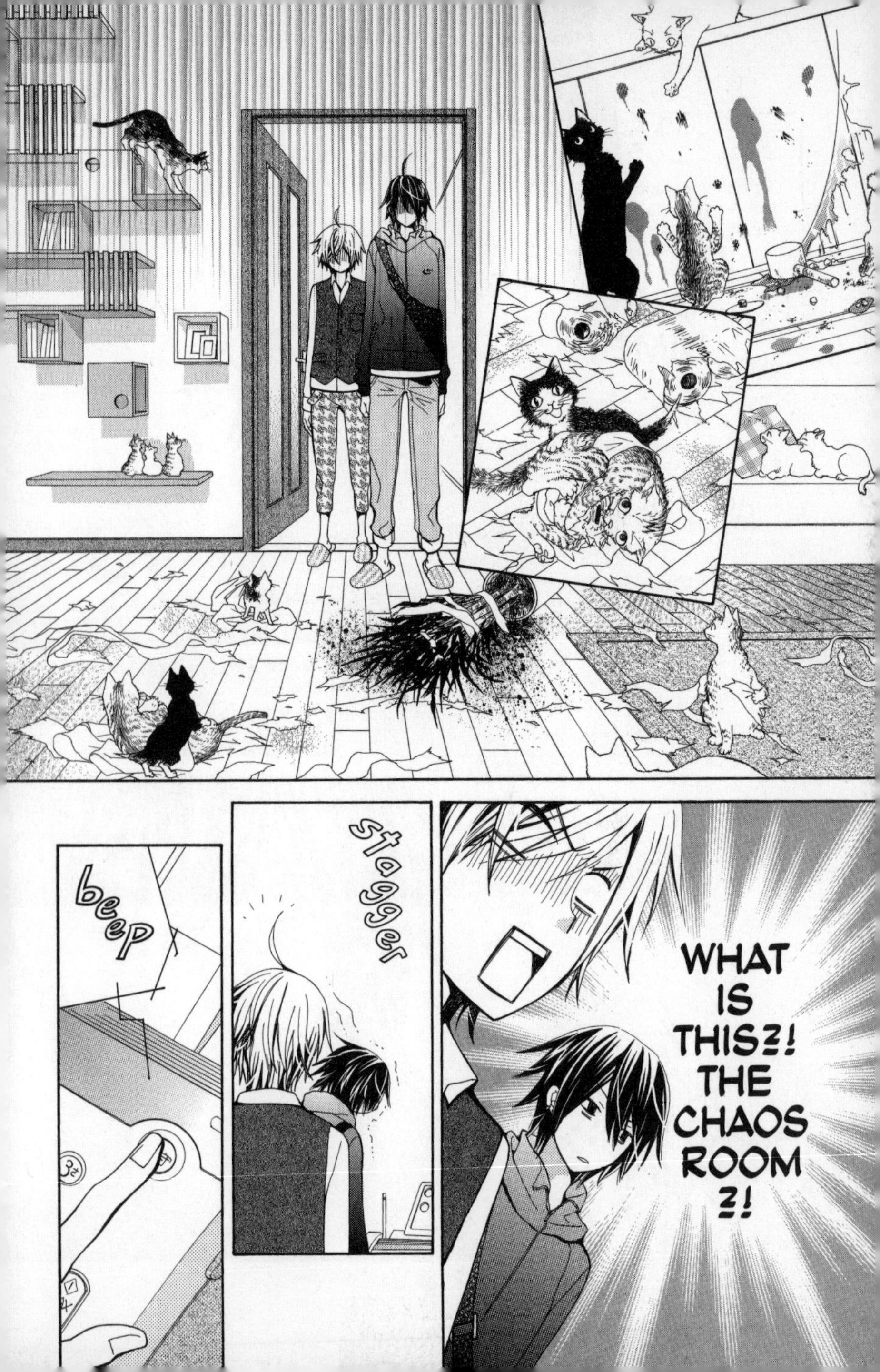
WHAT IS THIS?! THE CHAOS ROOM?!
stagger
beep

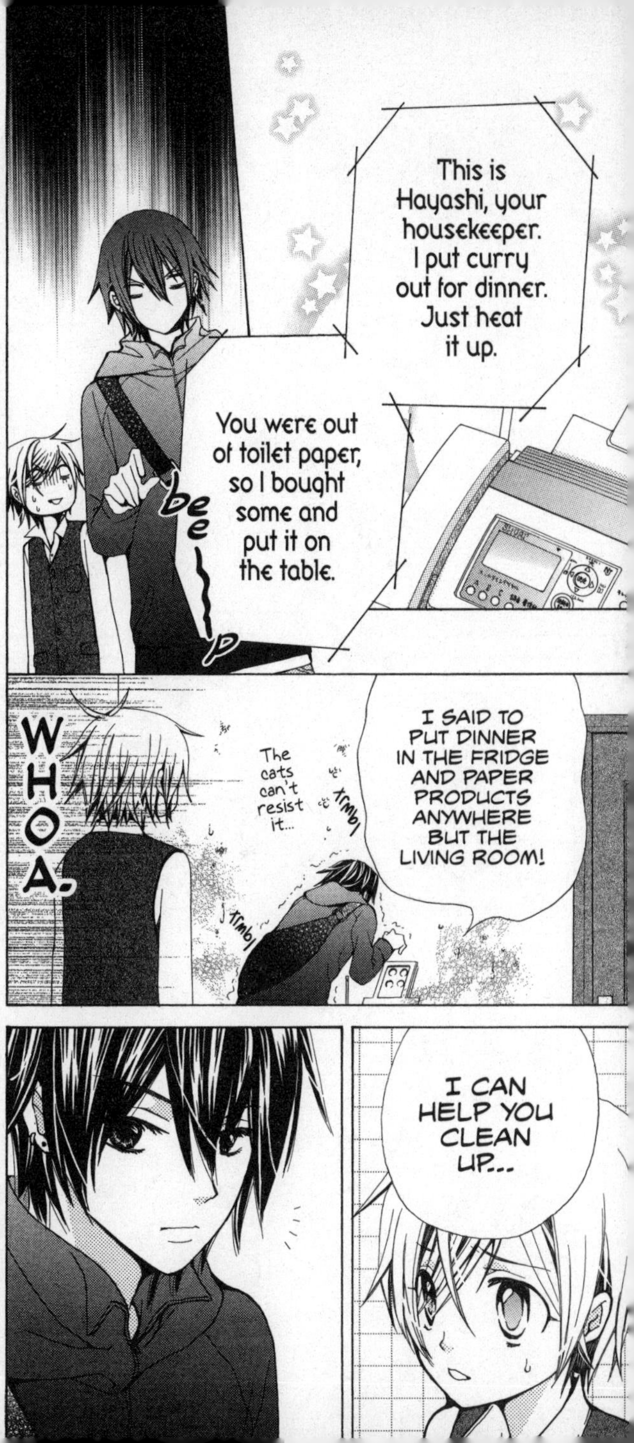
This is Hayashi, your housekeeper. I put curry out for dinner. Just heat it up.
You were out of toilet paper, so I bought some and put it on the table.
beeep
I SAID TO PUT DINNER IN THE FRIDGE AND PAPER PRODUCTS ANYWHERE BUT THE LIVING ROOM!
The cats can't resist it...
trmbl
trmbl
WHOA.
I CAN HELP YOU CLEAN UP...

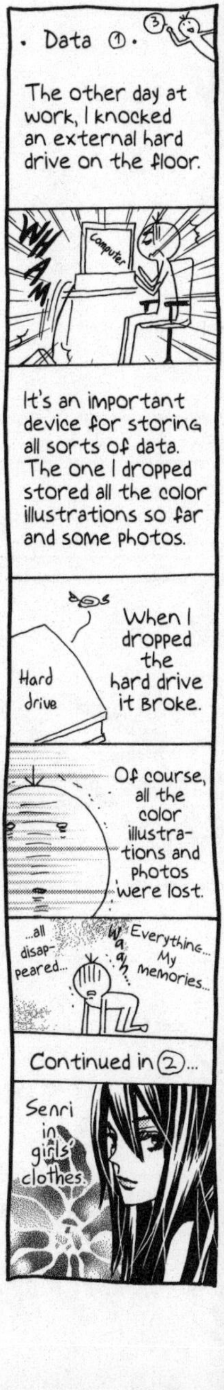
• Data ①•
The other day at work, I knocked an external hard drive on the floor.
WHAM
Computer
It's an important device for storing all sorts of data. The one I dropped stored all the color illustrations so far and some photos.
Hard drive
When I dropped the hard drive it broke.
Of course, all the color illustrations and photos were lost.
Everything... My memories...
Waah...
...all disappeared...
Continued in ②...
Senri in girls' clothes.

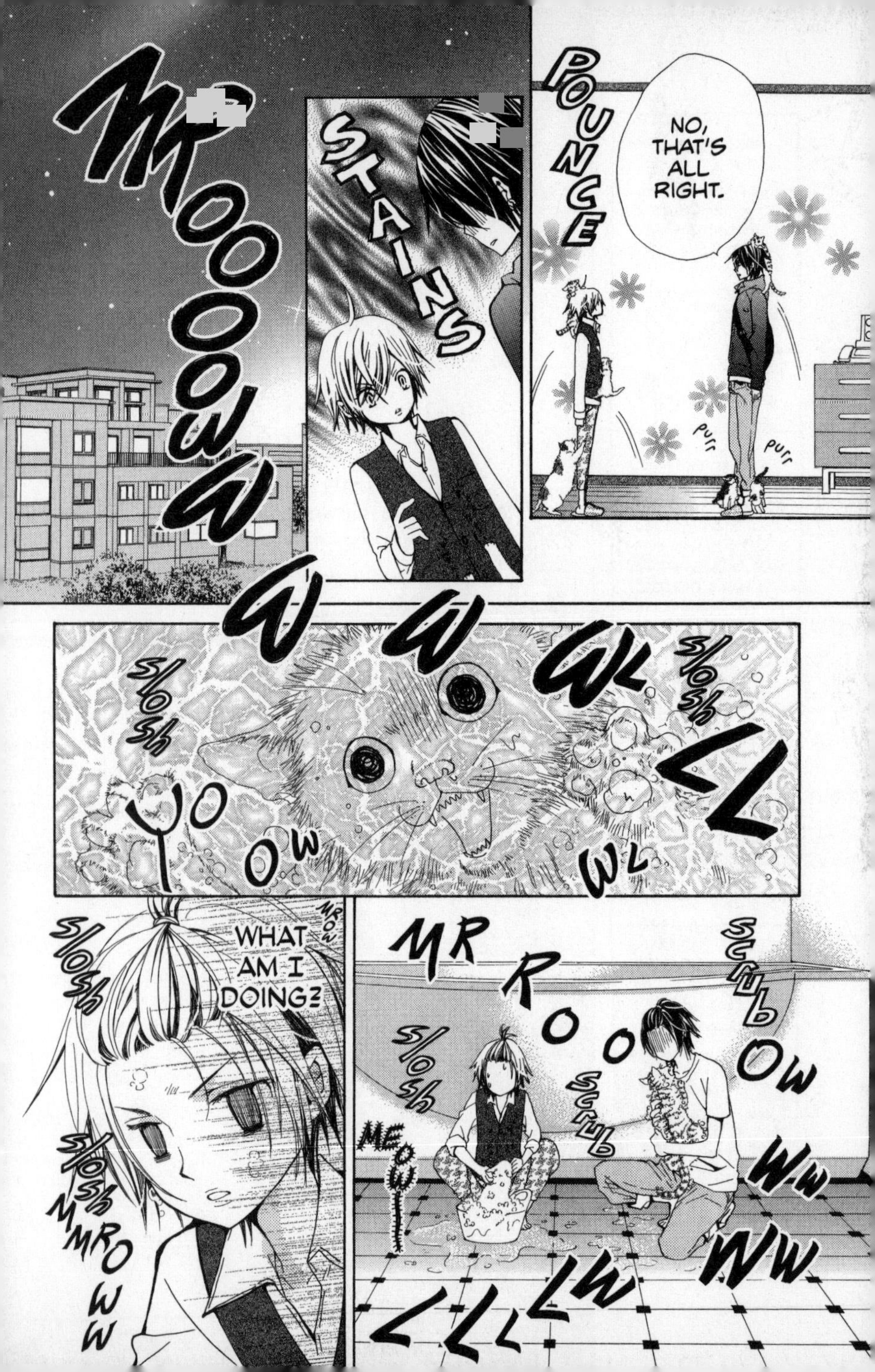
POUNCE
NO, THAT'S ALL RIGHT.
purr
purr
STAINS
MROOOOWWWWWL
slosh
LL
slosh
WL
YOOOW
SCRUB
MR ROOOWWWW
SCRUB
slosh
MEOW
LLLLL
WHAT AM I DOING?
MROW
slosh
slosh
MMROWWW

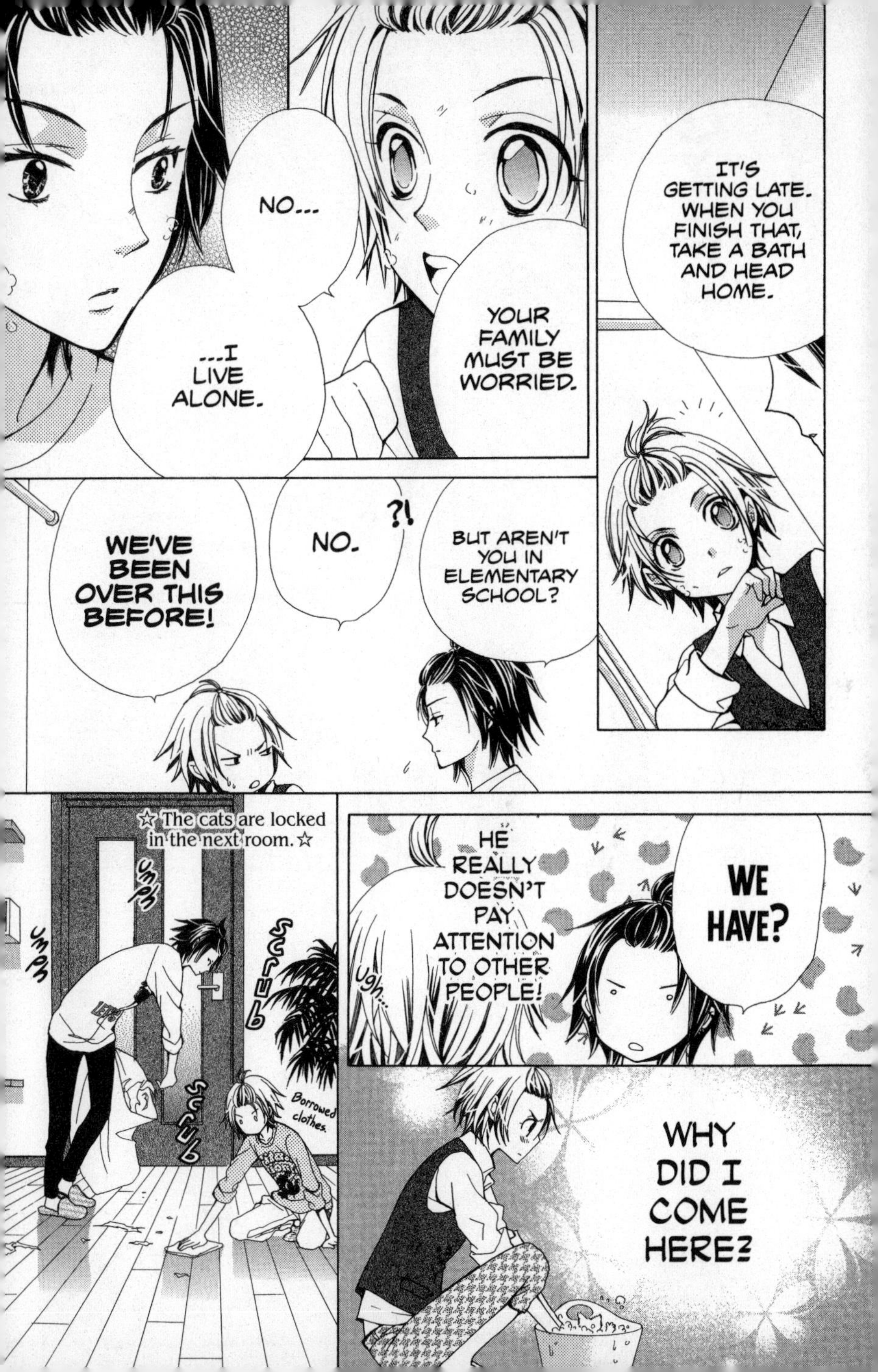
IT'S GETTING LATE. WHEN YOU FINISH THAT, TAKE A BATH AND HEAD HOME.
YOUR FAMILY MUST BE WORRIED.
NO...
...I LIVE ALONE.
BUT AREN'T YOU IN ELEMENTARY SCHOOL?
?!
NO.
WE'VE BEEN OVER THIS BEFORE!
WE HAVE?
HE REALLY DOESN'T PAY ATTENTION TO OTHER PEOPLE!
Ugh...
WHY DID I COME HERE?
☆ The cats are locked in the next room. ☆
umph
umph
scrub
scrub
Borrowed clothes.

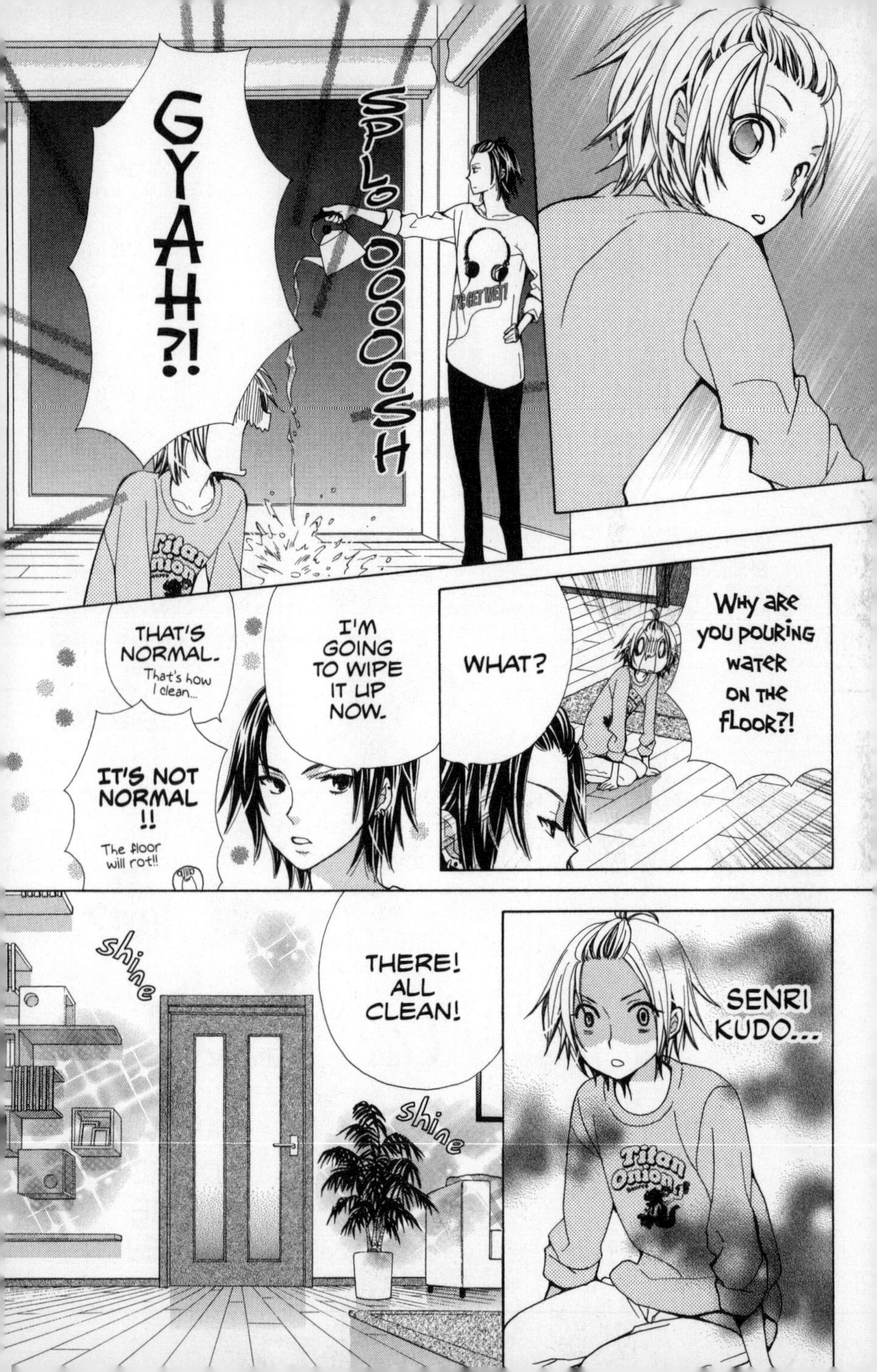
SPLOOOOOOSH
GYAH?!
Why are you pouring water on the floor?!
WHAT?
I'M GOING TO WIPE IT UP NOW.
THAT'S NORMAL.
That's how I clean...
IT'S NOT NORMAL!!
The floor will rot!!
SENRI KUDO...
Titan Onion
THERE! ALL CLEAN!
shine
shine

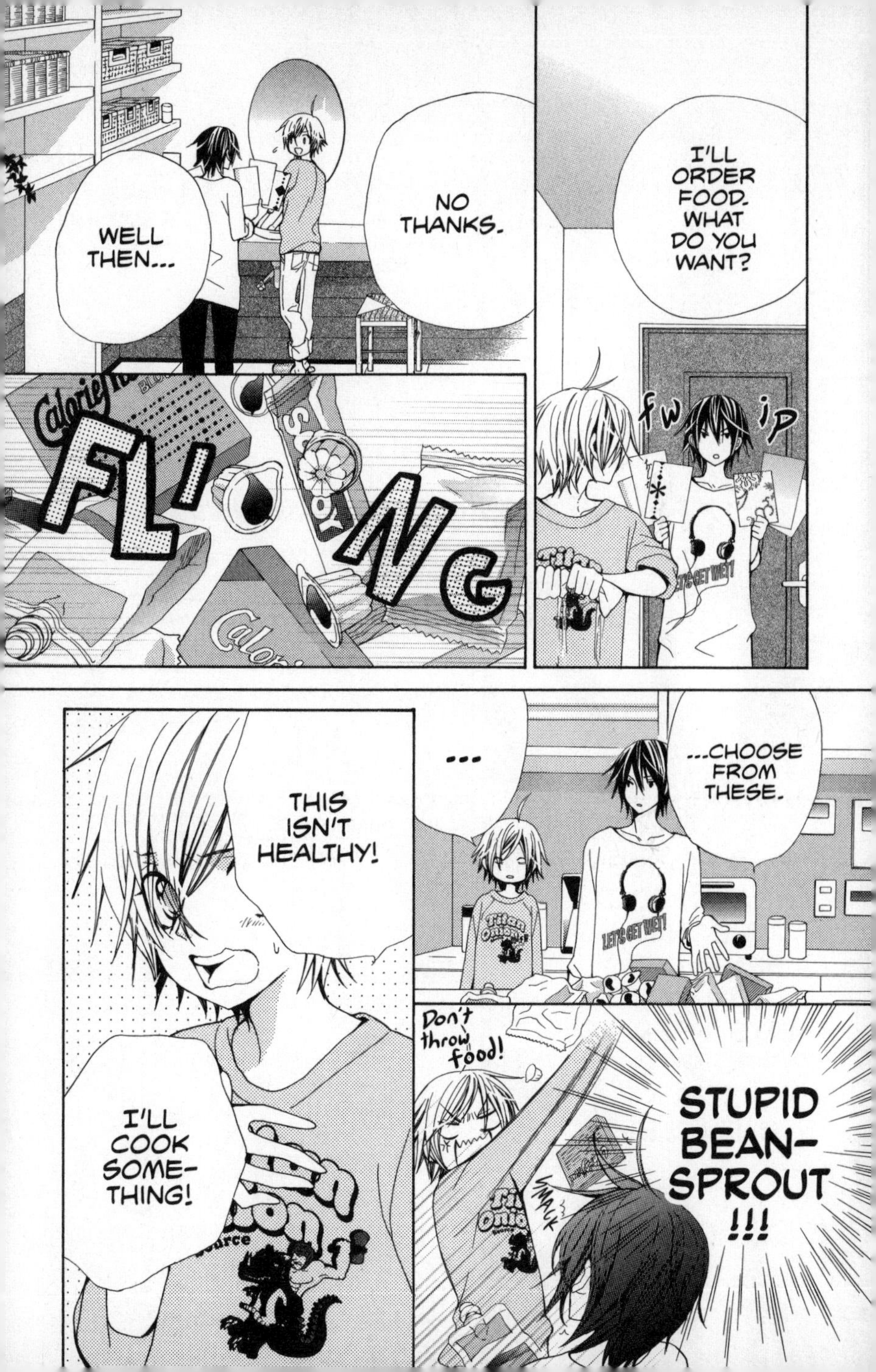
I'LL ORDER FOOD. WHAT DO YOU WANT?
fwip
NO THANKS.
WELL THEN...
FLING
...CHOOSE FROM THESE.
...
STUPID BEAN-SPROUT!!!
Don't throw food!
SMACK
THIS ISN'T HEALTHY!
I'LL COOK SOMETHING!

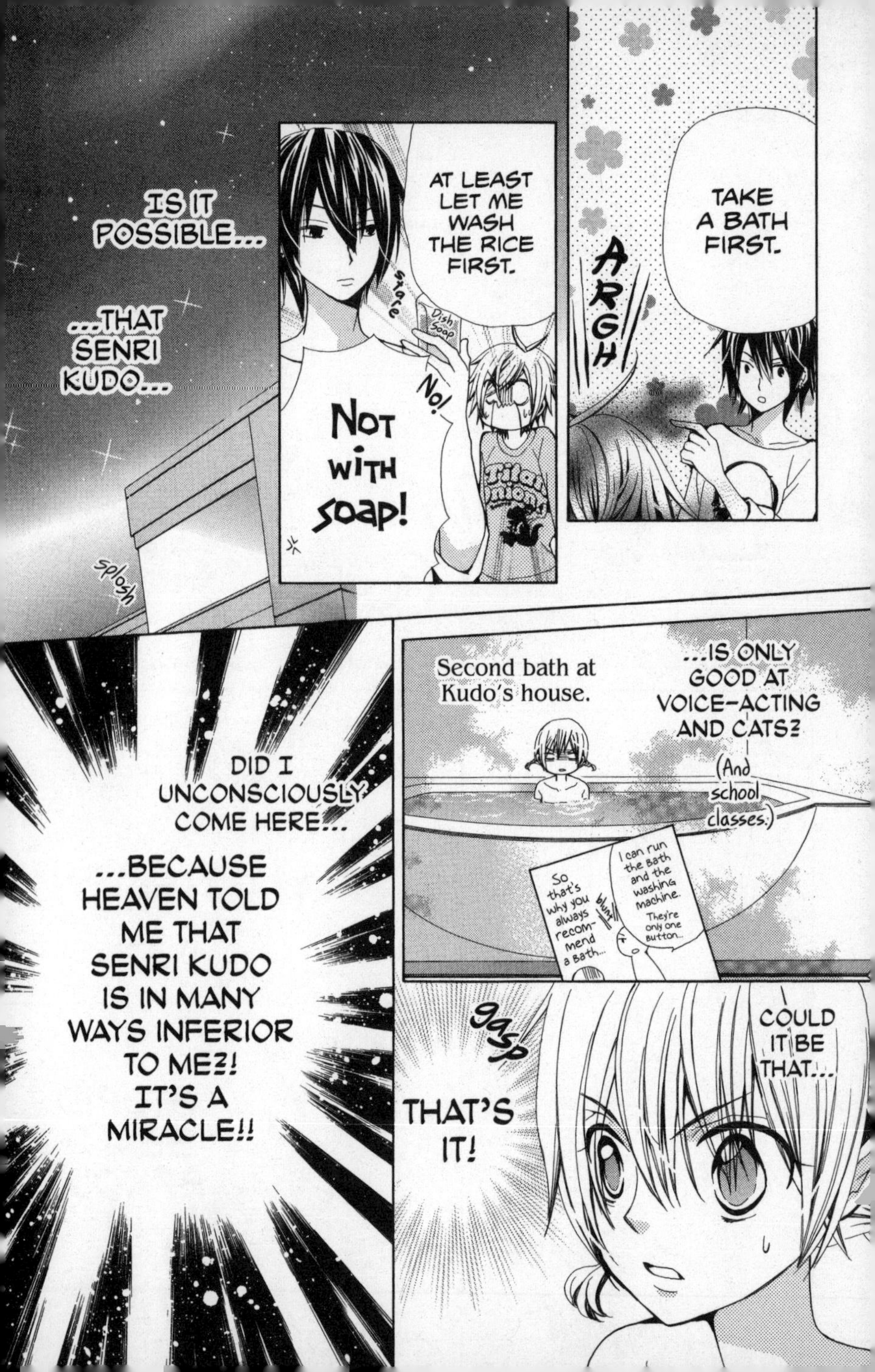
TAKE A BATH FIRST.
ARGH
AT LEAST LET ME WASH THE RICE FIRST.
stare
Dish Soap
No!
NOT WITH SOAP!
IS IT POSSIBLE...
...THAT SENRI KUDO...
splosh
Second bath at Kudo's house.
...IS ONLY GOOD AT VOICE-ACTING AND CATS?
(And school classes.)
I can run the Bath and the washing machine.
They're only one button...
So that's why you always recom-mend a Bath...
blunt
COULD IT BE THAT...
gasp
THAT'S IT!
DID I UNCONSCIOUSLY COME HERE...
...BECAUSE HEAVEN TOLD ME THAT SENRI KUDO IS IN MANY WAYS INFERIOR TO ME?! IT'S A MIRACLE!!

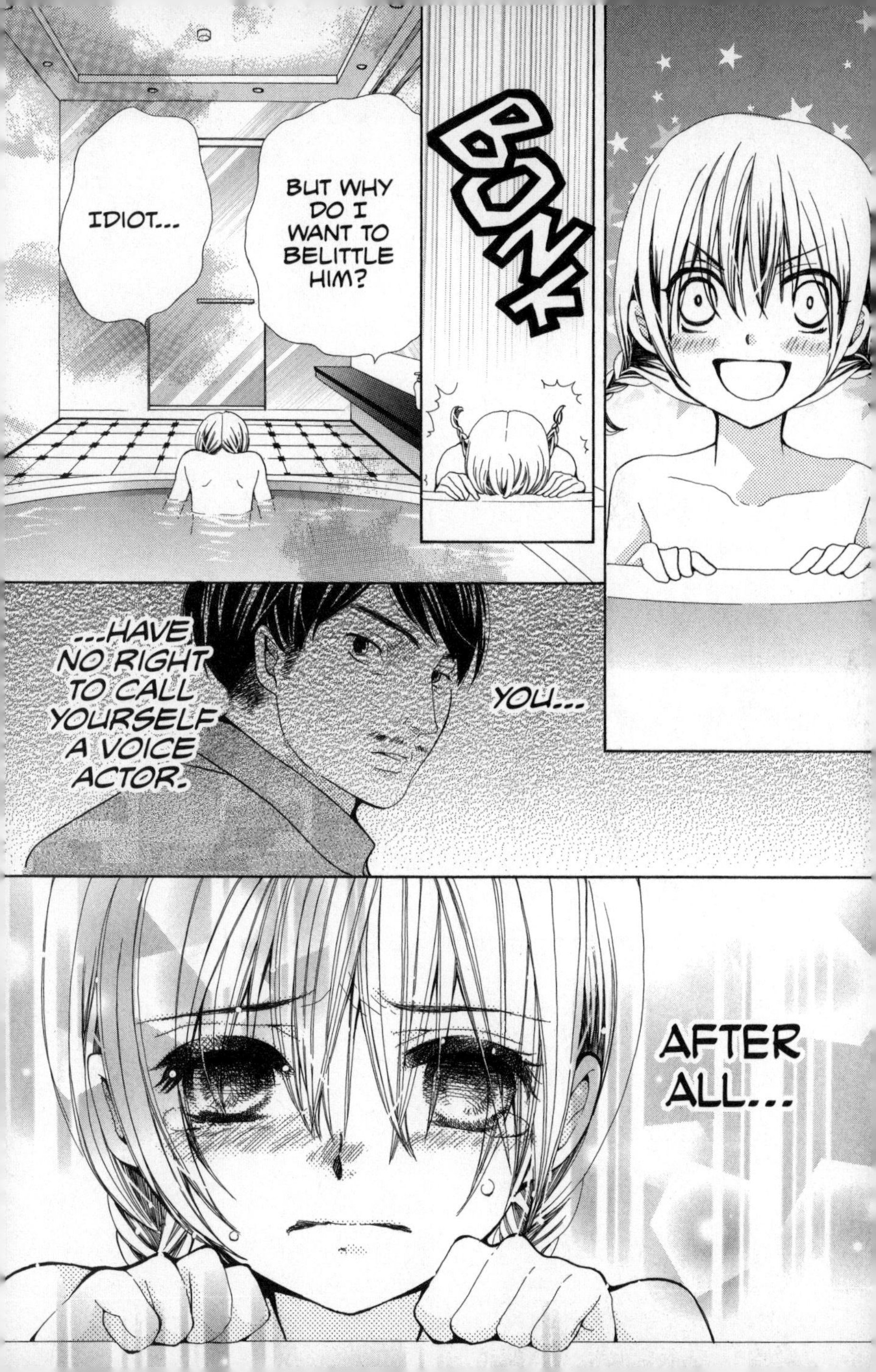
BONK
BUT WHY DO I WANT TO BELITTLE HIM?
IDIOT...
YOU...
...HAVE NO RIGHT TO CALL YOURSELF A VOICE ACTOR.
AFTER ALL...

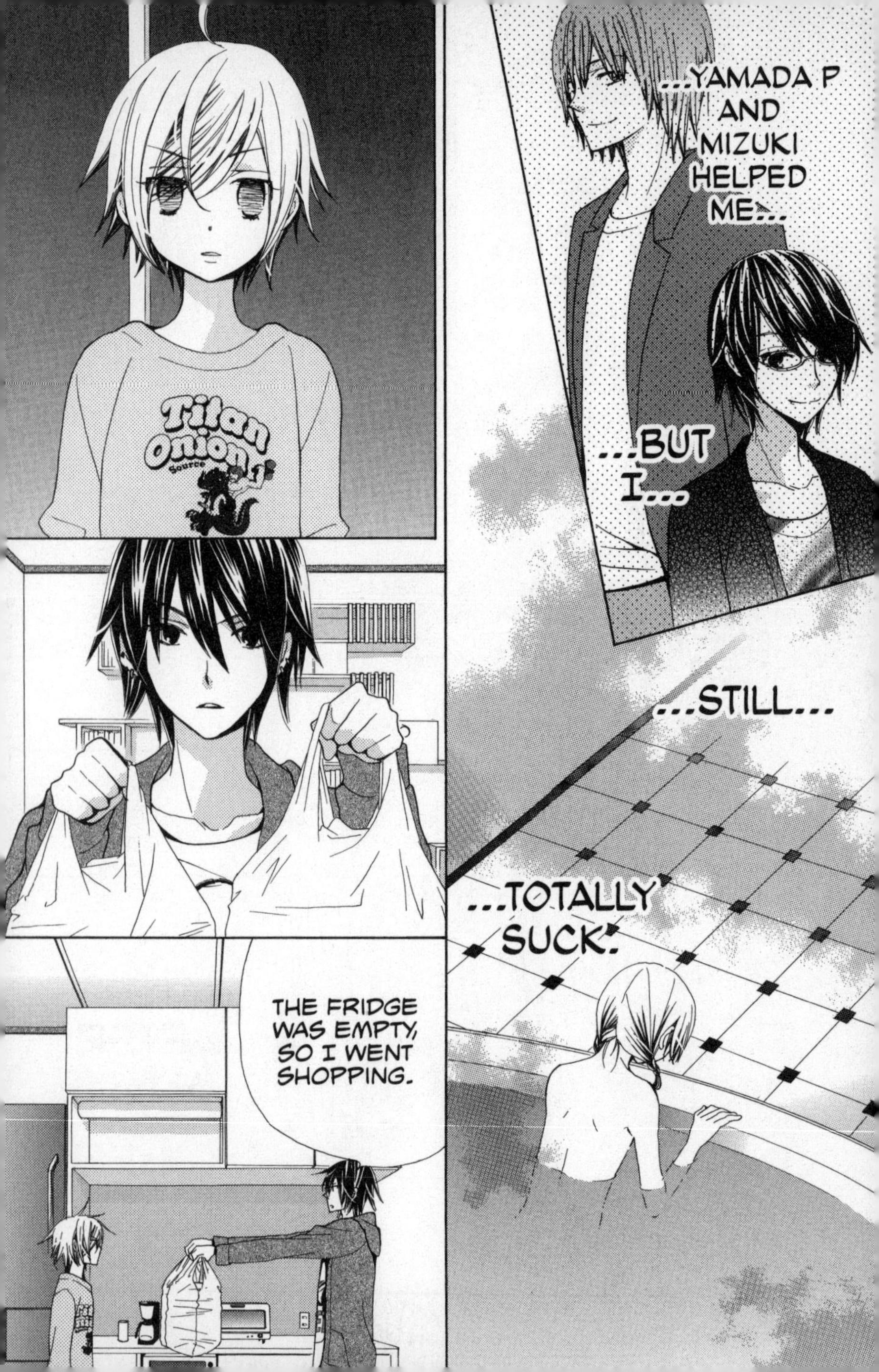
...YAMADA P AND MIZUKI HELPED ME...
...BUT I...
...STILL...
...TOTALLY SUCK.
Titan Onion Source
THE FRIDGE WAS EMPTY, SO I WENT SHOPPING.

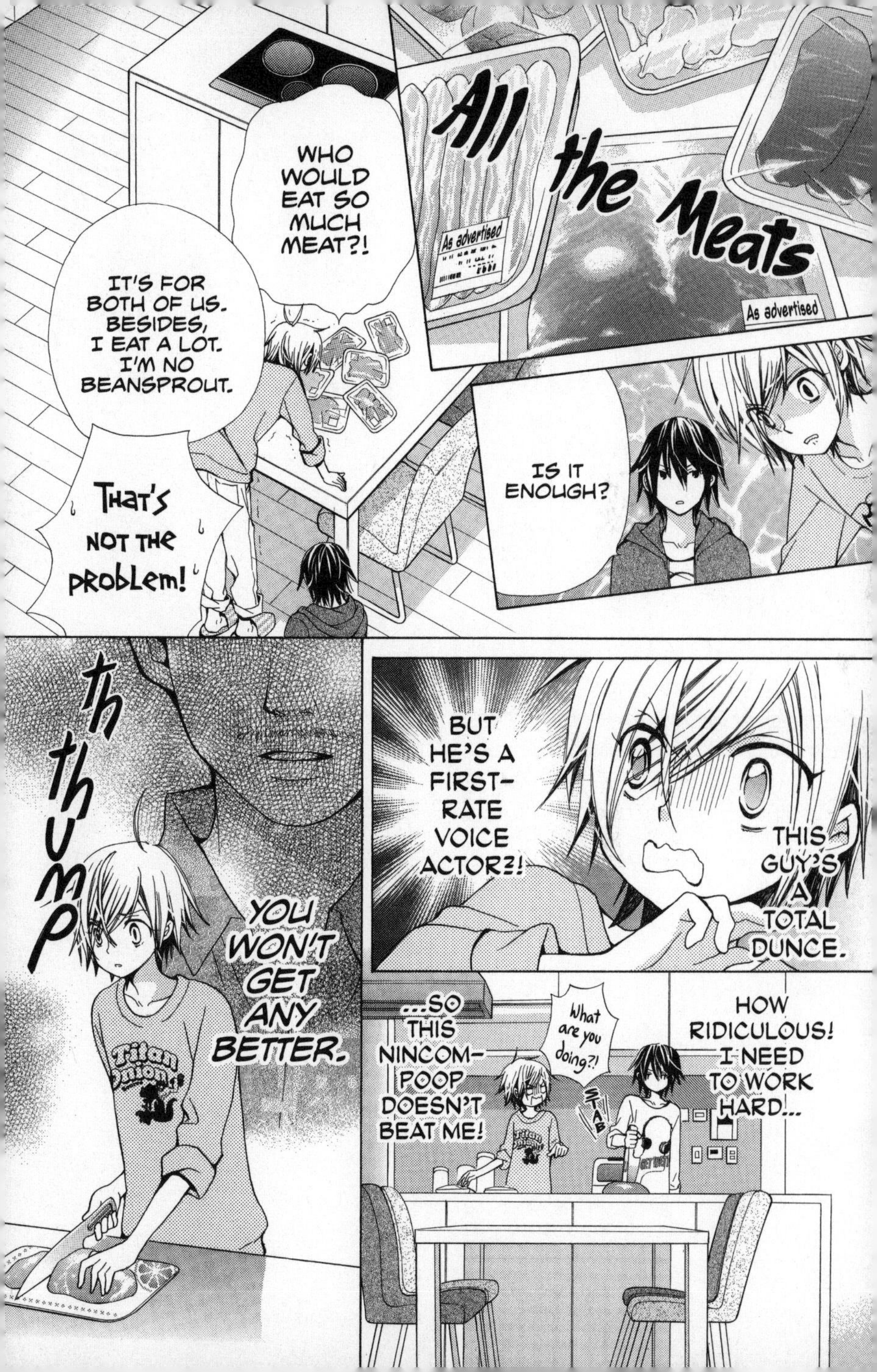
All the Meats
As advertised
As advertised
IS IT ENOUGH?
WHO WOULD EAT SO MUCH MEAT?!
IT'S FOR BOTH OF US. BESIDES, I EAT A LOT. I'M NO BEANSPROUT.
THAT'S NOT THE PROBLEM!
THIS GUY'S A TOTAL DUNCE.
BUT HE'S A FIRST-RATE VOICE ACTOR?!
HOW RIDICULOUS! I NEED TO WORK HARD...
What are you doing?!
STAB
...SO THIS NINCOMPOOP DOESN'T BEAT ME!
th thump
YOU WON'T GET ANY BETTER.

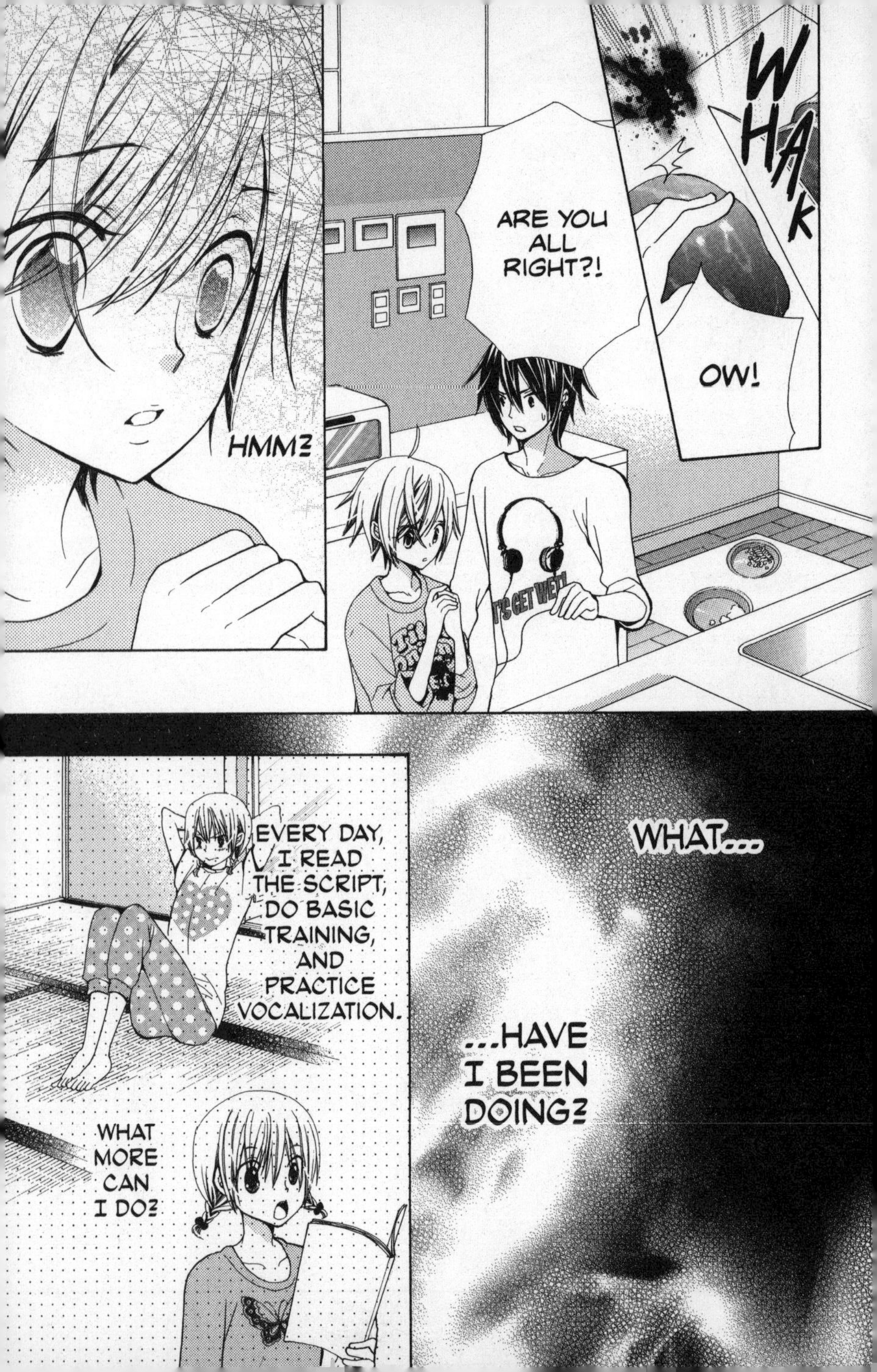
WHAK
OW!
ARE YOU ALL RIGHT?!
HMM?
WHAT...
...HAVE I BEEN DOING?
EVERY DAY, I READ THE SCRIPT, DO BASIC TRAINING, AND PRACTICE VOCALIZATION.
WHAT MORE CAN I DO?

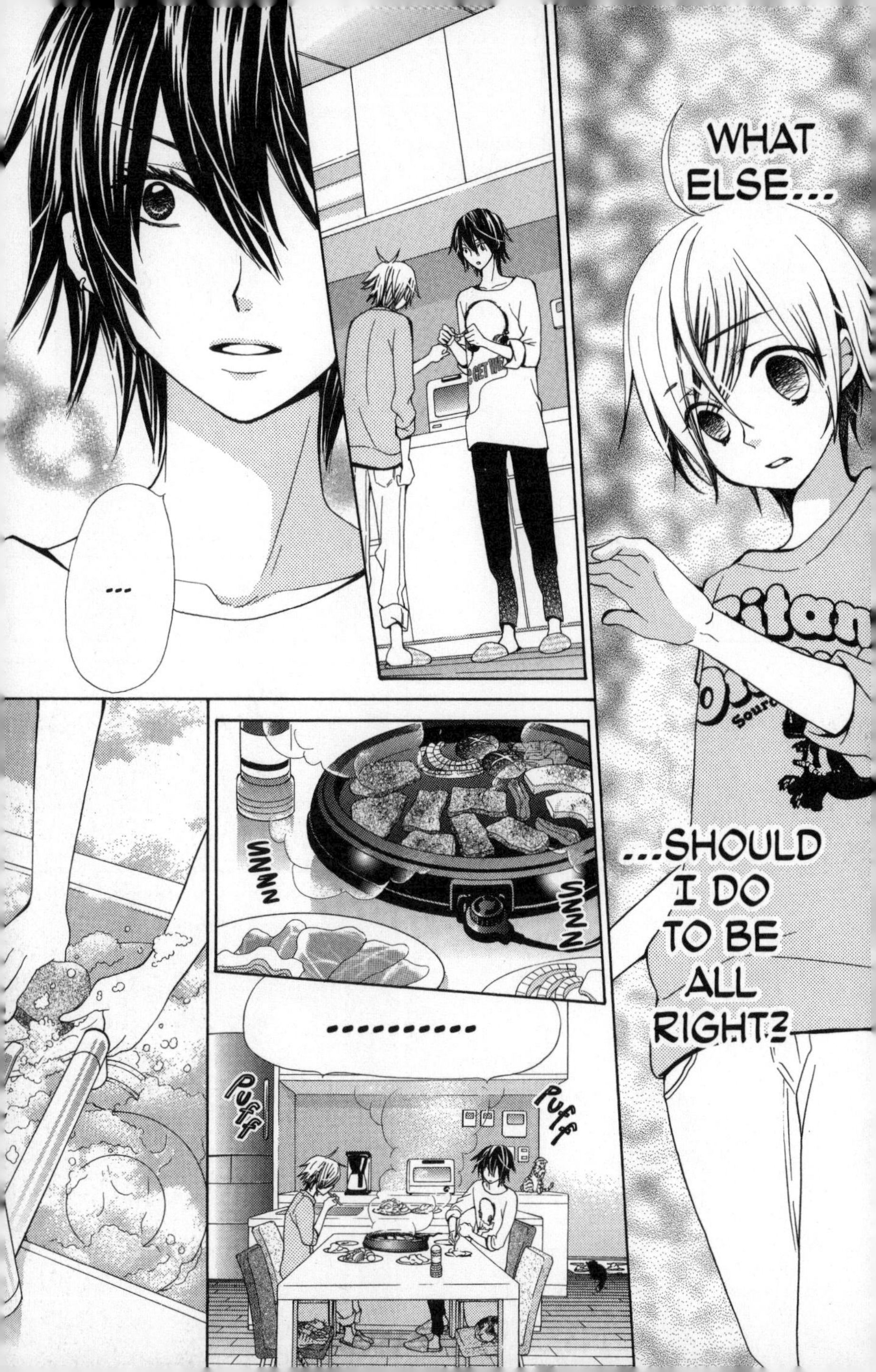
WHAT ELSE...
...SHOULD I DO TO BE ALL RIGHT?
...
SNNN
SNNN
....
Puff
Puff

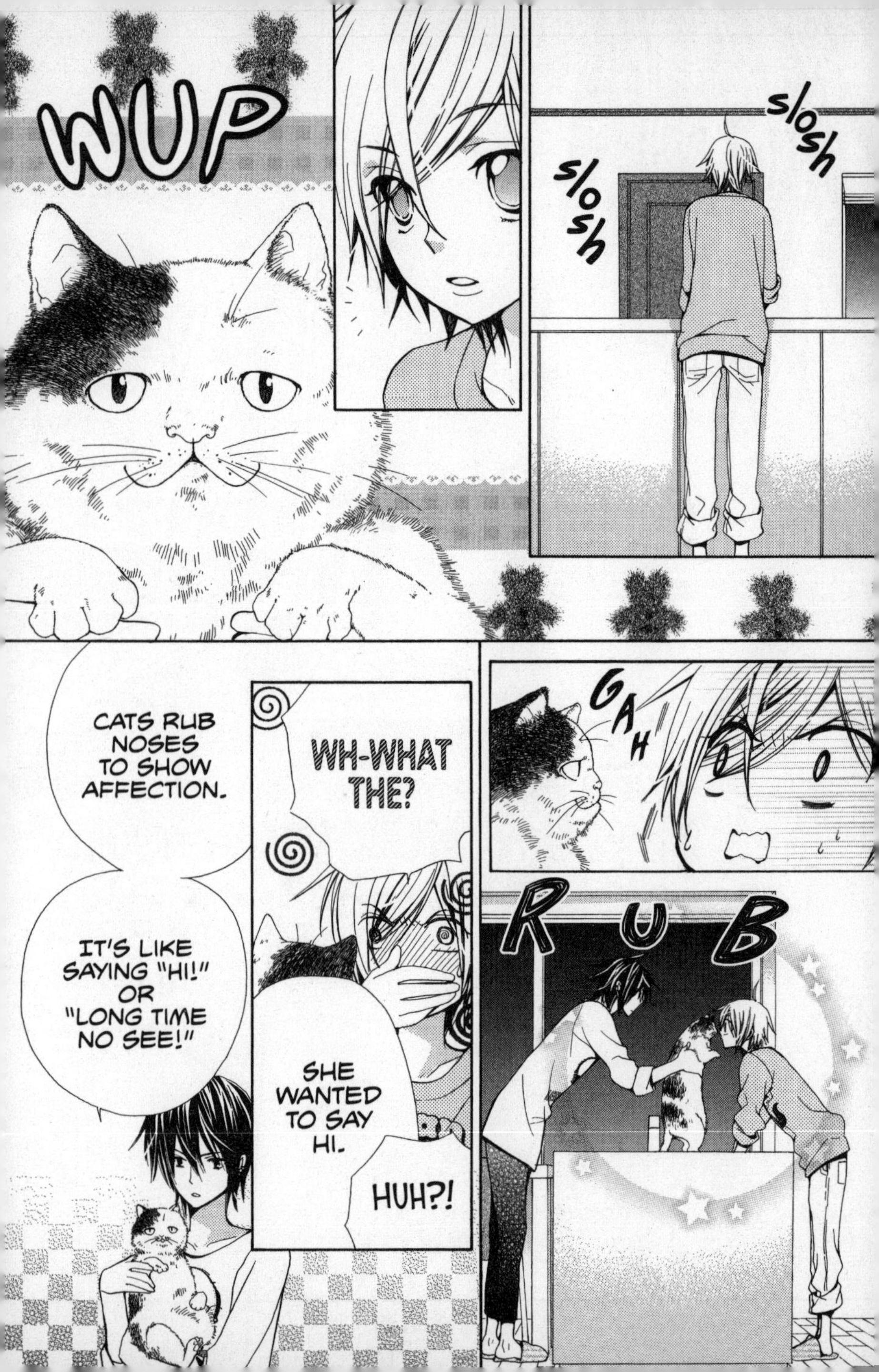
slosh
slosh
WUP
GAH
RUB
WH-WHAT THE?
SHE WANTED TO SAY HI.
HUH?!
CATS RUB NOSES TO SHOW AFFECTION.
IT'S LIKE SAYING "HI!" OR "LONG TIME NO SEE!"

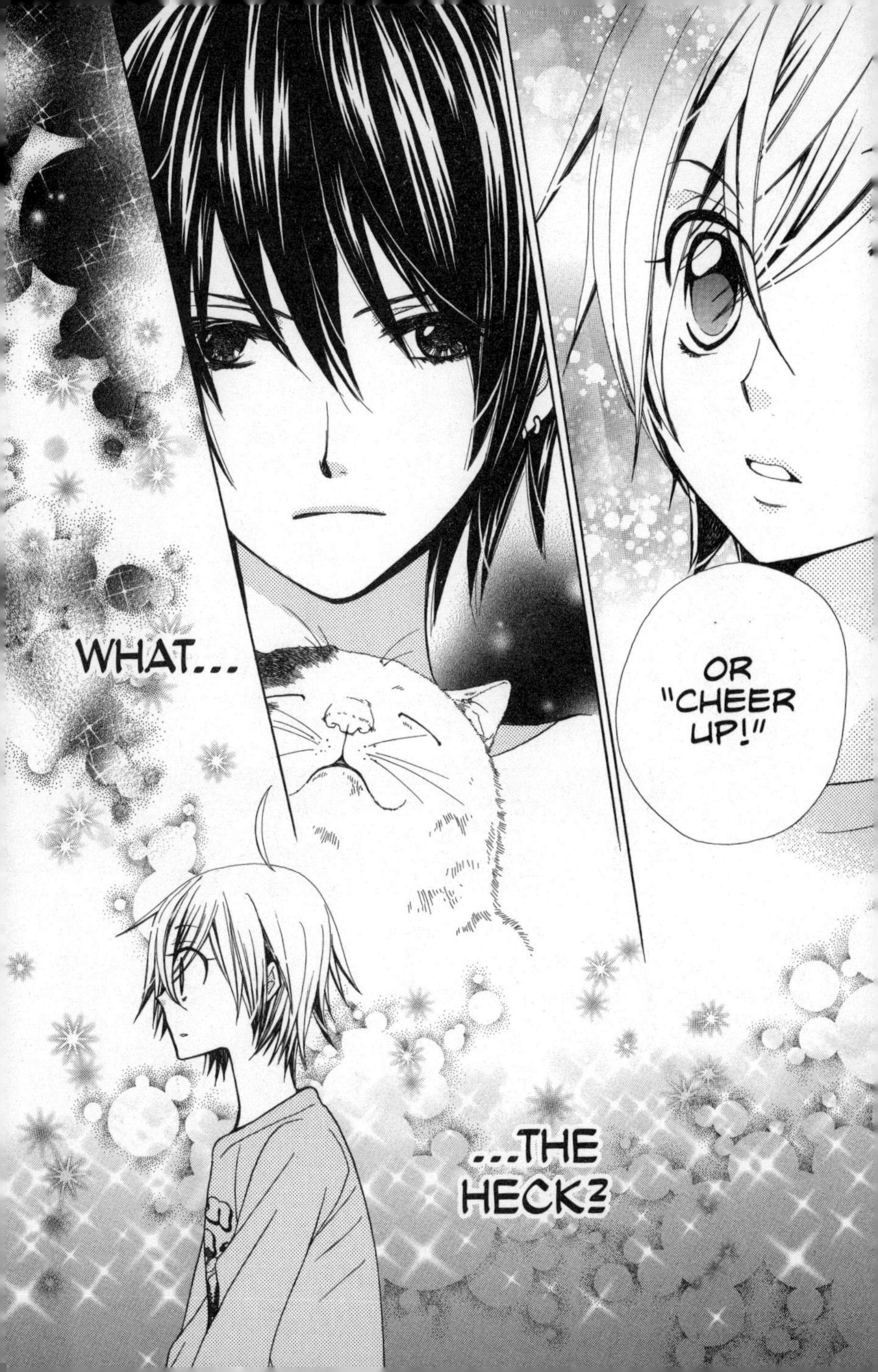
OR "CHEER UP!"
WHAT...
...THE HECK?

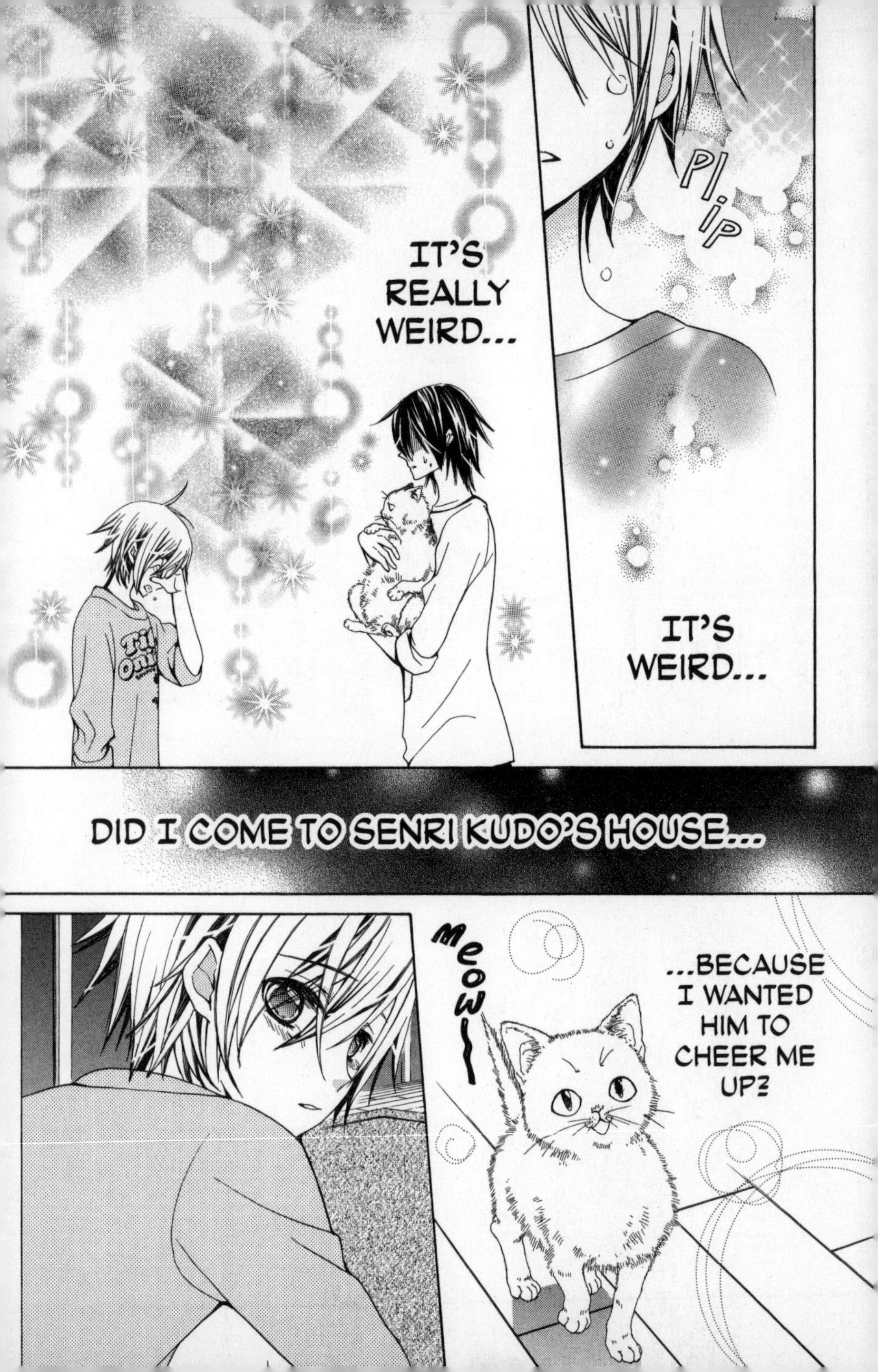
PLIP
IT'S WEIRD...
IT'S REALLY WEIRD...
DID I COME TO SENRI KUDO'S HOUSE...
...BECAUSE I WANTED HIM TO CHEER ME UP?
MEOW~

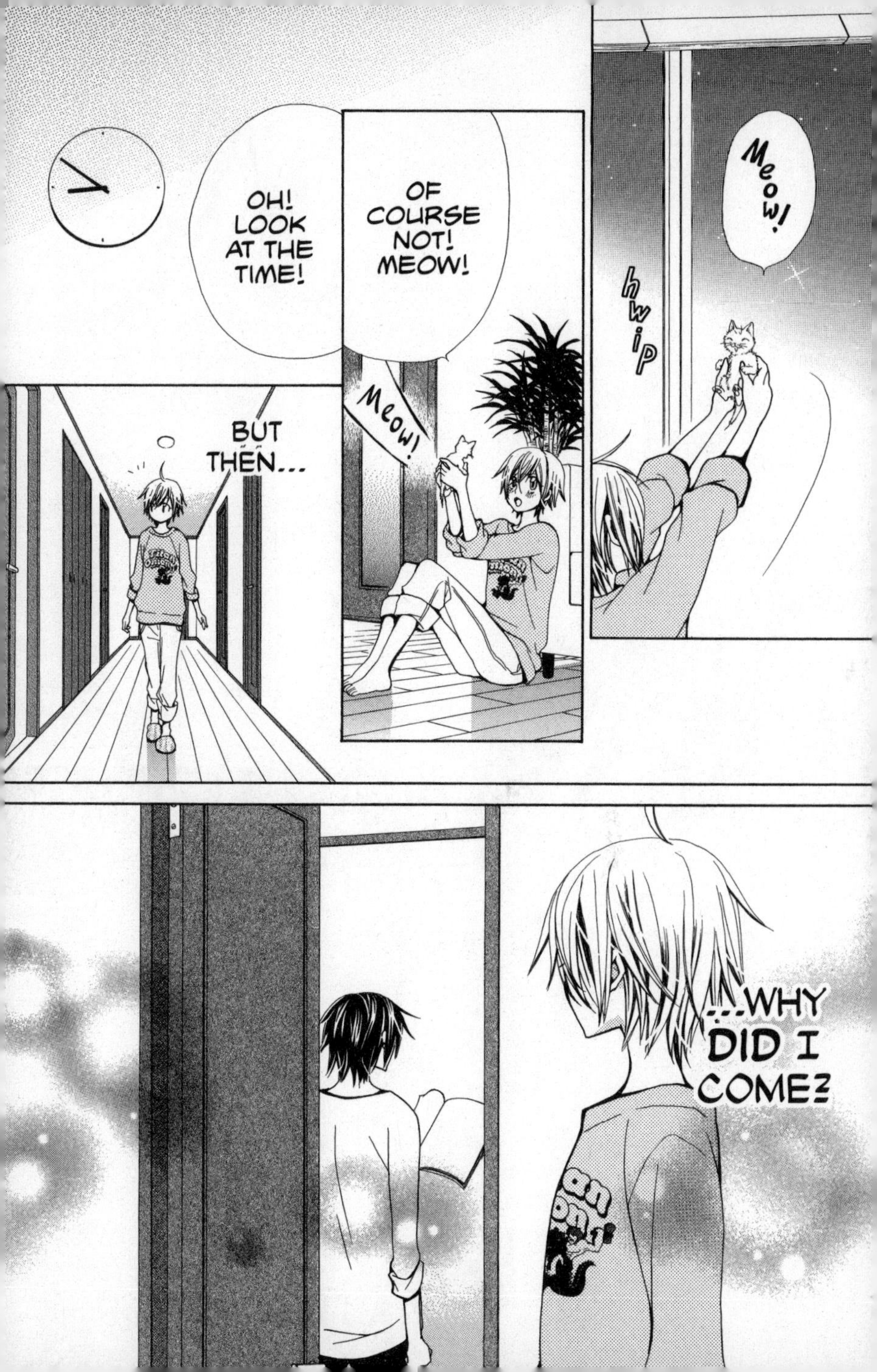
Meow!
hwip
OF COURSE NOT! MEOW!
Meow!
OH! LOOK AT THE TIME!
BUT THEN...
...WHY DID I COME?

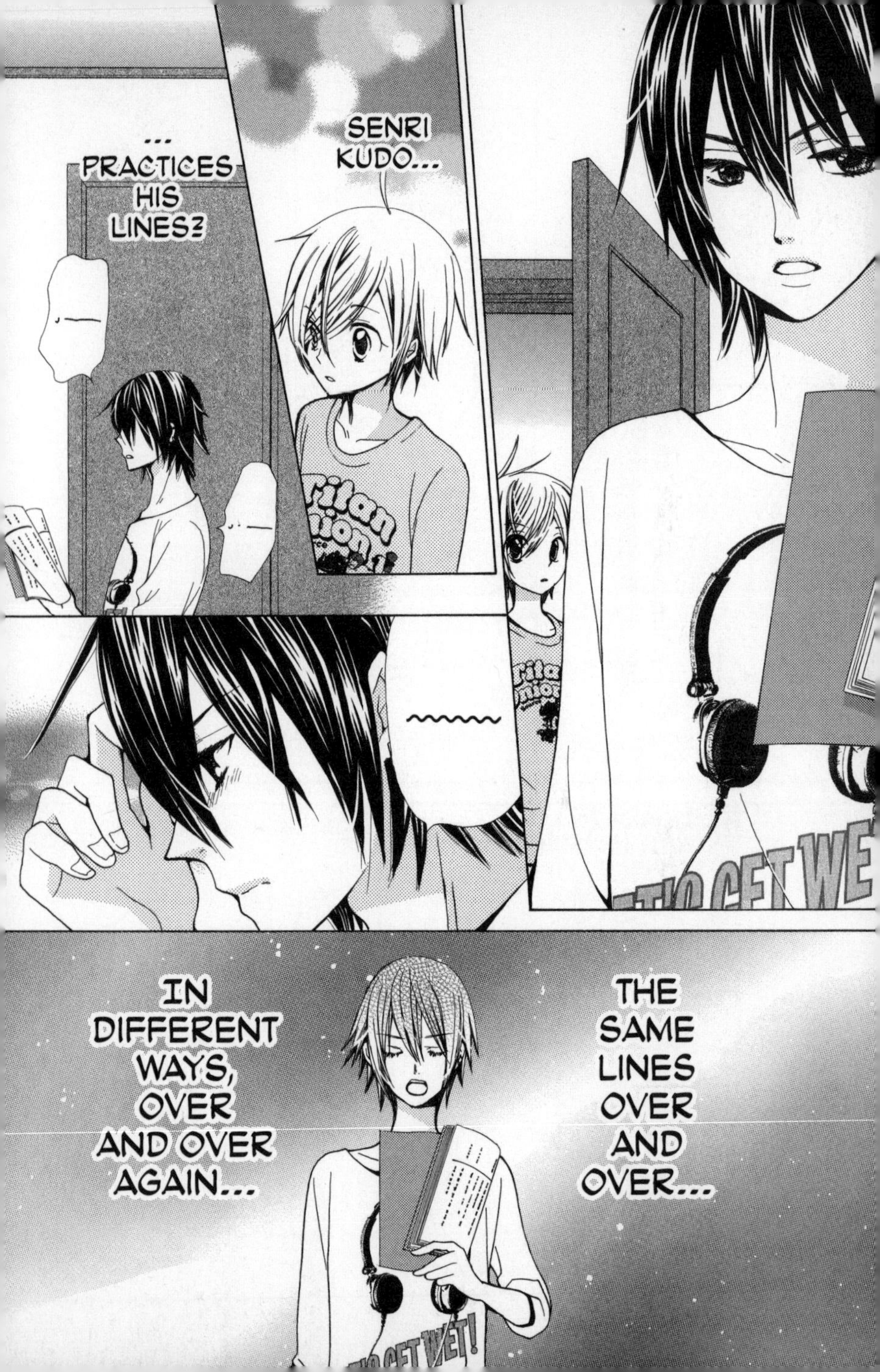
SENRI KUDO...
...PRACTICES HIS LINES?
THE SAME LINES OVER AND OVER...
IN DIFFERENT WAYS, OVER AND OVER AGAIN...

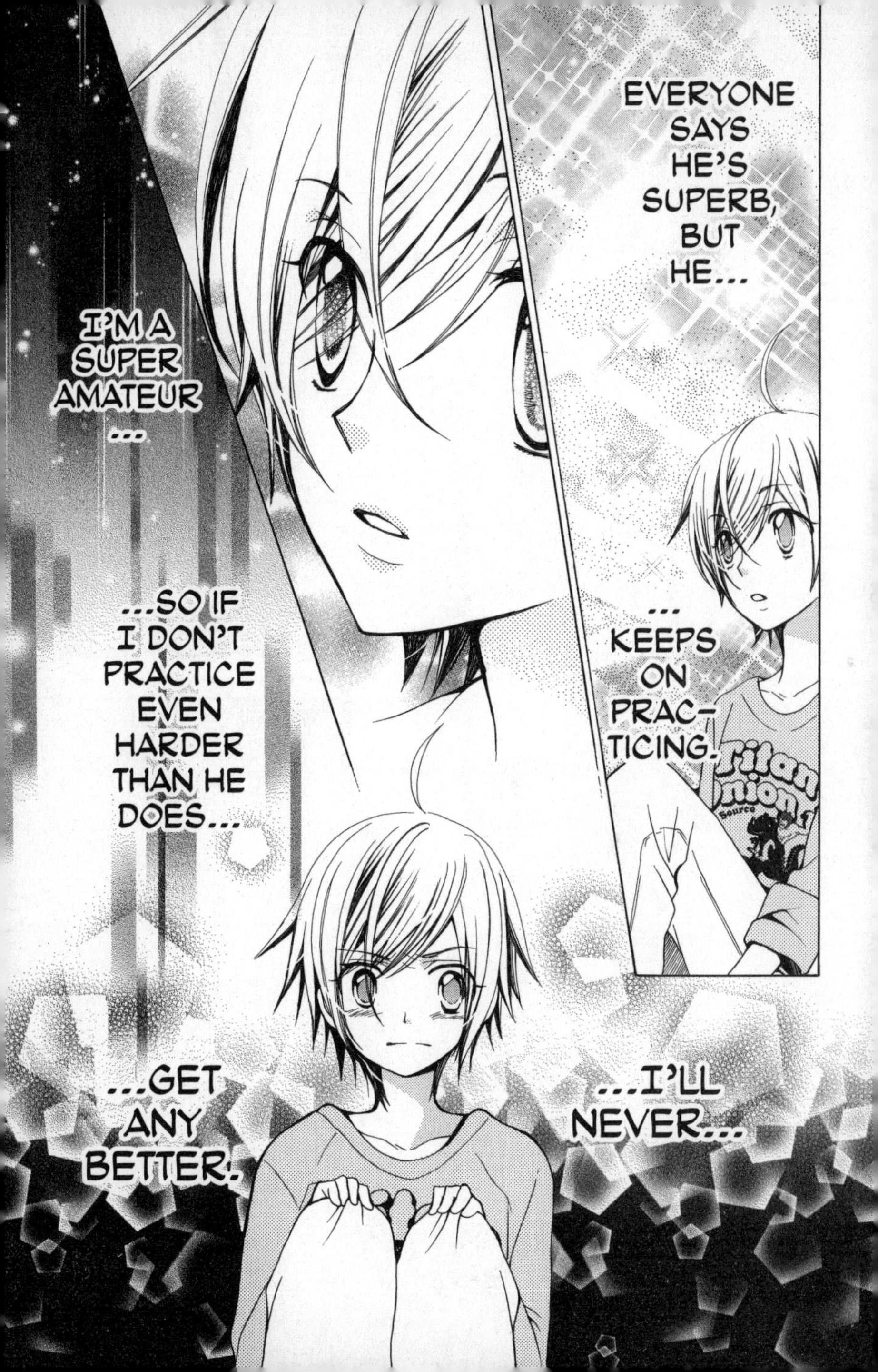
EVERYONE SAYS HE'S SUPERB, BUT HE...
...KEEPS ON PRAC-TICING.
I'M A SUPER AMATEUR...
...SO IF I DON'T PRACTICE EVEN HARDER THAN HE DOES...
...I'LL NEVER...
...GET ANY BETTER.

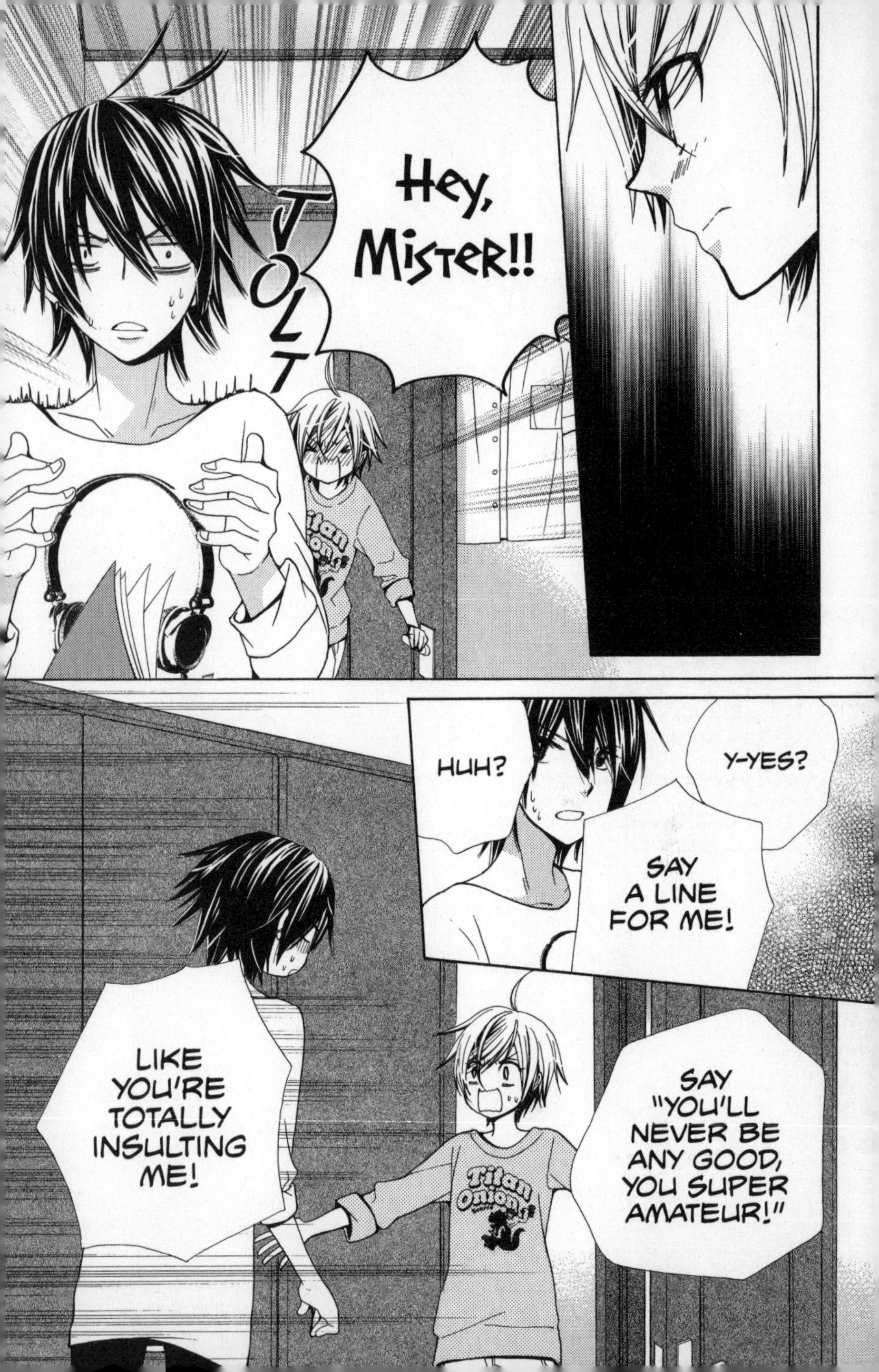
Hey, Mister!!
JOLT
HUH?
Y-YES?
SAY A LINE FOR ME!
SAY "YOU'LL NEVER BE ANY GOOD, YOU SUPER AMATEUR!"
LIKE YOU'RE TOTALLY INSULTING ME!

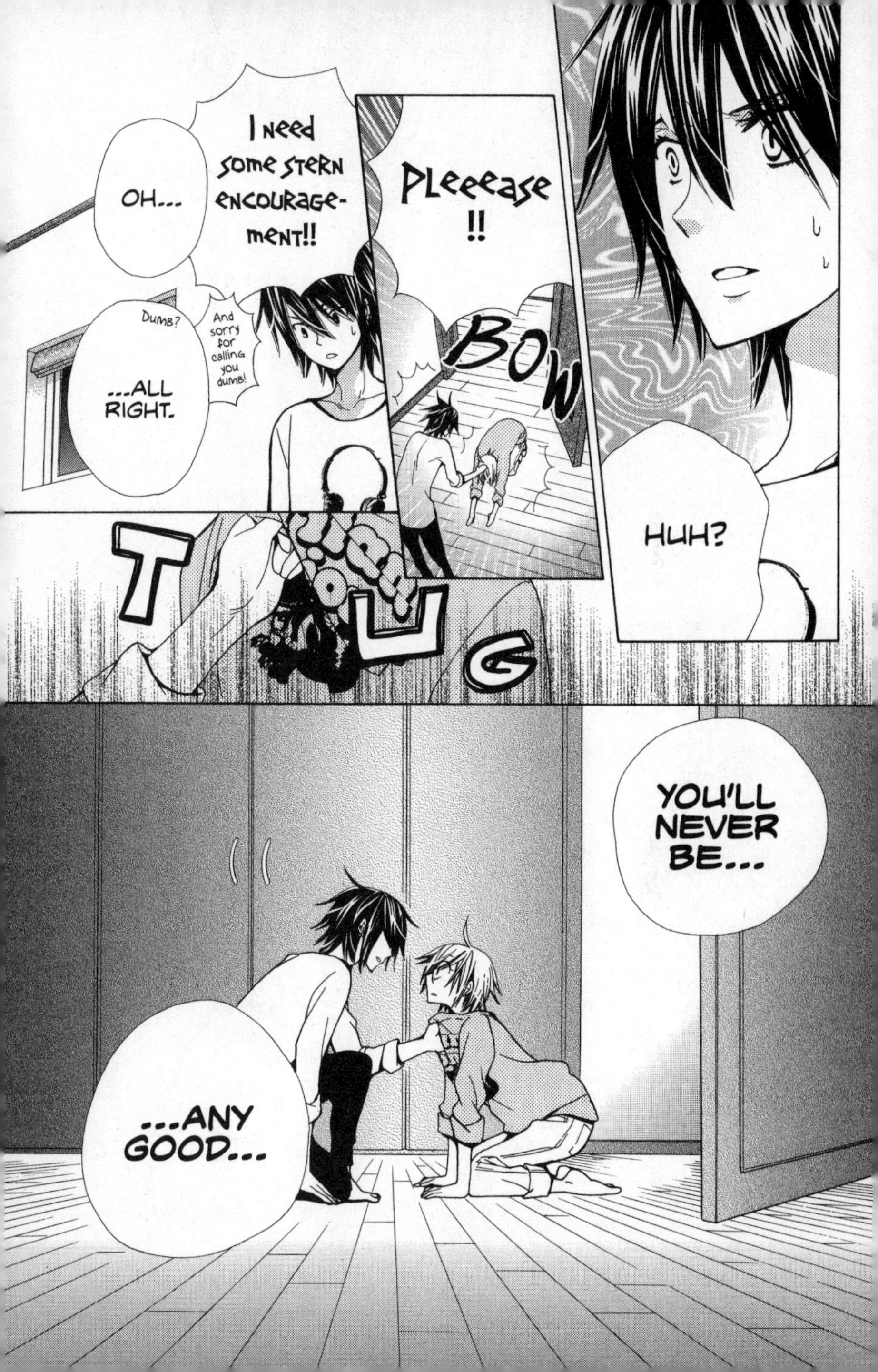
HUH?
Pleeease !!
BOW
I need some stern encourage-ment!!
OH...
And sorry for calling you dumb!
Dumb?
...ALL RIGHT.
TUG
YOU'LL NEVER BE...
...ANY GOOD...

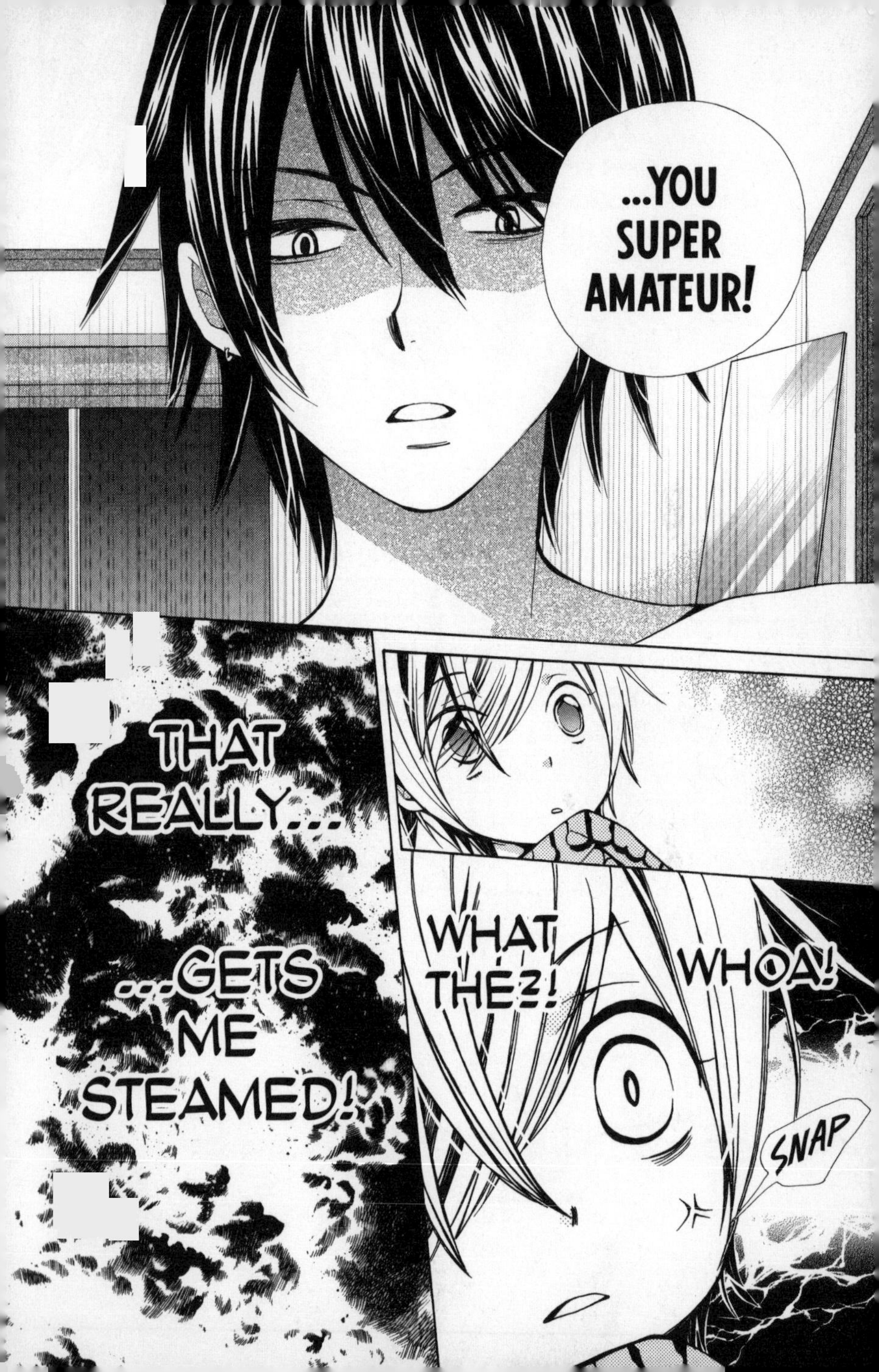
...YOU SUPER AMATEUR!
WHOA!
WHAT THE?!
SNAP
THAT REALLY...
...GETS ME STEAMED!

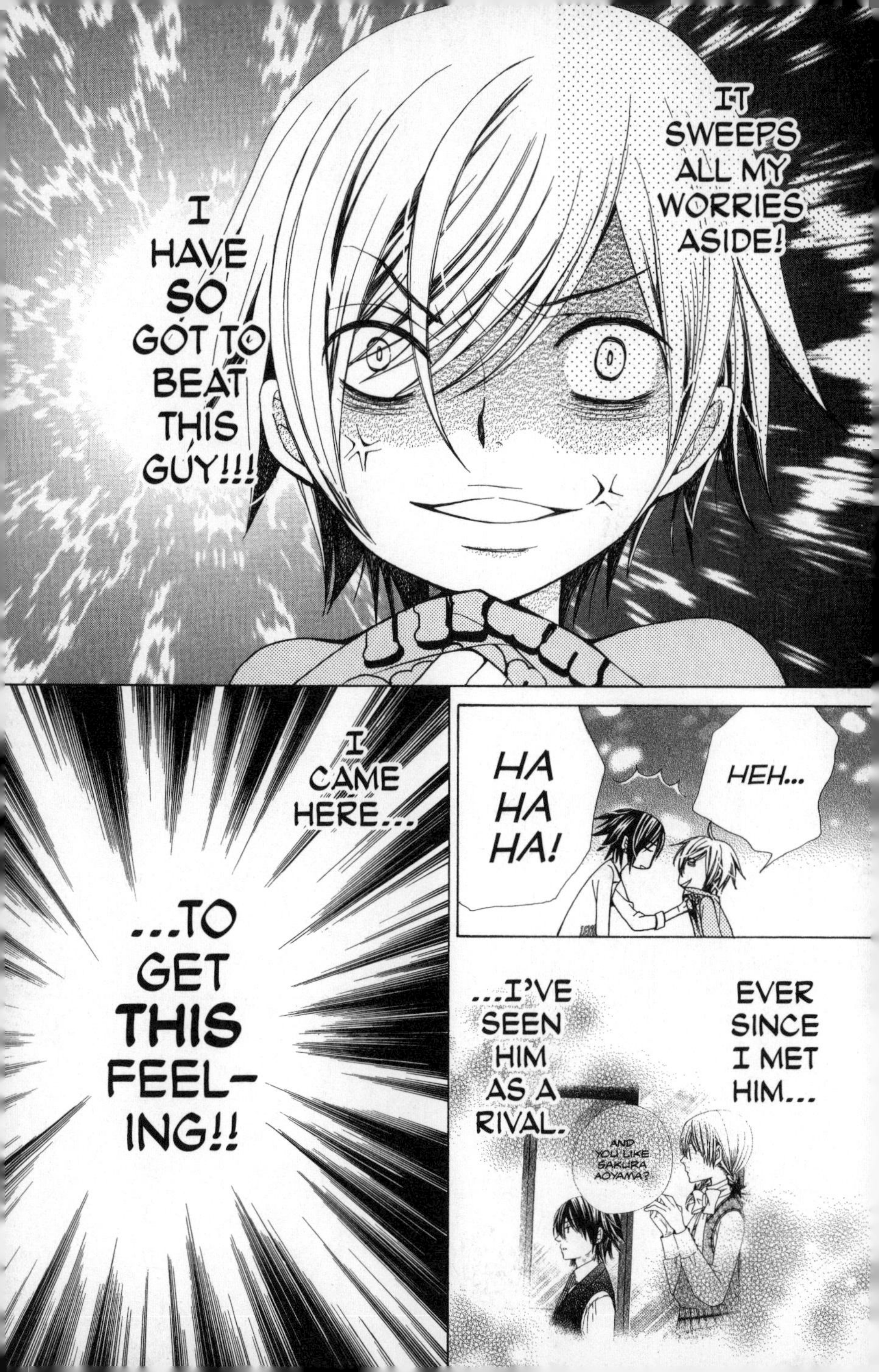
IT SWEEPS ALL MY WORRIES ASIDE!
I HAVE SO GOT TO BEAT THIS GUY!!!
HEH...
HA HA HA!
EVER SINCE I MET HIM...
...I'VE SEEN HIM AS A RIVAL.
AND YOU LIKE SAKURA AOYAMA?
I CAME HERE...
...TO GET THIS FEELING!!

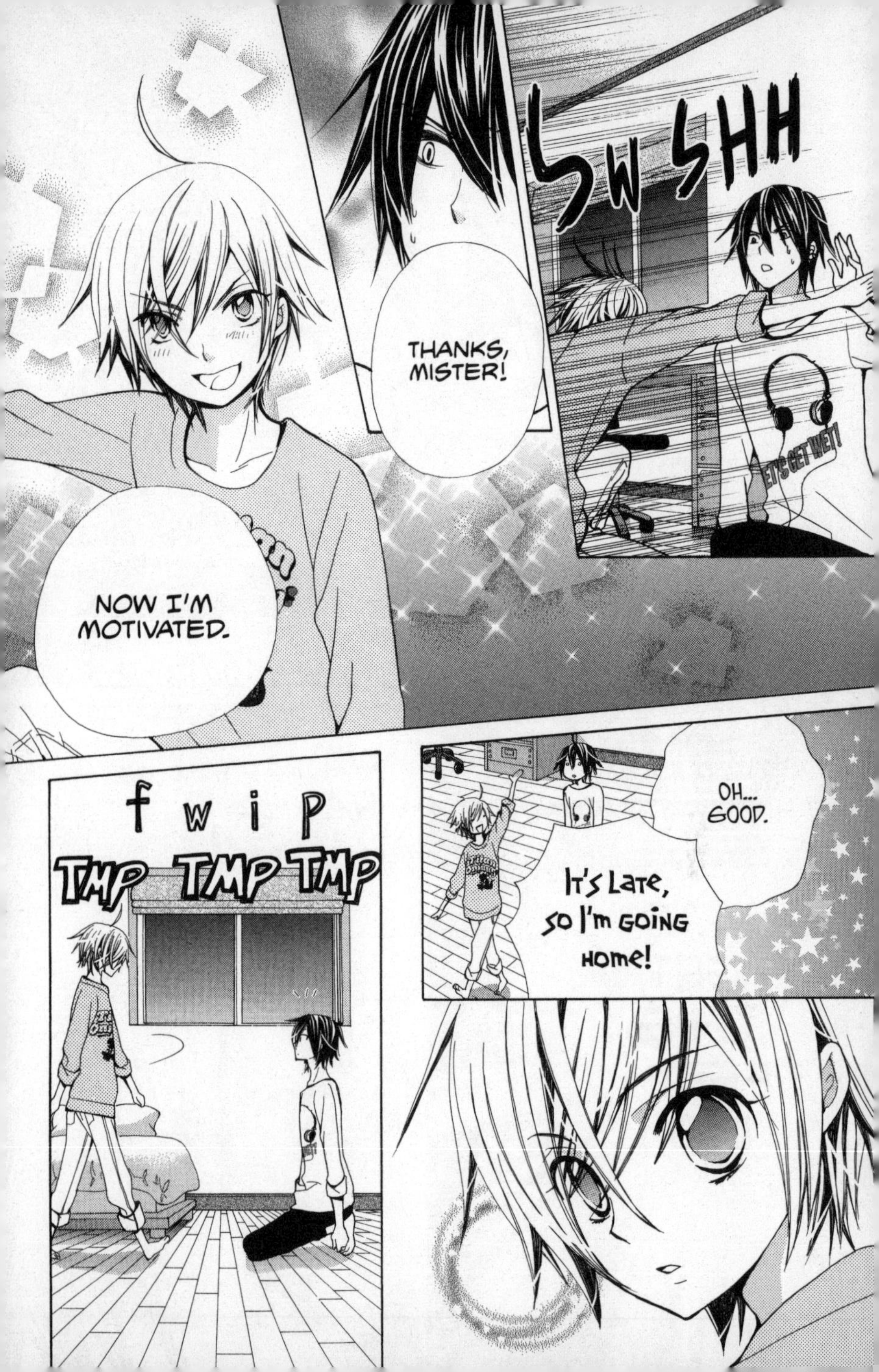
SWSHH
ET'S GET WET!
THANKS, MISTER!
NOW I'M MOTIVATED.
OH... GOOD.
It's late, so I'm going home!
fwip
TMP TMP TMP

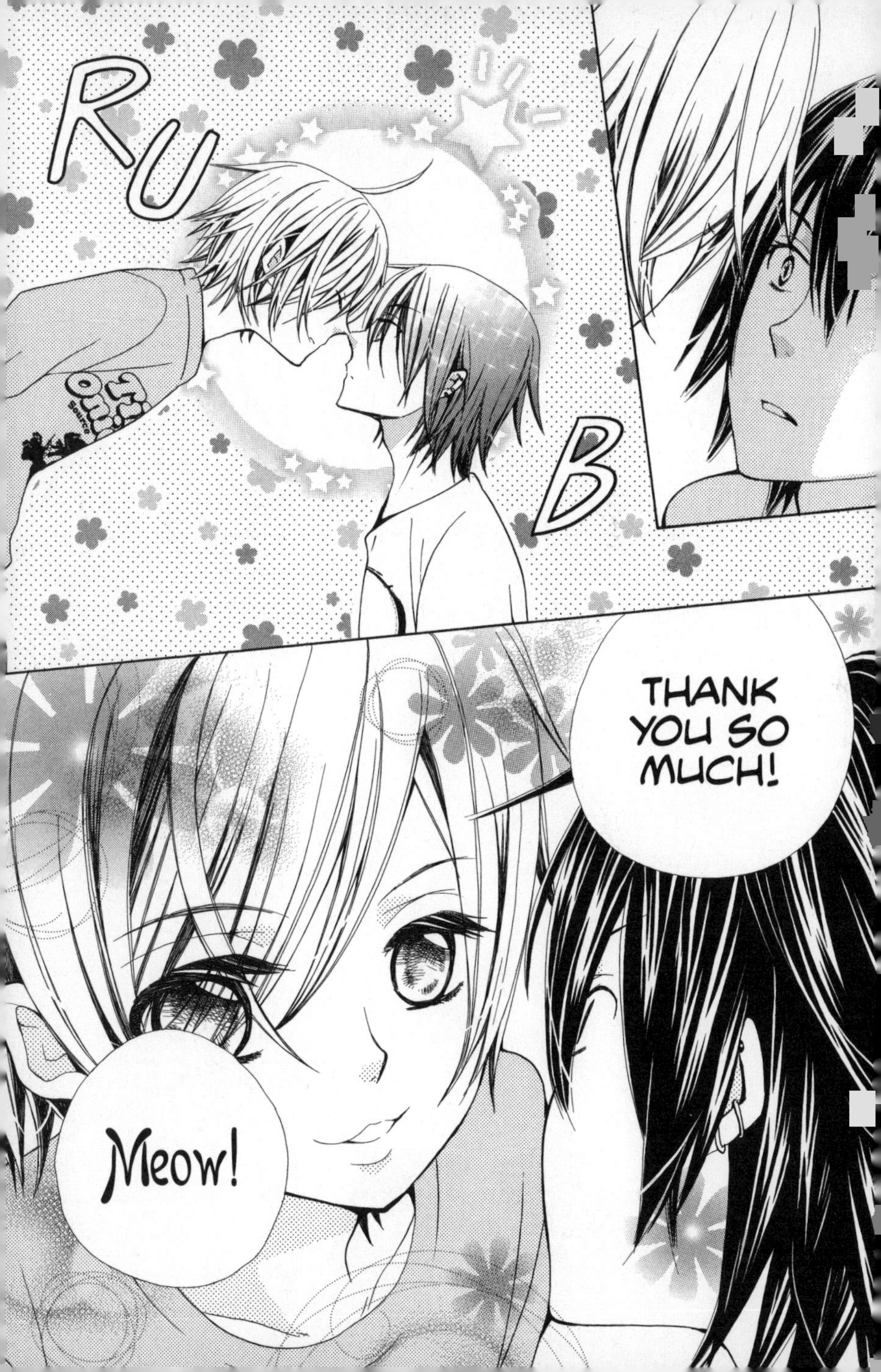
RUB
THANK YOU SO MUCH!
Meow!

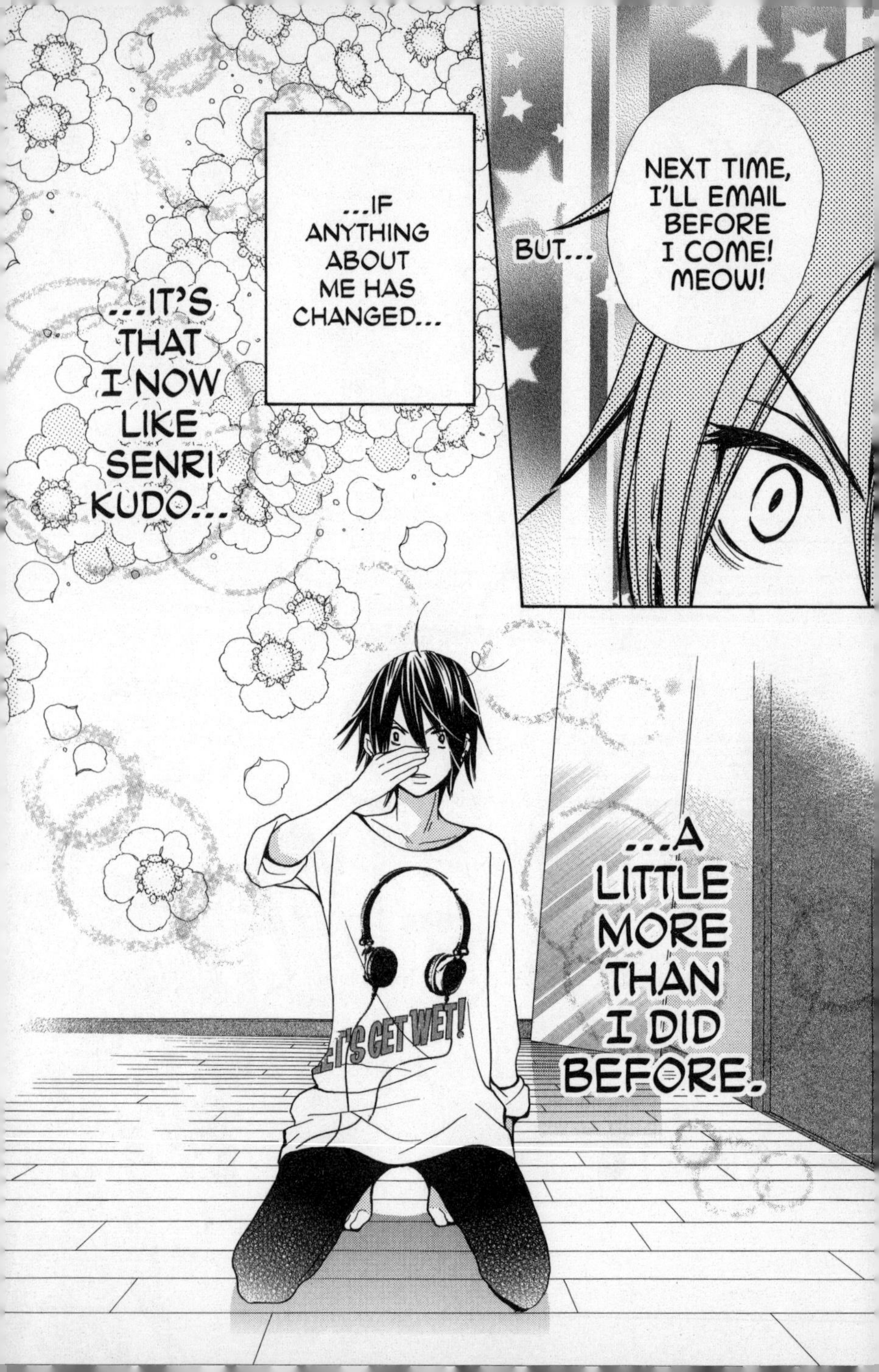
NEXT TIME, I'LL EMAIL BEFORE I COME! MEOW!
BUT...
...IF ANYTHING ABOUT ME HAS CHANGED...
...IT'S THAT I NOW LIKE SENRI KUDO...
...A LITTLE MORE THAN I DID BEFORE.
LET'S GET WET!

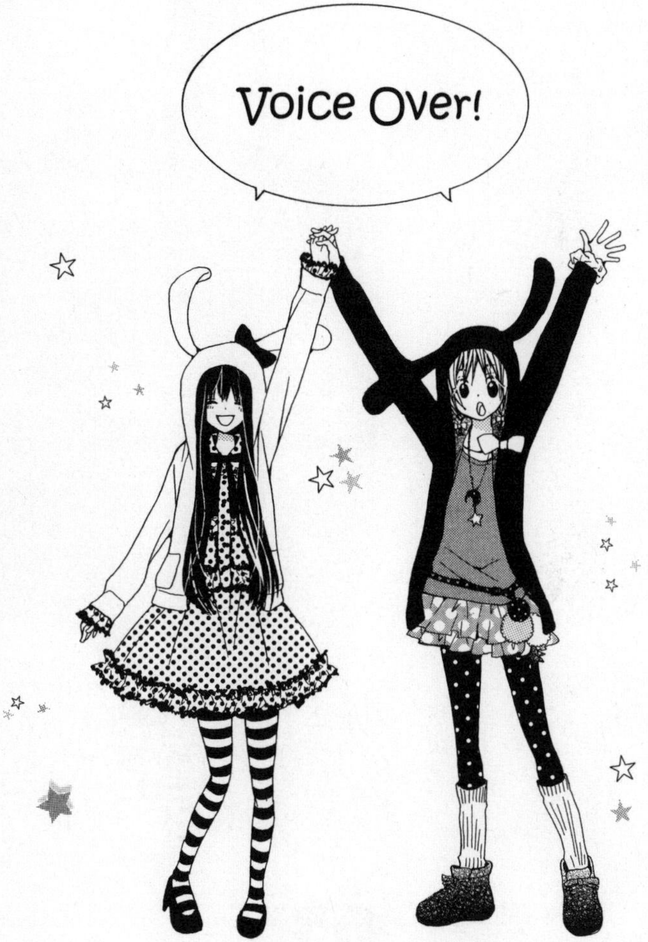
Voice Over!

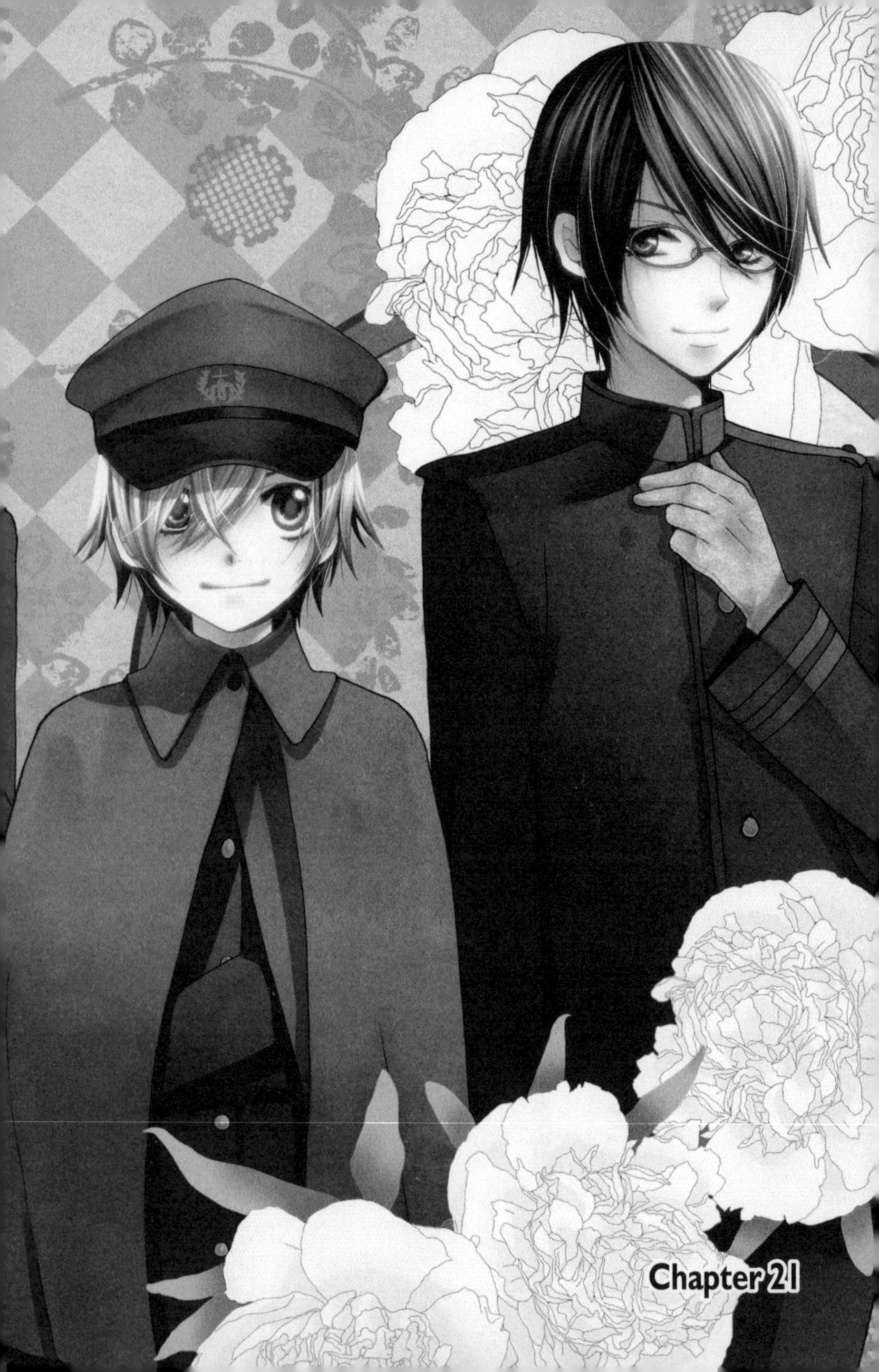
Chapter 21

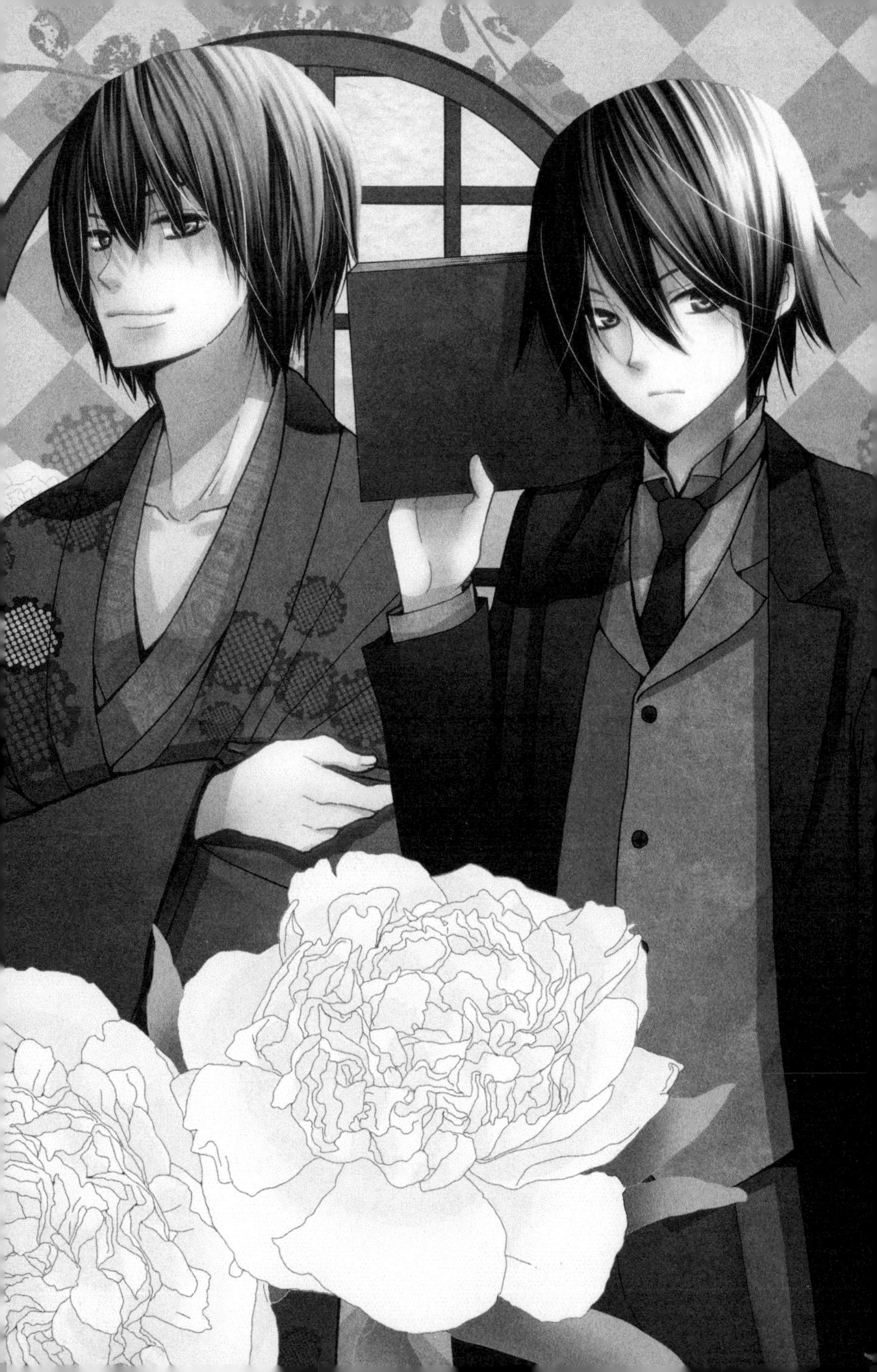

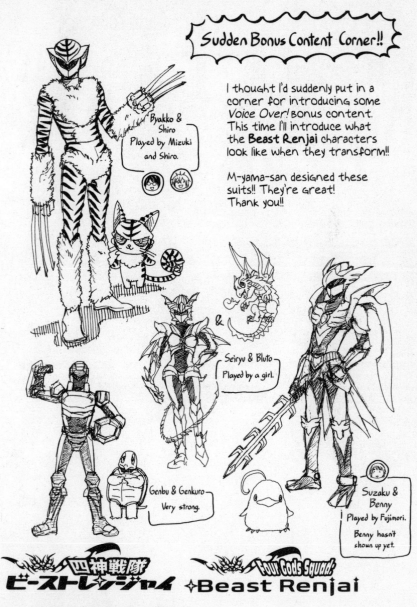

Sudden Bonus Content Corner!!

I thought I'd suddenly put in a corner for introducing some *Voice Over!* bonus content. This time I'll introduce what the **Beast Renjai** characters look like when they transform!!

M-yama-san designed these suits!! They're great! Thank you!!

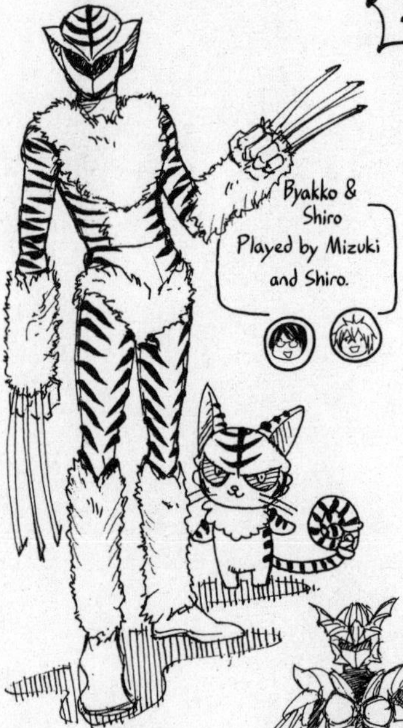

Byakko & Shiro
Played by Mizuki and Shiro.

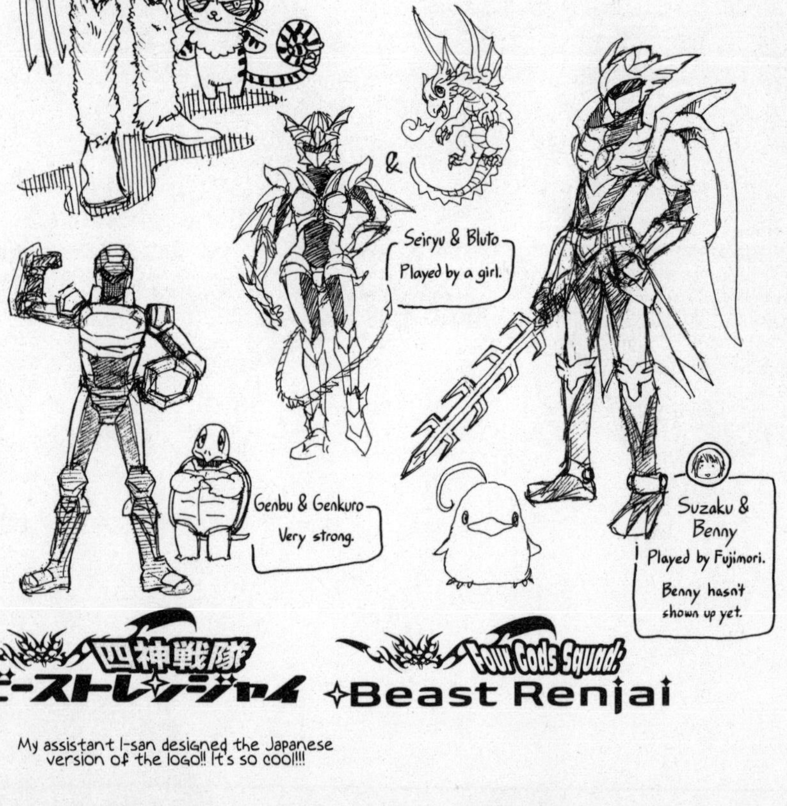

&
Seiryu & Bluto
Played by a girl.
Genbu & Genkuro
Very strong.
Suzaku & Benny
Played by Fujimori.
Benny hasn't shown up yet.

四神戦隊 ビーストレンジャイ

Four Gods Squad: Beast Renjai

My assistant I-san designed the Japanese version of the logo!! It's so cool!!!

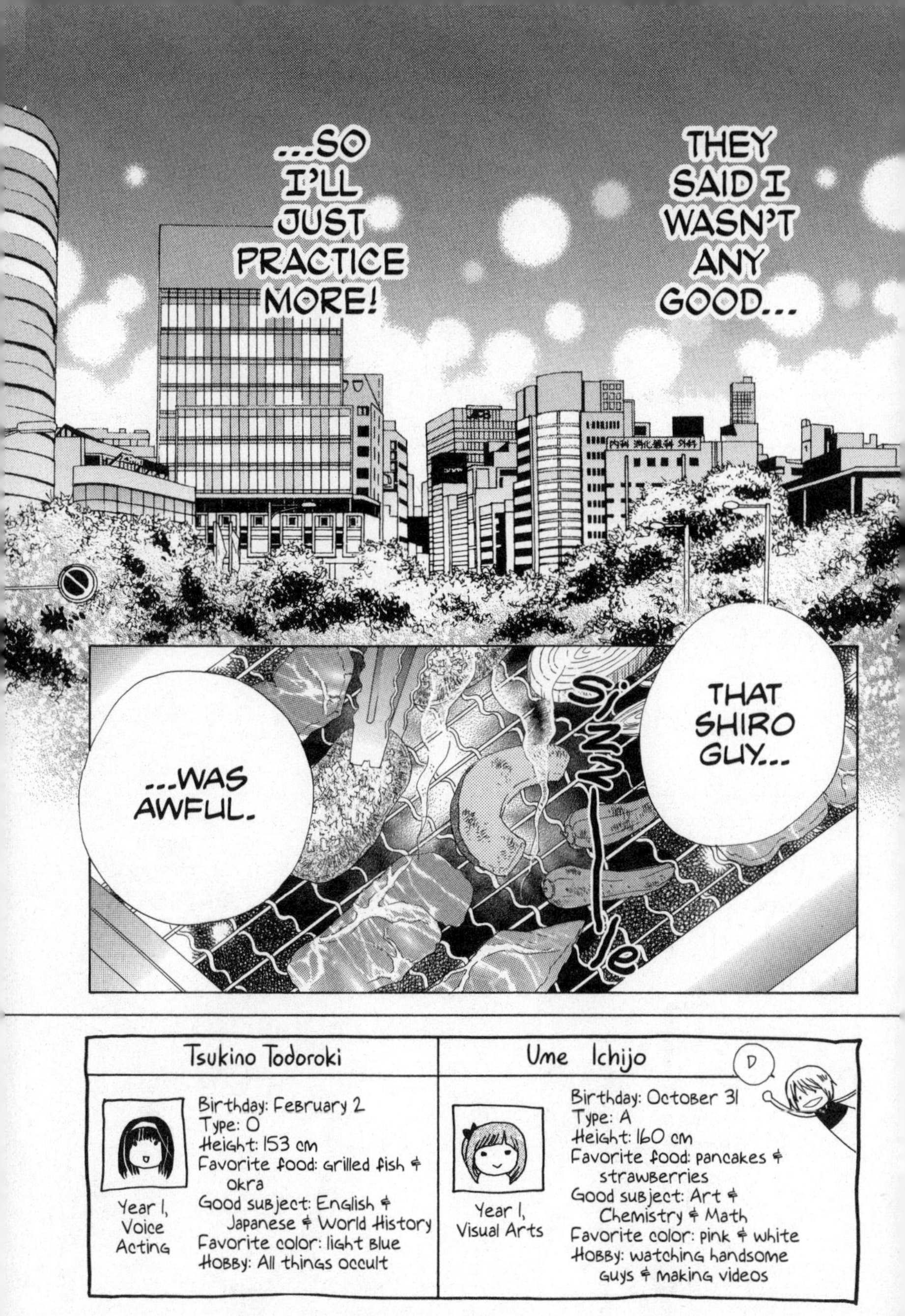
THEY SAID I WASN'T ANY GOOD...
...SO I'LL JUST PRACTICE MORE!
THAT SHIRO GUY...
...WAS AWFUL.

Tsukino Todoroki	Ume Ichijo
Year 1, Voice Acting	Year 1, Visual Arts
Birthday: February 2 Type: O Height: 153 cm Favorite food: Grilled fish & okra Good subject: English & Japanese & World History Favorite color: light Blue Hobby: All things occult	Birthday: October 31 Type: A Height: 160 cm Favorite food: pancakes & strawberries Good subject: Art & Chemistry & Math Favorite color: pink & white Hobby: watching handsome guys & making videos

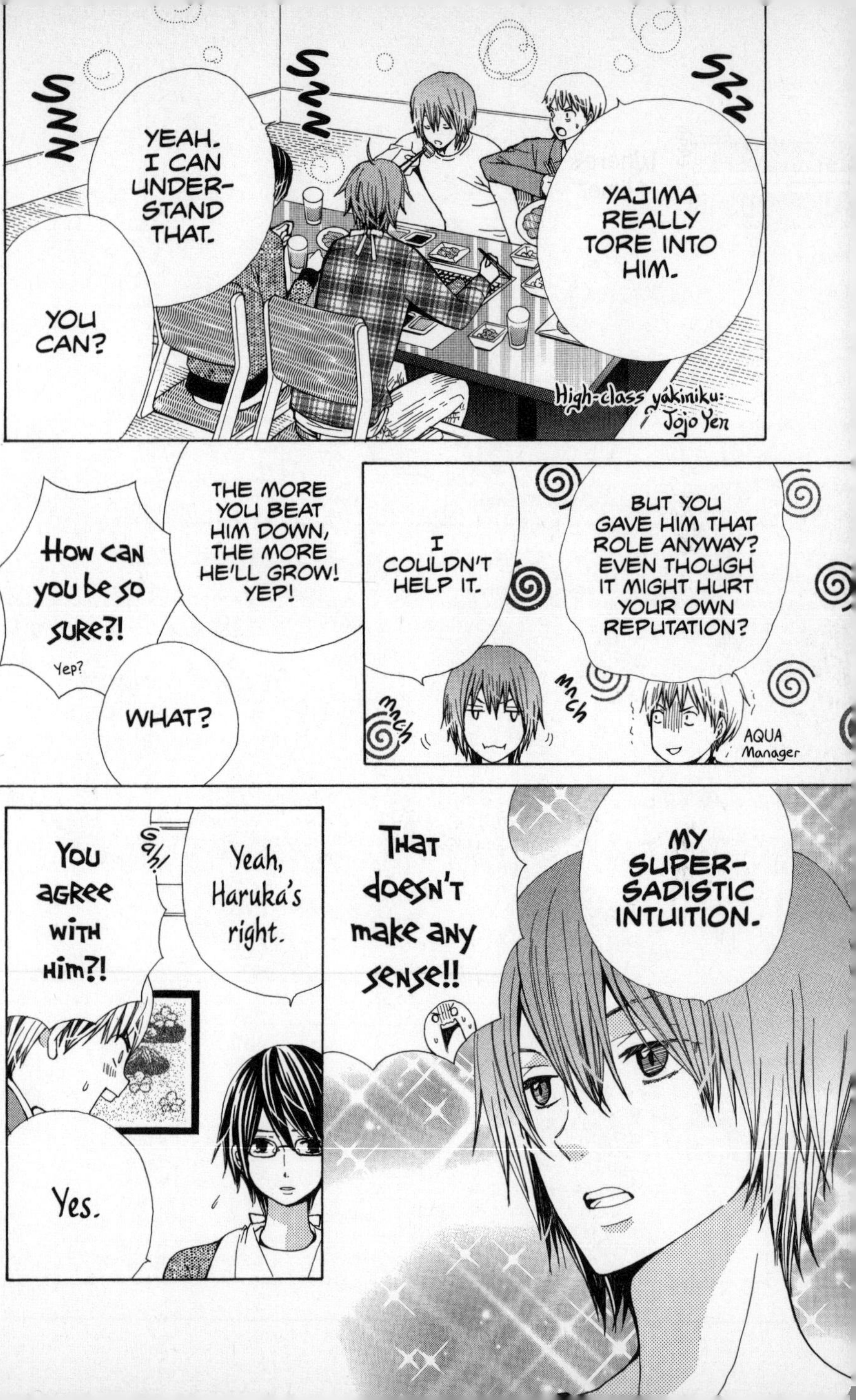
SZZ
YAJIMA REALLY TORE INTO HIM.
SZZ
SZZ
YEAH. I CAN UNDERSTAND THAT.
YOU CAN?
High-class yakiniku: Jojo Yen
BUT YOU GAVE HIM THAT ROLE ANYWAY? EVEN THOUGH IT MIGHT HURT YOUR OWN REPUTATION?
I COULDN'T HELP IT.
mnch
mnch
AQUA Manager
THE MORE YOU BEAT HIM DOWN, THE MORE HE'LL GROW! YEP!
How can you be so sure?!
Yep?
WHAT?
MY SUPER-SADISTIC INTUITION.
That doesn't make any sense!!
Yeah, Haruka's right.
Gah!
You agree with him?!
Yes.

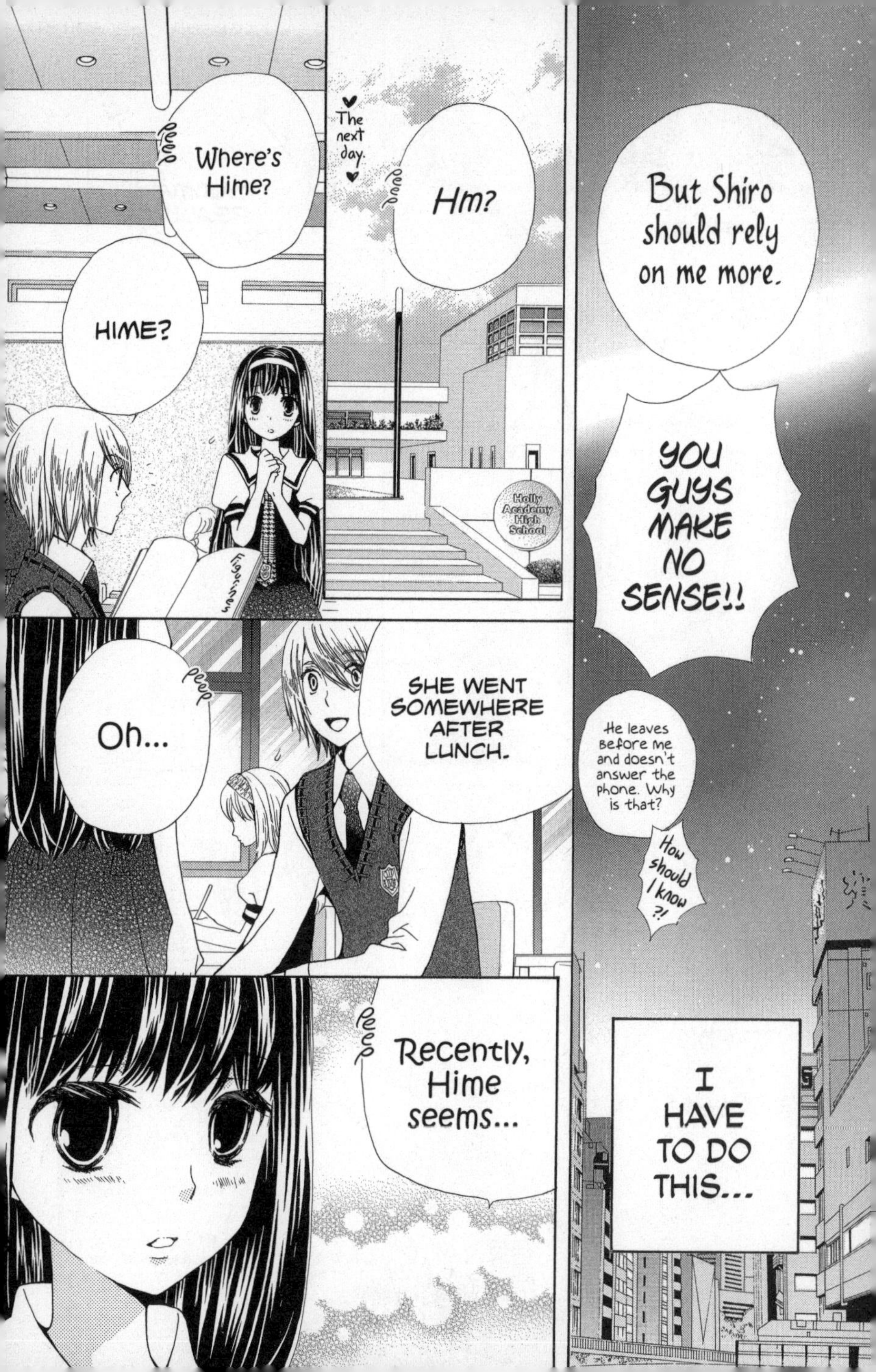
But Shiro should rely on me more.
YOU GUYS MAKE NO SENSE!!
He leaves before me and doesn't answer the phone. Why is that?
How should I know?!
I HAVE TO DO THIS...
The next day.
peep
Hm?
Holly Academy High School
peep
Where's Hime?
HIME?
Figurines
SHE WENT SOMEWHERE AFTER LUNCH.
peep
Oh...
peep
Recently, Hime seems...

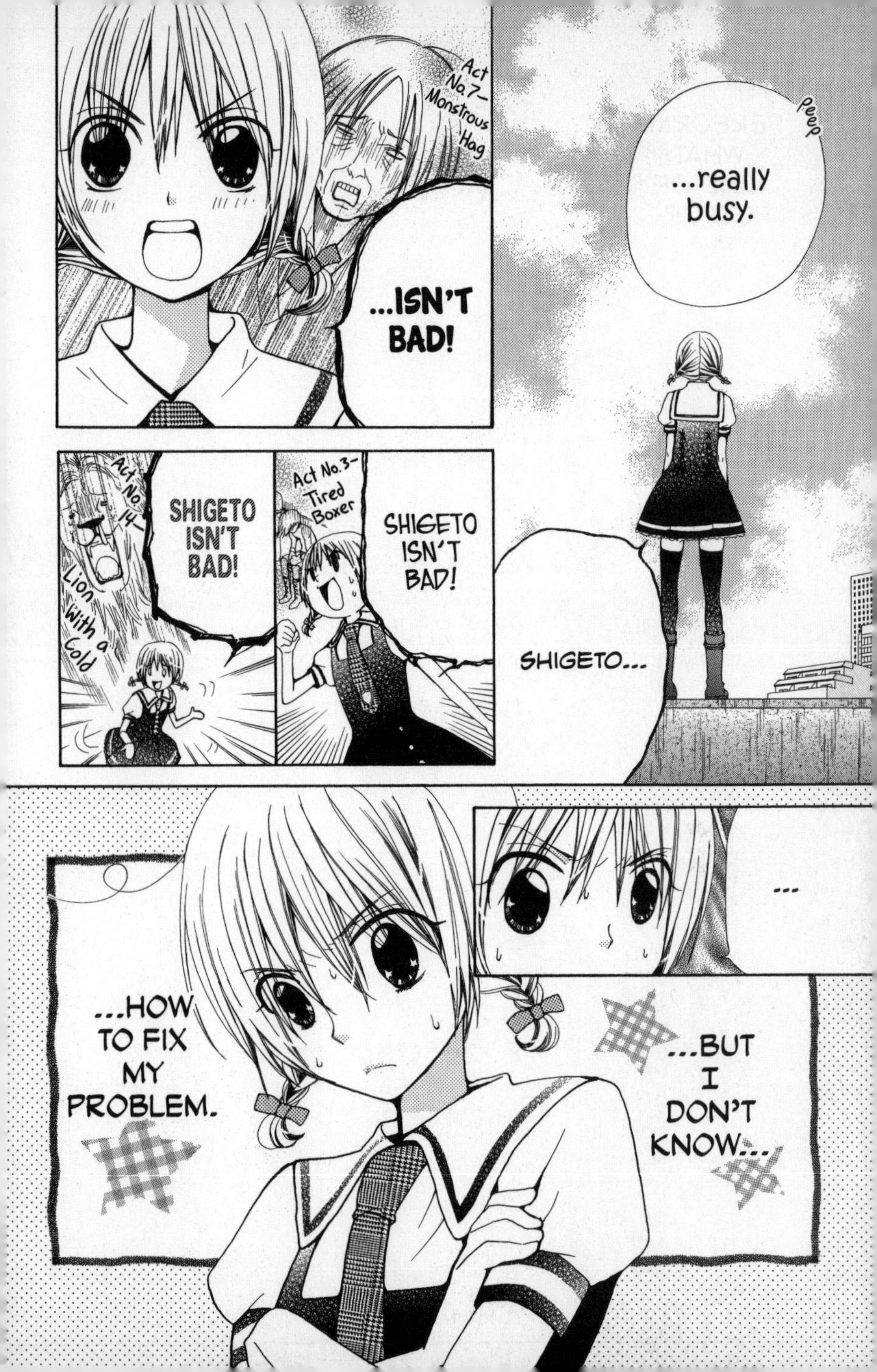
Peep
...really busy.
SHIGETO...
Act No.7—Monstrous Hag
...ISN'T BAD!
Act No.3—Tired Boxer
SHIGETO ISN'T BAD!
SHIGETO ISN'T BAD!
Act No.14—Lion with a Cold
...
...BUT I DON'T KNOW...
...HOW TO FIX MY PROBLEM.

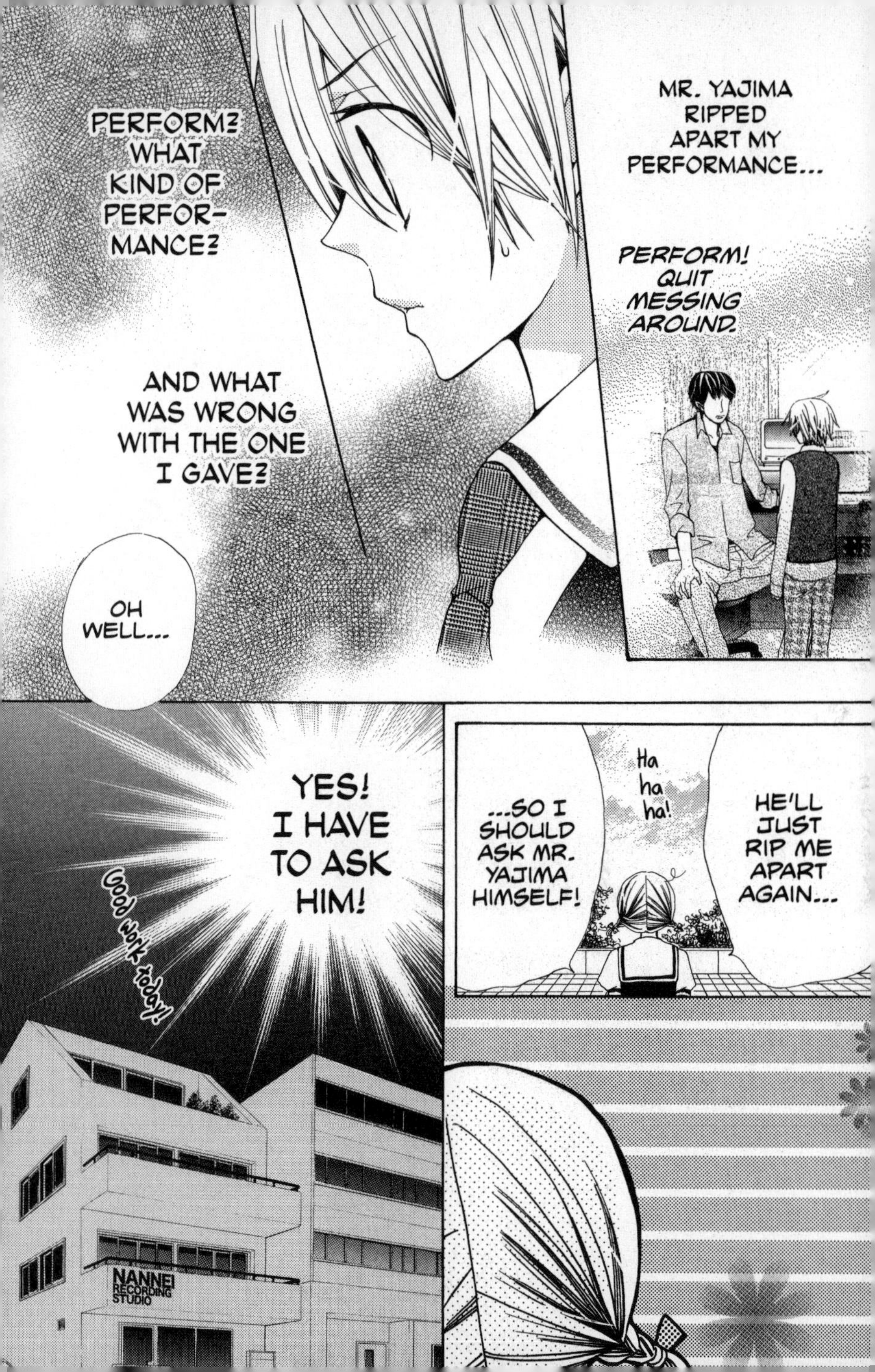
MR. YAJIMA RIPPED APART MY PERFORMANCE...
PERFORM! QUIT MESSING AROUND.
PERFORM? WHAT KIND OF PERFOR-MANCE?
AND WHAT WAS WRONG WITH THE ONE I GAVE?
OH WELL...
HE'LL JUST RIP ME APART AGAIN...
Ha ha ha!
...SO I SHOULD ASK MR. YAJIMA HIMSELF!
YES! I HAVE TO ASK HIM!
Good work today!
NANNEI RECORDING STUDIO

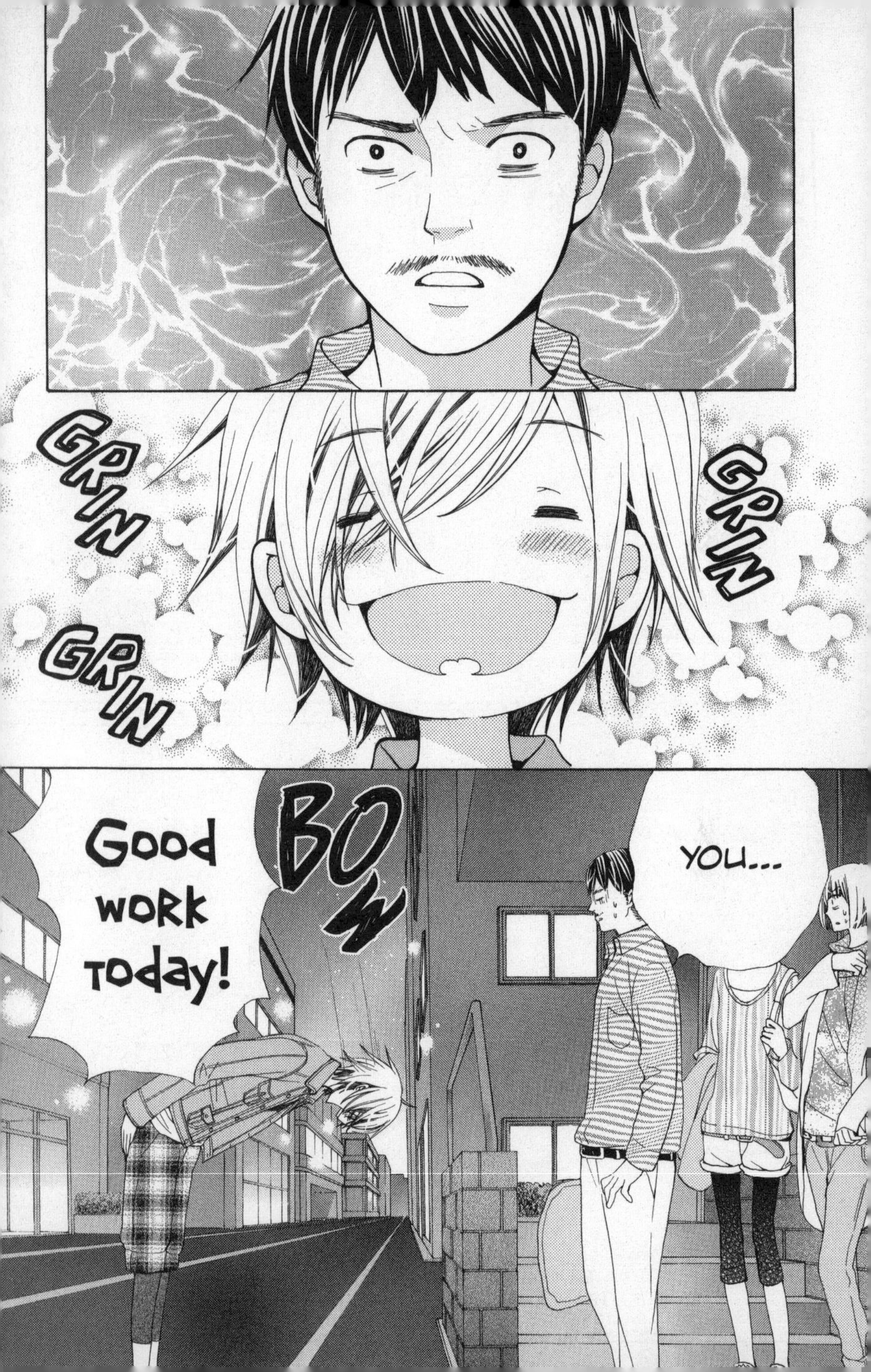
GRIN
GRIN
GRIN
YOU...
BOW
Good work today!

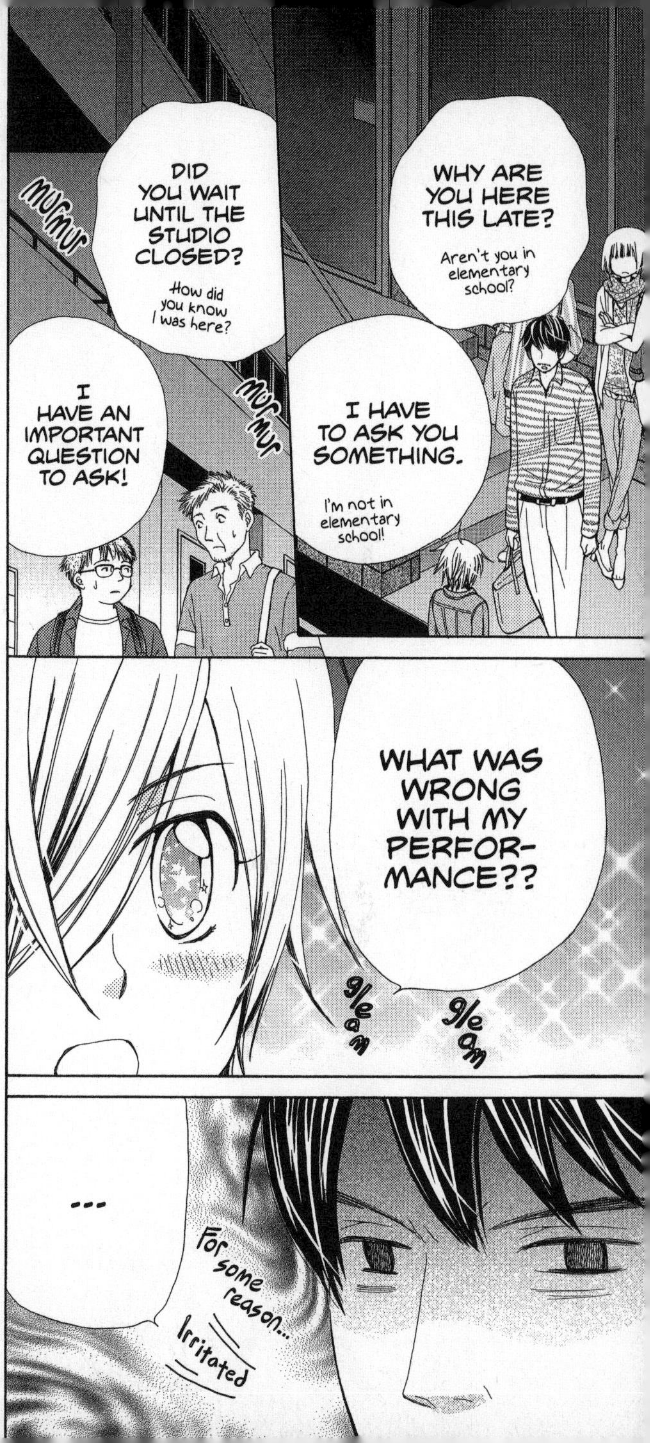
WHY ARE YOU HERE THIS LATE?
Aren't you in elementary school?
I HAVE TO ASK YOU SOMETHING.
I'm not in elementary school!
DID YOU WAIT UNTIL THE STUDIO CLOSED?
How did you know I was here?
murmur
I HAVE AN IMPORTANT QUESTION TO ASK!
murmur
WHAT WAS WRONG WITH MY PERFORMANCE??
gleam
gleam
...
For some reason...
Irritated

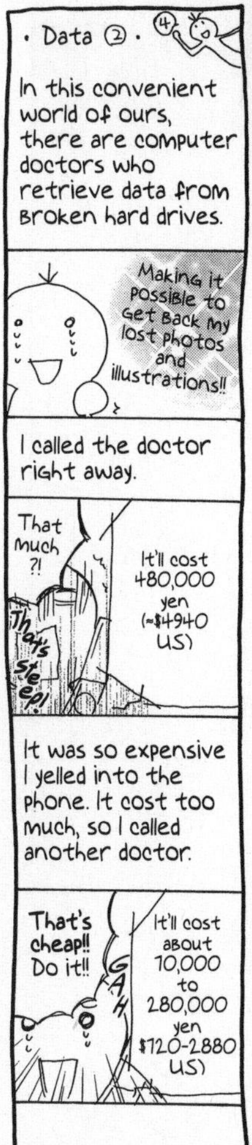
• Data ② •
④
In this convenient world of ours, there are computer doctors who retrieve data from broken hard drives.
Making it possible to get back my lost photos and illustrations!!
I called the doctor right away.
That much?!
It'll cost 480,000 yen (≈$4940 US)
That's steep!
It was so expensive I yelled into the phone. It cost too much, so I called another doctor.
That's cheap!! Do it!!
It'll cost about 10,000 to 280,000 yen $120-2880 US)
GAH
The first price was so expensive that the second one sounded dirt-cheap.
But that's expensive, too!
GASP

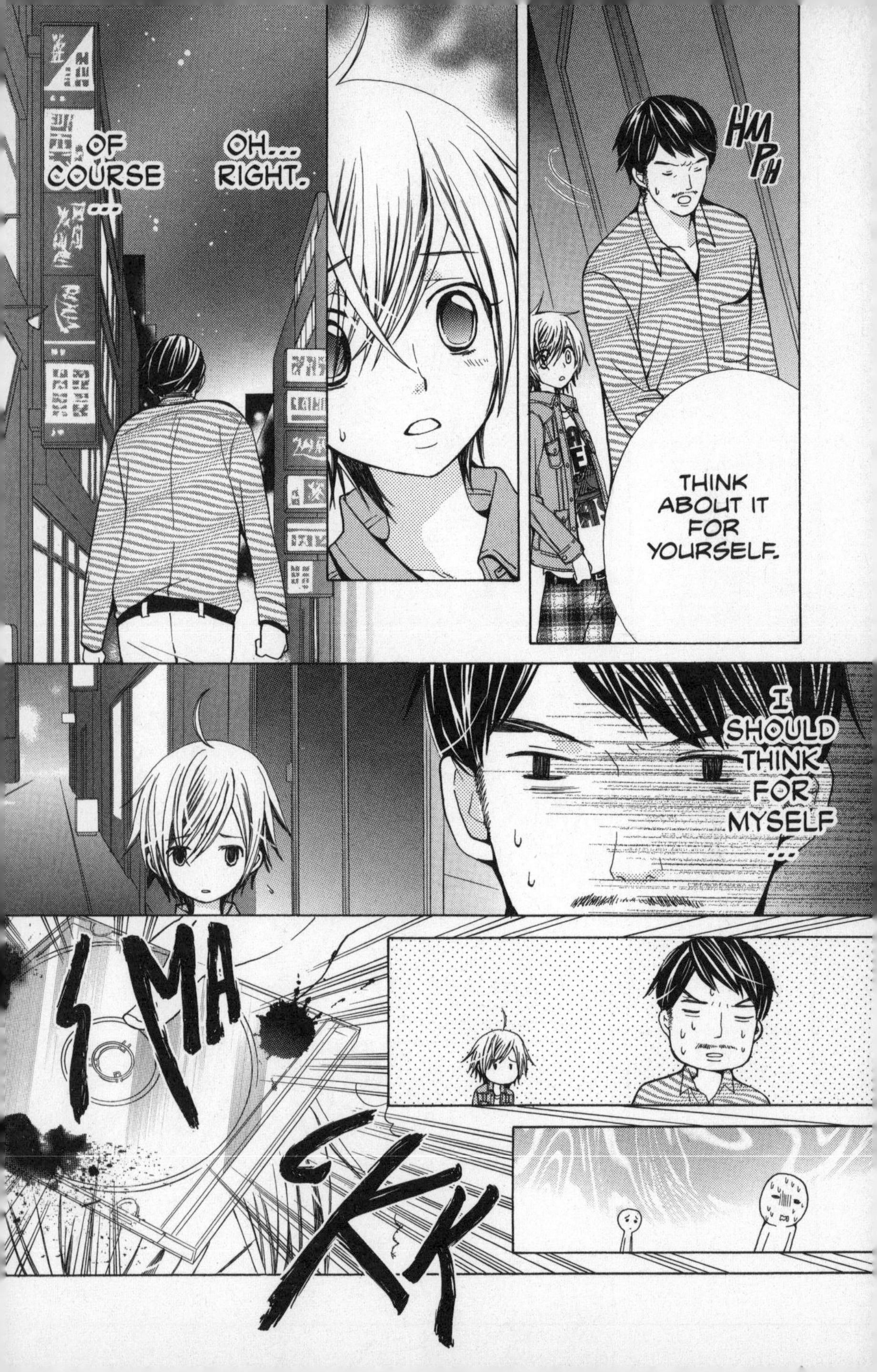
HMPH
THINK ABOUT IT FOR YOURSELF.
OH... RIGHT.
OF COURSE...
I SHOULD THINK FOR MYSELF...
SMACK

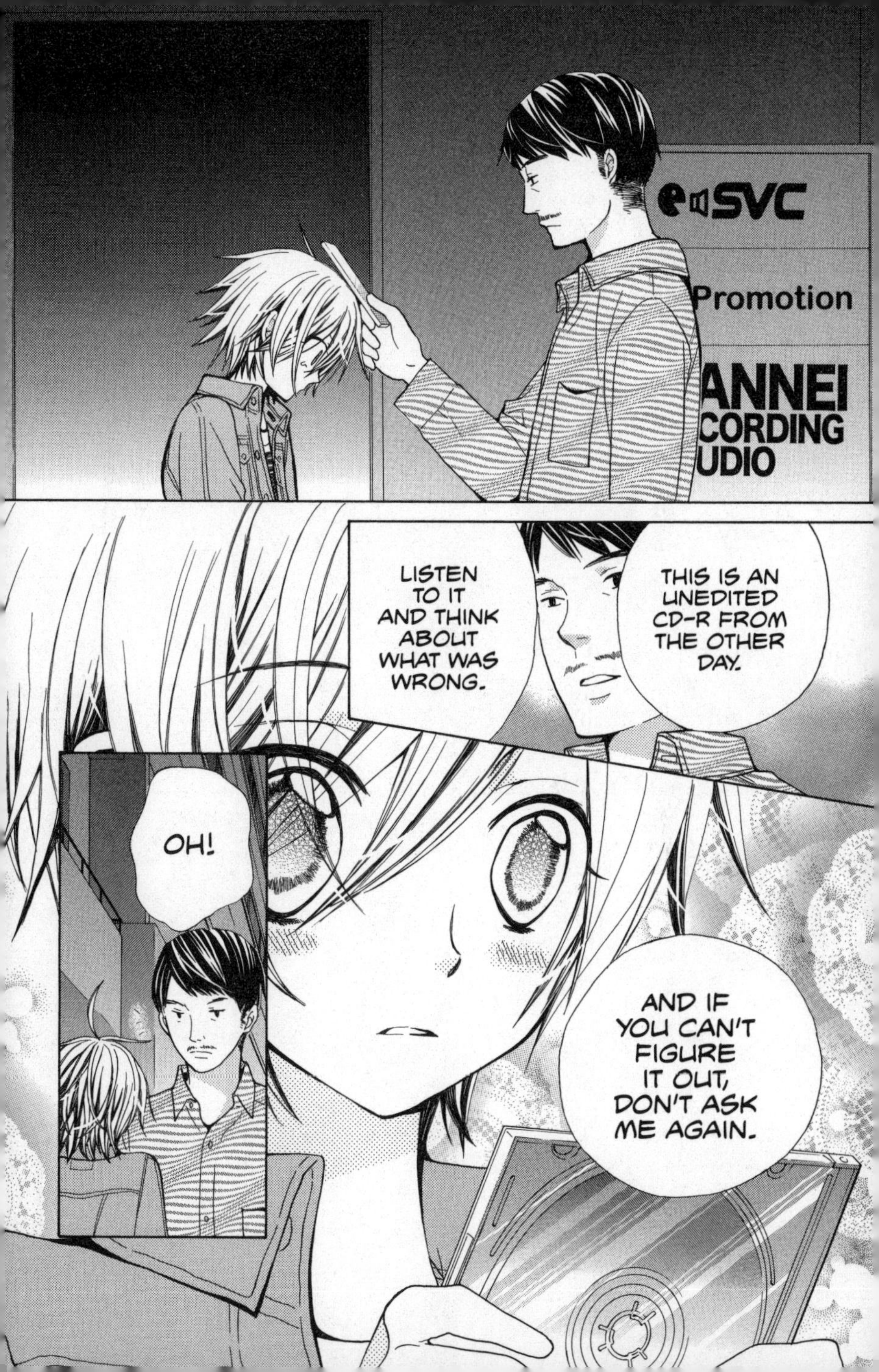
SVC
Promotion
ANNEI
CORDING
UDIO
THIS IS AN UNEDITED CD-R FROM THE OTHER DAY.
LISTEN TO IT AND THINK ABOUT WHAT WAS WRONG.
AND IF YOU CAN'T FIGURE IT OUT, DON'T ASK ME AGAIN.
OH!

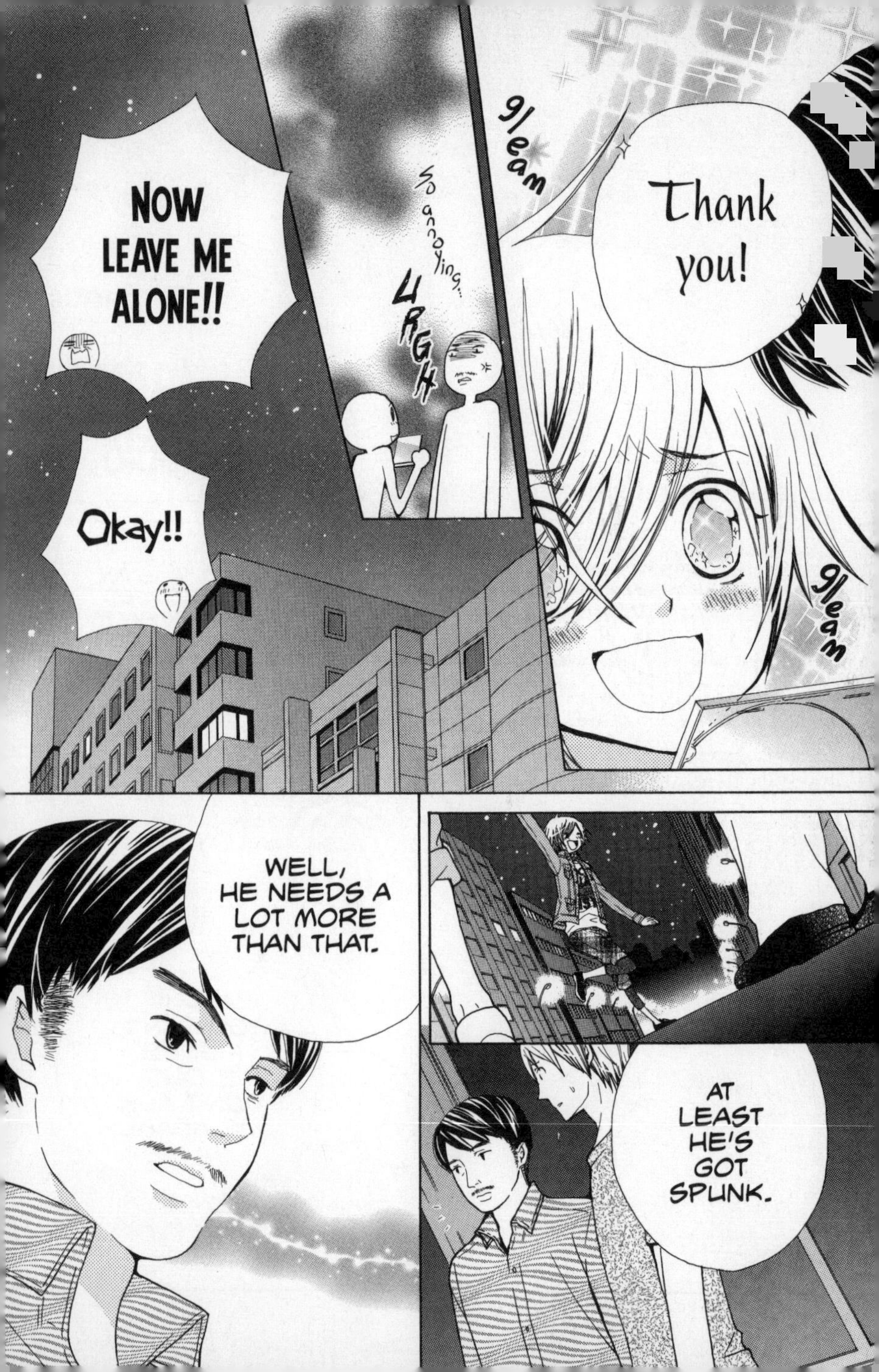
gleam
Thank you!
gleam
So annoying...
URGH
NOW LEAVE ME ALONE!!
Okay!!
AT LEAST HE'S GOT SPUNK.
WELL, HE NEEDS A LOT MORE THAN THAT.

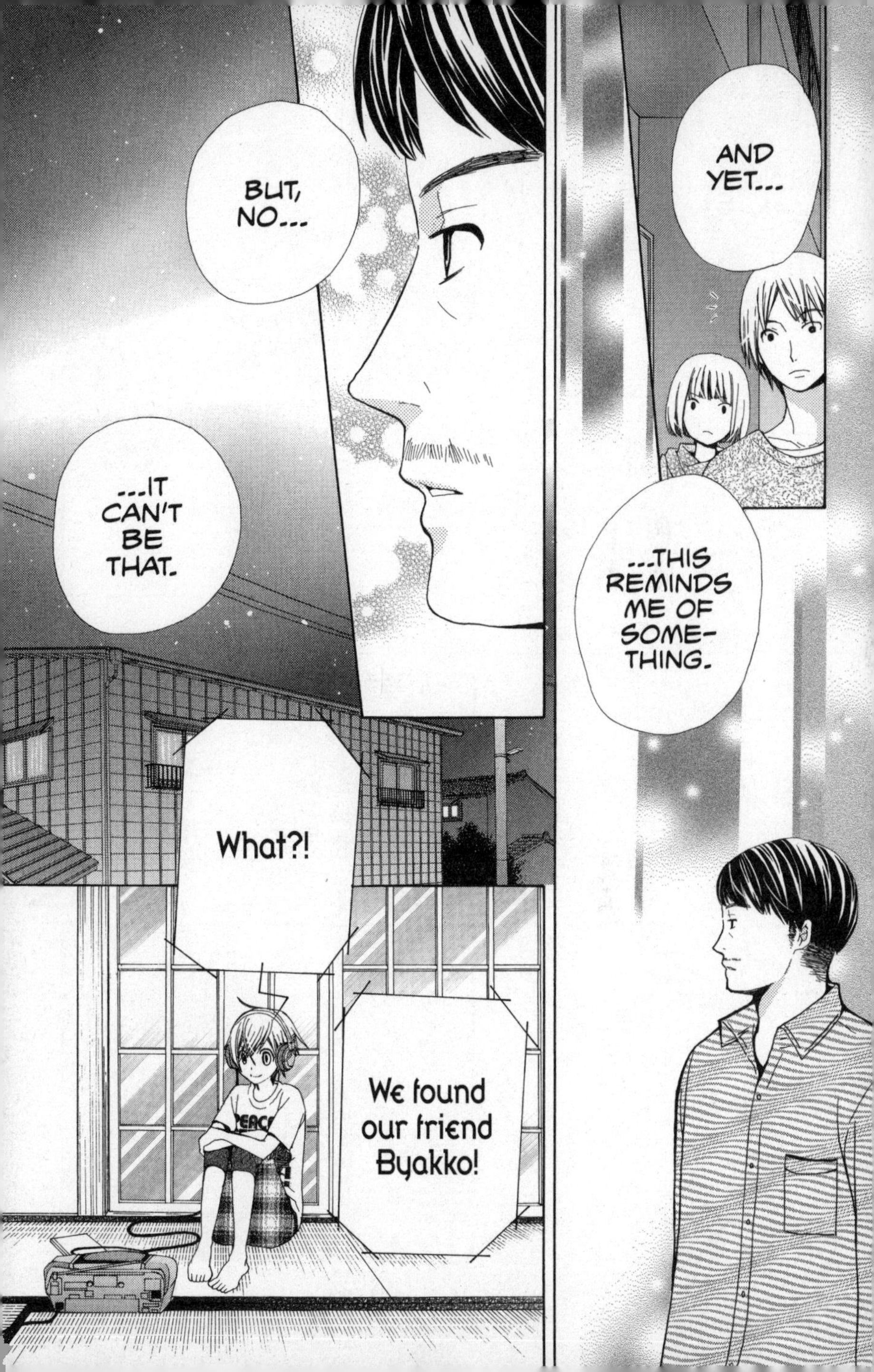
AND YET...
...THIS REMINDS ME OF SOME-THING.
BUT, NO...
...IT CAN'T BE THAT.
What?!
We found our friend Byakko!

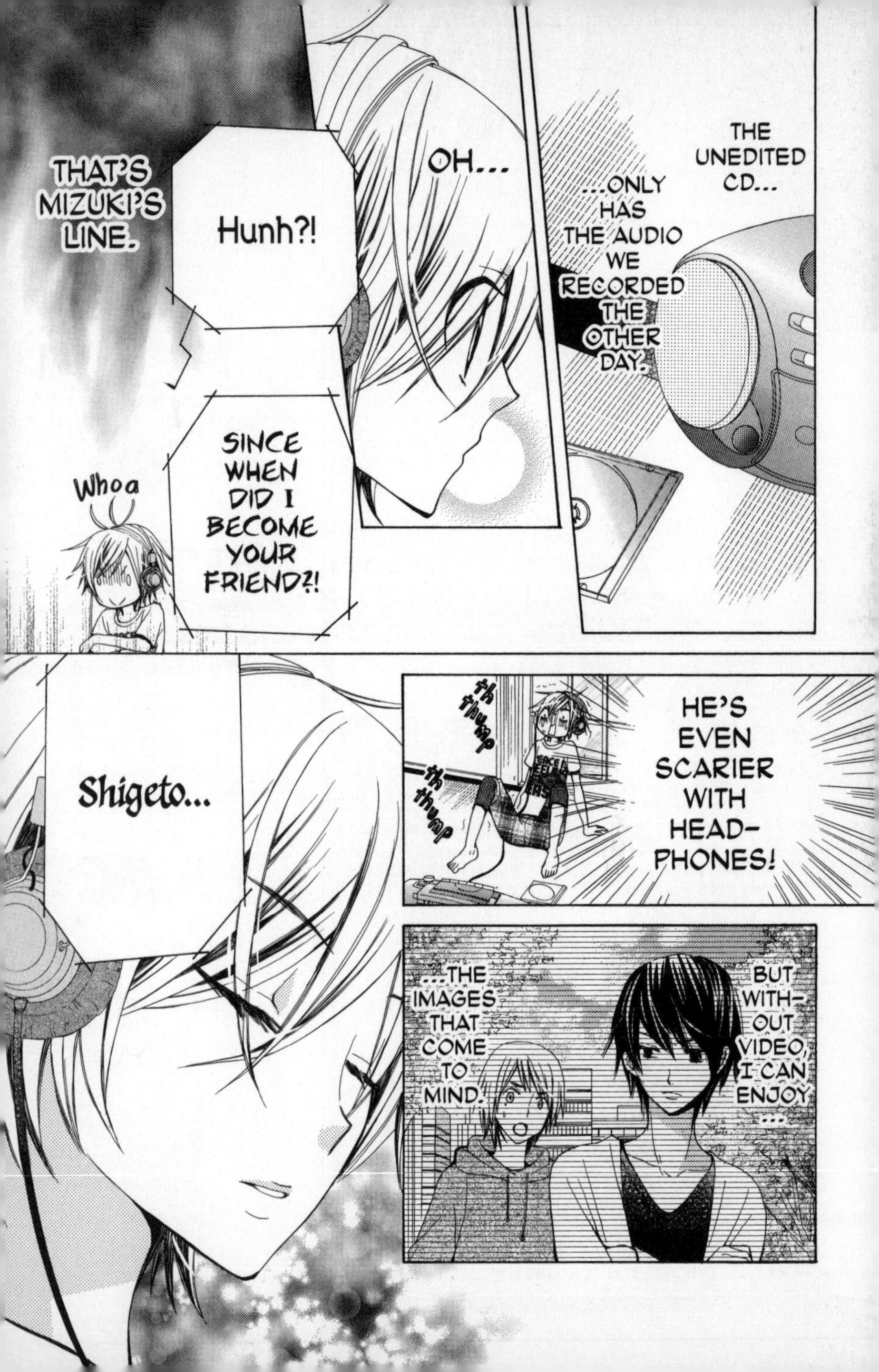
THE UNEDITED CD...
...ONLY HAS THE AUDIO WE RECORDED THE OTHER DAY.
OH...
Hunh?!
SINCE WHEN DID I BECOME YOUR FRIEND?!
THAT'S MIZUKI'S LINE.
Whoa
HE'S EVEN SCARIER WITH HEAD-PHONES!
th thump
th thump
BUT WITH-OUT VIDEO, I CAN ENJOY...
...THE IMAGES THAT COME TO MIND.
Shigeto...

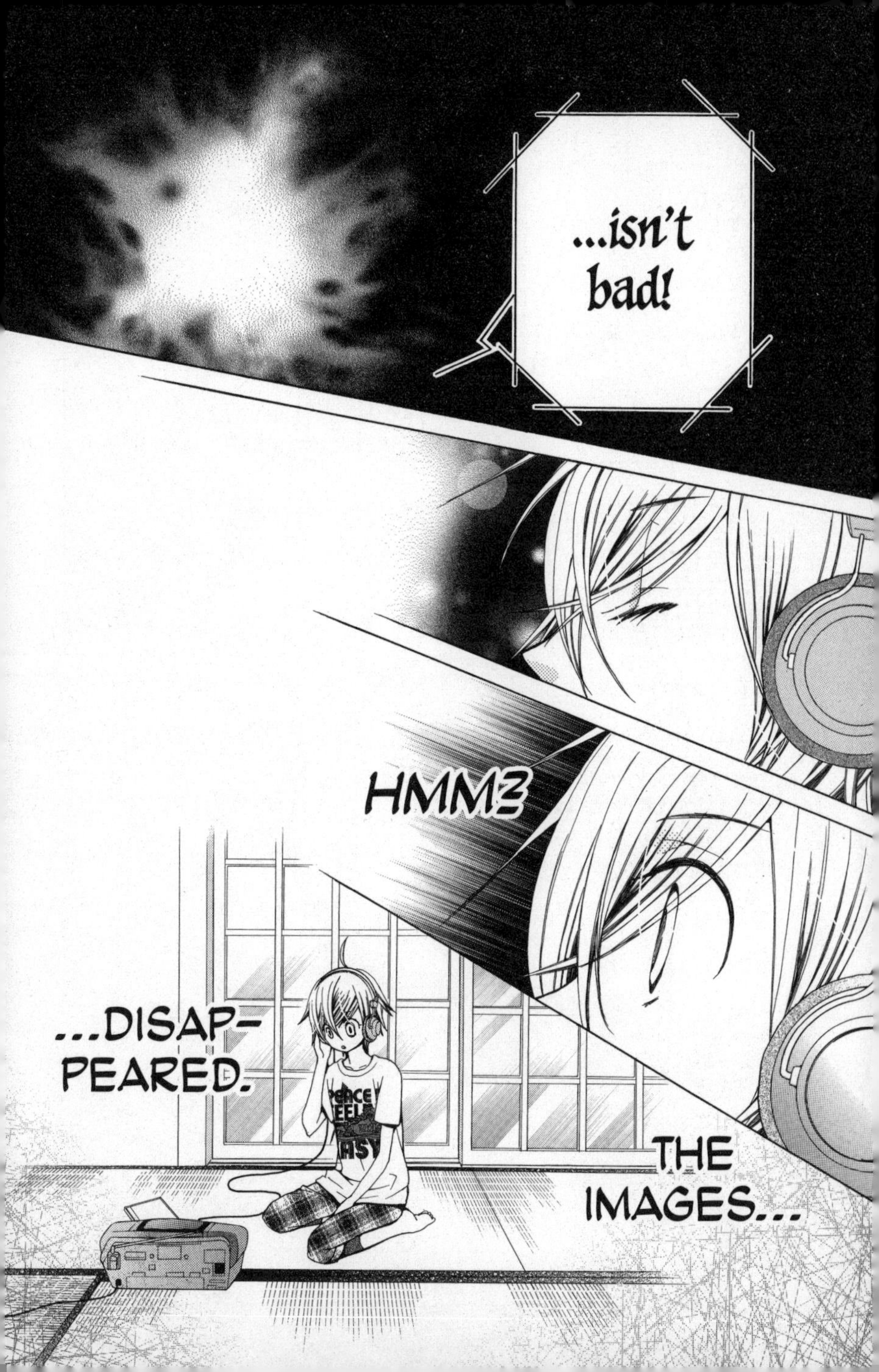
...isn't bad!
HMM?
THE IMAGES...
...DISAP-PEARED.

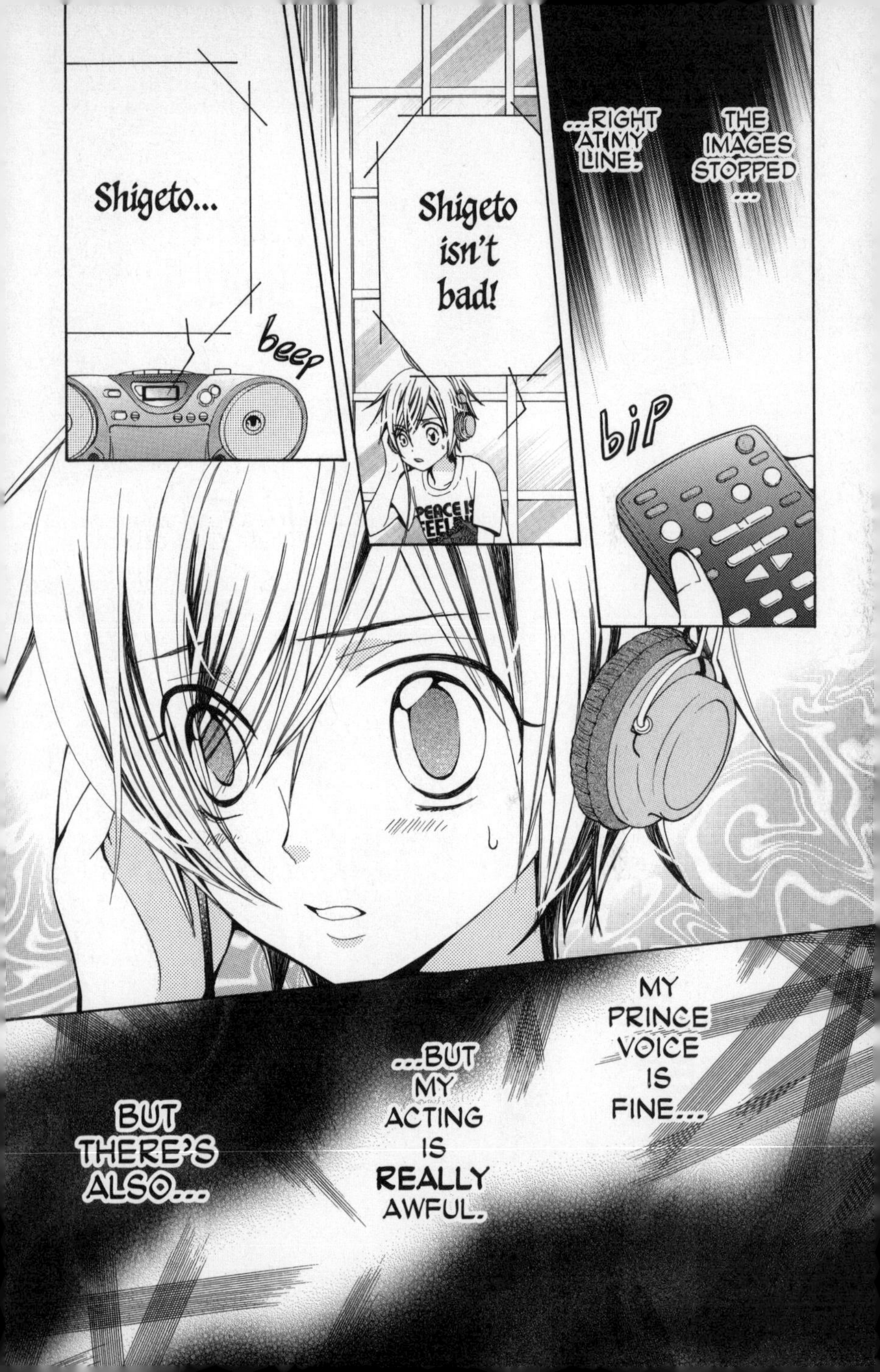
THE IMAGES STOPPED...
...RIGHT AT MY LINE.
bip
Shigeto isn't bad!
Shigeto...
beep
MY PRINCE VOICE IS FINE...
...BUT MY ACTING IS REALLY AWFUL.
BUT THERE'S ALSO...

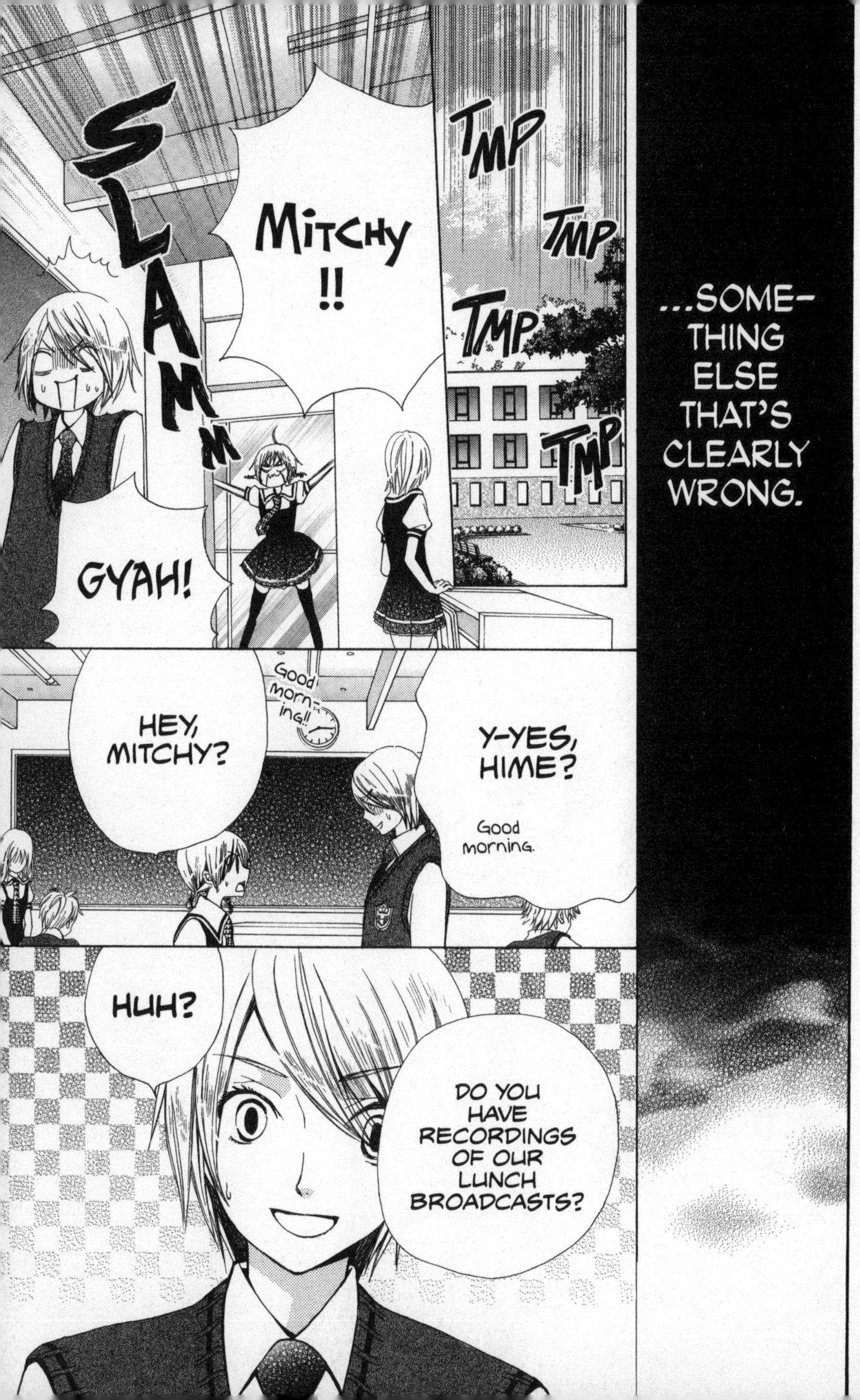
...SOME-THING ELSE THAT'S CLEARLY WRONG.
TMP
TMP
TMP
TMP
MITCHY!!
SLAMM
GYAH!
Y-YES, HIME?
Good morning.
Good morn-ing!!
HEY, MITCHY?
DO YOU HAVE RECORDINGS OF OUR LUNCH BROADCASTS?
HUH?

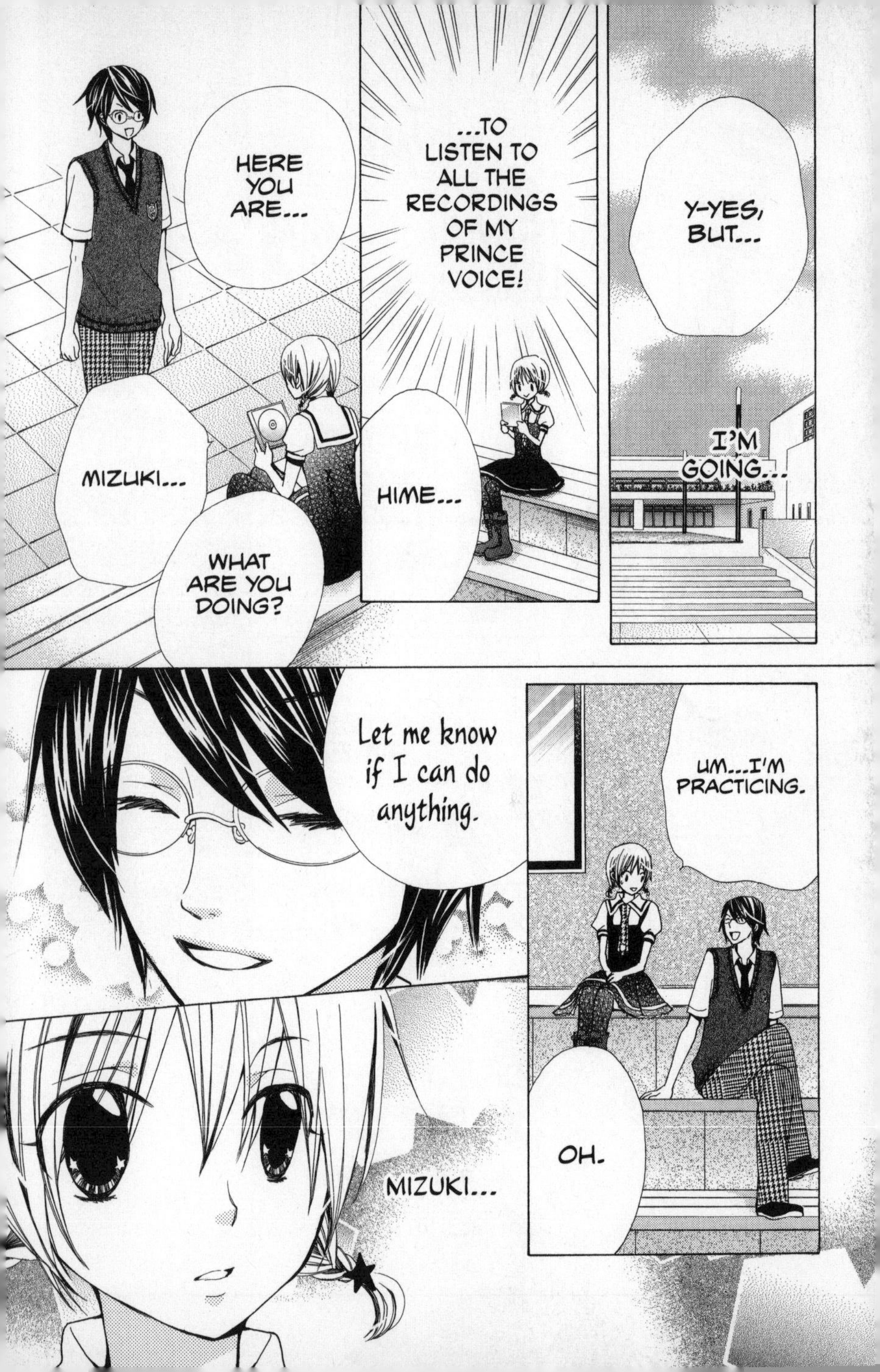
Y-YES, BUT...
I'M GOING...
...TO LISTEN TO ALL THE RECORDINGS OF MY PRINCE VOICE!
HIME...
HERE YOU ARE...
MIZUKI...
WHAT ARE YOU DOING?
UM...I'M PRACTICING.
OH.
Let me know if I can do anything.
MIZUKI...

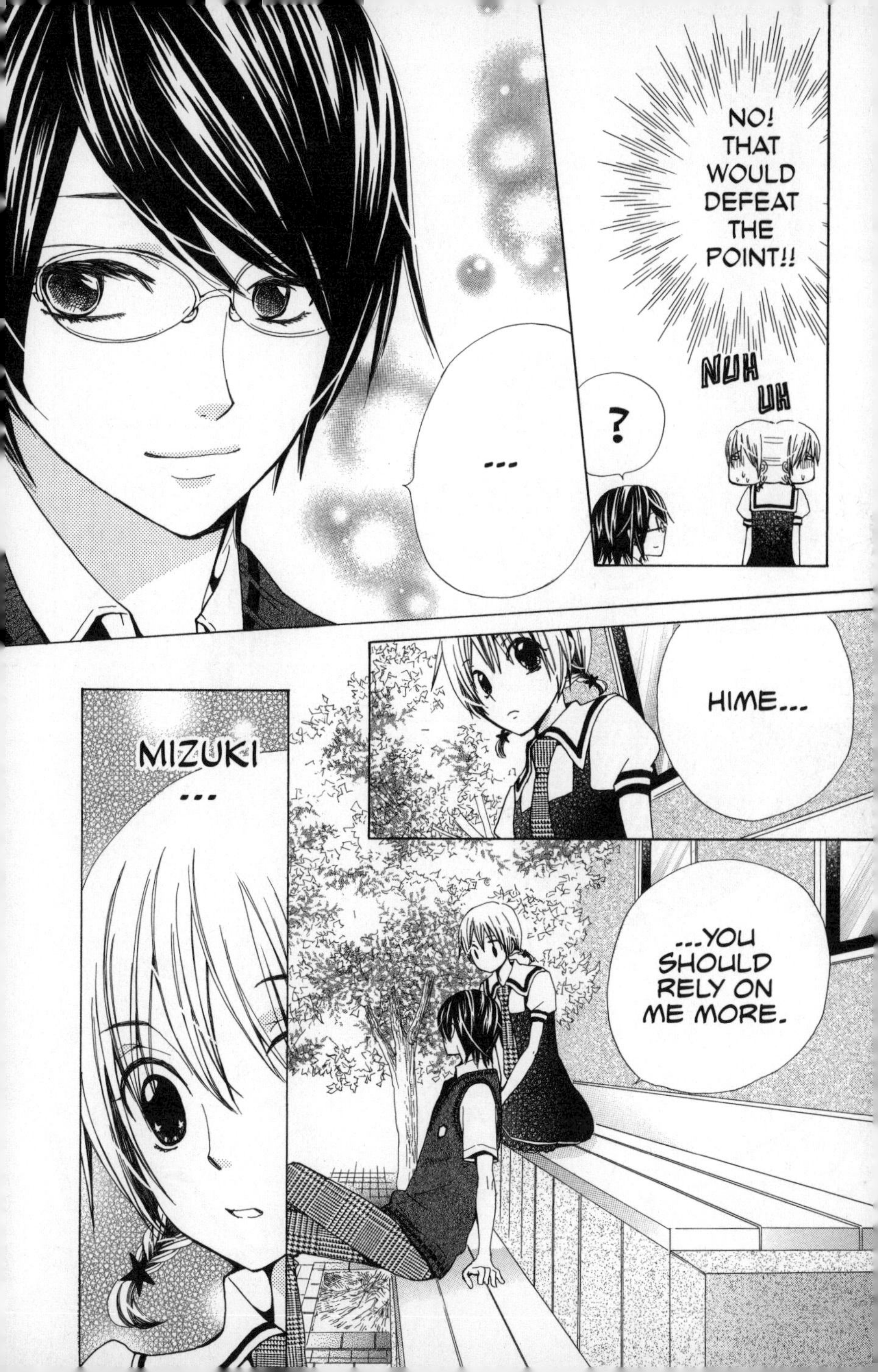
NO! THAT WOULD DEFEAT THE POINT!!
NUH UH
?
...
HIME...
...YOU SHOULD RELY ON ME MORE.
MIZUKI ...

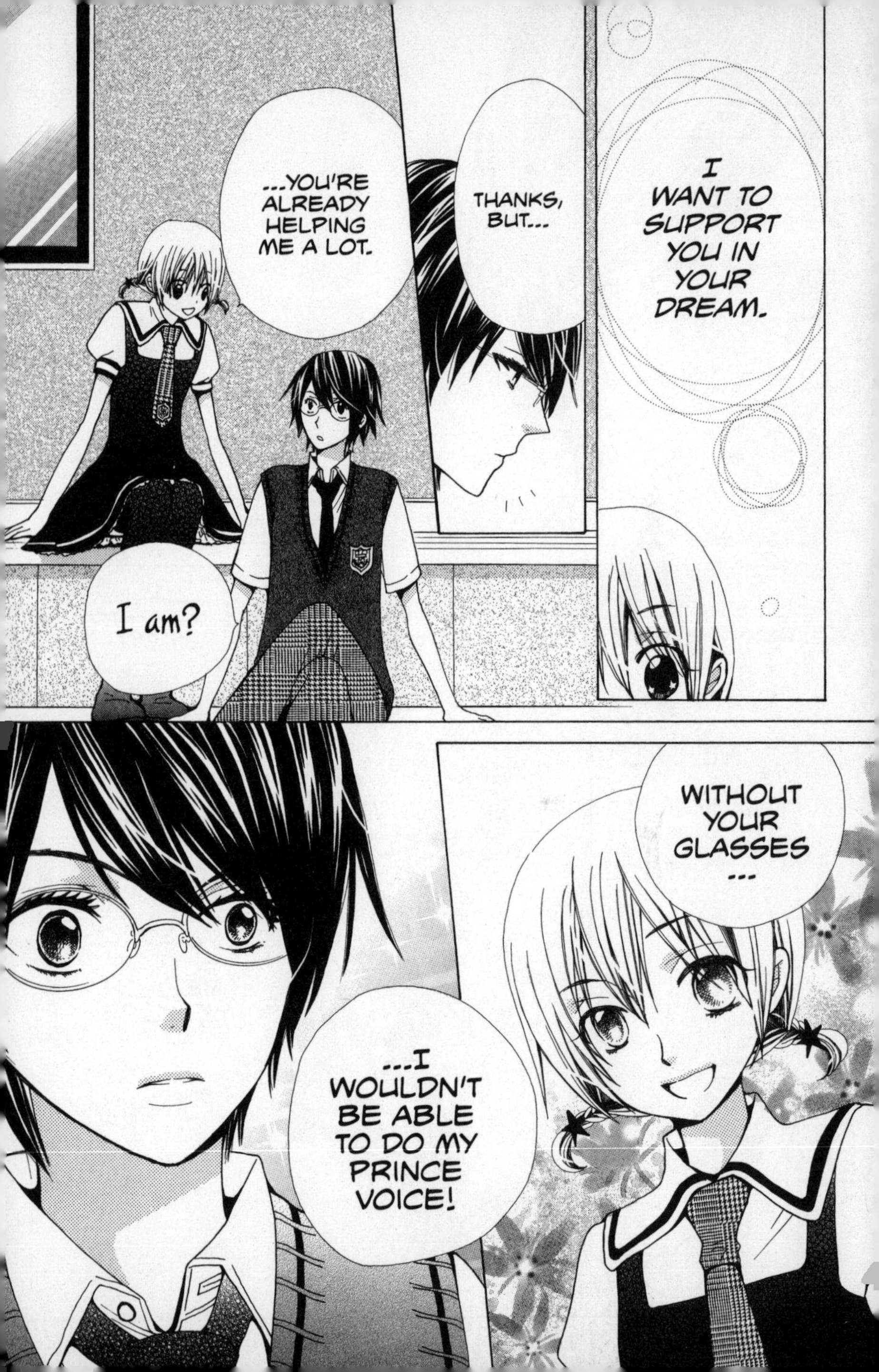
I WANT TO SUPPORT YOU IN YOUR DREAM.
THANKS, BUT...
...YOU'RE ALREADY HELPING ME A LOT.
I am?
WITHOUT YOUR GLASSES...
...I WOULDN'T BE ABLE TO DO MY PRINCE VOICE!

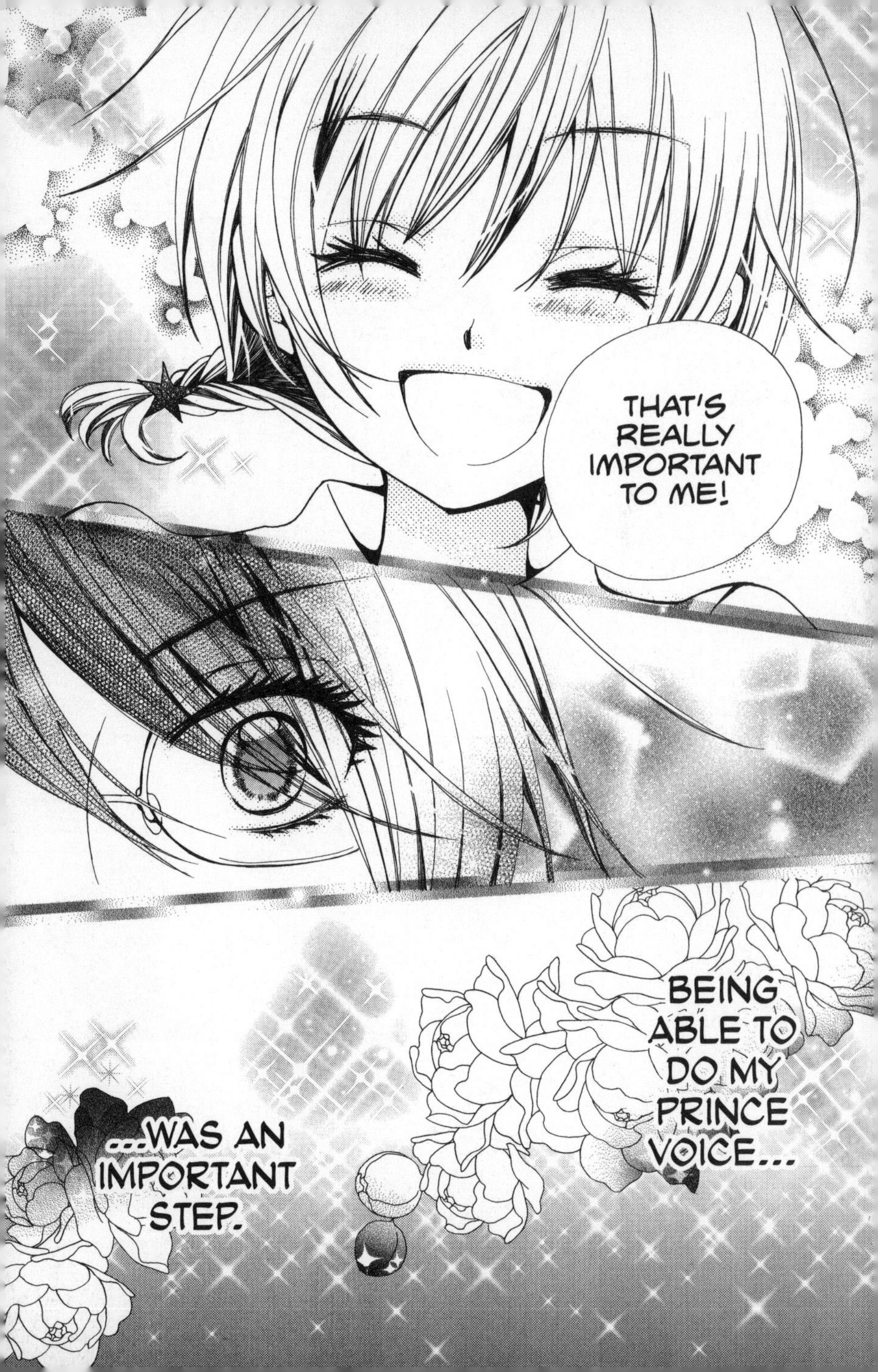
THAT'S REALLY IMPORTANT TO ME!
BEING ABLE TO DO MY PRINCE VOICE...
...WAS AN IMPORTANT STEP.

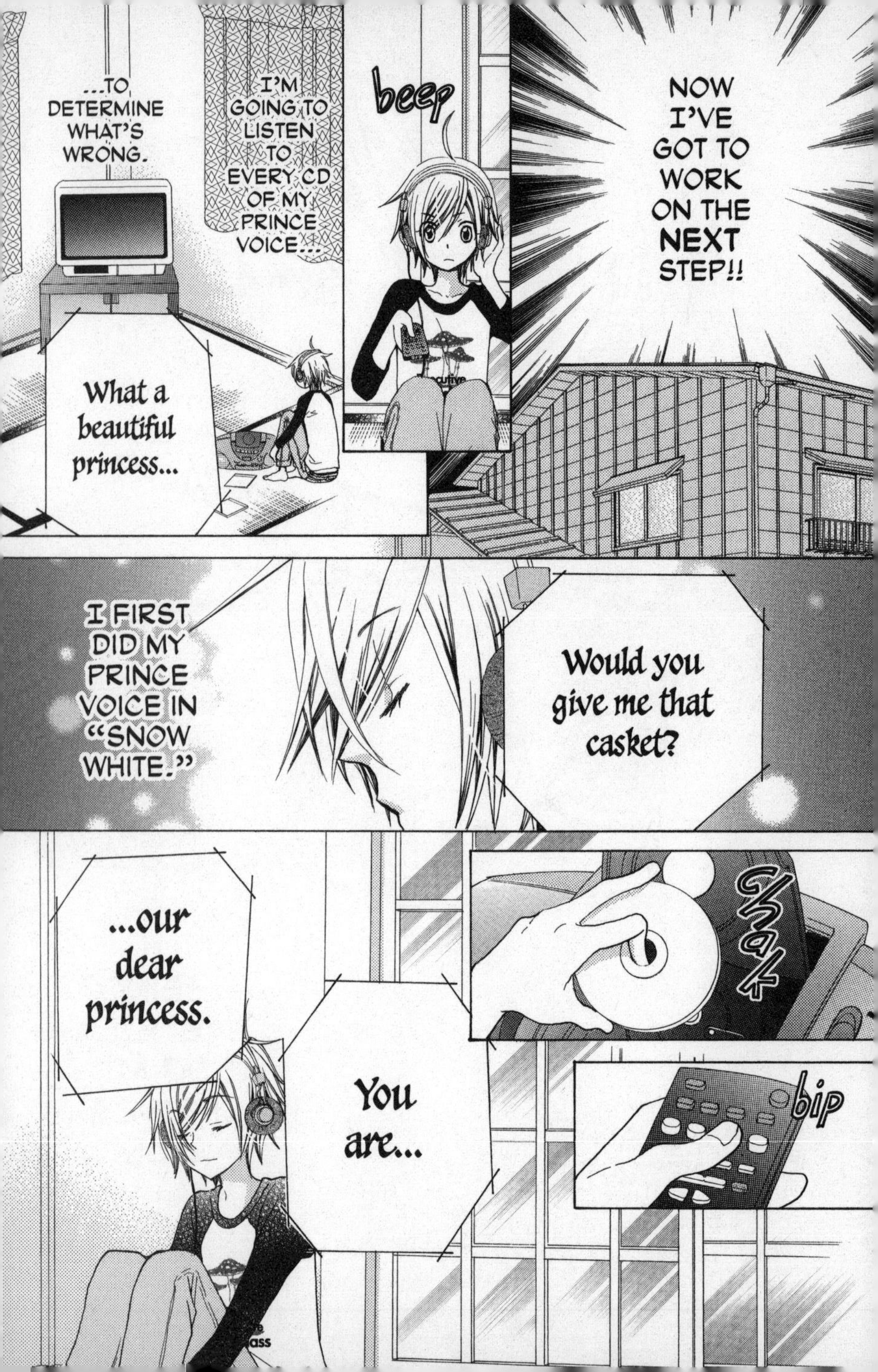
NOW I'VE GOT TO WORK ON THE NEXT STEP!!
beep
I'M GOING TO LISTEN TO EVERY CD OF MY PRINCE VOICE...
...TO DETERMINE WHAT'S WRONG.
What a beautiful princess...
Would you give me that casket?
I FIRST DID MY PRINCE VOICE IN "SNOW WHITE."
Chak
bip
You are...
...our dear princess.

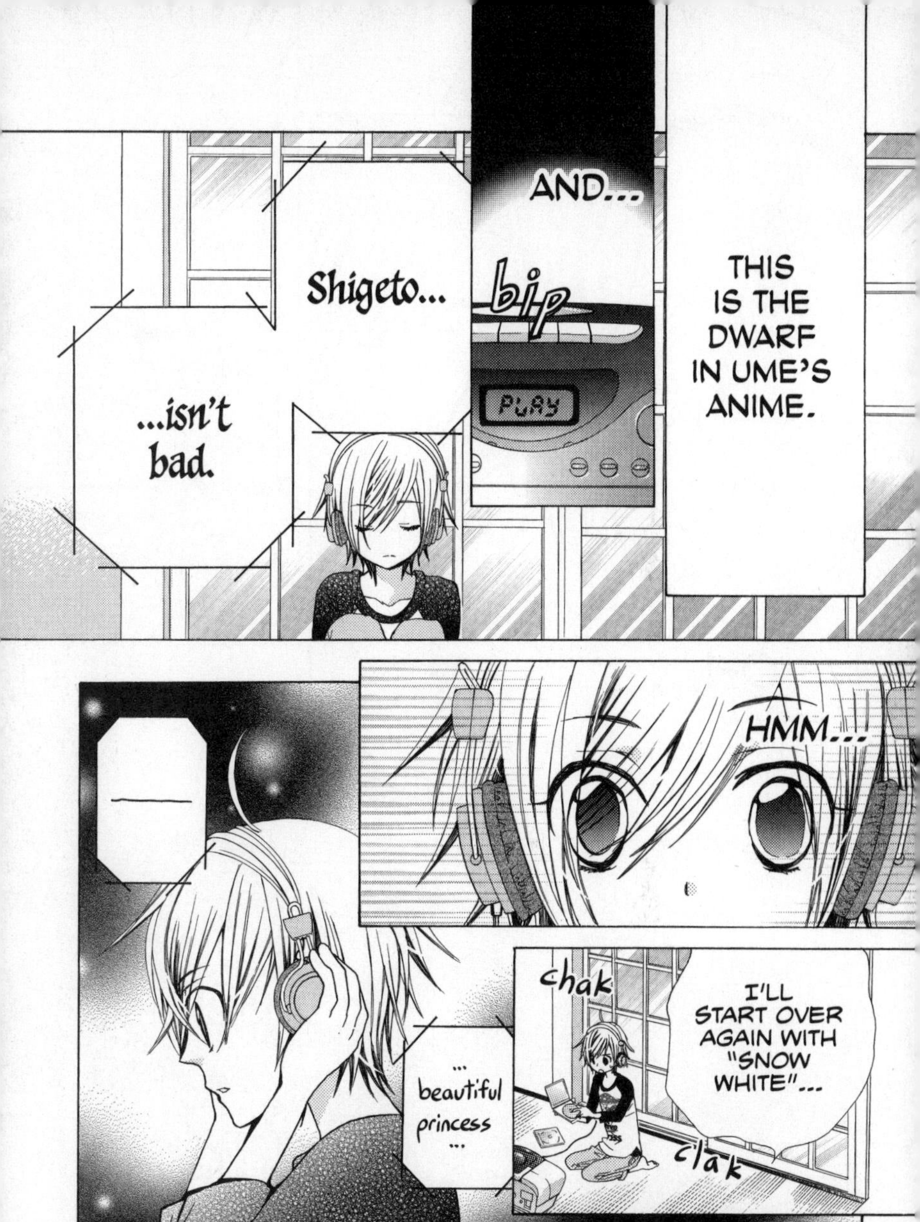
THIS IS THE DWARF IN UME'S ANIME.
AND...
bip
PLAY
Shigeto...
...isn't bad.
HMM...
I'LL START OVER AGAIN WITH "SNOW WHITE"...
chak
clak
—
...beautiful princess...

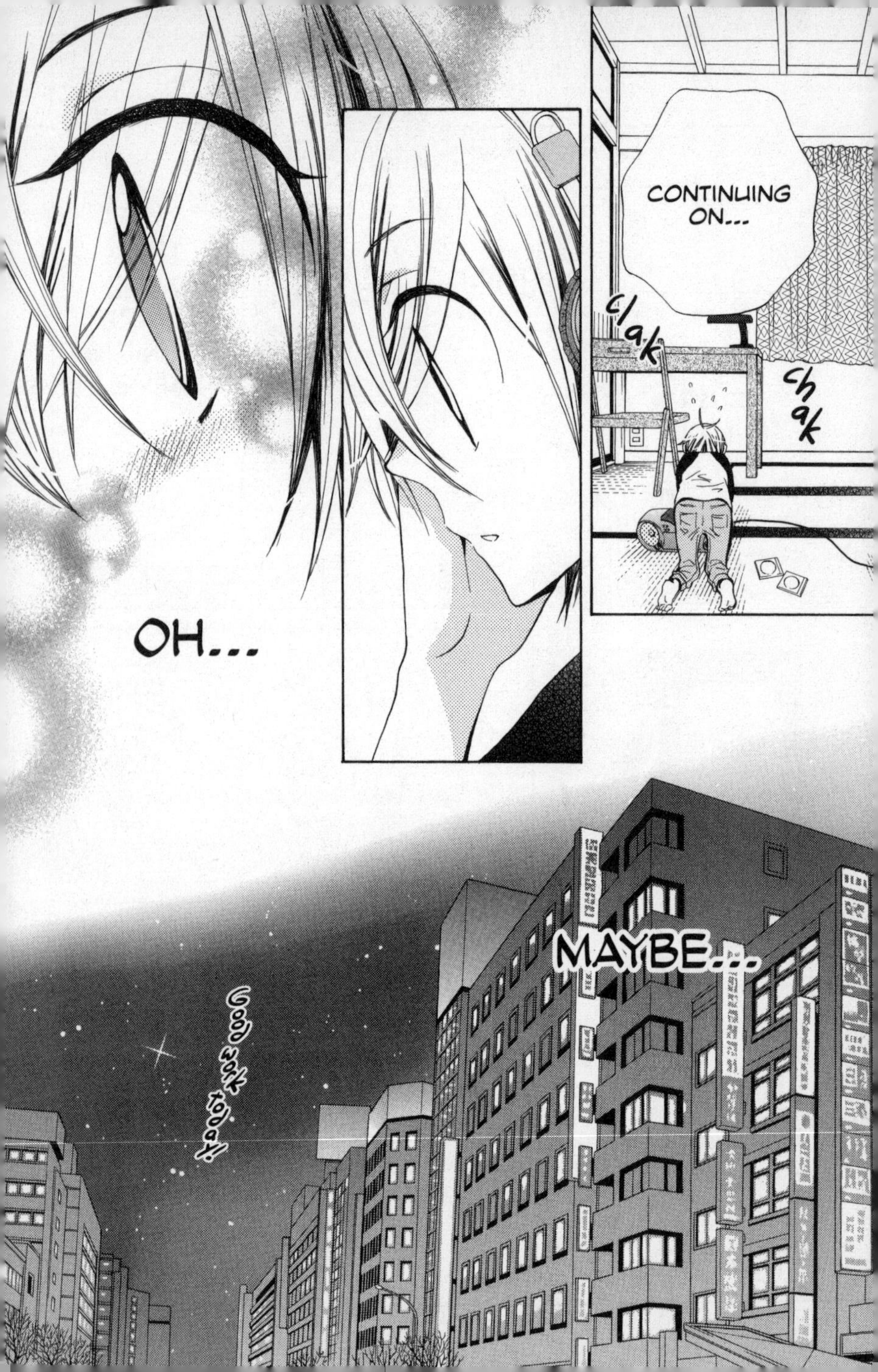
CONTINUING ON...
clak
chak
OH...
MAYBE...
Good work today!

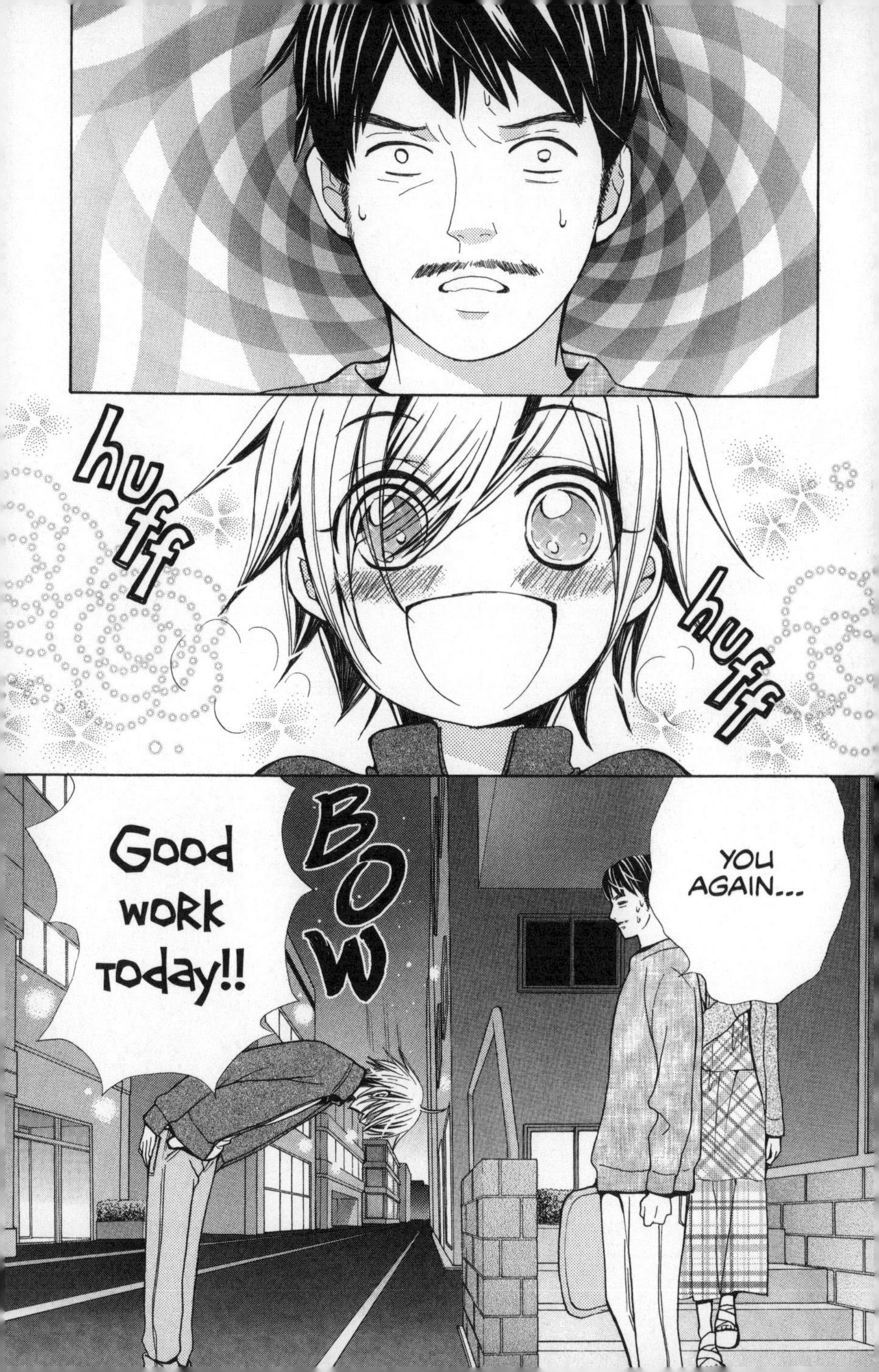
huff
huff
YOU AGAIN...
BOW
Good work today!!

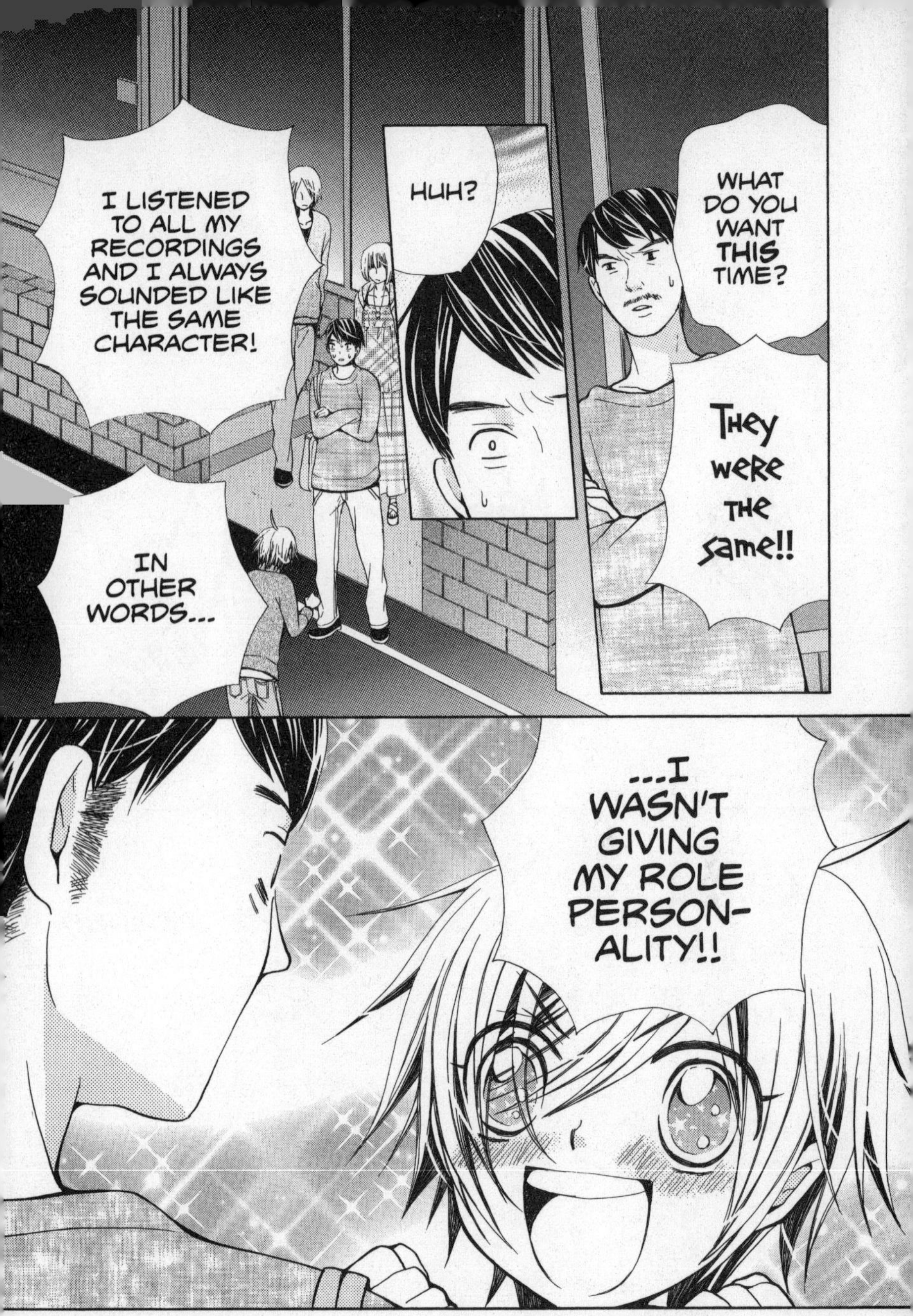
WHAT DO YOU WANT THIS TIME?
They were the same!!
HUH?
I LISTENED TO ALL MY RECORDINGS AND I ALWAYS SOUNDED LIKE THE SAME CHARACTER!
IN OTHER WORDS...
...I WASN'T GIVING MY ROLE PERSON-ALITY!!

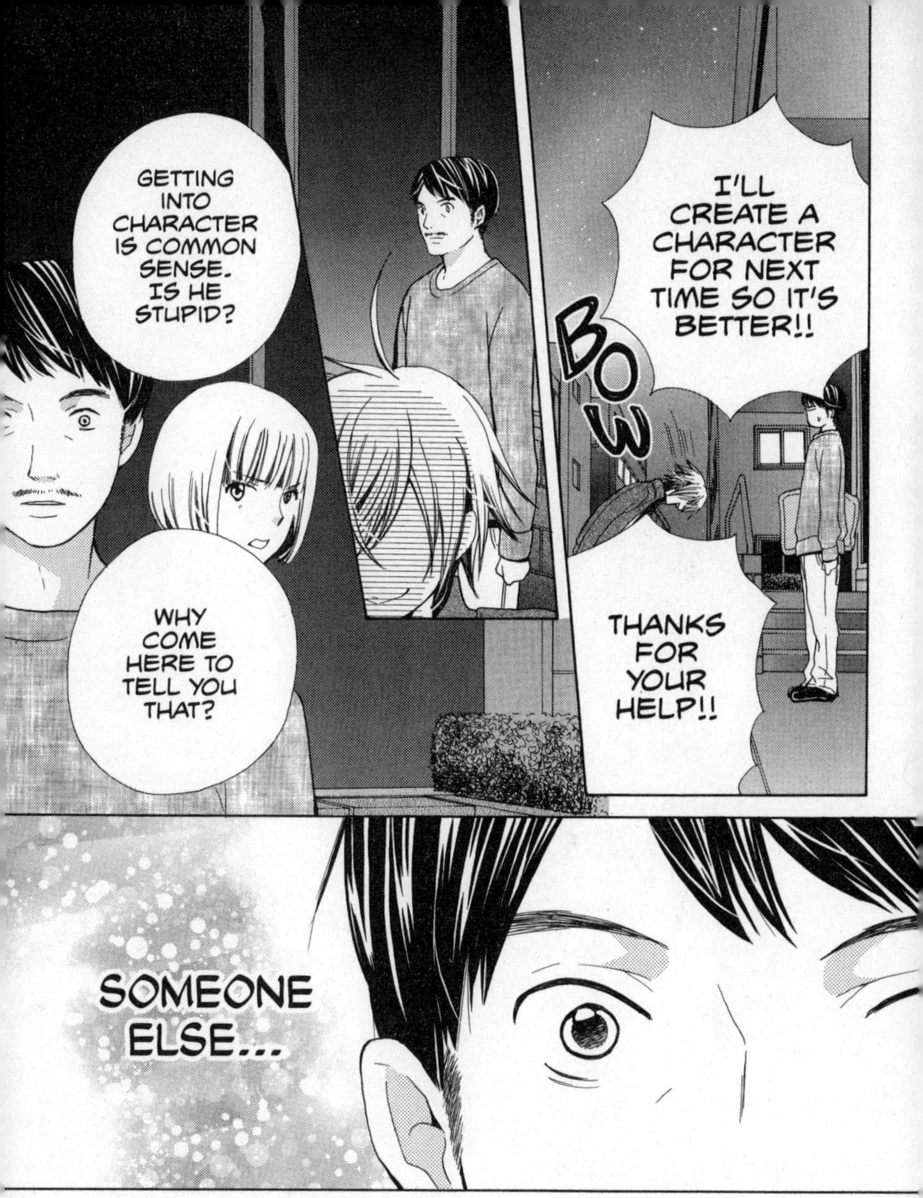
I'LL CREATE A CHARACTER FOR NEXT TIME SO IT'S BETTER!!
BOW
THANKS FOR YOUR HELP!!
GETTING INTO CHARACTER IS COMMON SENSE. IS HE STUPID?
WHY COME HERE TO TELL YOU THAT?
SOMEONE ELSE...
...ONCE DID THE SAME THING...

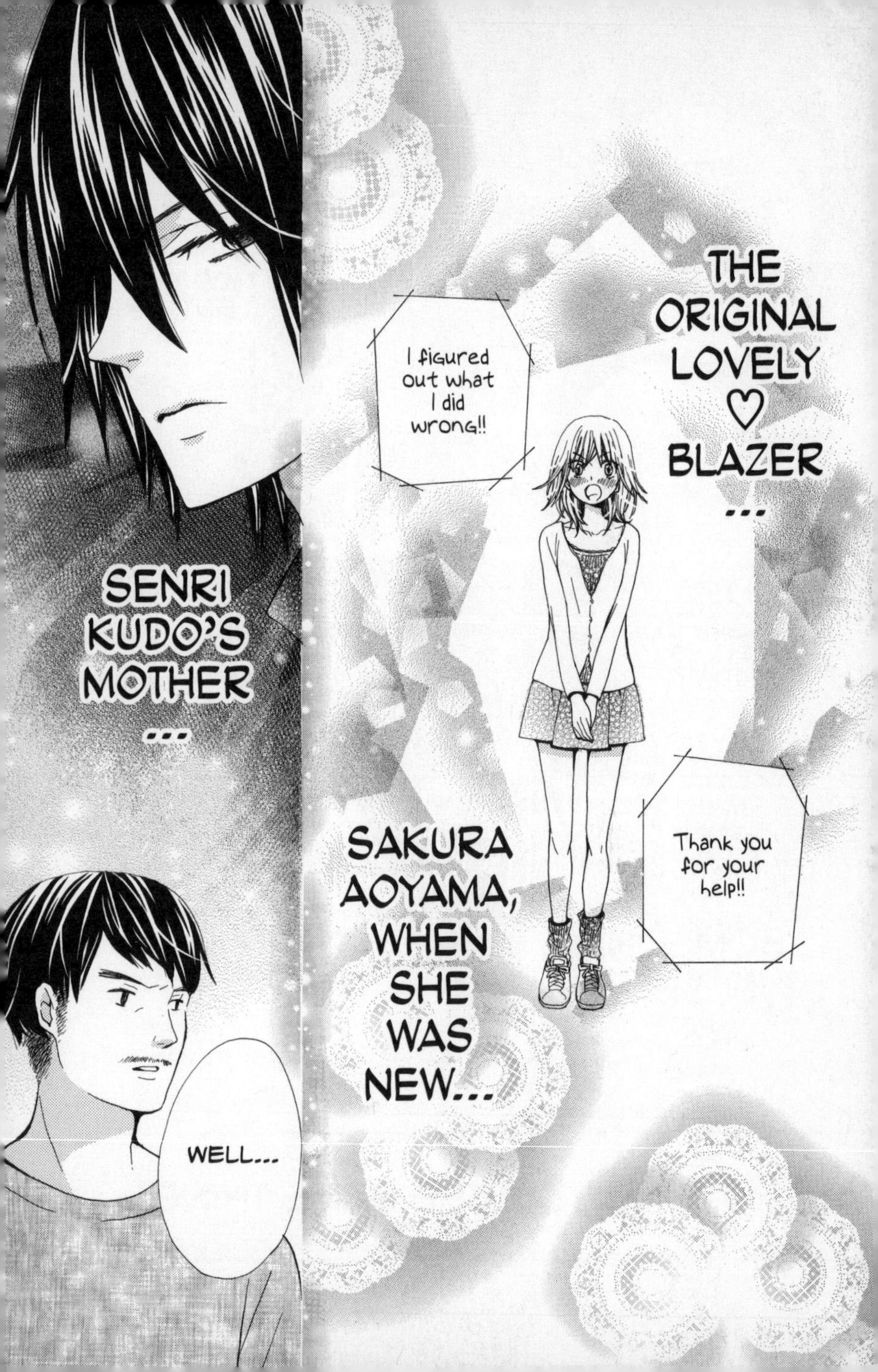
THE ORIGINAL LOVELY ♡ BLAZER...
I figured out what I did wrong!!
Thank you for your help!!
SAKURA AOYAMA, WHEN SHE WAS NEW...
SENRI KUDO'S MOTHER...
WELL...

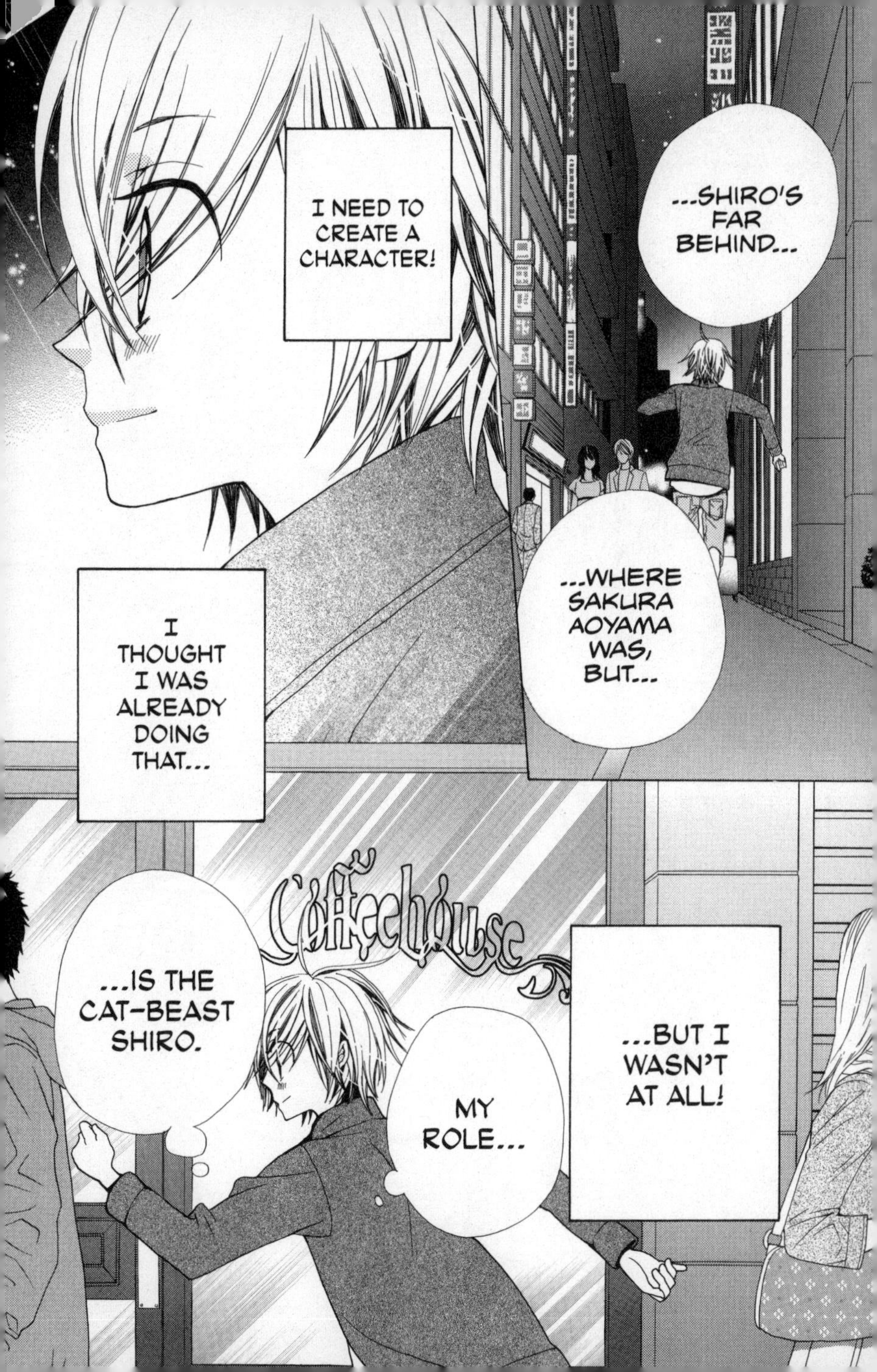
...SHIRO'S FAR BEHIND...
...WHERE SAKURA AOYAMA WAS, BUT...
I NEED TO CREATE A CHARACTER!
I THOUGHT I WAS ALREADY DOING THAT...
Coffeehouse
...BUT I WASN'T AT ALL!
MY ROLE...
...IS THE CAT-BEAST SHIRO.

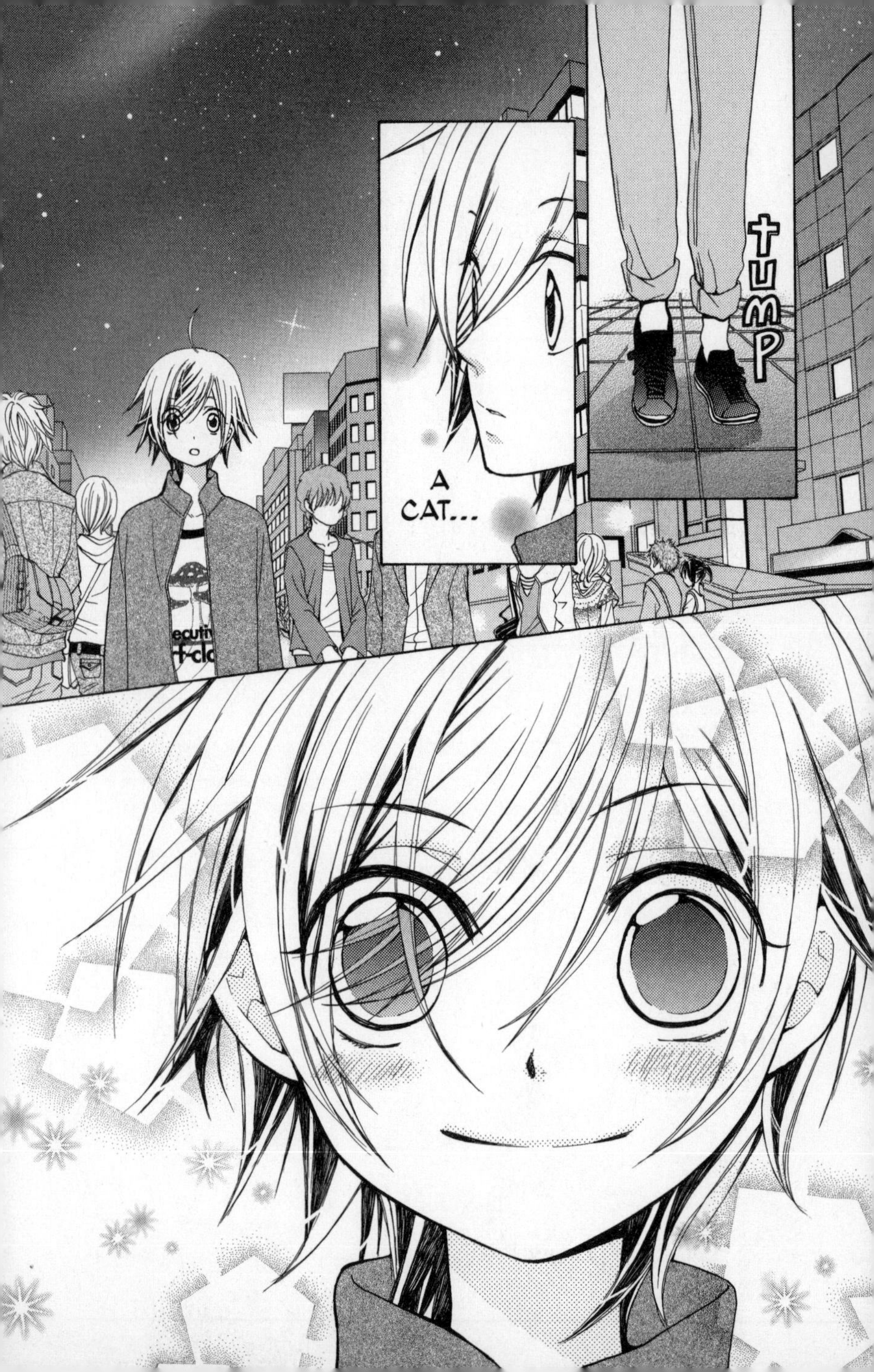
TUMP
A CAT...

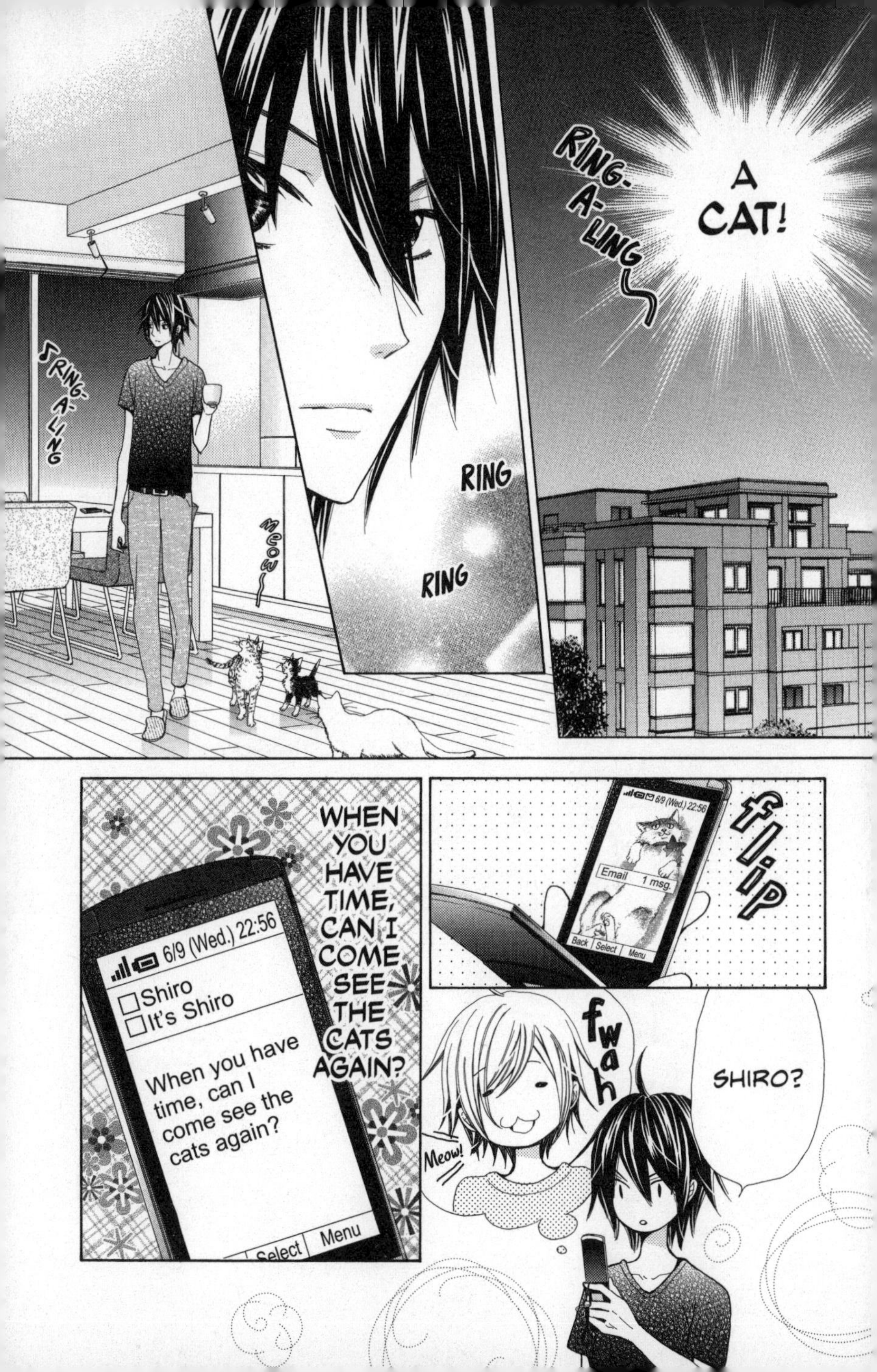

RING-A-LING~
A CAT!
RING
RING
SRING-A-LING
MEOW~
6/9 (Wed.) 22:56
Email 1 msg.
Back Select Menu
flip
SHIRO?
fwah
Meow!
6/9 (Wed.) 22:56
Shiro
It's Shiro
When you have time, can I come see the cats again?
Select Menu
WHEN YOU HAVE TIME, CAN I COME SEE THE CATS AGAIN?

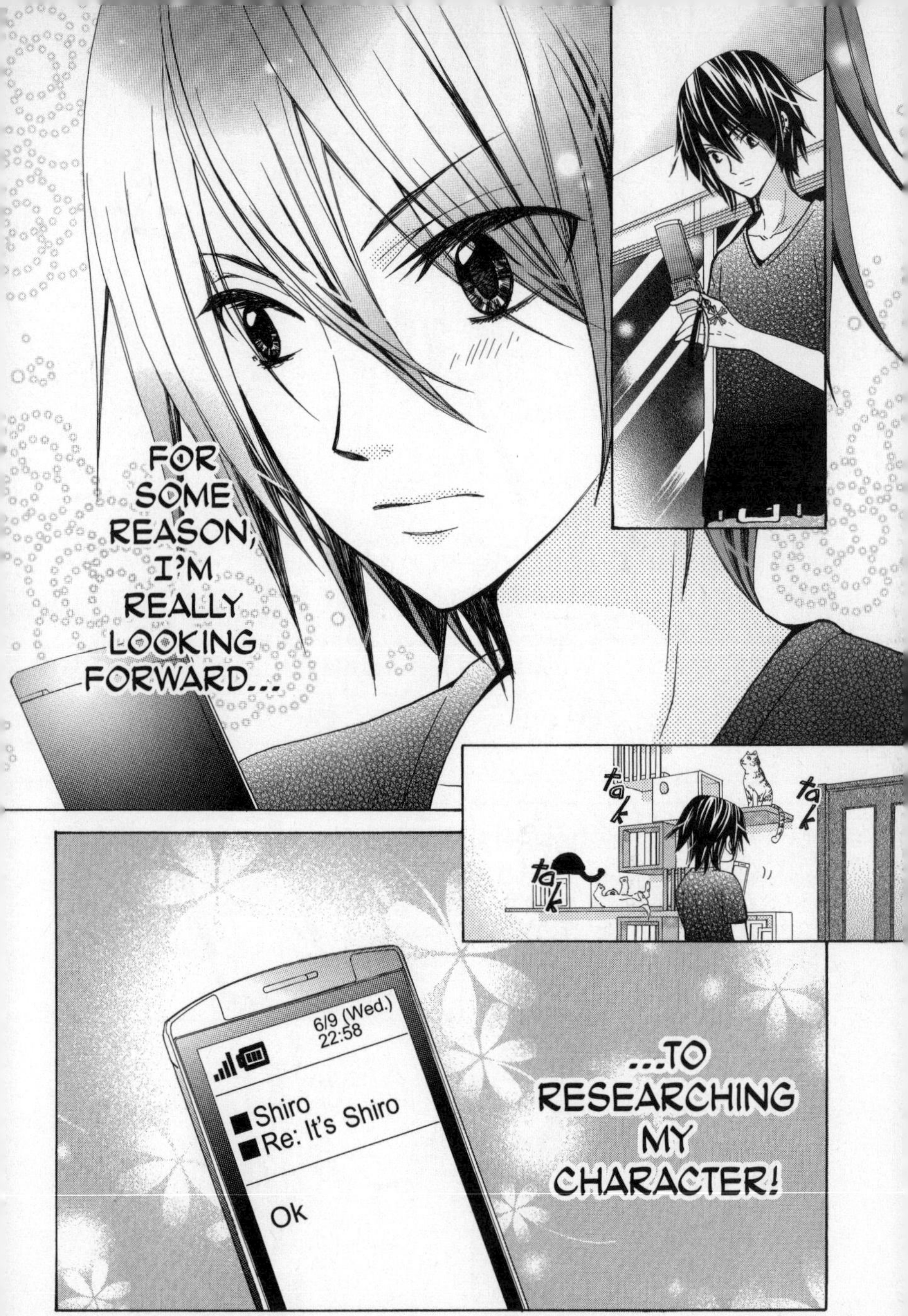
FOR SOME REASON, I'M REALLY LOOKING FORWARD...
tak
tak
tak
6/9 (Wed.)
22:58
Shiro
Re: It's Shiro
Ok
...TO RESEARCHING MY CHARACTER!

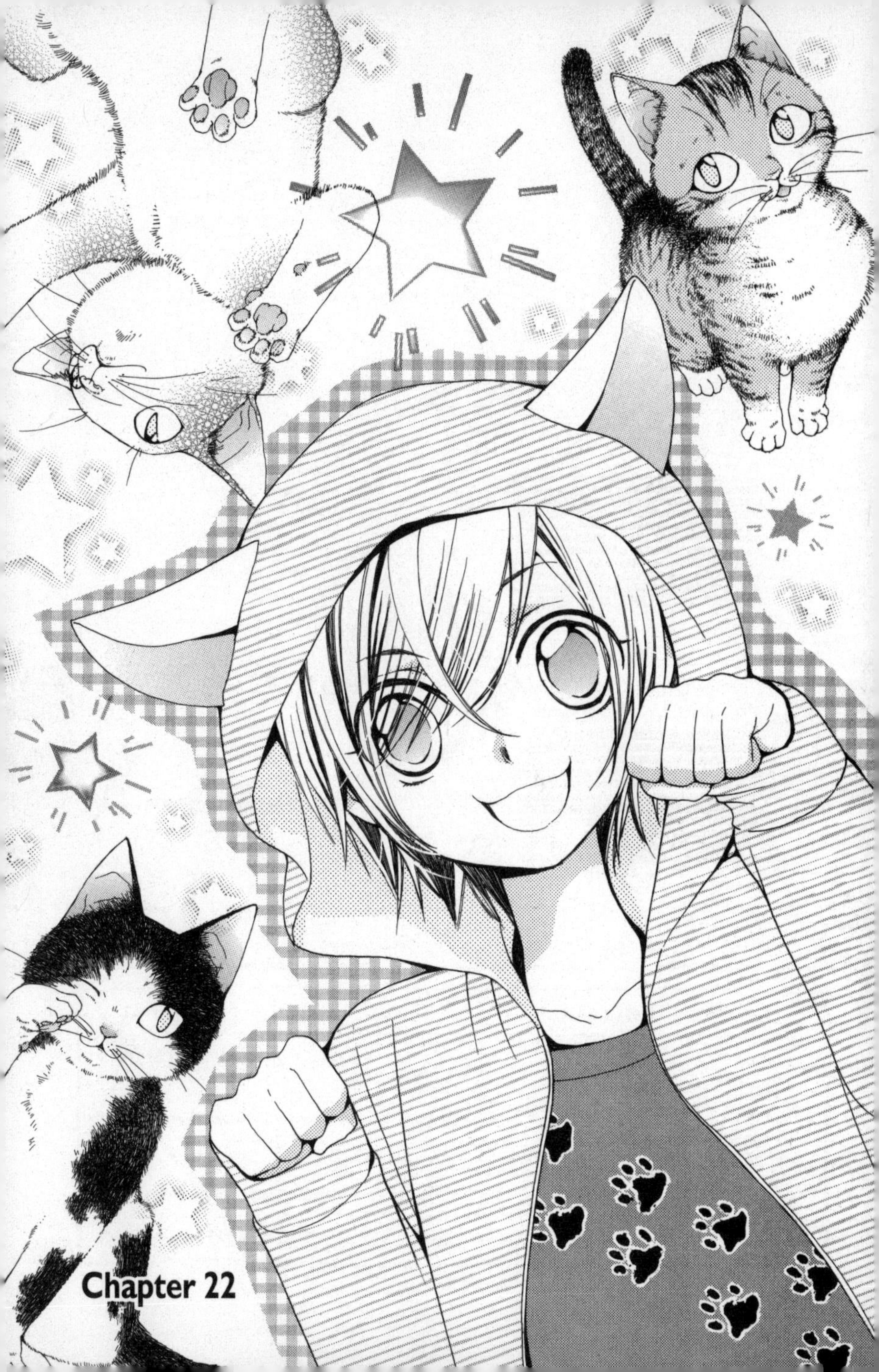
Chapter 22

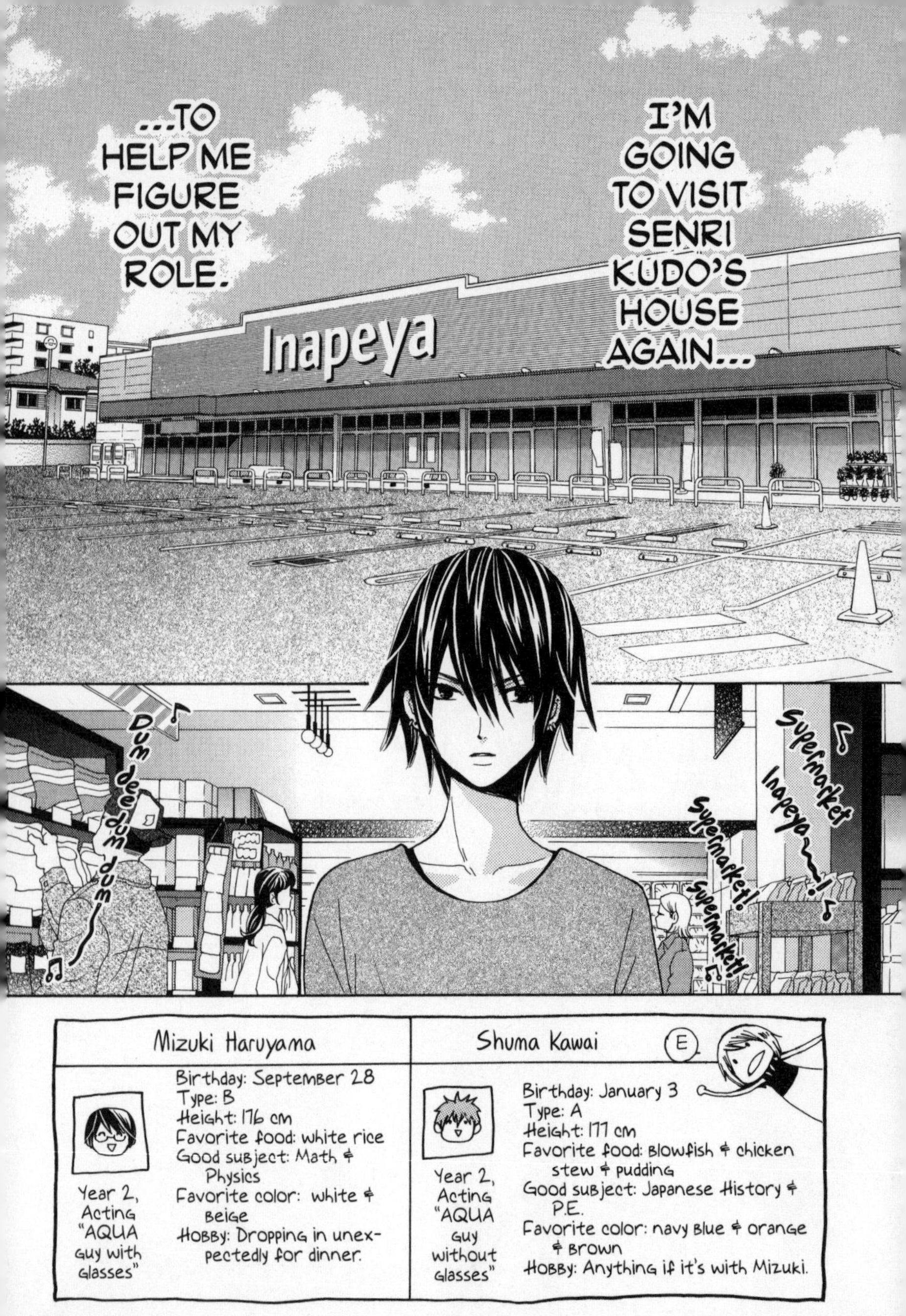
I'M GOING TO VISIT SENRI KUDO'S HOUSE AGAIN...
...TO HELP ME FIGURE OUT MY ROLE.
Inapeya
Supermarket Inapeya~~!
Supermarket! Supermarket!
Dum dee dum dum~

Mizuki Haruyama	Shuma Kawai (E)
Birthday: September 28 Type: B Height: 176 cm Favorite food: white rice Good subject: Math & Physics Favorite color: white & beige Hobby: Dropping in unexpectedly for dinner. Year 2, Acting "AQUA Guy with Glasses"	Birthday: January 3 Type: A Height: 177 cm Favorite food: Blowfish & chicken stew & pudding Good subject: Japanese History & P.E. Favorite color: navy blue & orange & brown Hobby: Anything if it's with Mizuki. Year 2, Acting "AQUA Guy without Glasses"

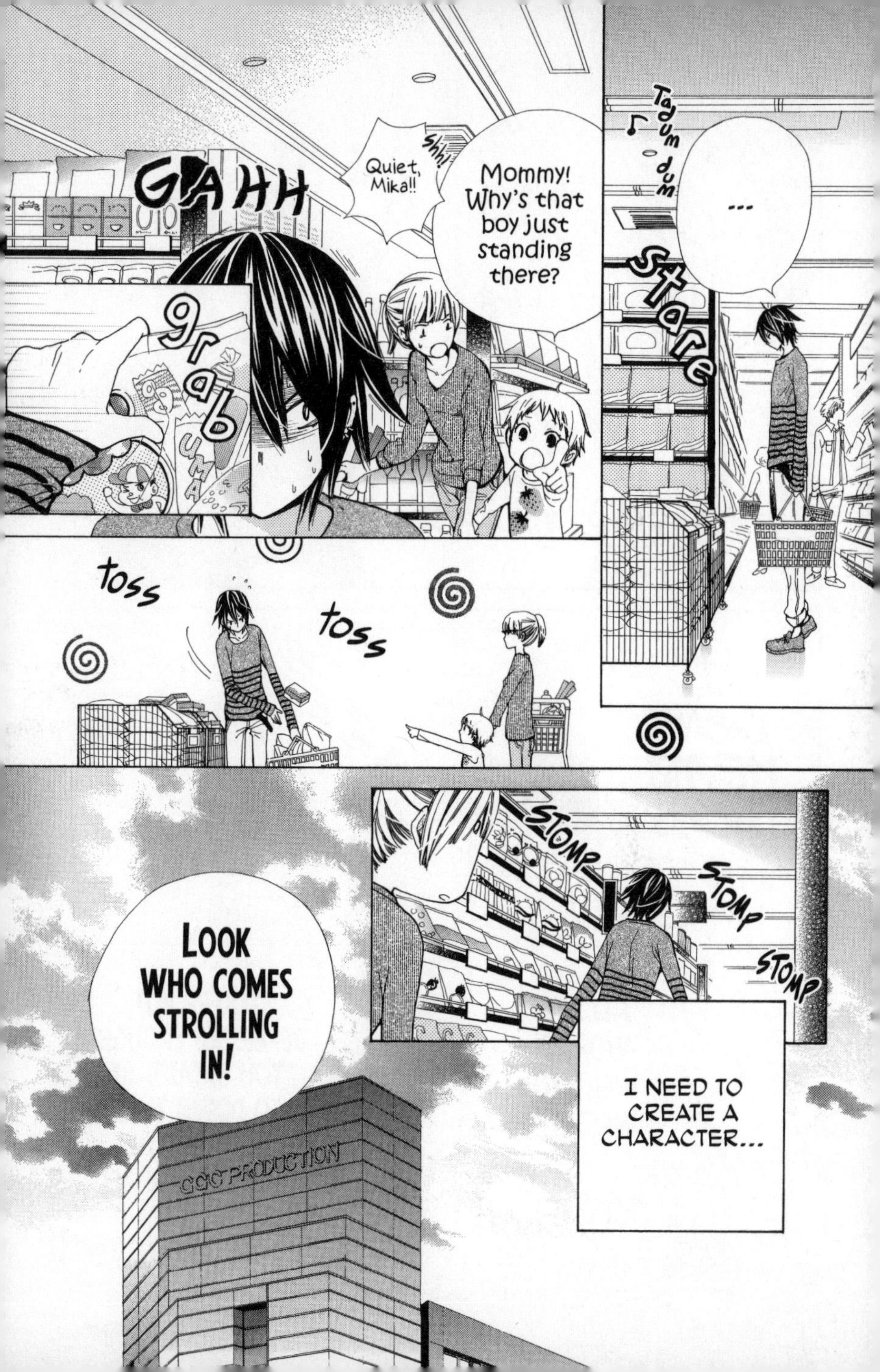
Ta dum dum
...
stare
Mommy! Why's that boy just standing there?
Shh!
Quiet, Mika!!
GAHH
grab
toss
toss
STOMP
STOMP
STOMP
I NEED TO CREATE A CHARACTER...
LOOK WHO COMES STROLLING IN!

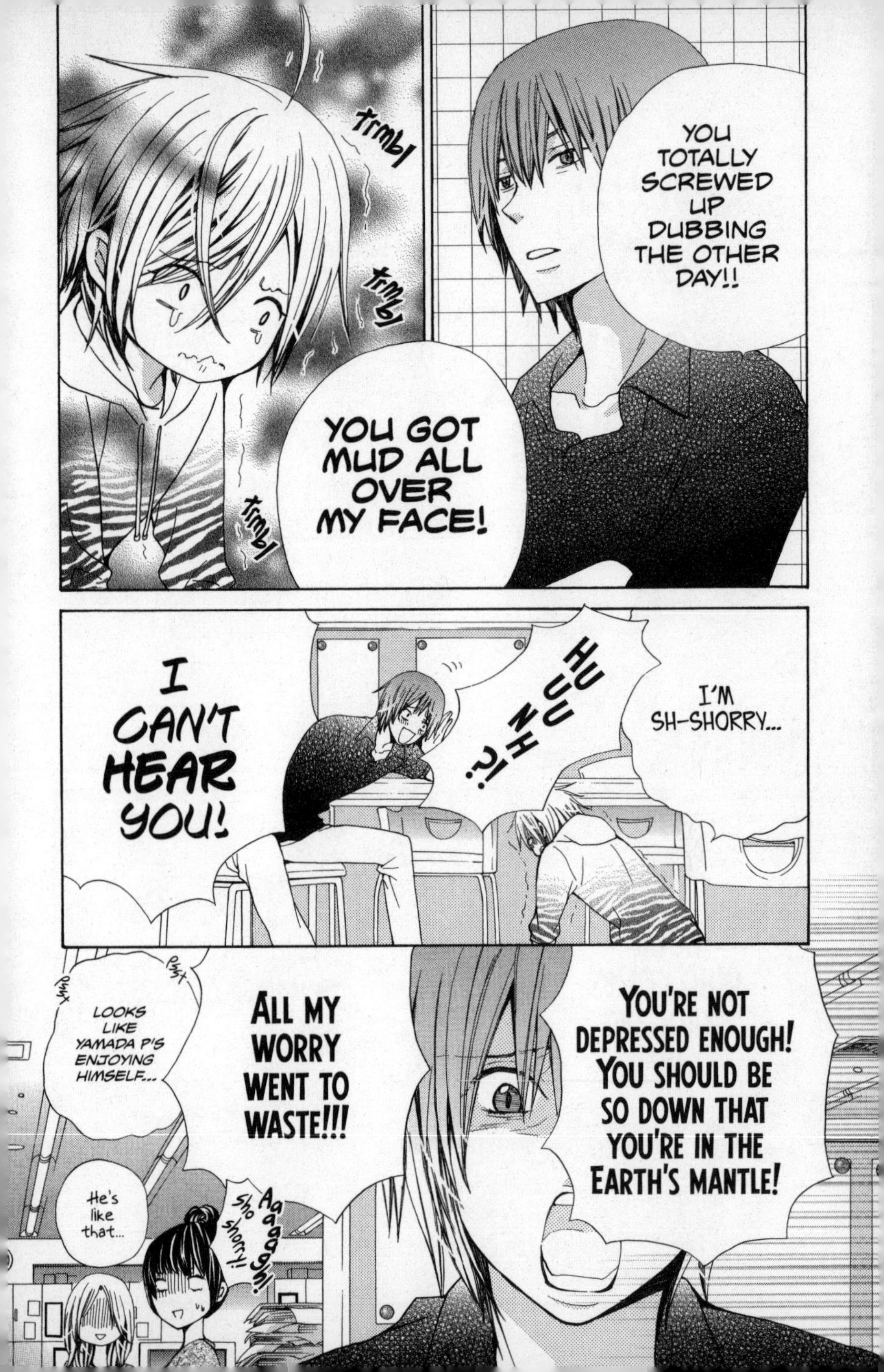
YOU TOTALLY SCREWED UP DUBBING THE OTHER DAY!!
YOU GOT MUD ALL OVER MY FACE!
trmbl
trmbl
trmbl
I'M SH-SHORRY...
HUUNH?!
I CAN'T HEAR YOU!
YOU'RE NOT DEPRESSED ENOUGH! YOU SHOULD BE SO DOWN THAT YOU'RE IN THE EARTH'S MANTLE!
ALL MY WORRY WENT TO WASTE!!!
Aaaaagh! Sho shorry!
Pssst
Pssst
LOOKS LIKE YAMADA P'S ENJOYING HIMSELF...
He's like that...

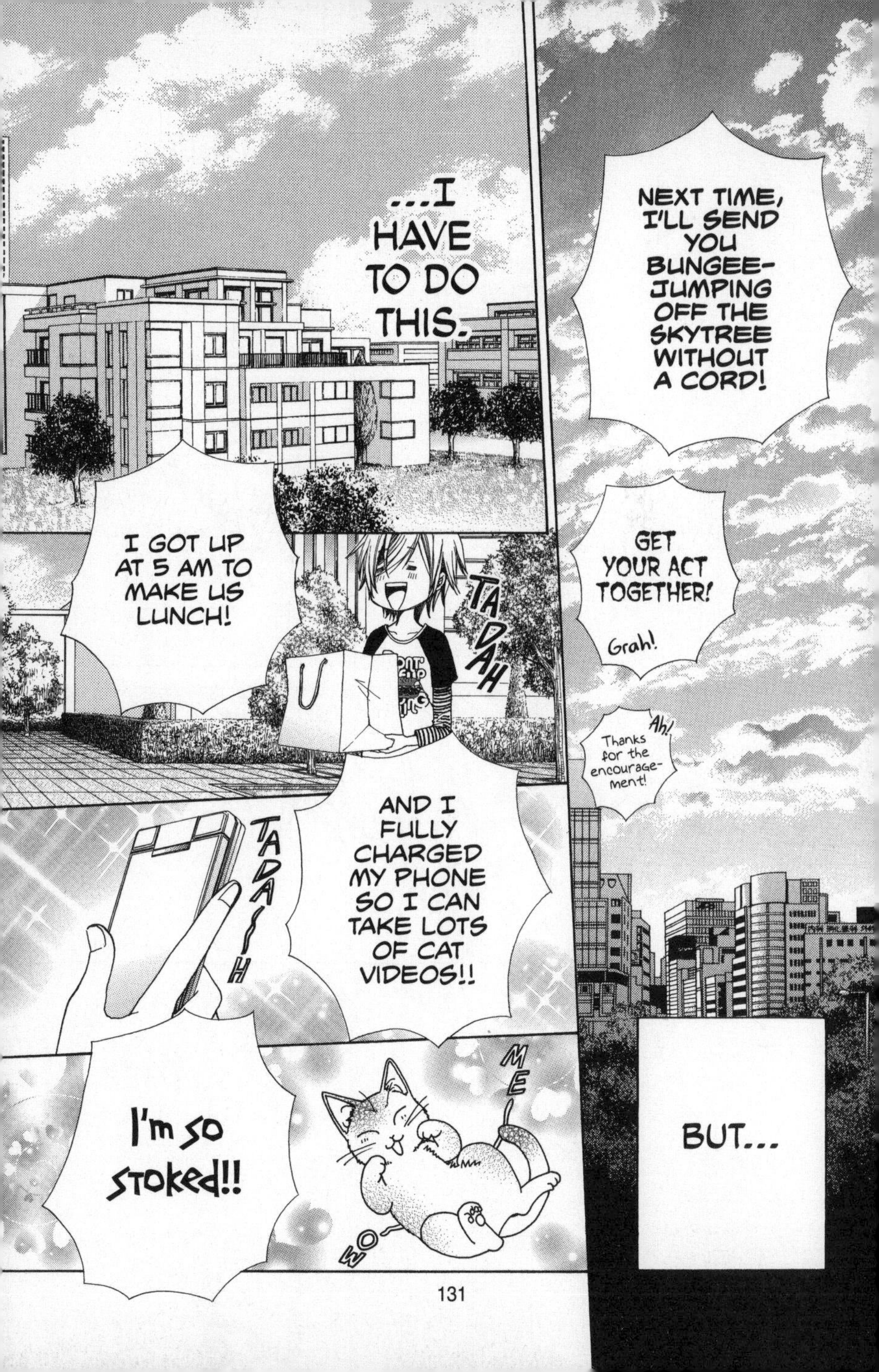
NEXT TIME, I'LL SEND YOU BUNGEE-JUMPING OFF THE SKYTREE WITHOUT A CORD!
GET YOUR ACT TOGETHER!
Grah!
Ah!
Thanks for the encourage-ment!
...I HAVE TO DO THIS.
I GOT UP AT 5 AM TO MAKE US LUNCH!
TADAH
AND I FULLY CHARGED MY PHONE SO I CAN TAKE LOTS OF CAT VIDEOS!!
TADAISH
I'm so stoked!!
ME
OW
BUT...

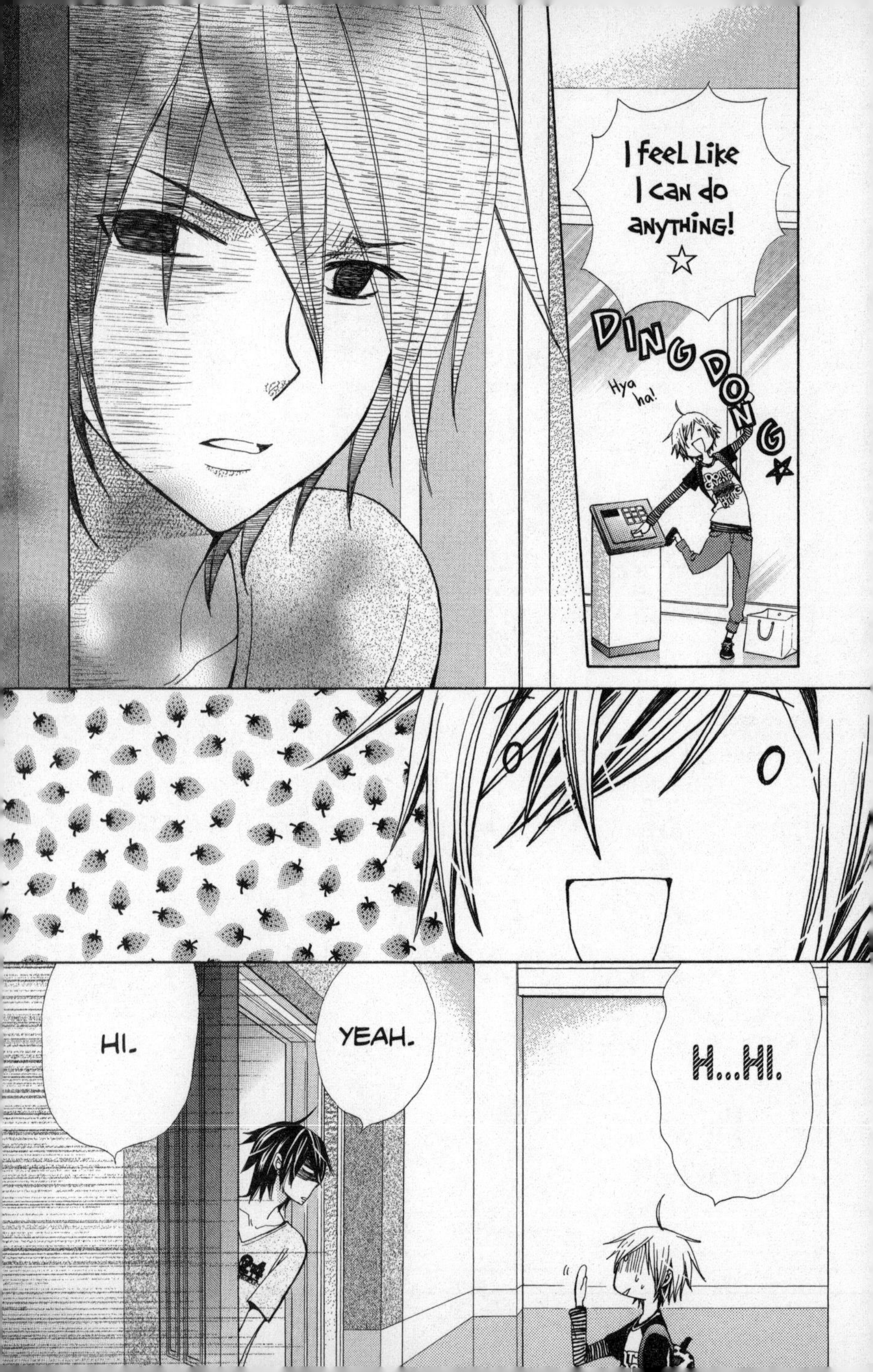
I feel Like I can do anything! ☆
DING DONG ☆
Hya ha!
H...HI.
YEAH.
HI.

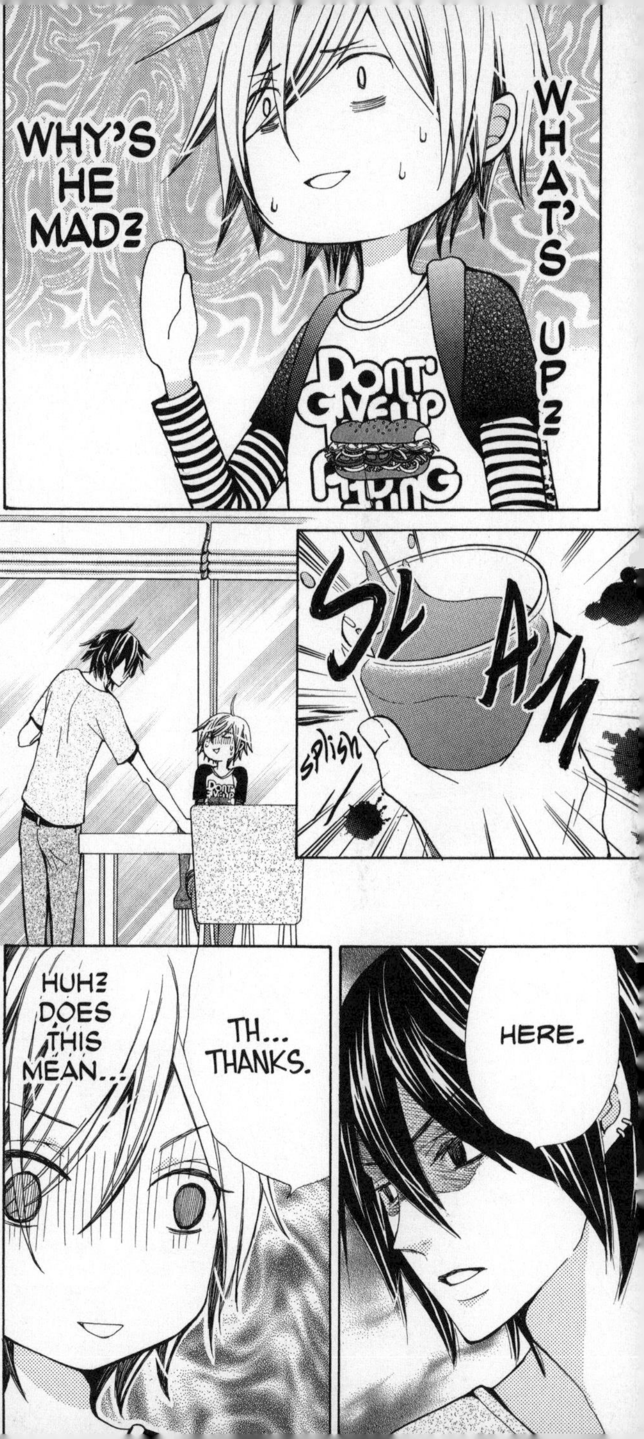
WHAT'S UP?
WHY'S HE MAD?
SLAM
splish
HERE.
TH... THANKS.
HUH? DOES THIS MEAN...

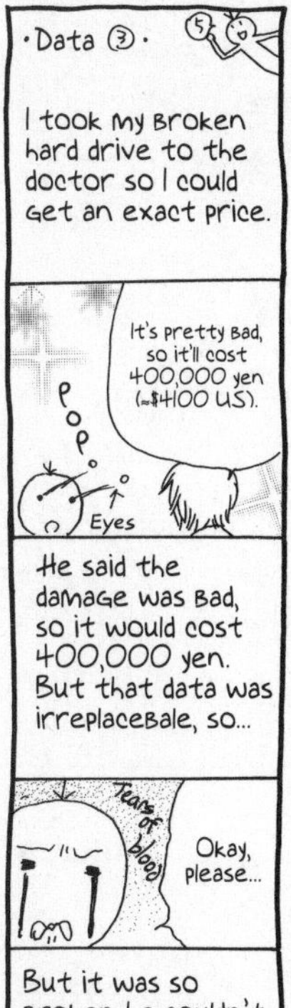
•Data ③•
I took my broken hard drive to the doctor so I could get an exact price.
It's pretty bad, so it'll cost 400,000 yen (≈$4100 US).
Pop
Eyes
He said the damage was bad, so it would cost 400,000 yen. But that data was irreplacebale, so...
Tears of blood
Okay, please...
But it was so broken he couldn't retrieve all the data.
It didn't work, so that'll be 300,000 (≈$3075).
Wow! A 100,000-yen discount!
The doctor really helped me.
Always save your data...
...in more places than one!
Backing up is important!!
It was my fault!!

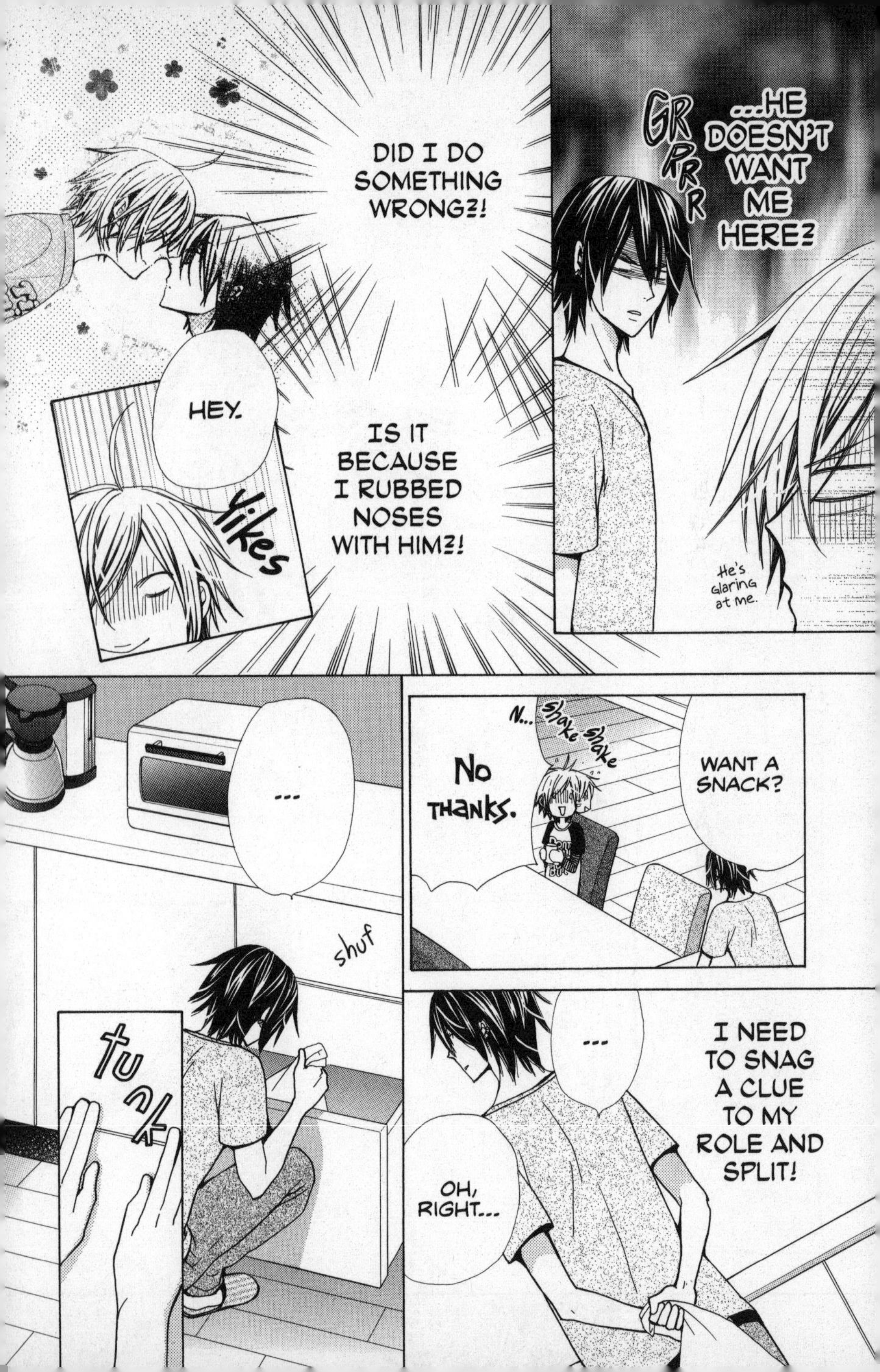
GRRR
...HE DOESN'T WANT ME HERE?
He's glaring at me.
DID I DO SOMETHING WRONG?!
IS IT BECAUSE I RUBBED NOSES WITH HIM?!
HEY.
Yikes
WANT A SNACK?
shake shake
N...
No thanks.
I NEED TO SNAG A CLUE TO MY ROLE AND SPLIT!
...
OH, RIGHT...
...
shuf
tunk

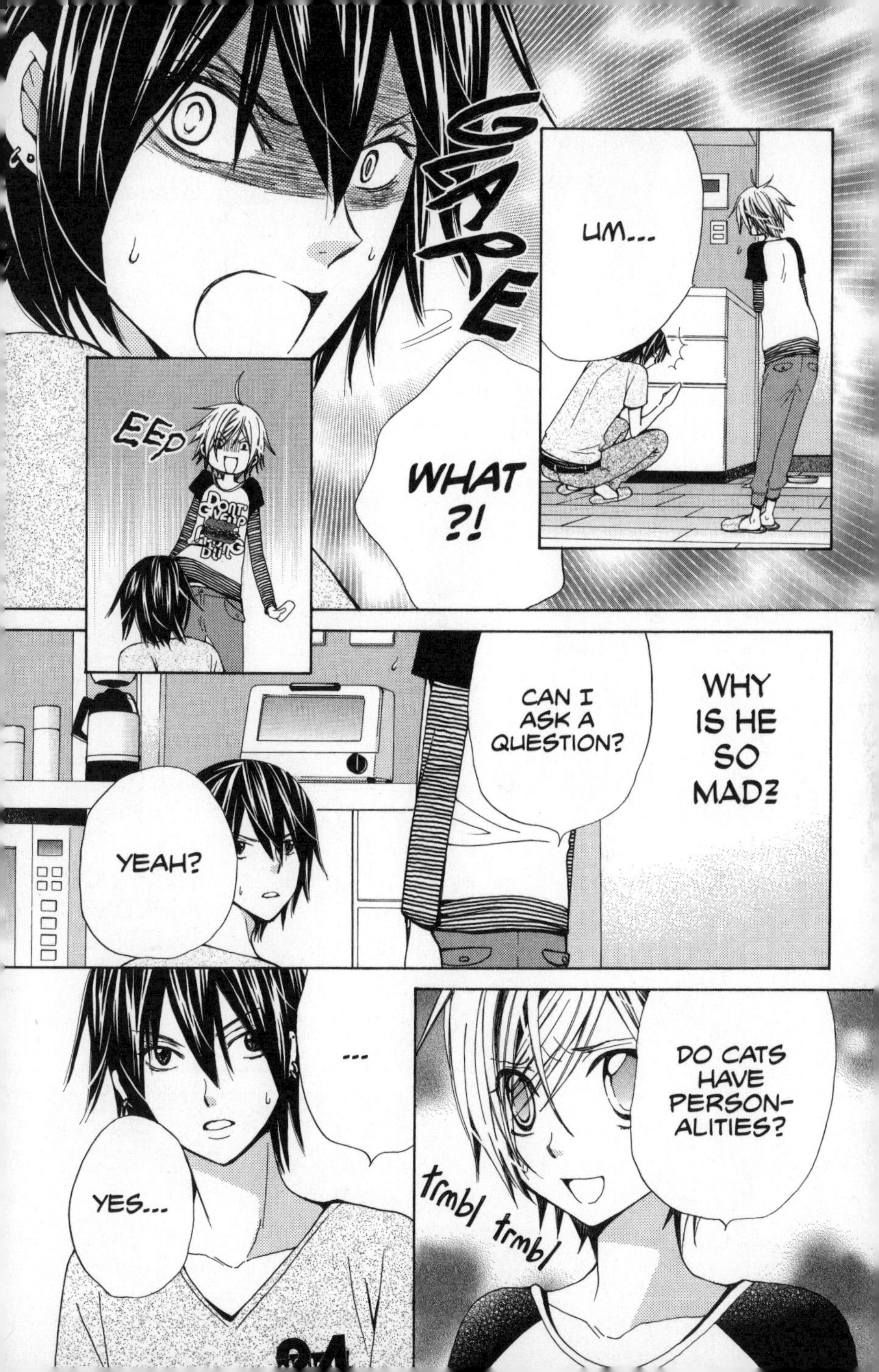
UM...
GLARE
WHAT ?!
EEP
DON'T GIVE UP
WHY IS HE SO MAD?
CAN I ASK A QUESTION?
YEAH?
DO CATS HAVE PERSON-ALITIES?
trmbl trmbl
...
YES...

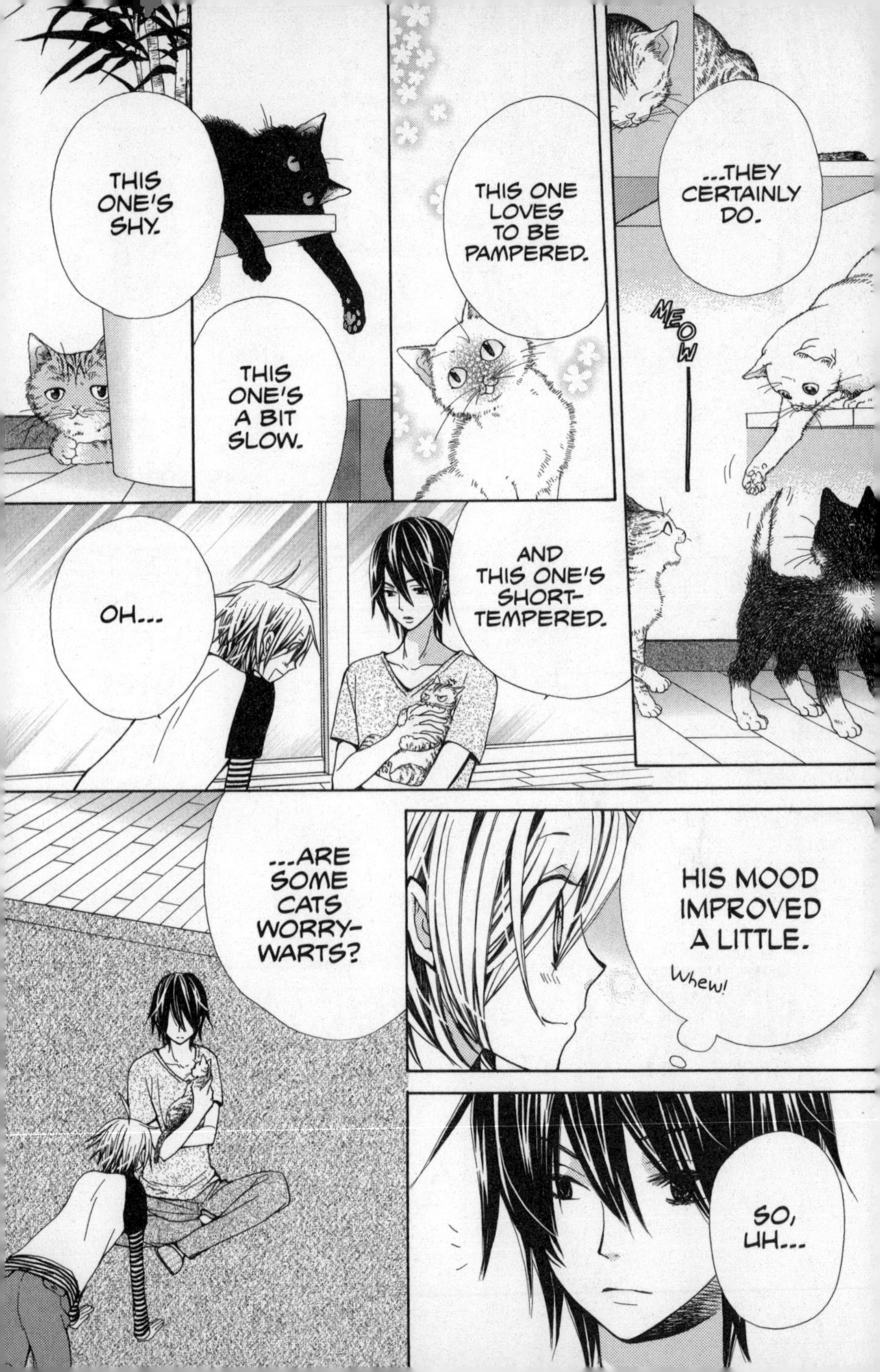
...THEY CERTAINLY DO.
MEOW
THIS ONE LOVES TO BE PAMPERED.
THIS ONE'S SHY.
THIS ONE'S A BIT SLOW.
AND THIS ONE'S SHORT-TEMPERED.
OH...
HIS MOOD IMPROVED A LITTLE.
Whew!
SO, UH...
...ARE SOME CATS WORRY-WARTS?

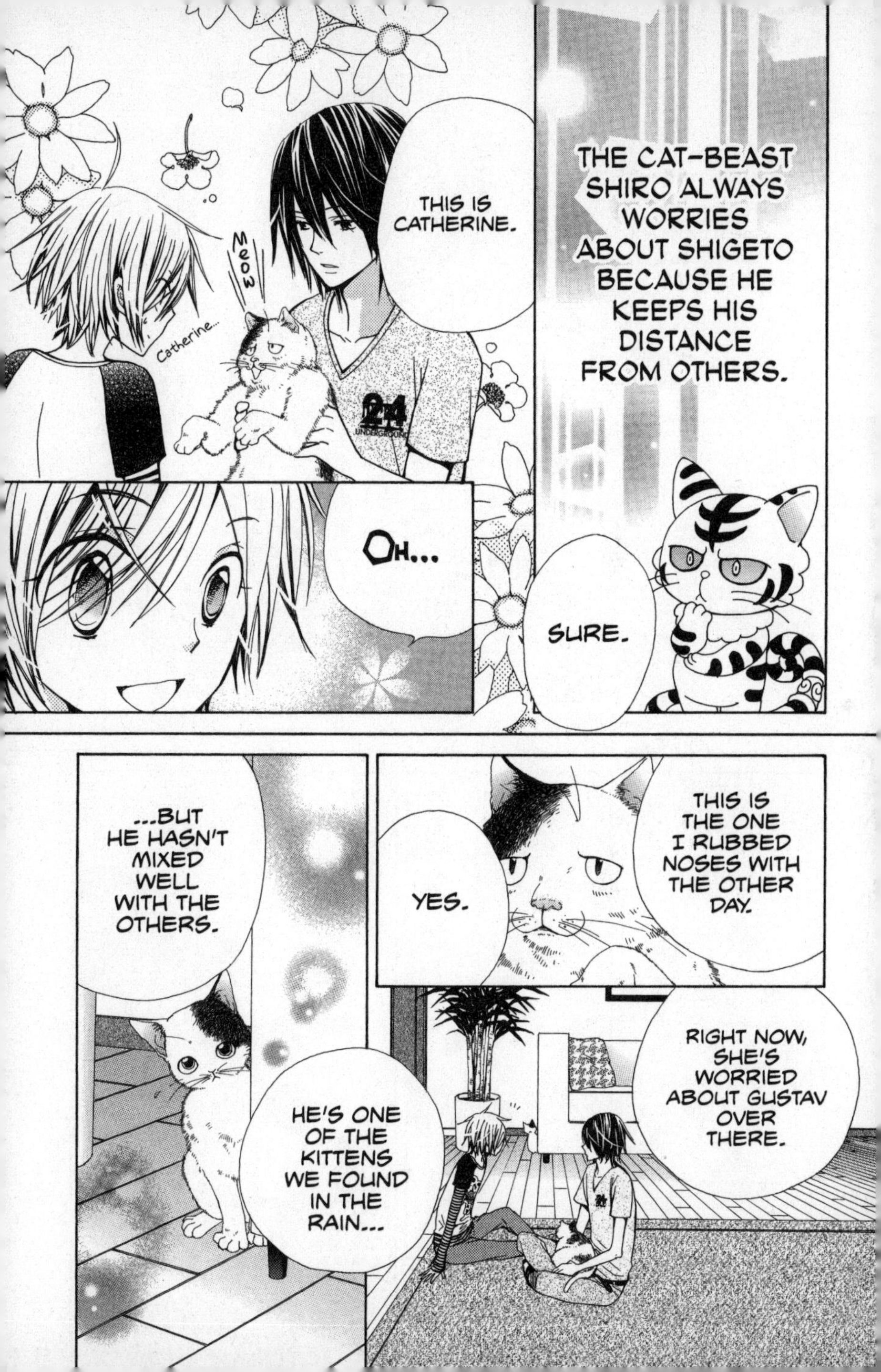
THE CAT-BEAST SHIRO ALWAYS WORRIES ABOUT SHIGETO BECAUSE HE KEEPS HIS DISTANCE FROM OTHERS.
SURE.
THIS IS CATHERINE.
Meow
Catherine...
OH...
THIS IS THE ONE I RUBBED NOSES WITH THE OTHER DAY.
YES.
RIGHT NOW, SHE'S WORRIED ABOUT GUSTAV OVER THERE.
HE'S ONE OF THE KITTENS WE FOUND IN THE RAIN...
...BUT HE HASN'T MIXED WELL WITH THE OTHERS.

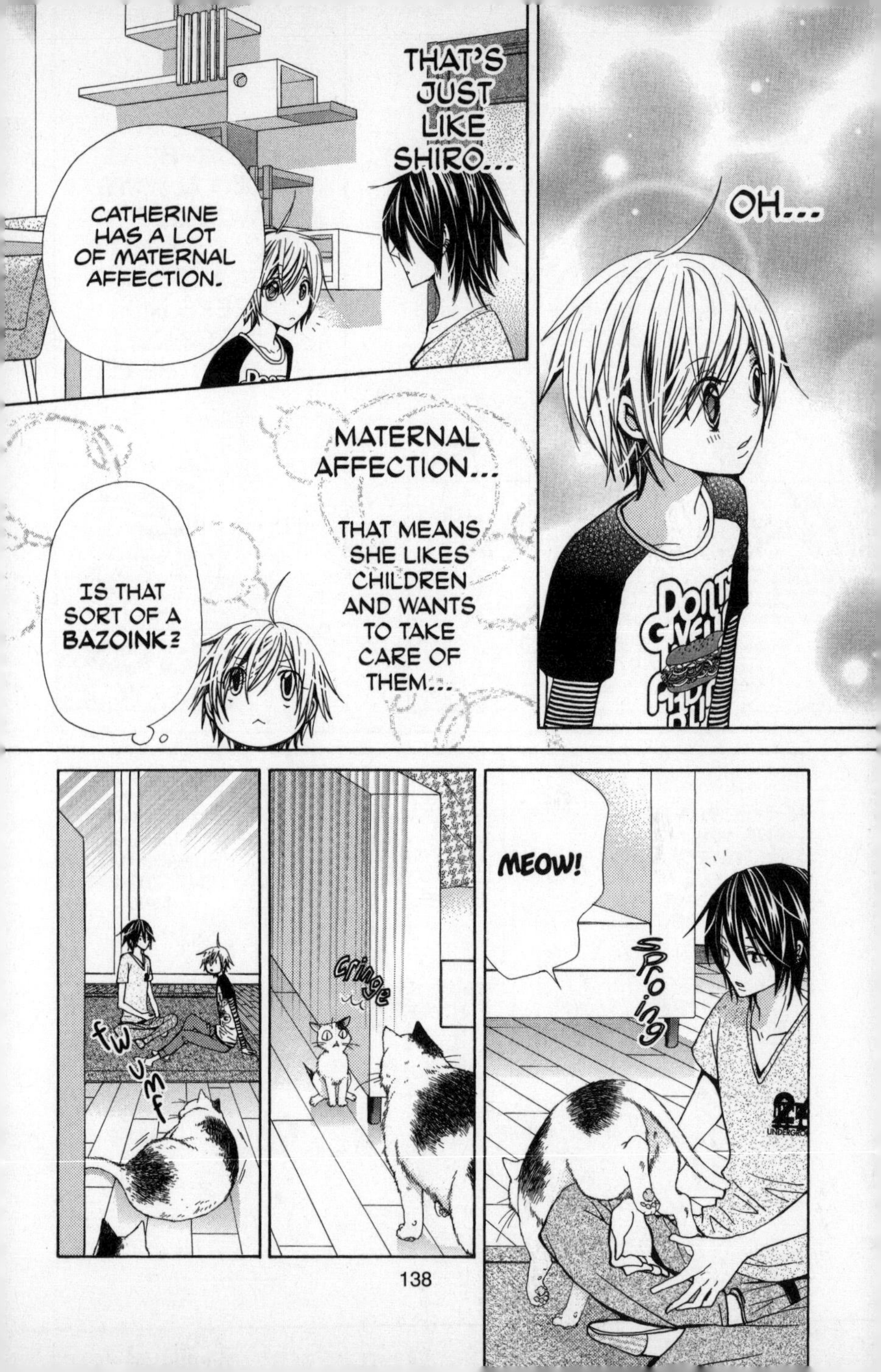
OH...
THAT'S JUST LIKE SHIRO...
CATHERINE HAS A LOT OF MATERNAL AFFECTION.
MATERNAL AFFECTION...
THAT MEANS SHE LIKES CHILDREN AND WANTS TO TAKE CARE OF THEM...
IS THAT SORT OF A BAZOINK?
MEOW!
SPROING
CRINGE
FWUMF

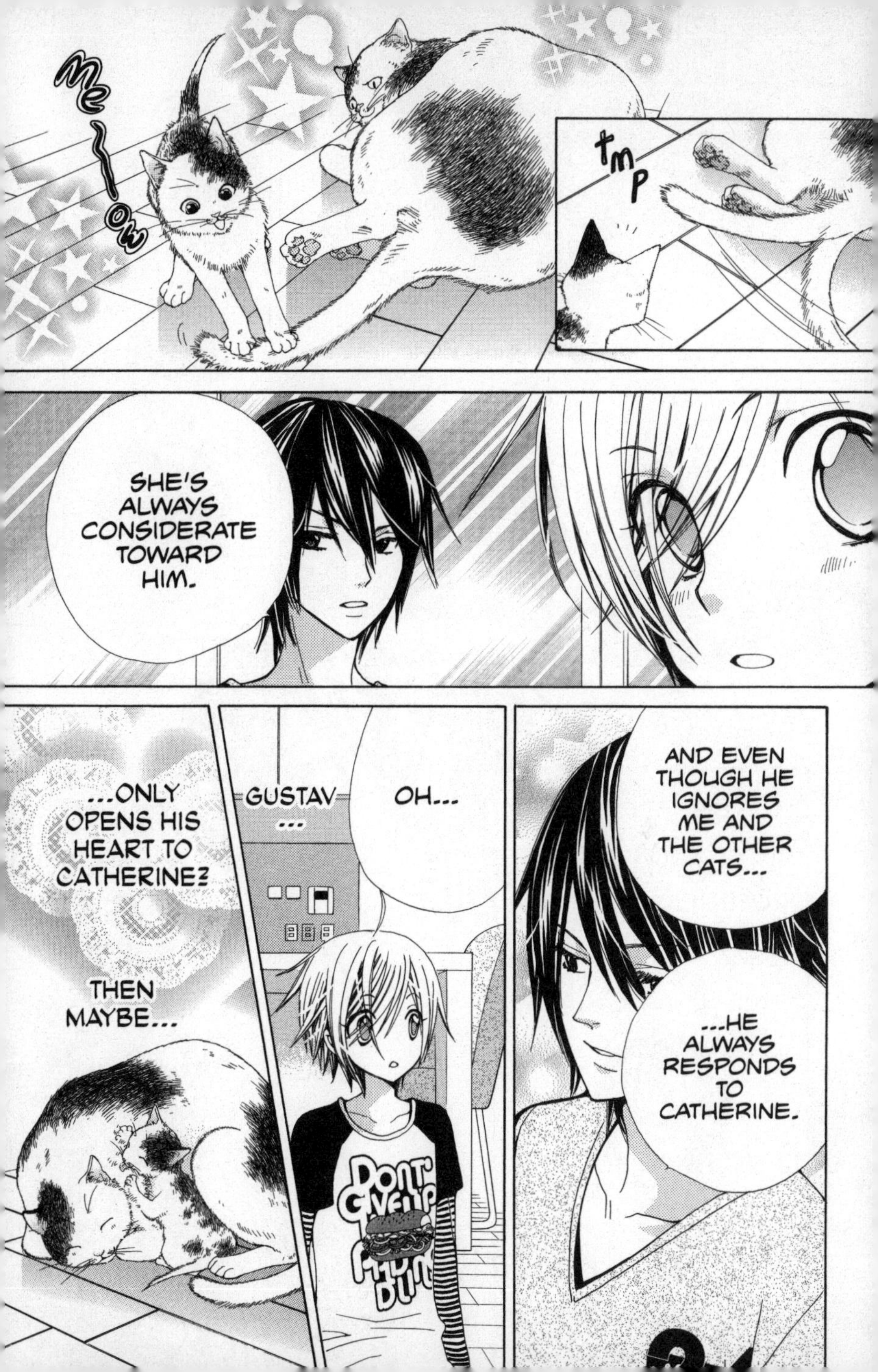
tmp
me~~ow
SHE'S ALWAYS CONSIDERATE TOWARD HIM.
AND EVEN THOUGH HE IGNORES ME AND THE OTHER CATS...
...HE ALWAYS RESPONDS TO CATHERINE.
OH...
GUSTAV ...
...ONLY OPENS HIS HEART TO CATHERINE?
THEN MAYBE...

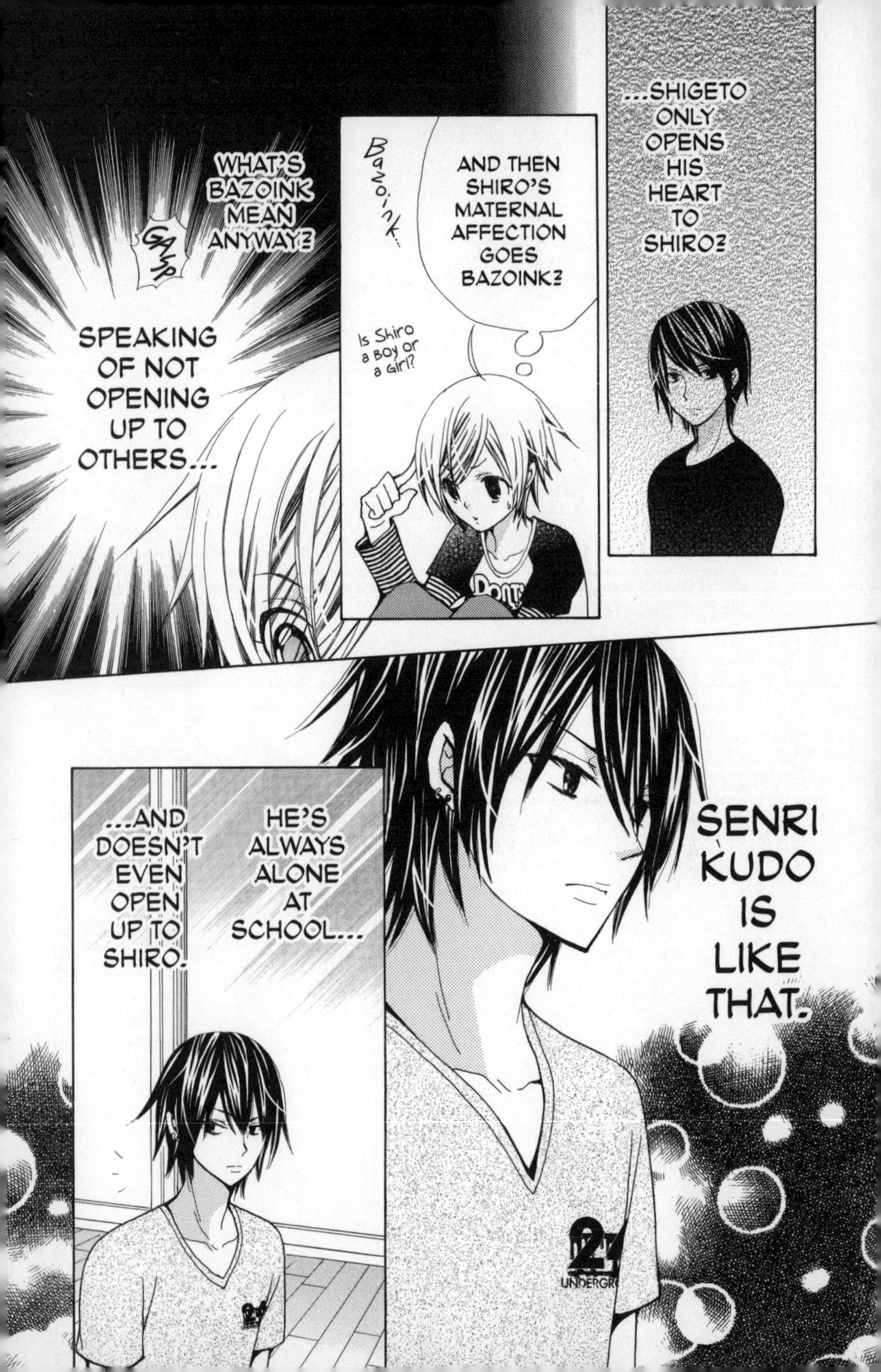
...SHIGETO ONLY OPENS HIS HEART TO SHIRO?
AND THEN SHIRO'S MATERNAL AFFECTION GOES BAZOINK?
Bazoink...
Is Shiro a Boy or a Girl?
WHAT'S BAZOINK MEAN ANYWAY?
GASP
SPEAKING OF NOT OPENING UP TO OTHERS...
SENRI KUDO IS LIKE THAT.
HE'S ALWAYS ALONE AT SCHOOL...
...AND DOESN'T EVEN OPEN UP TO SHIRO.

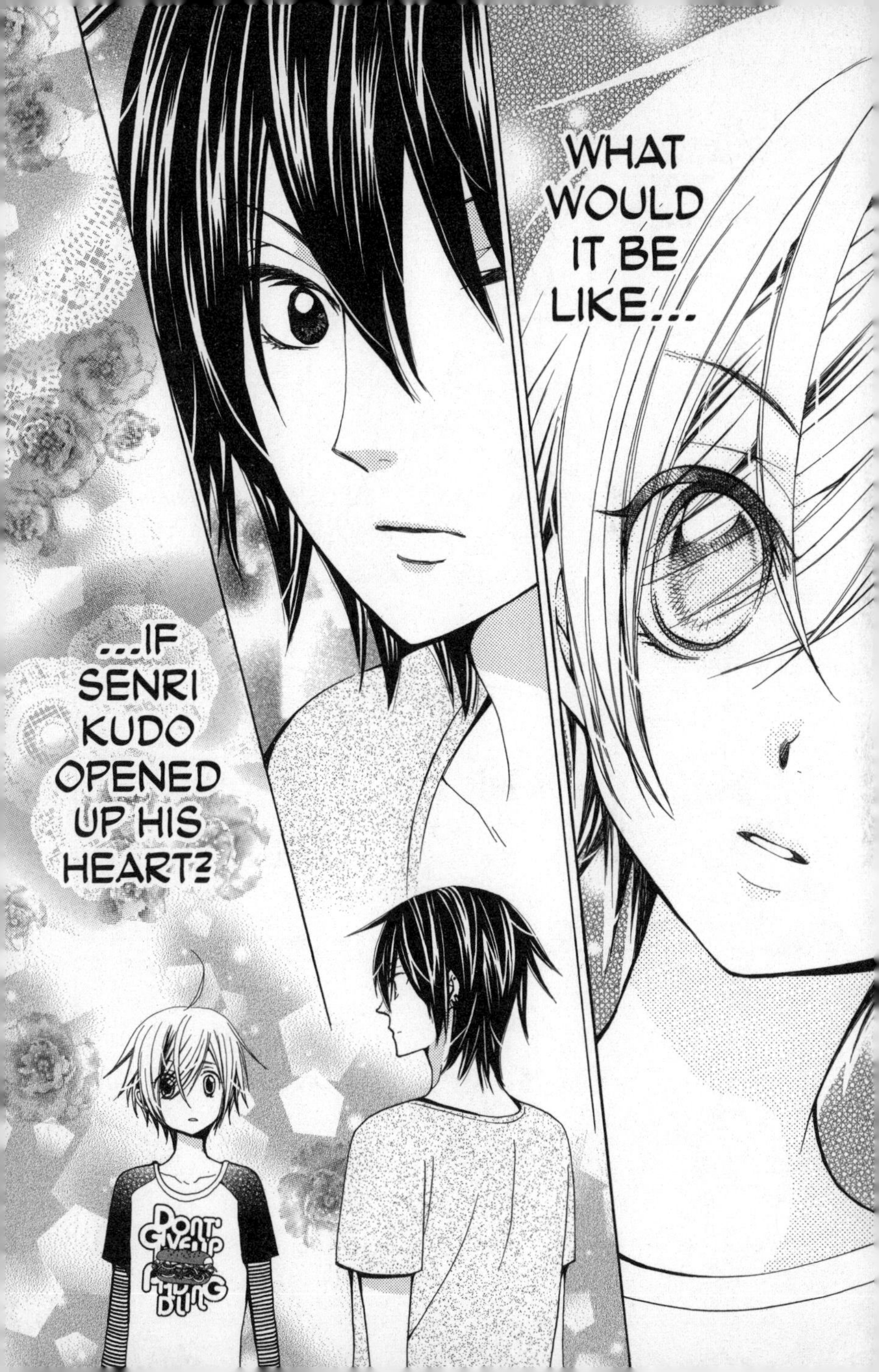
WHAT WOULD IT BE LIKE...
...IF SENRI KUDO OPENED UP HIS HEART?
DON'T GIVE UP

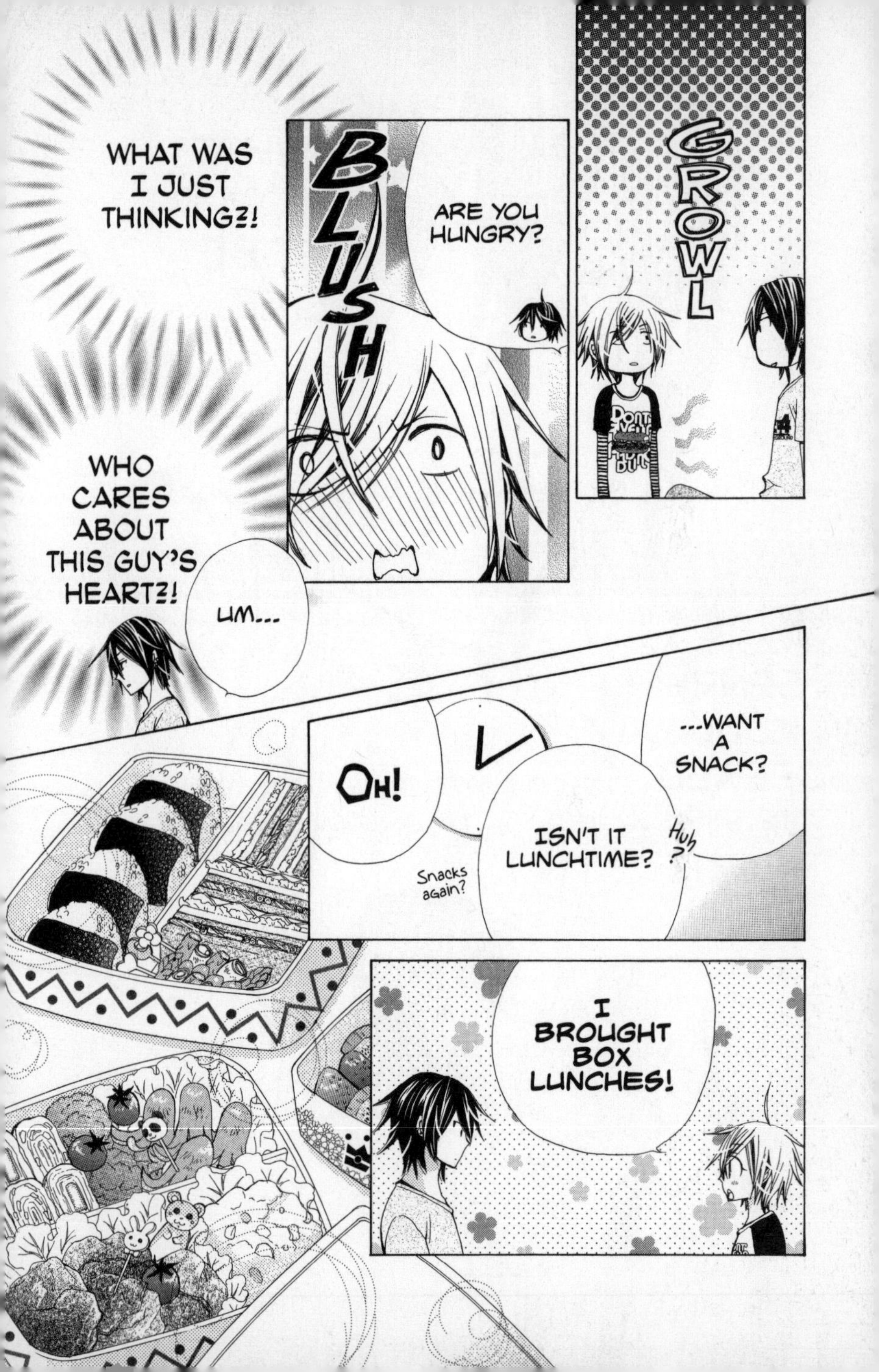
GROWL
ARE YOU HUNGRY?
BLUSH
WHAT WAS I JUST THINKING?!
WHO CARES ABOUT THIS GUY'S HEART?!
UM...
...WANT A SNACK?
Huh?
ISN'T IT LUNCHTIME?
Snacks again?
OH!
I BROUGHT BOX LUNCHES!

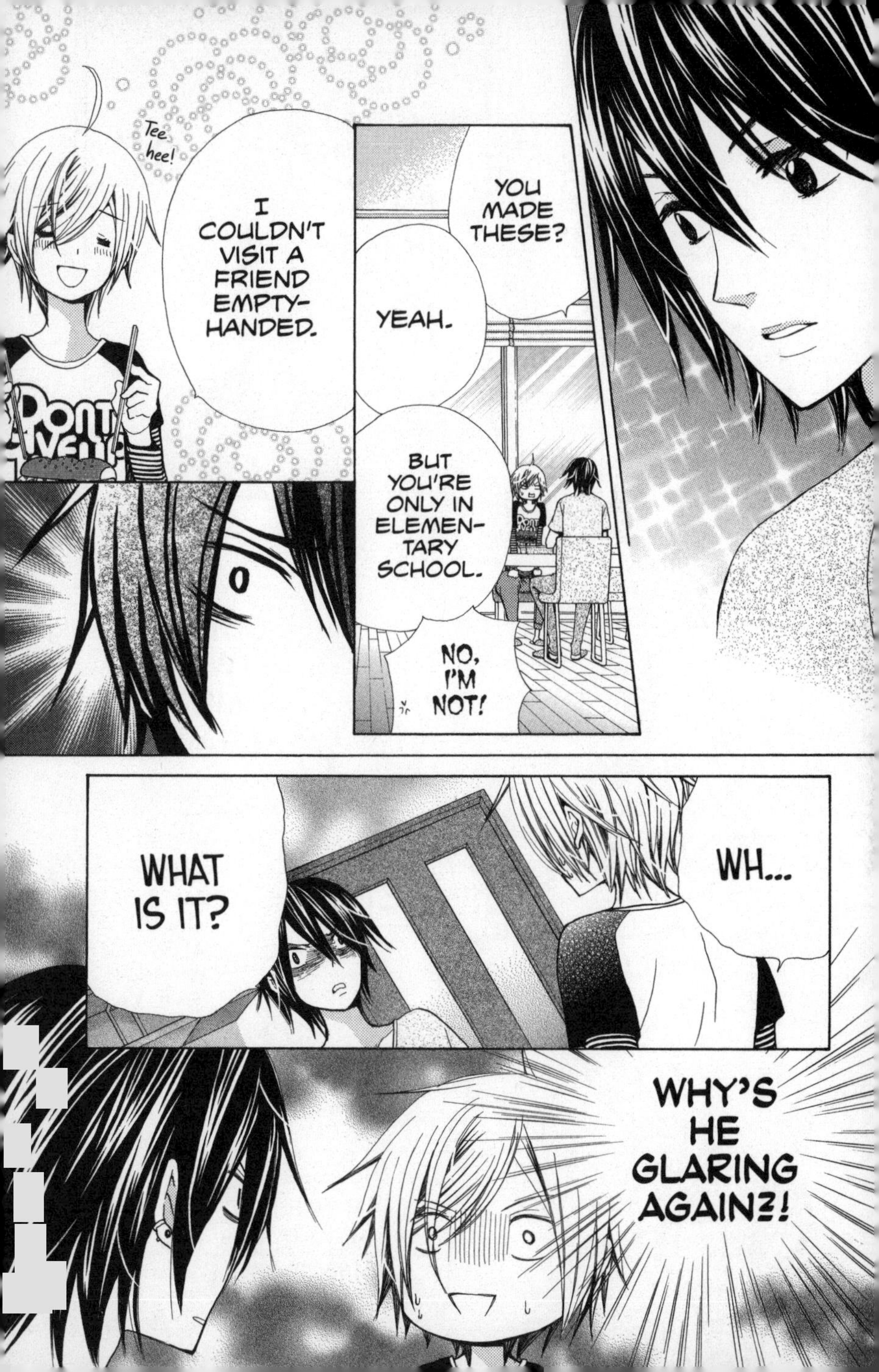
YOU MADE THESE?
YEAH.
BUT YOU'RE ONLY IN ELEMENTARY SCHOOL.
NO, I'M NOT!
Tee hee!
I COULDN'T VISIT A FRIEND EMPTY-HANDED.
WH...
WHAT IS IT?
WHY'S HE GLARING AGAIN?!

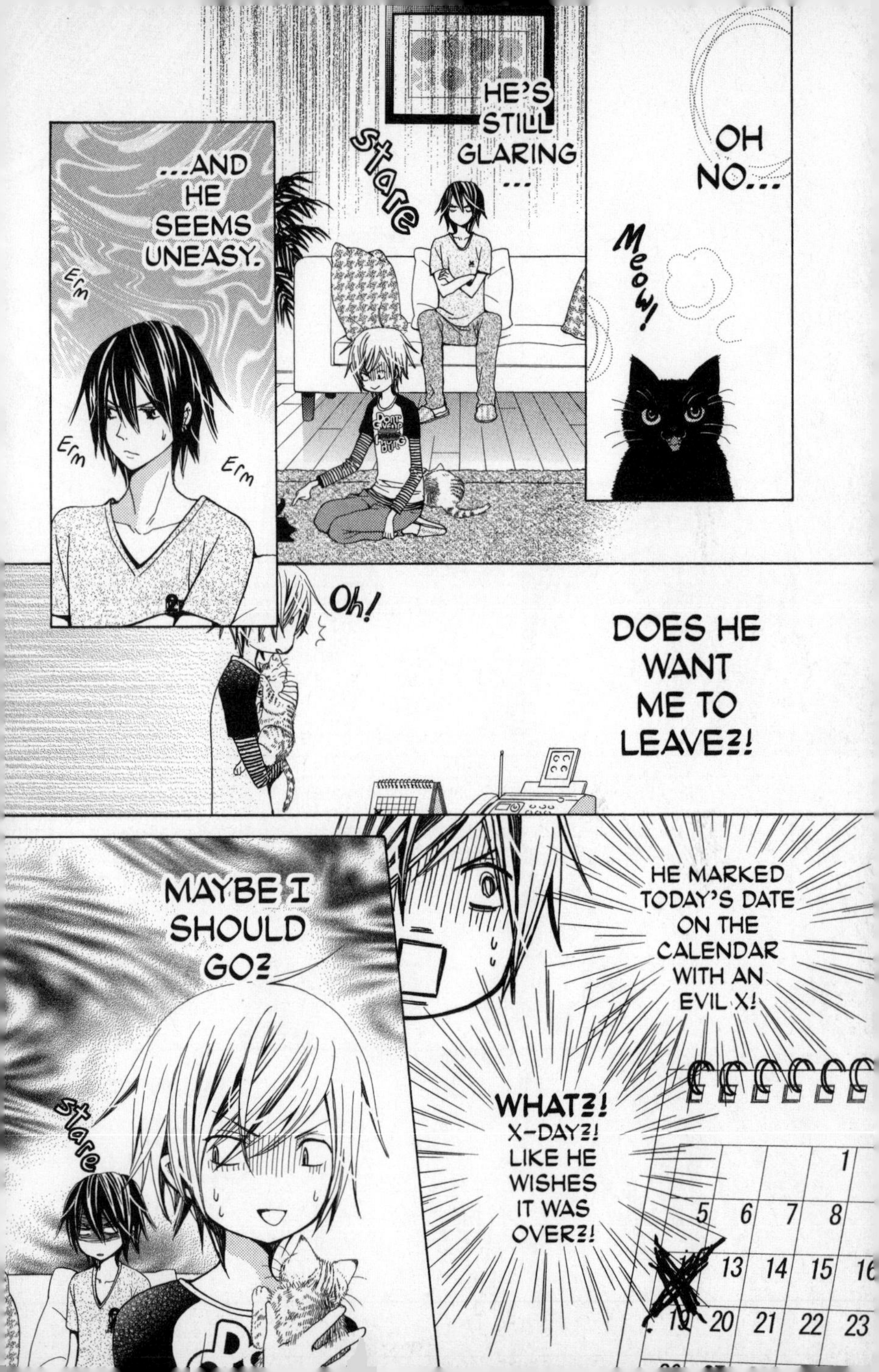
OH NO...
Meow!
HE'S STILL GLARING...
stare
...AND HE SEEMS UNEASY.
Erm
Erm
Erm
DOES HE WANT ME TO LEAVE?!
Oh!
HE MARKED TODAY'S DATE ON THE CALENDAR WITH AN EVIL X!
WHAT?! X-DAY?! LIKE HE WISHES IT WAS OVER?!
1
5 6 7 8
13 14 15
20 21 22 23
MAYBE I SHOULD GO?
stare

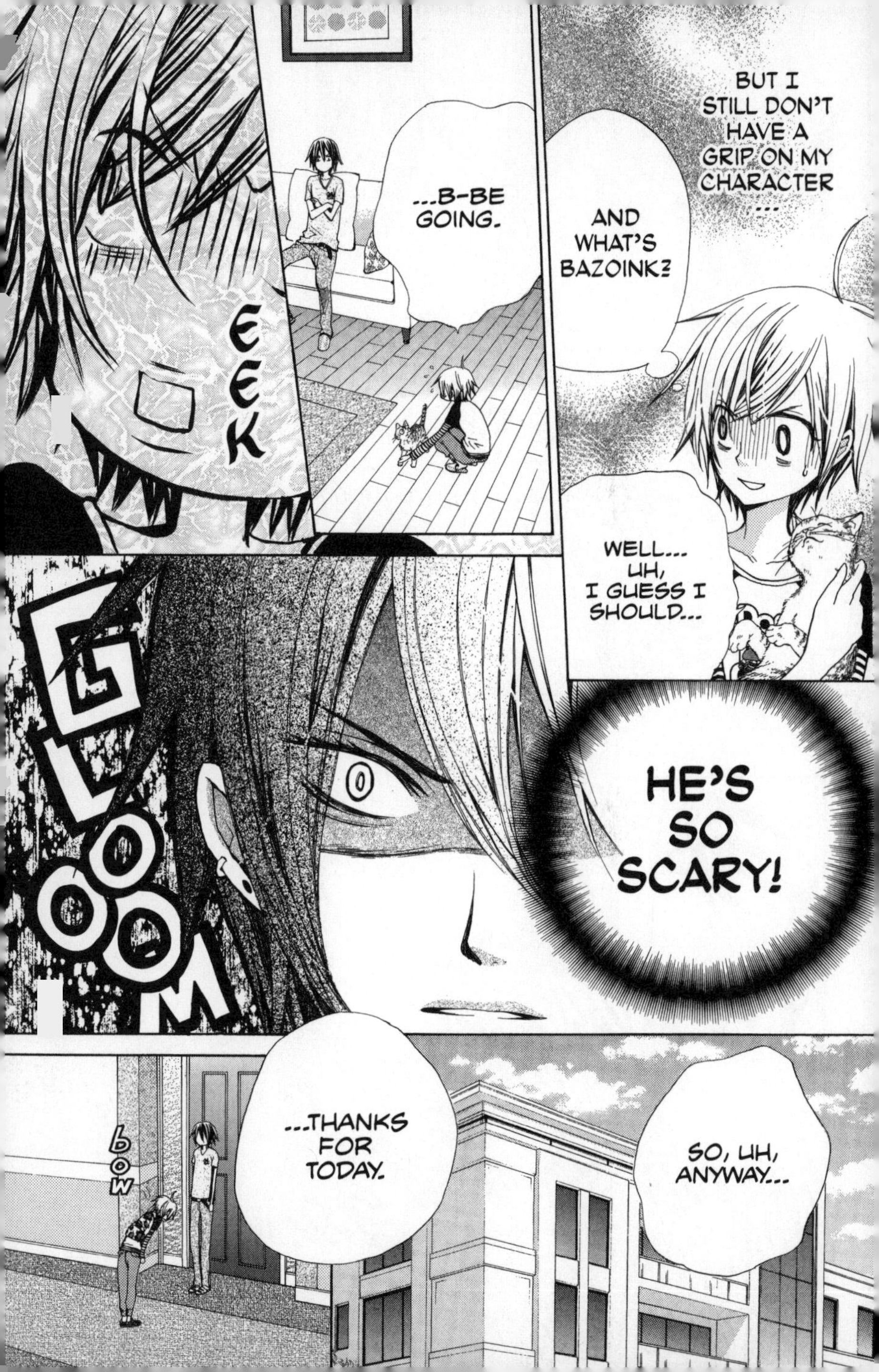
BUT I STILL DON'T HAVE A GRIP ON MY CHARACTER...
AND WHAT'S BAZOINK?
WELL... UH, I GUESS I SHOULD...
...B-BE GOING.
EEK
HE'S SO SCARY!
GLOOOM
SO, UH, ANYWAY...
...THANKS FOR TODAY.
bow

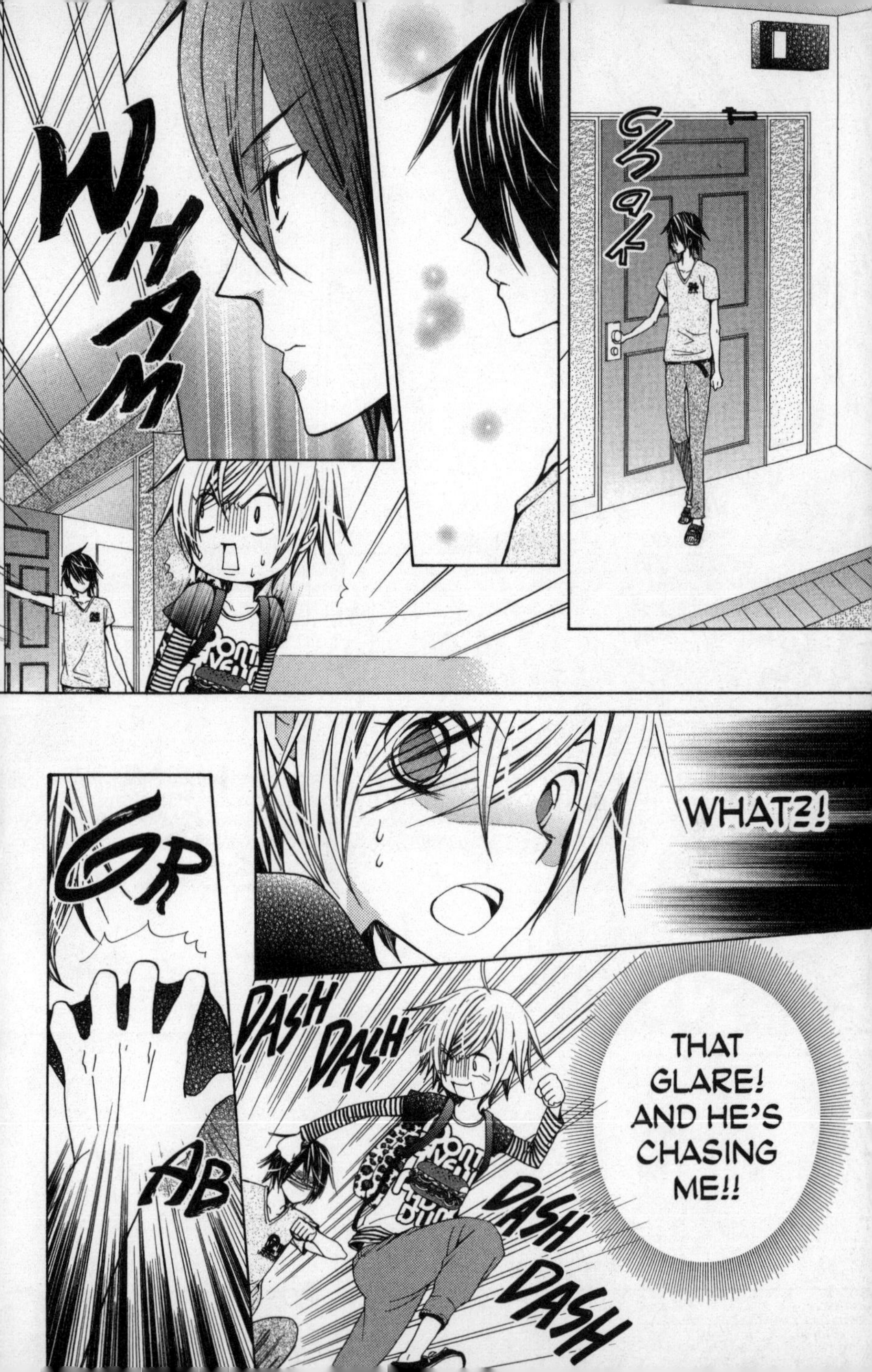
Creak
WHAM
WHAT?!
THAT GLARE! AND HE'S CHASING ME!!
DASH DASH
DASH DASH
GRAB

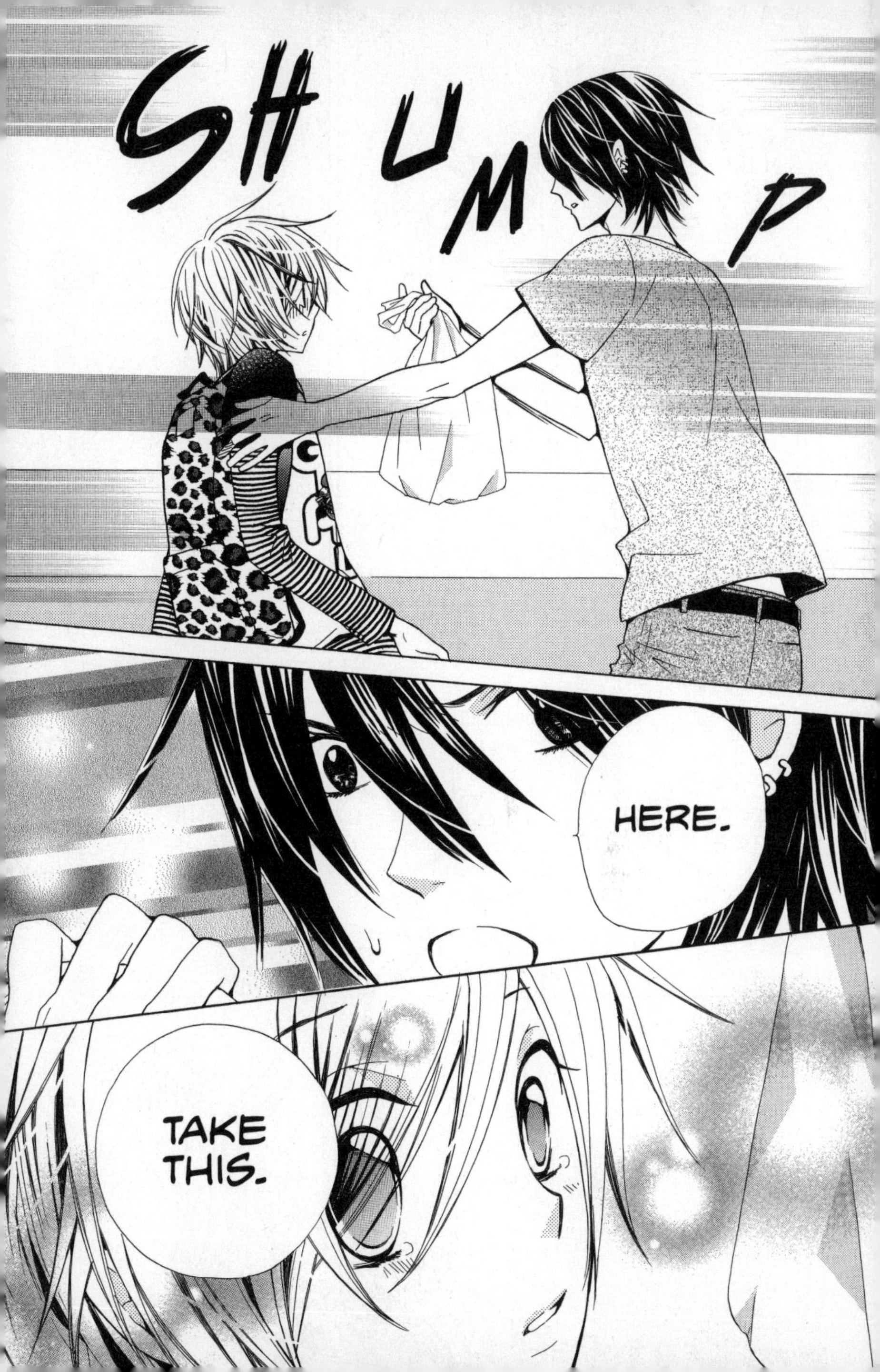
SHUMP
HERE.
TAKE THIS.

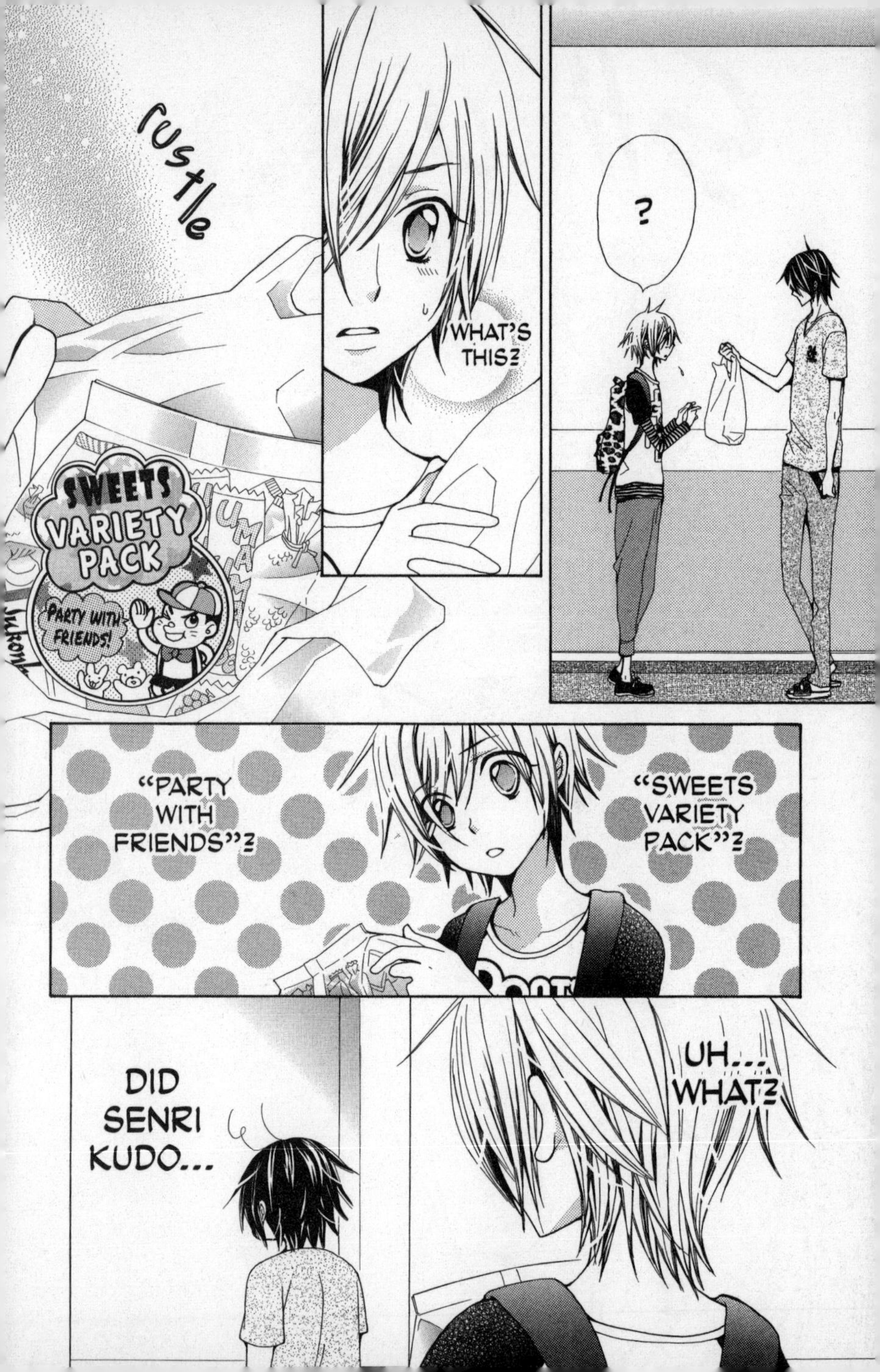
?
WHAT'S THIS?
rustle
SWEETS VARIETY PACK
PARTY WITH FRIENDS!
"SWEETS VARIETY PACK"?
"PARTY WITH FRIENDS"?
UH... WHAT?
DID SENRI KUDO...

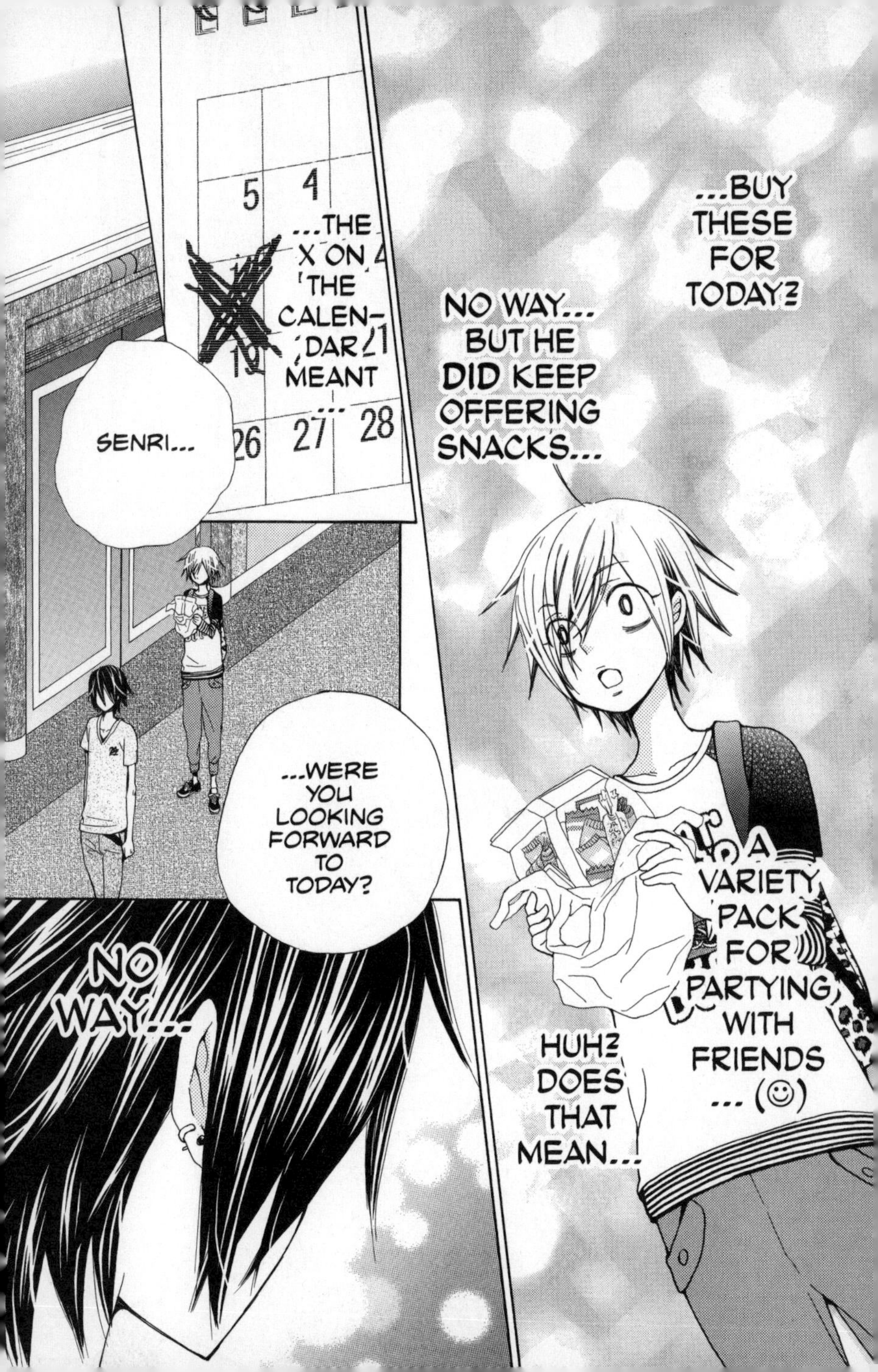
...BUY THESE FOR TODAY?
NO WAY... BUT HE DID KEEP OFFERING SNACKS...
A VARIETY PACK FOR PARTYING WITH FRIENDS ... (☺)
HUH? DOES THAT MEAN...
...THE X ON THE CALENDAR MEANT ...
SENRI...
...WERE YOU LOOKING FORWARD TO TODAY?
NO WAY...

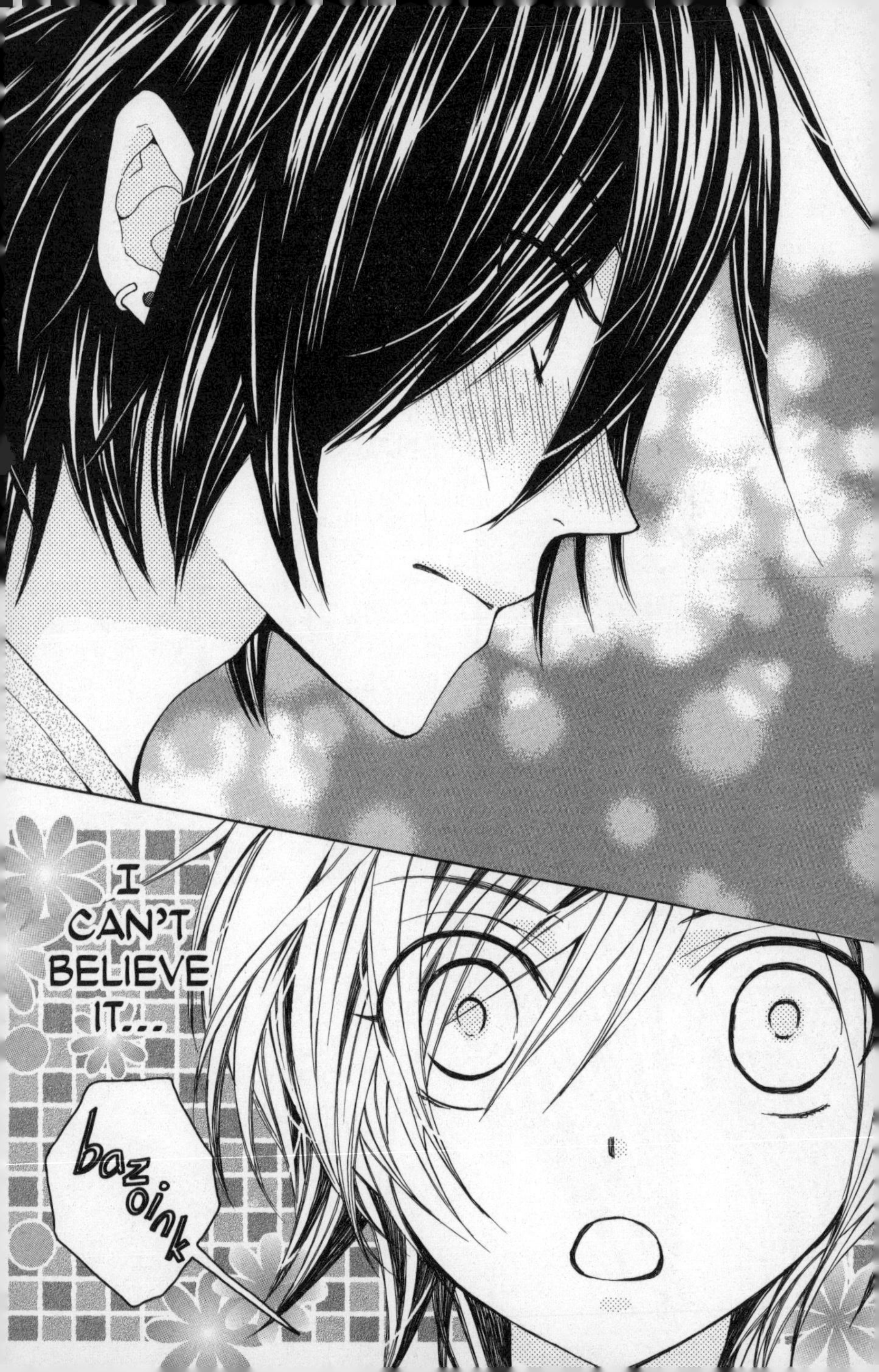
I CAN'T BELIEVE IT...
bazoink

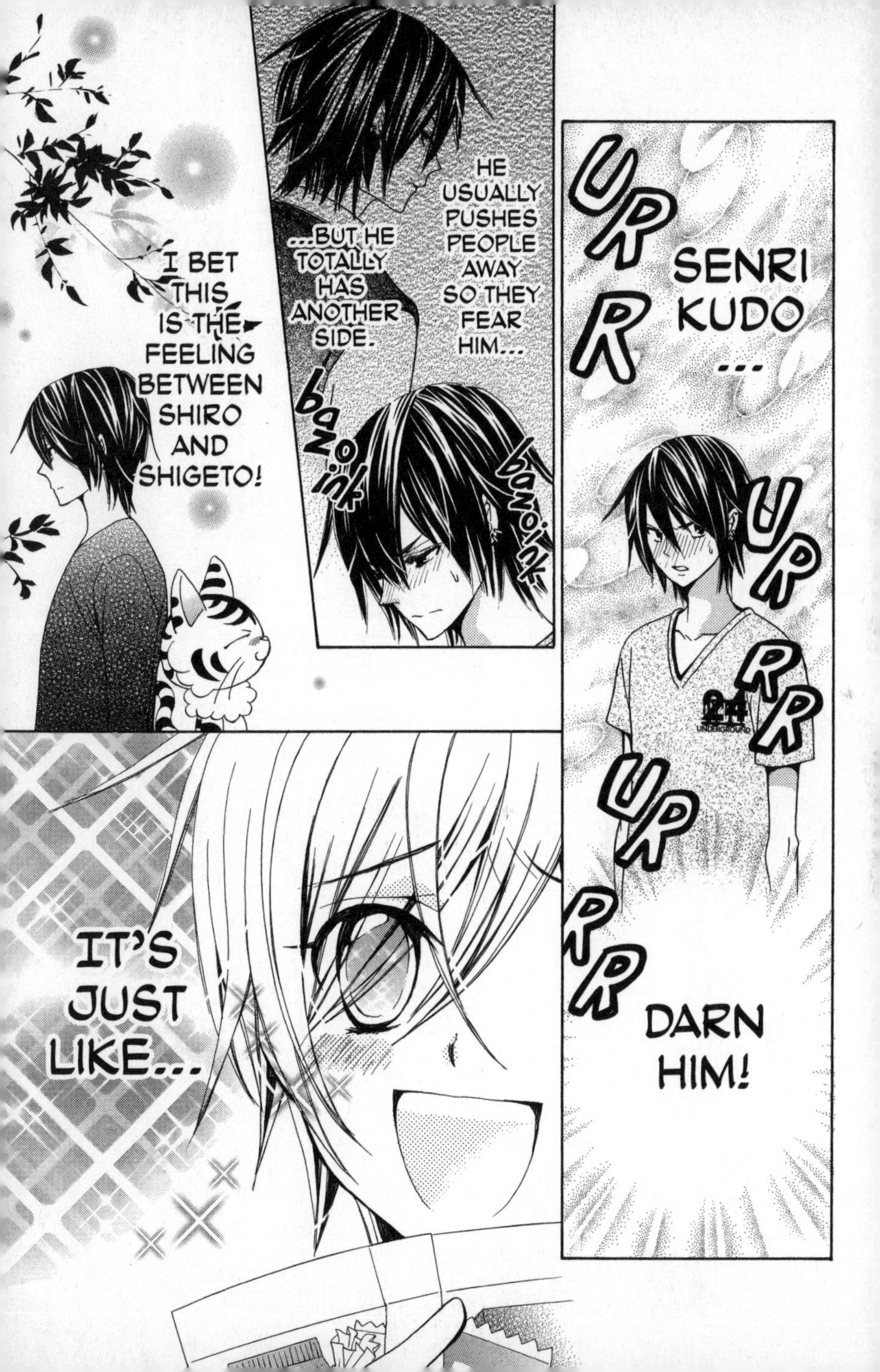
URR
SENRI KUDO...
URRR
URRR
DARN HIM!
HE USUALLY PUSHES PEOPLE AWAY SO THEY FEAR HIM...
...BUT HE TOTALLY HAS ANOTHER SIDE.
bazoink
bazoink
I BET THIS IS THE FEELING BETWEEN SHIRO AND SHIGETO!
IT'S JUST LIKE...

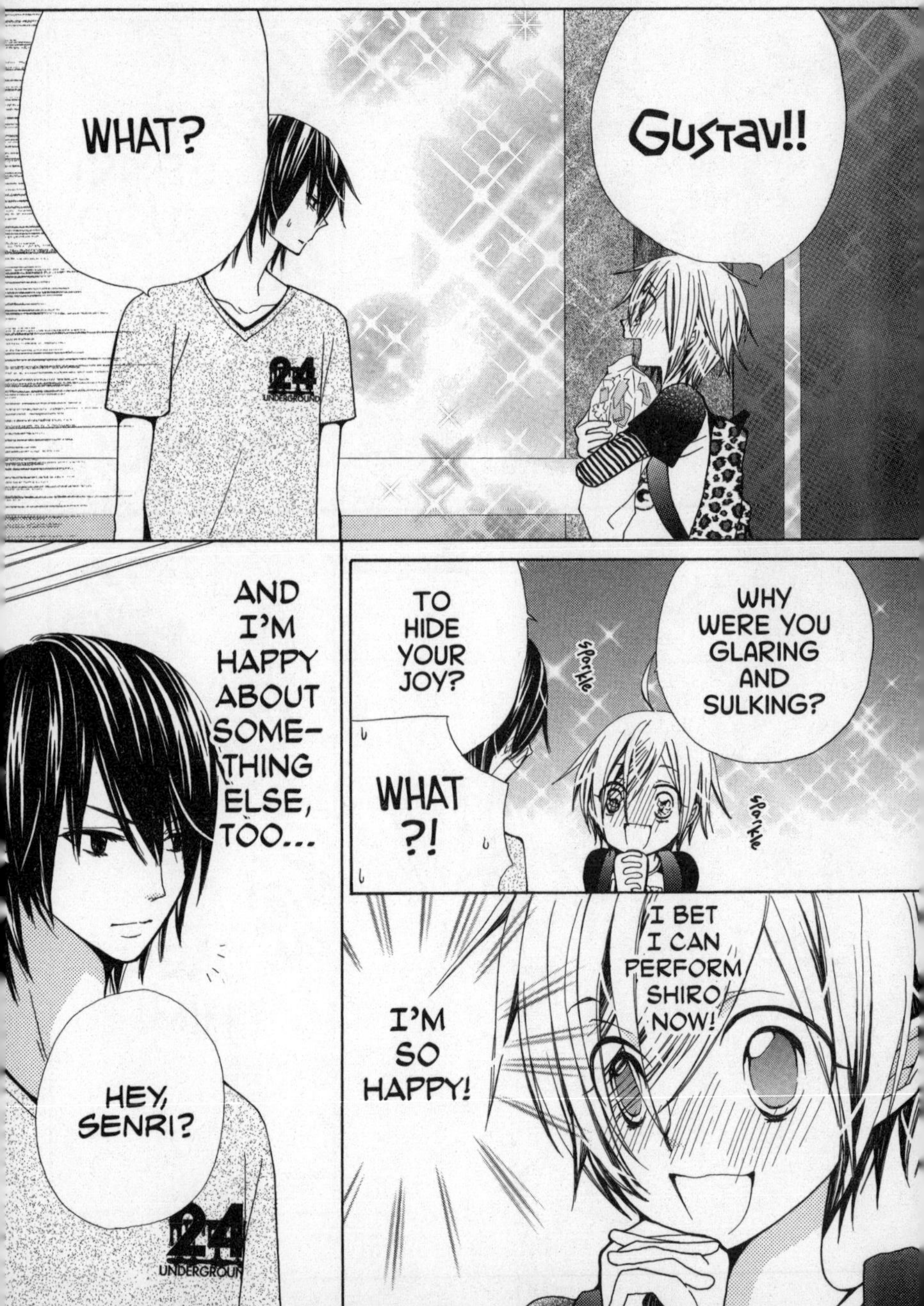
GUSTAV!!
WHAT?
WHY WERE YOU GLARING AND SULKING?
sparkle
sparkle
TO HIDE YOUR JOY?
WHAT?!
I BET I CAN PERFORM SHIRO NOW!
I'M SO HAPPY!
AND I'M HAPPY ABOUT SOMETHING ELSE, TOO...
HEY, SENRI?

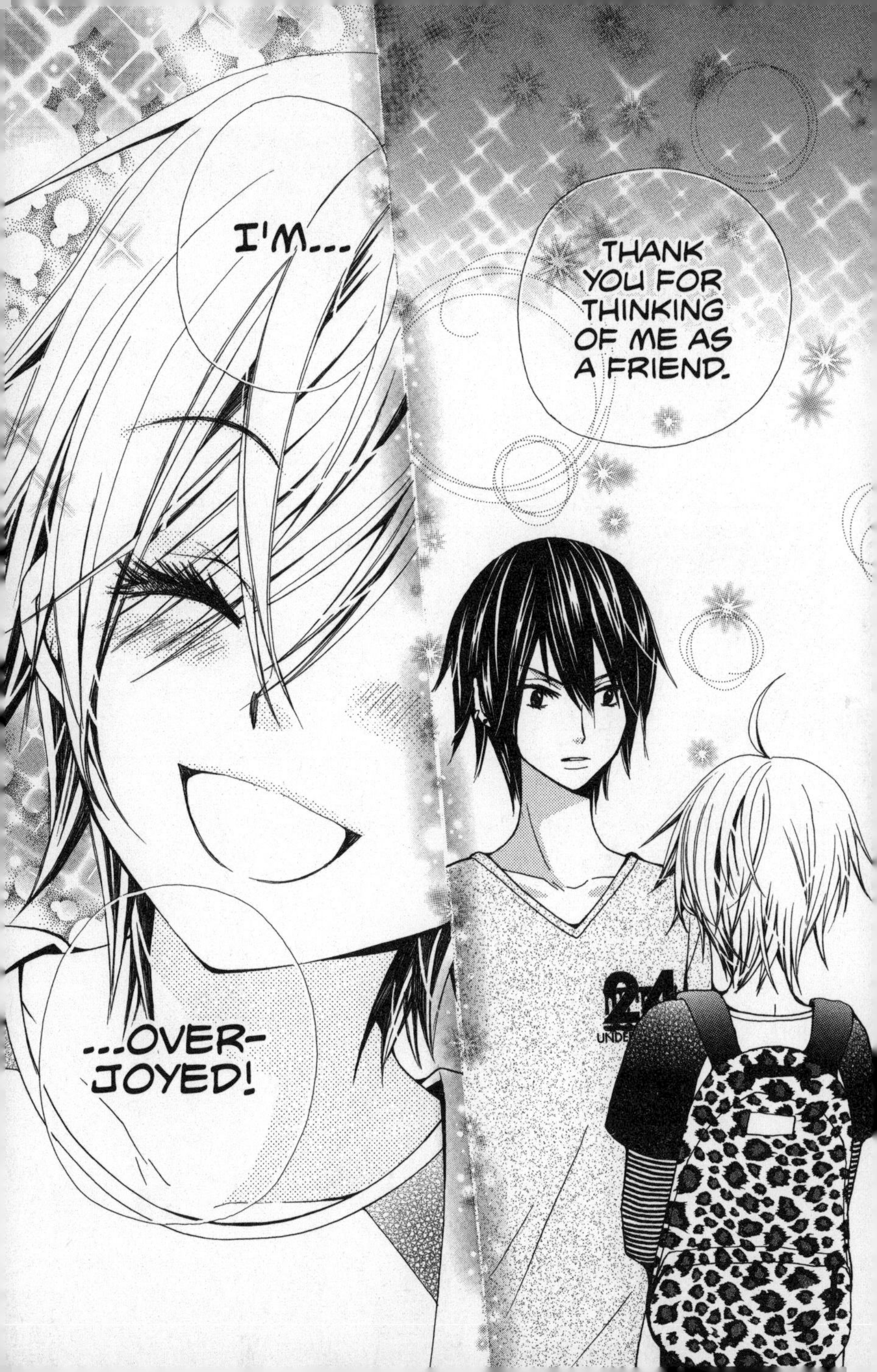
THANK YOU FOR THINKING OF ME AS A FRIEND.
I'M...
...OVER-JOYED!

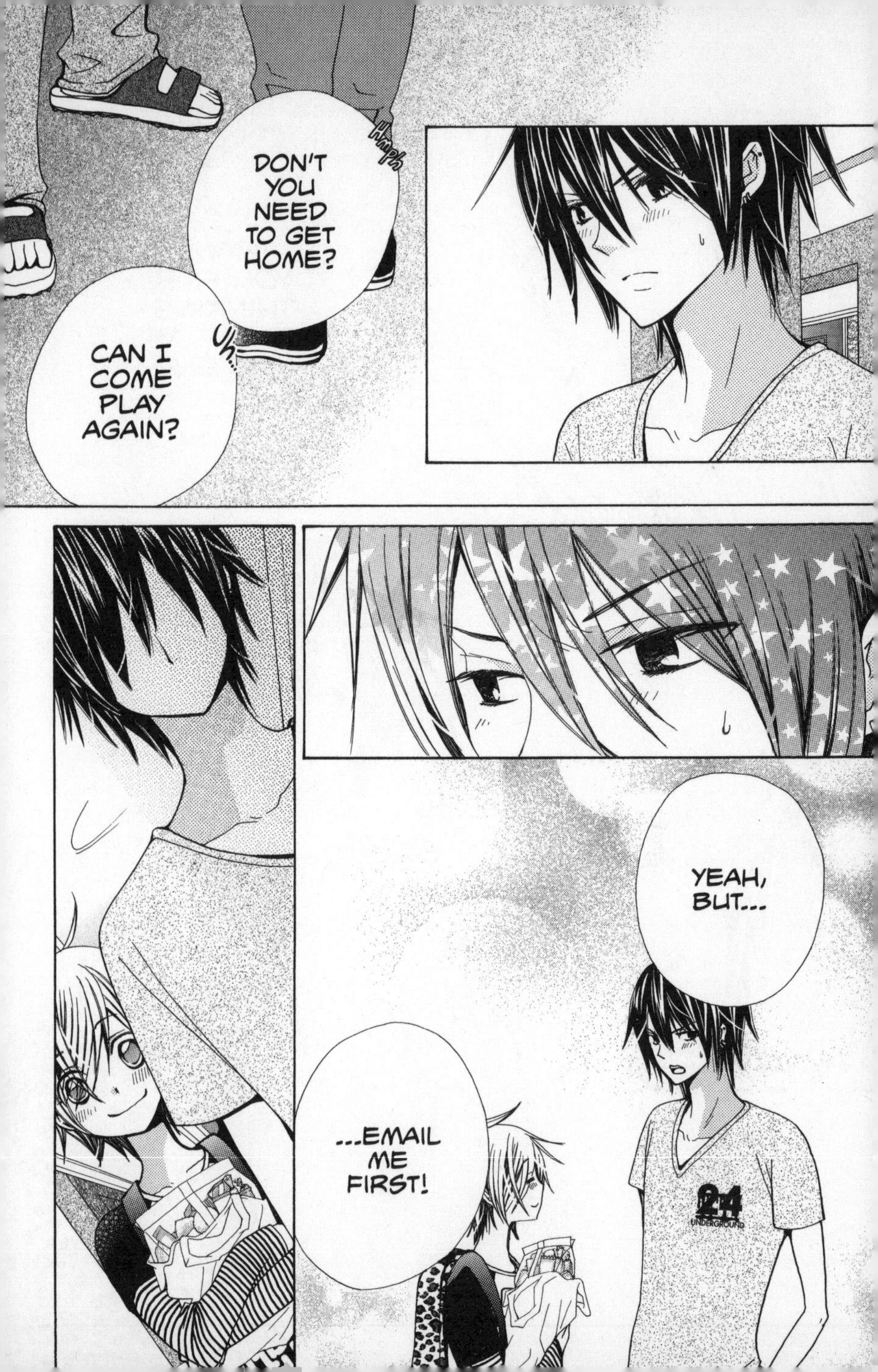
Hmph
DON'T YOU NEED TO GET HOME?
Uh...
CAN I COME PLAY AGAIN?
YEAH, BUT...
...EMAIL ME FIRST!
24 UNDERGROUND

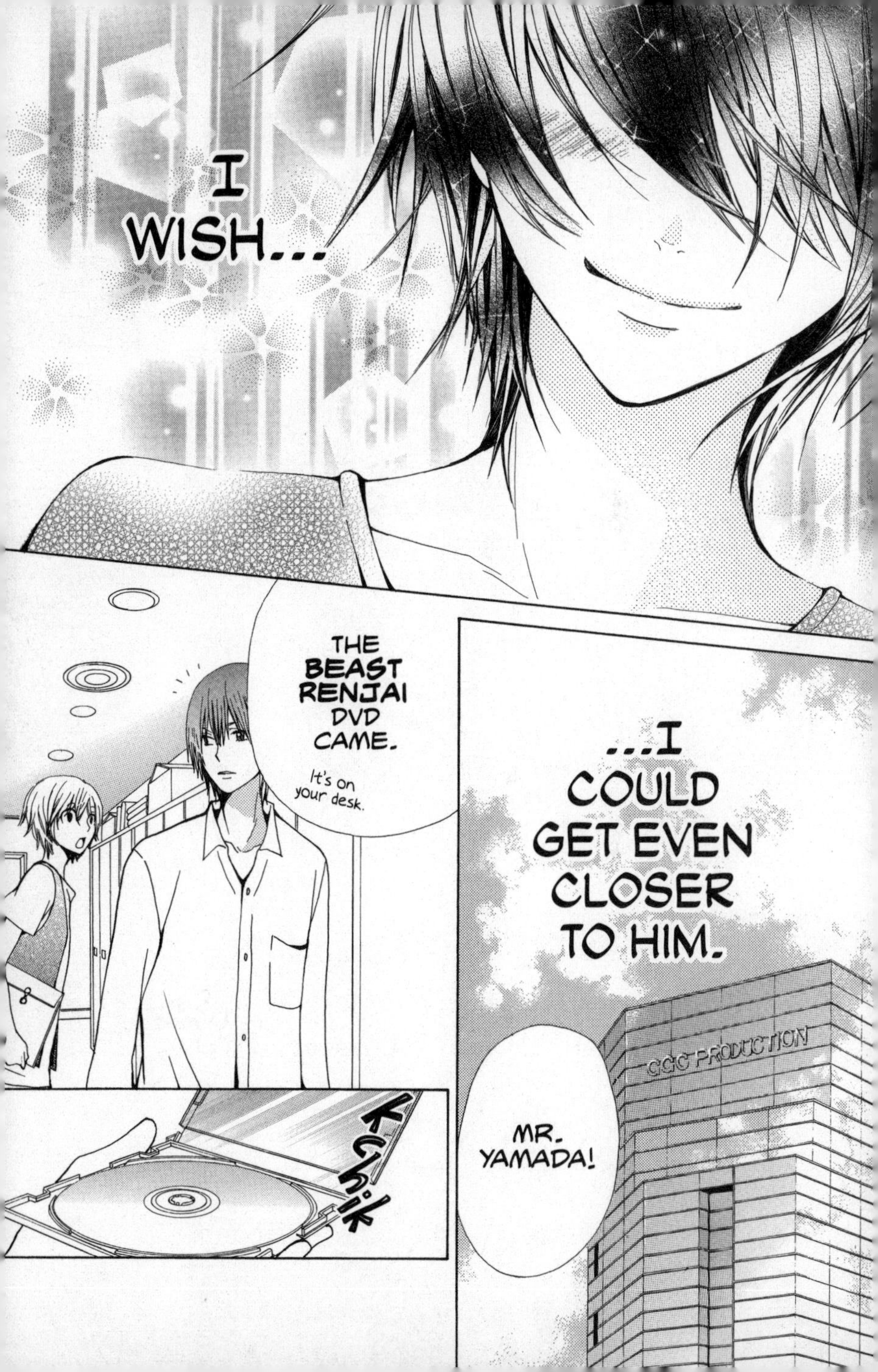
I WISH...
...I COULD GET EVEN CLOSER TO HIM.
GGG PRODUCTION
MR. YAMADA!
THE BEAST RENJAI DVD CAME.
It's on your desk.
Kchik

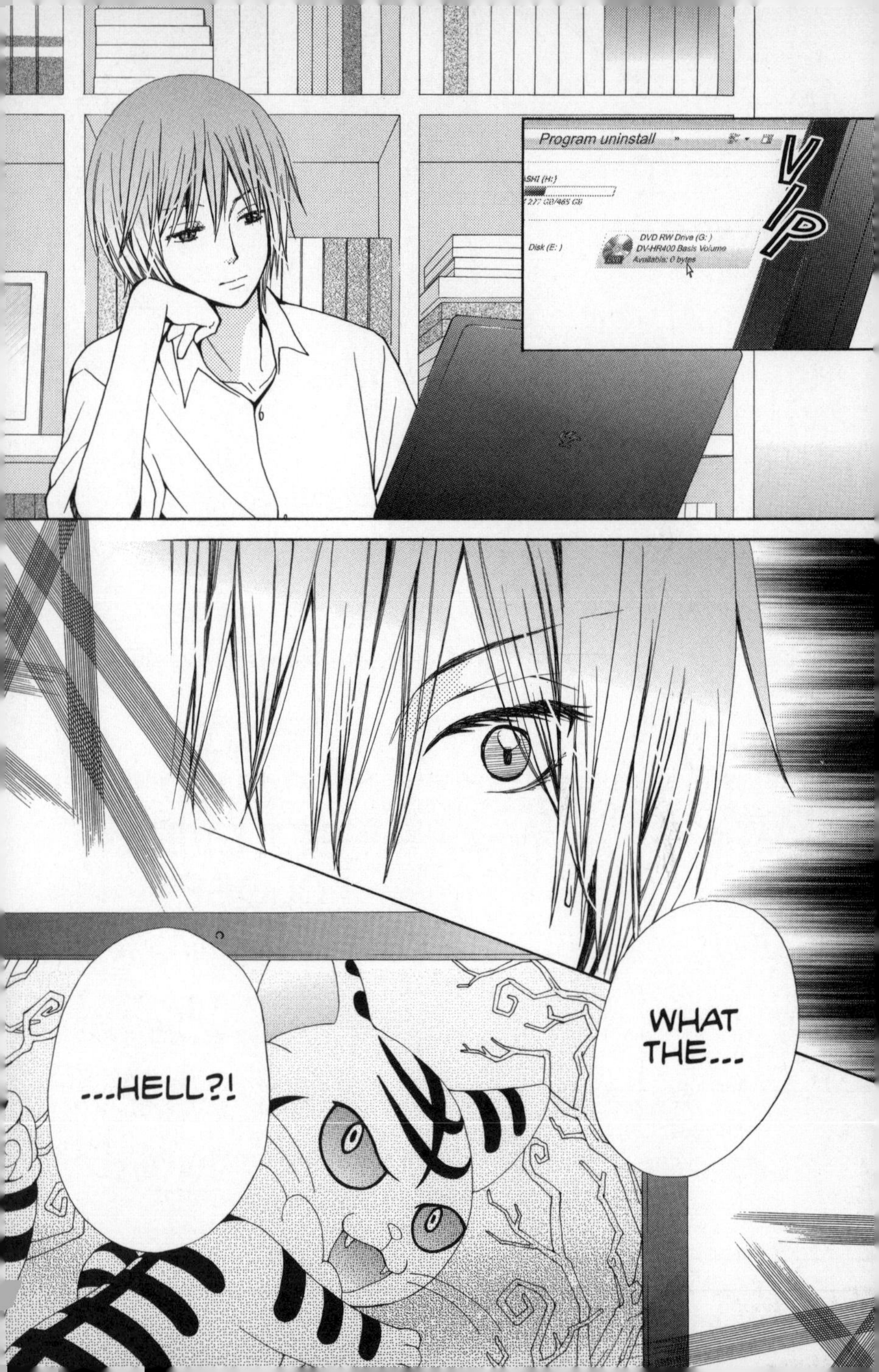
Program uninstall
Disk (E:)
DVD RW Drive (G:)
DV-HR400 Basis Volume
Available: 0 bytes
VIP
WHAT THE...
...HELL?!

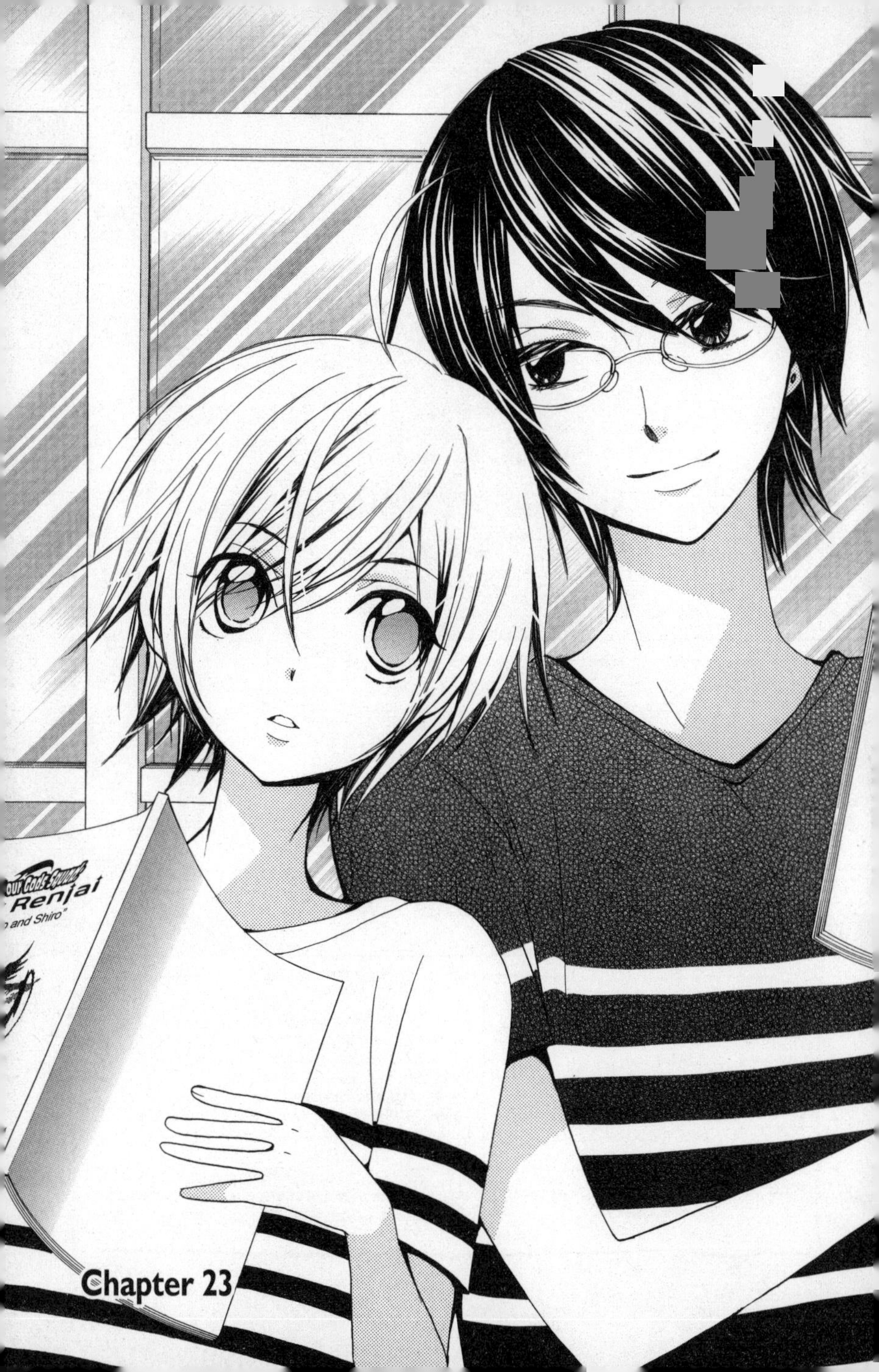
Renjai
and Shiro"
Chapter 23

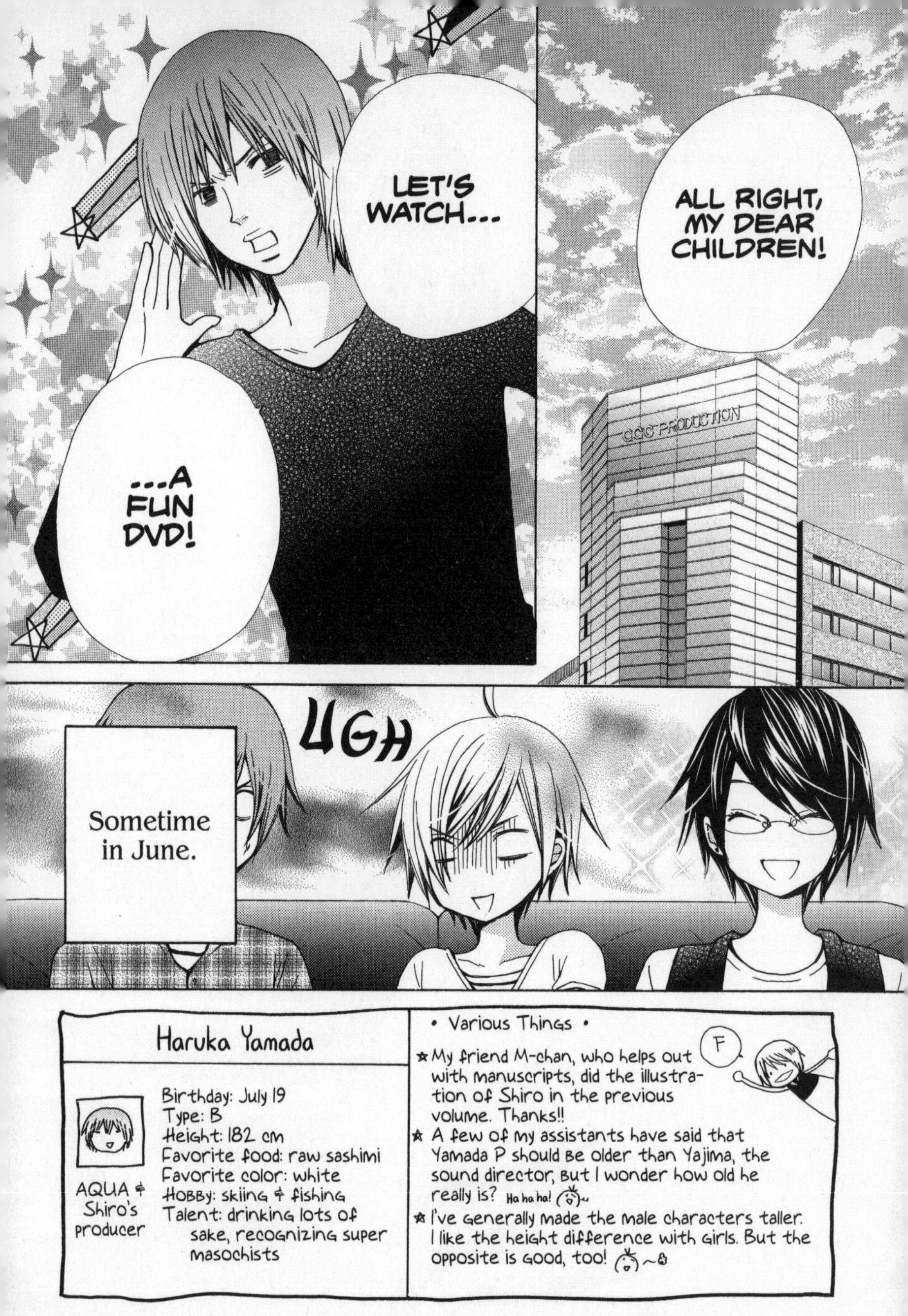
ALL RIGHT, MY DEAR CHILDREN!
LET'S WATCH...
...A FUN DVD!
UGH
Sometime in June.

Haruka Yamada

Birthday: July 19
Type: B
Height: 182 cm
Favorite food: raw sashimi
Favorite color: white
Hobby: skiing & fishing
Talent: drinking lots of sake, recognizing super masochists

AQUA & Shiro's producer

• Various Things •

☆ My friend M-chan, who helps out with manuscripts, did the illustration of Shiro in the previous volume. Thanks!!

☆ A few of my assistants have said that Yamada P should be older than Yajima, the sound director, but I wonder how old he really is? Ha ha ha!

☆ I've generally made the male characters taller. I like the height difference with girls. But the opposite is good, too!

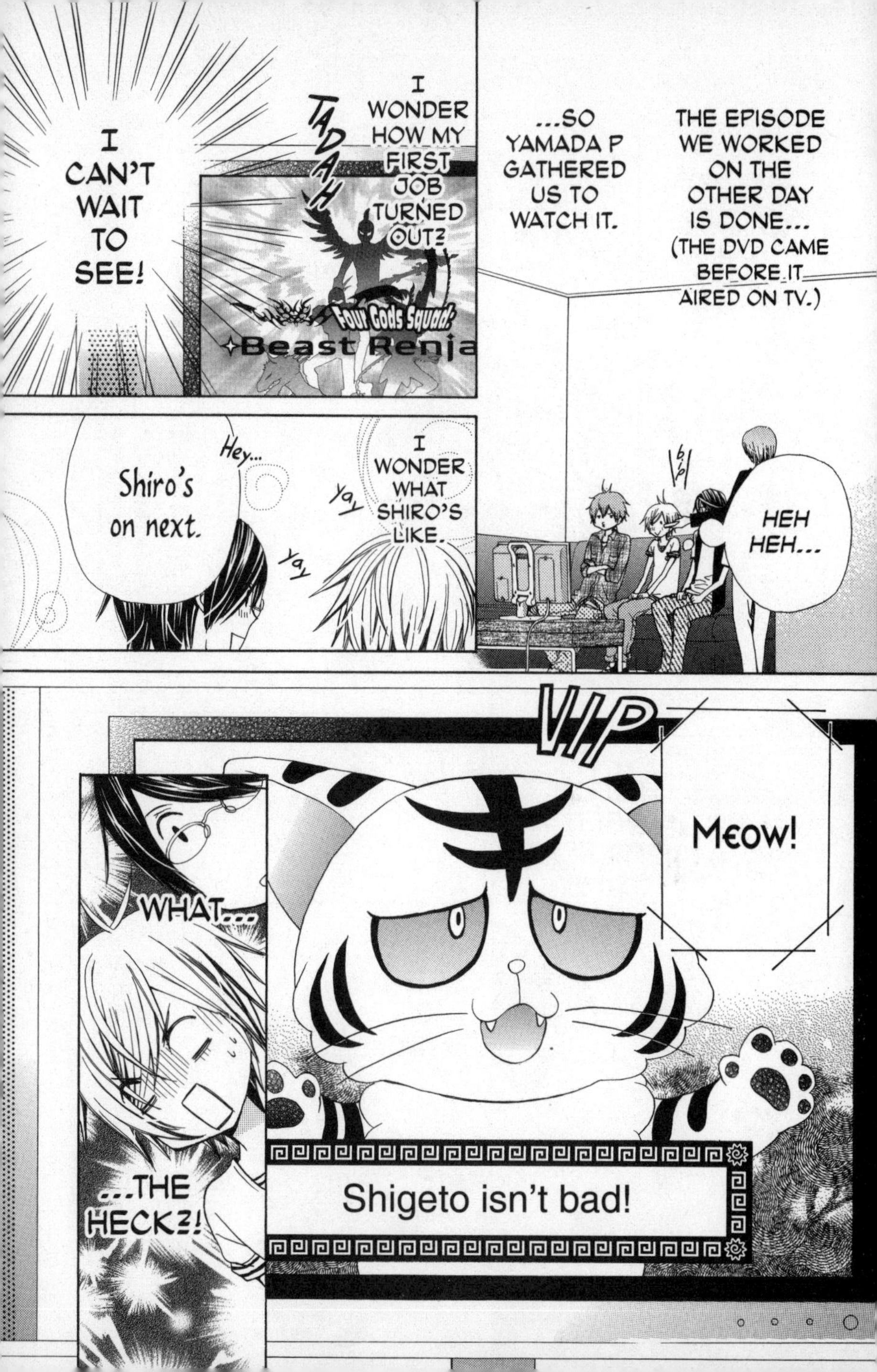
THE EPISODE WE WORKED ON THE OTHER DAY IS DONE... (THE DVD CAME BEFORE IT AIRED ON TV.)
...SO YAMADA P GATHERED US TO WATCH IT.
I WONDER HOW MY FIRST JOB TURNED OUT?
TADAH
Four Gods Squad:
Beast Renja
I CAN'T WAIT TO SEE!
b.p
HEH HEH...
I WONDER WHAT SHIRO'S LIKE.
yay
yay
Hey...
Shiro's on next.
VIP
Meow!
Shigeto isn't bad!
WHAT...
...THE HECK?!

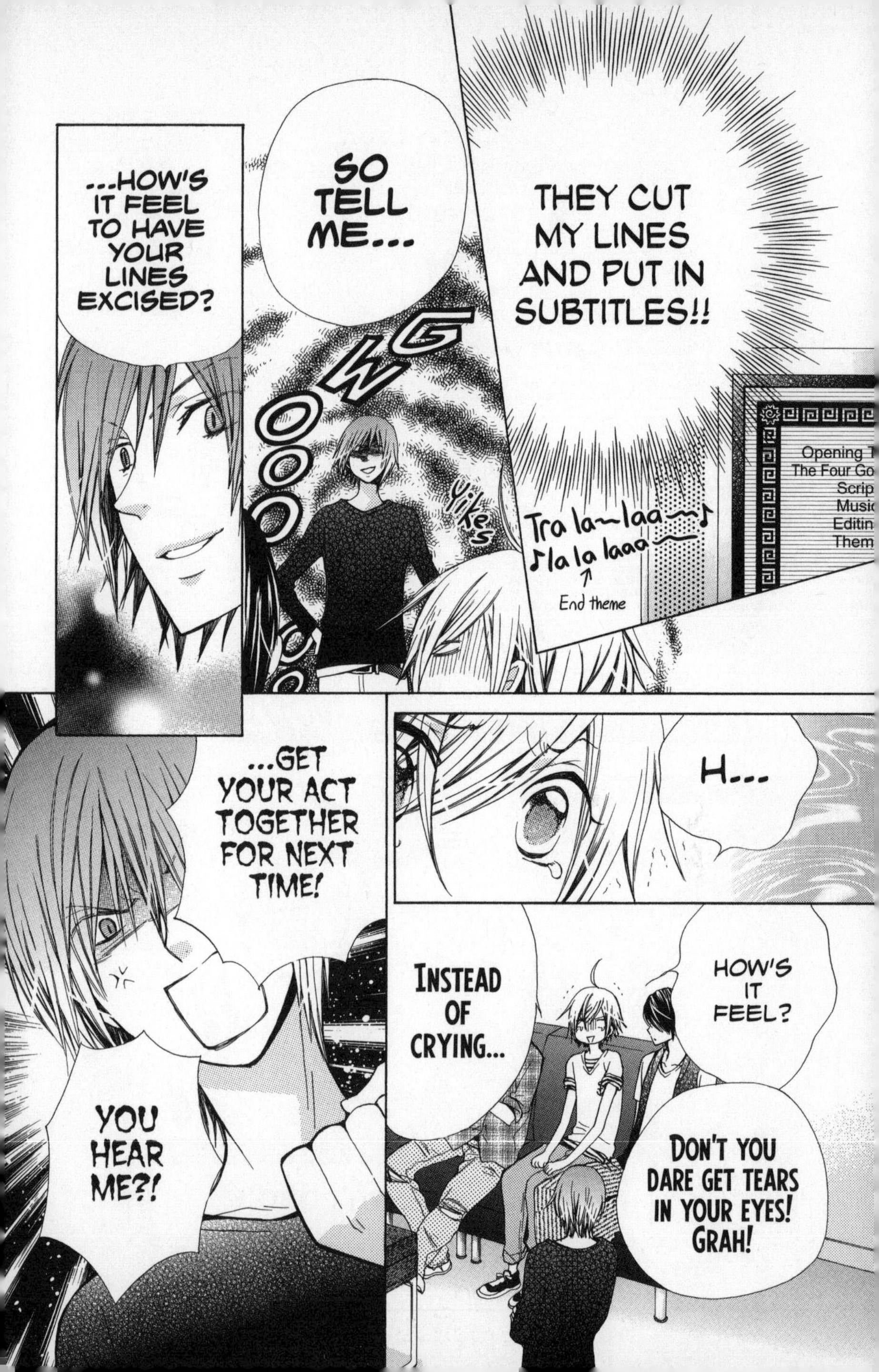
THEY CUT MY LINES AND PUT IN SUBTITLES!!
Opening T
The Four Go
Scrip
Music
Editin
Them
Tra la~laa~♪ ♪la la laaa~
End theme
SO TELL ME...
GWOOOO
Yikes
...HOW'S IT FEEL TO HAVE YOUR LINES EXCISED?
H...
HOW'S IT FEEL?
INSTEAD OF CRYING...
DON'T YOU DARE GET TEARS IN YOUR EYES! GRAH!
...GET YOUR ACT TOGETHER FOR NEXT TIME!
YOU HEAR ME?!

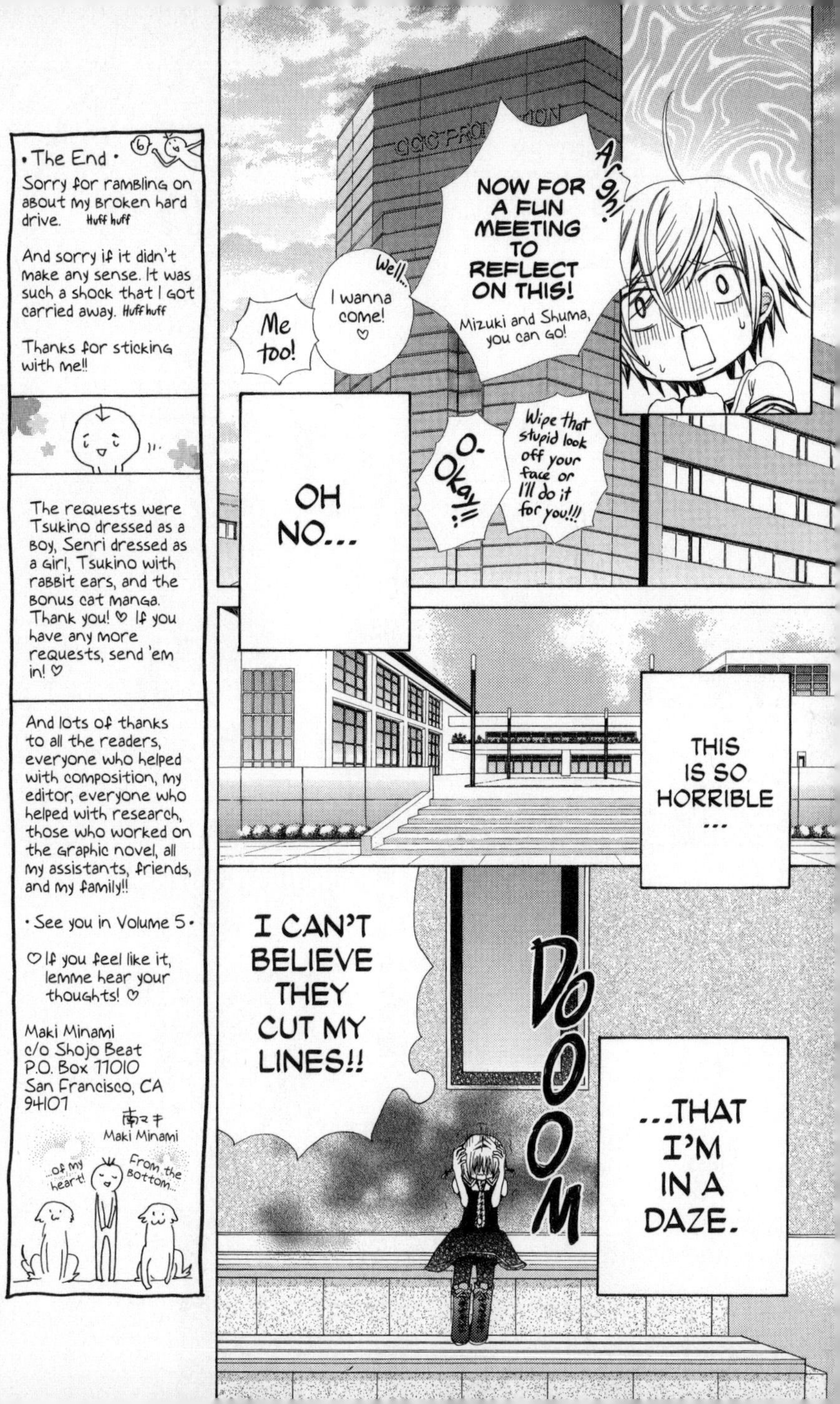
Argh!
NOW FOR A FUN MEETING TO REFLECT ON THIS!
Mizuki and Shuma, you can go!
Well... I wanna come! ♡
Me too!
Wipe that stupid look off your face or I'll do it for you!!!
O-Okay!!
OH NO...
THIS IS SO HORRIBLE...
...THAT I'M IN A DAZE.
DOOOOM
I CAN'T BELIEVE THEY CUT MY LINES!!

• The End • ⑥

Sorry for rambling on about my broken hard drive. Huff huff

And sorry if it didn't make any sense. It was such a shock that I got carried away. Huff huff

Thanks for sticking with me!!

The requests were Tsukino dressed as a boy, Senri dressed as a girl, Tsukino with rabbit ears, and the bonus cat manga. Thank you! ♡ If you have any more requests, send 'em in! ♡

And lots of thanks to all the readers, everyone who helped with composition, my editor, everyone who helped with research, those who worked on the graphic novel, all my assistants, friends, and my family!!

• See you in Volume 5 •

♡ If you feel like it, lemme hear your thoughts! ♡

Maki Minami
c/o Shojo Beat
P.O. Box 77010
San Francisco, CA
94107

南マキ
Maki Minami

From the bottom... ...of my heart!

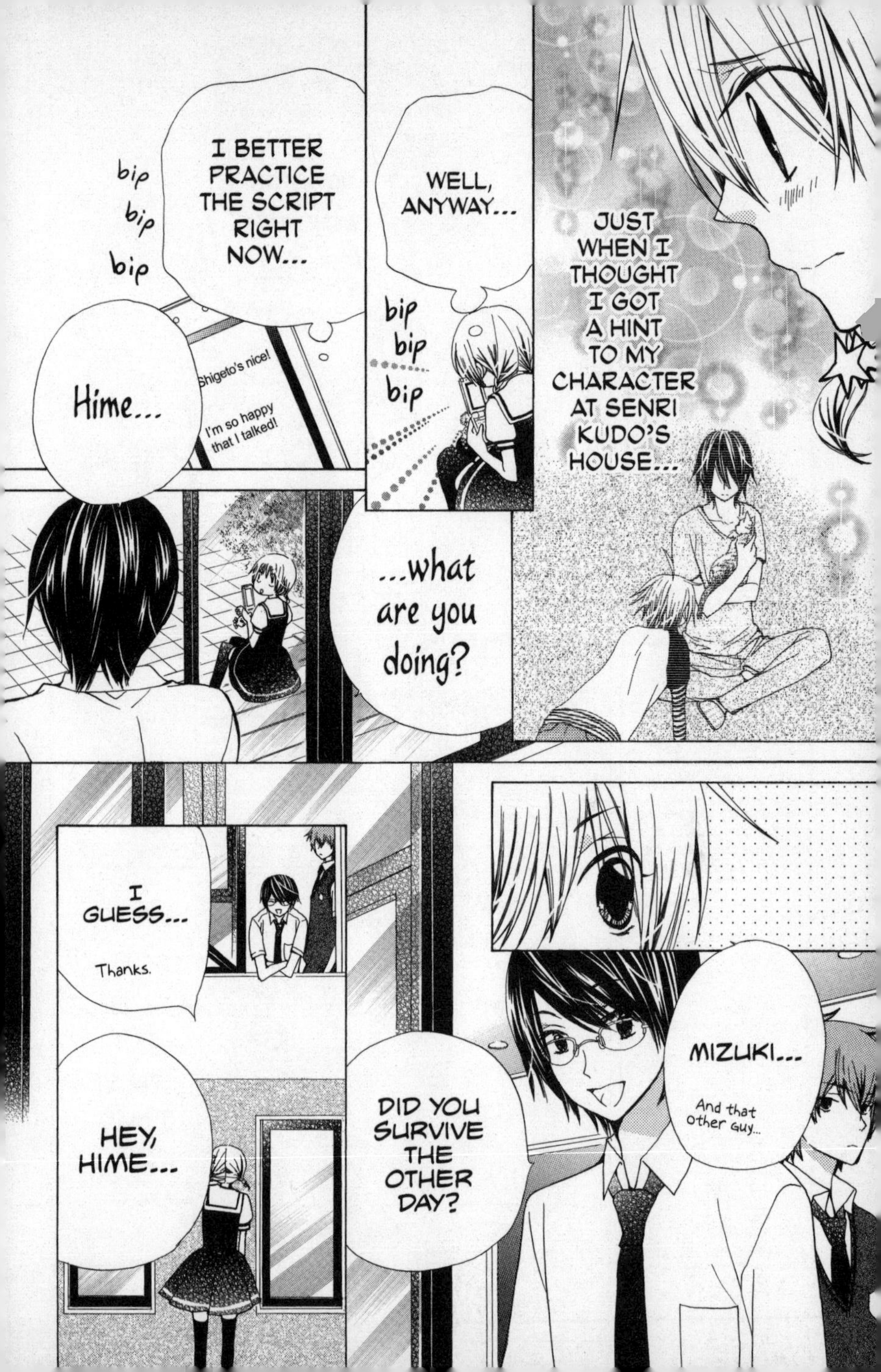

JUST WHEN I THOUGHT I GOT A HINT TO MY CHARACTER AT SENRI KUDO'S HOUSE...
WELL, ANYWAY...
bip bip bip
I BETTER PRACTICE THE SCRIPT RIGHT NOW...
bip bip bip
Shigeto's nice!
I'm so happy that I talked!
Hime...
...what are you doing?
MIZUKI...
And that other guy...
DID YOU SURVIVE THE OTHER DAY?
I GUESS...
Thanks.
HEY, HIME...

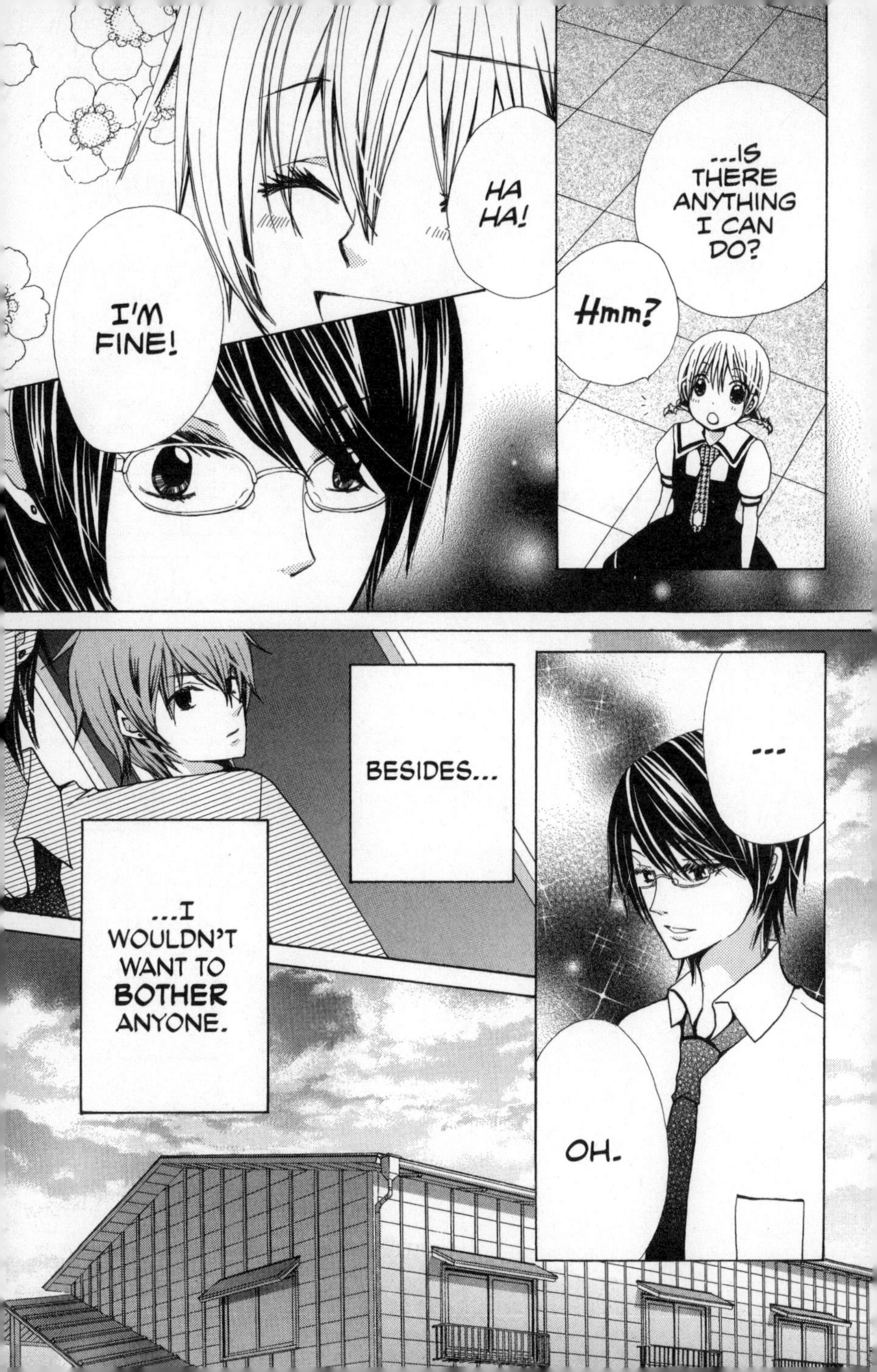
...IS THERE ANYTHING I CAN DO?
Hmm?
HA HA!
I'M FINE!
...
OH.
BESIDES...
...I WOULDN'T WANT TO BOTHER ANYONE.

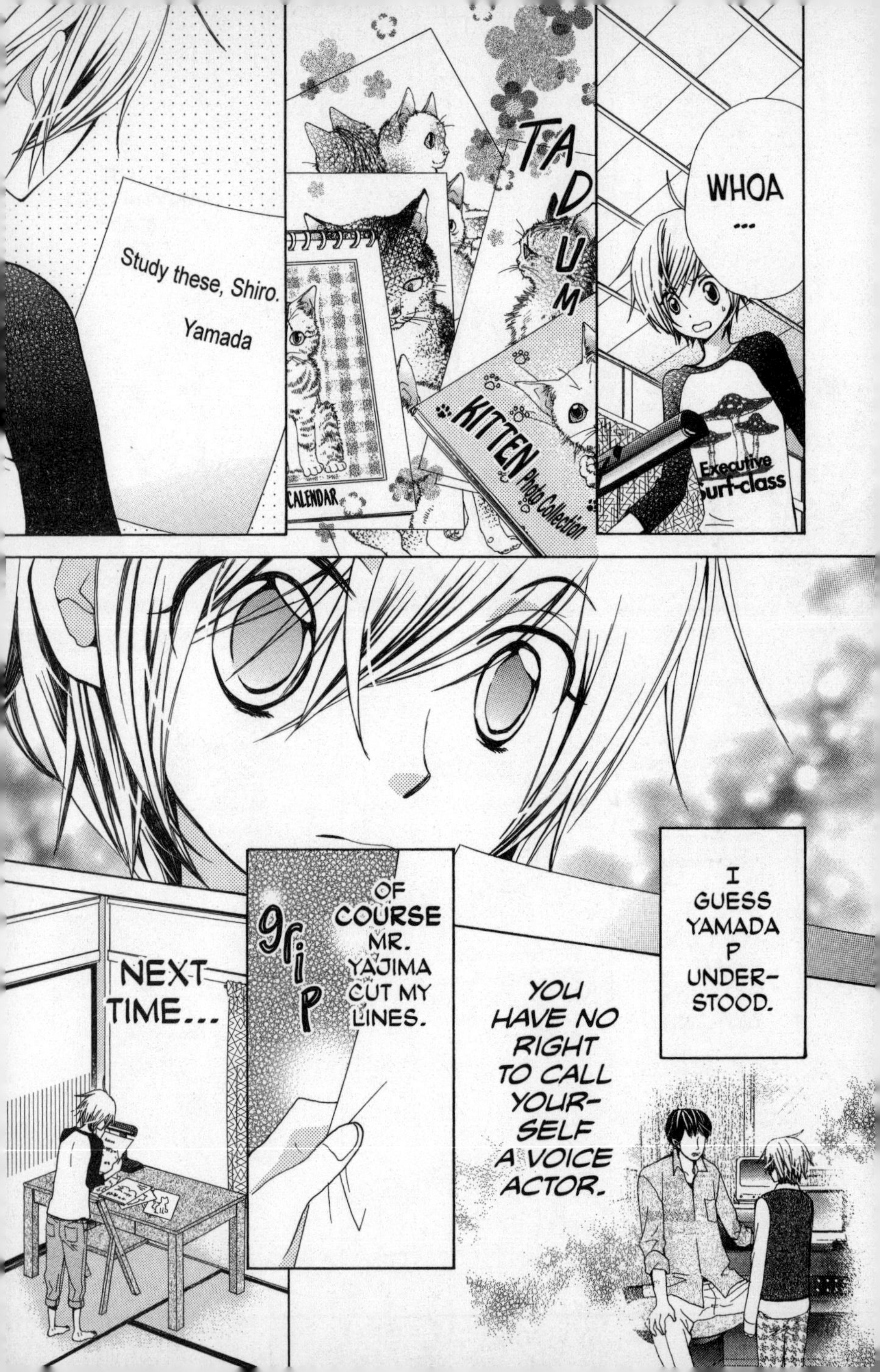
WHOA ...
TADUM
KITTEN Photo Collection
CALENDAR
Executive Surf-class
Study these, Shiro.
Yamada
I GUESS YAMADA P UNDERSTOOD.
YOU HAVE NO RIGHT TO CALL YOURSELF A VOICE ACTOR.
OF COURSE MR. YAJIMA CUT MY LINES.
grip
NEXT TIME...

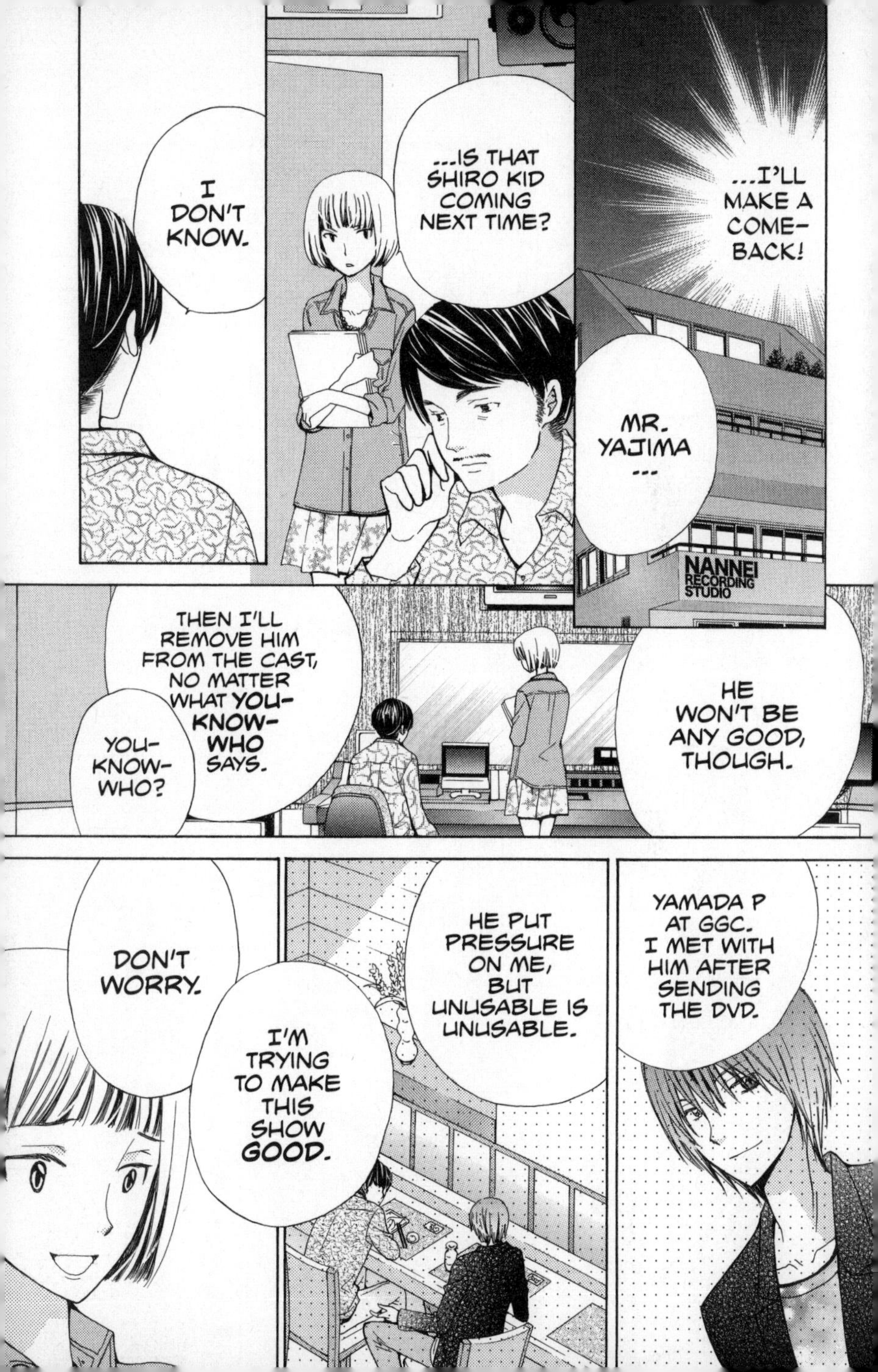
...I'LL MAKE A COME-BACK!
MR. YAJIMA...
NANNEI RECORDING STUDIO
...IS THAT SHIRO KID COMING NEXT TIME?
I DON'T KNOW.
HE WON'T BE ANY GOOD, THOUGH.
THEN I'LL REMOVE HIM FROM THE CAST, NO MATTER WHAT YOU-KNOW-WHO SAYS.
YOU-KNOW-WHO?
YAMADA P AT GGC. I MET WITH HIM AFTER SENDING THE DVD.
HE PUT PRESSURE ON ME, BUT UNUSABLE IS UNUSABLE.
DON'T WORRY.
I'M TRYING TO MAKE THIS SHOW GOOD.

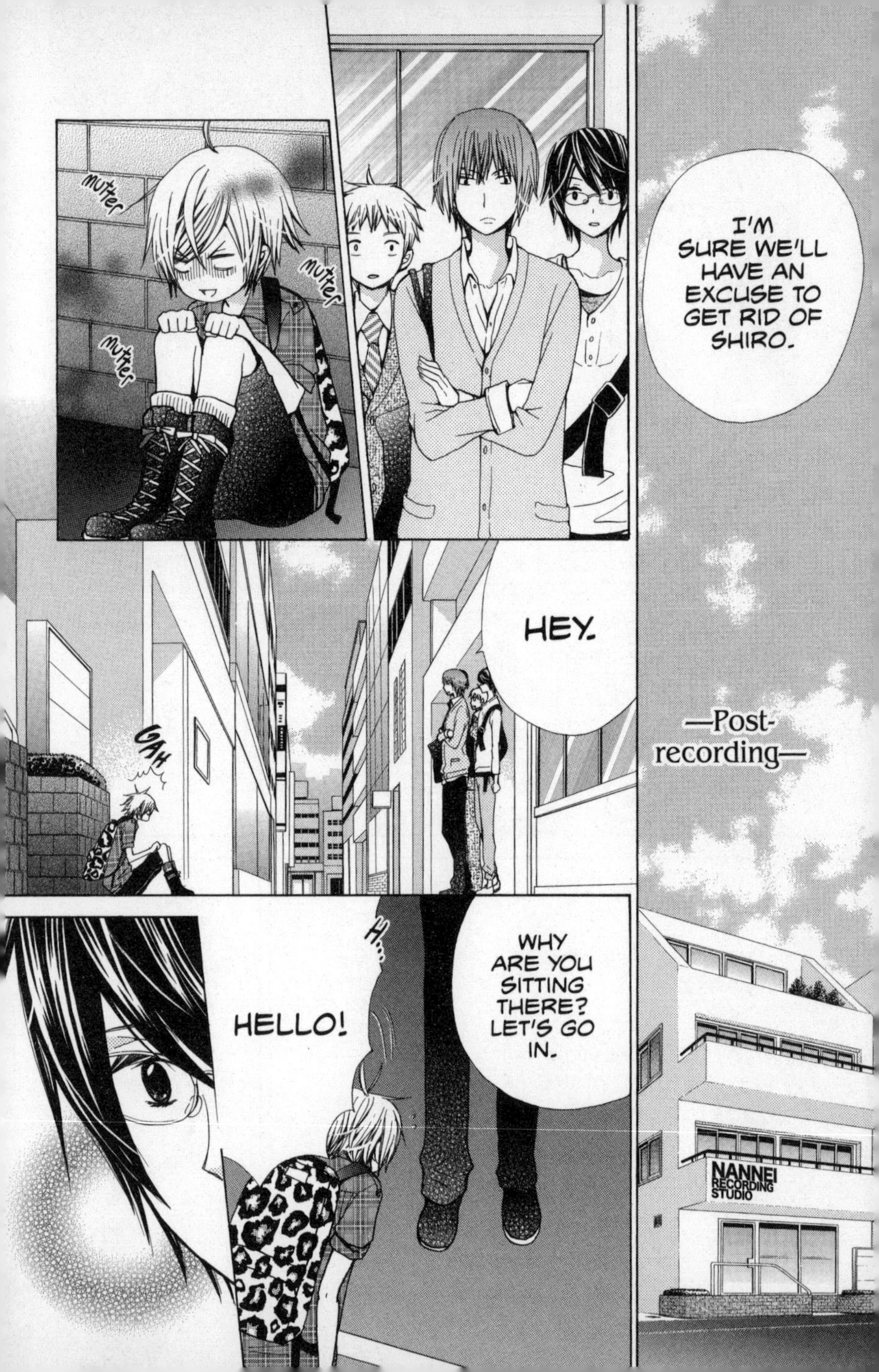
I'M SURE WE'LL HAVE AN EXCUSE TO GET RID OF SHIRO.
—Post-recording—
NANNEI RECORDING STUDIO
mutter
mutter
mutter
HEY.
GAH
WHY ARE YOU SITTING THERE? LET'S GO IN.
H...
HELLO!

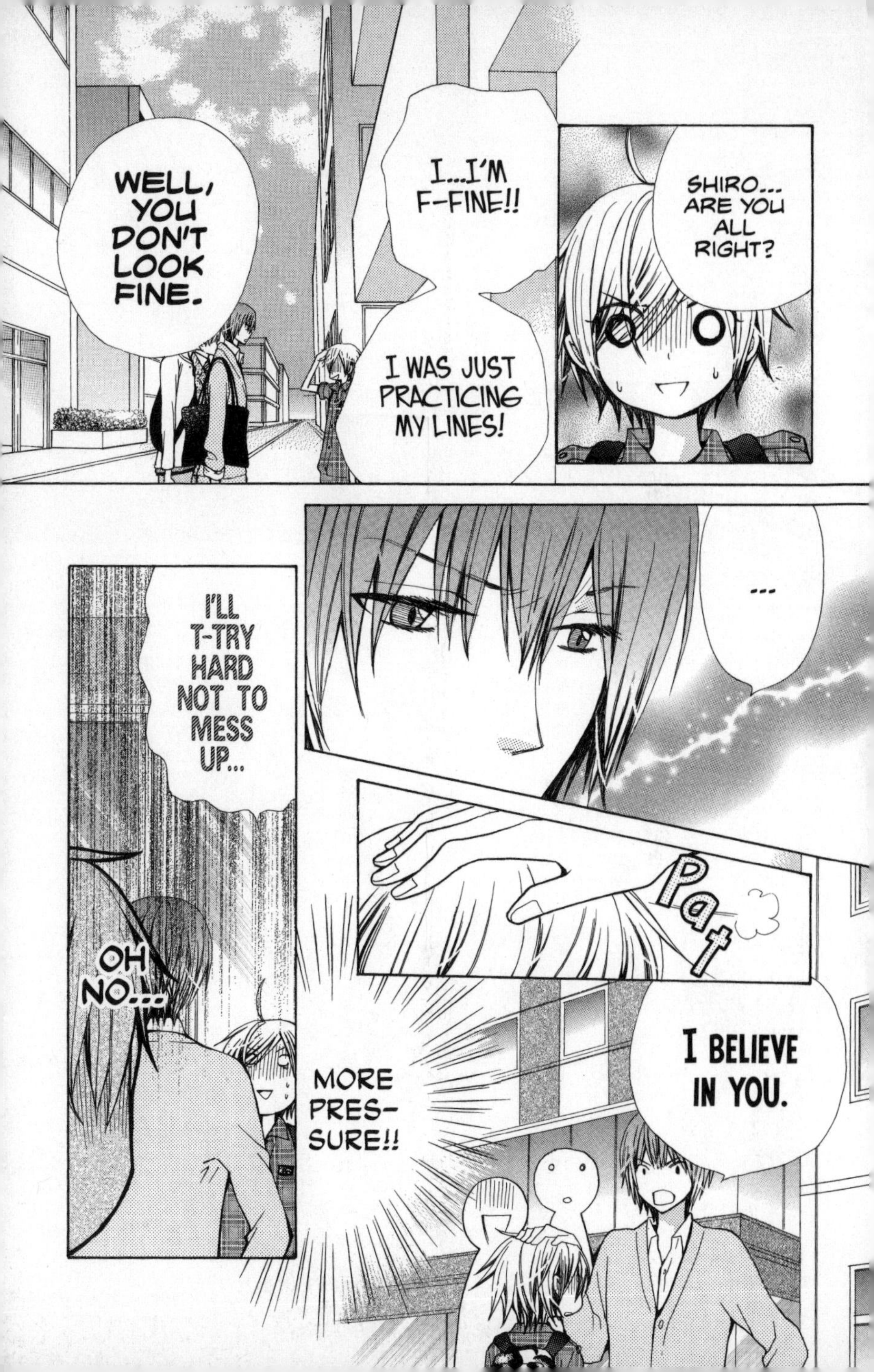
SHIRO... ARE YOU ALL RIGHT?
I...I'M F-FINE!!
I WAS JUST PRACTICING MY LINES!
WELL, YOU DON'T LOOK FINE.
...
Pat
I BELIEVE IN YOU.
MORE PRES-SURE!!
I'LL T-TRY HARD NOT TO MESS UP...
OH NO...

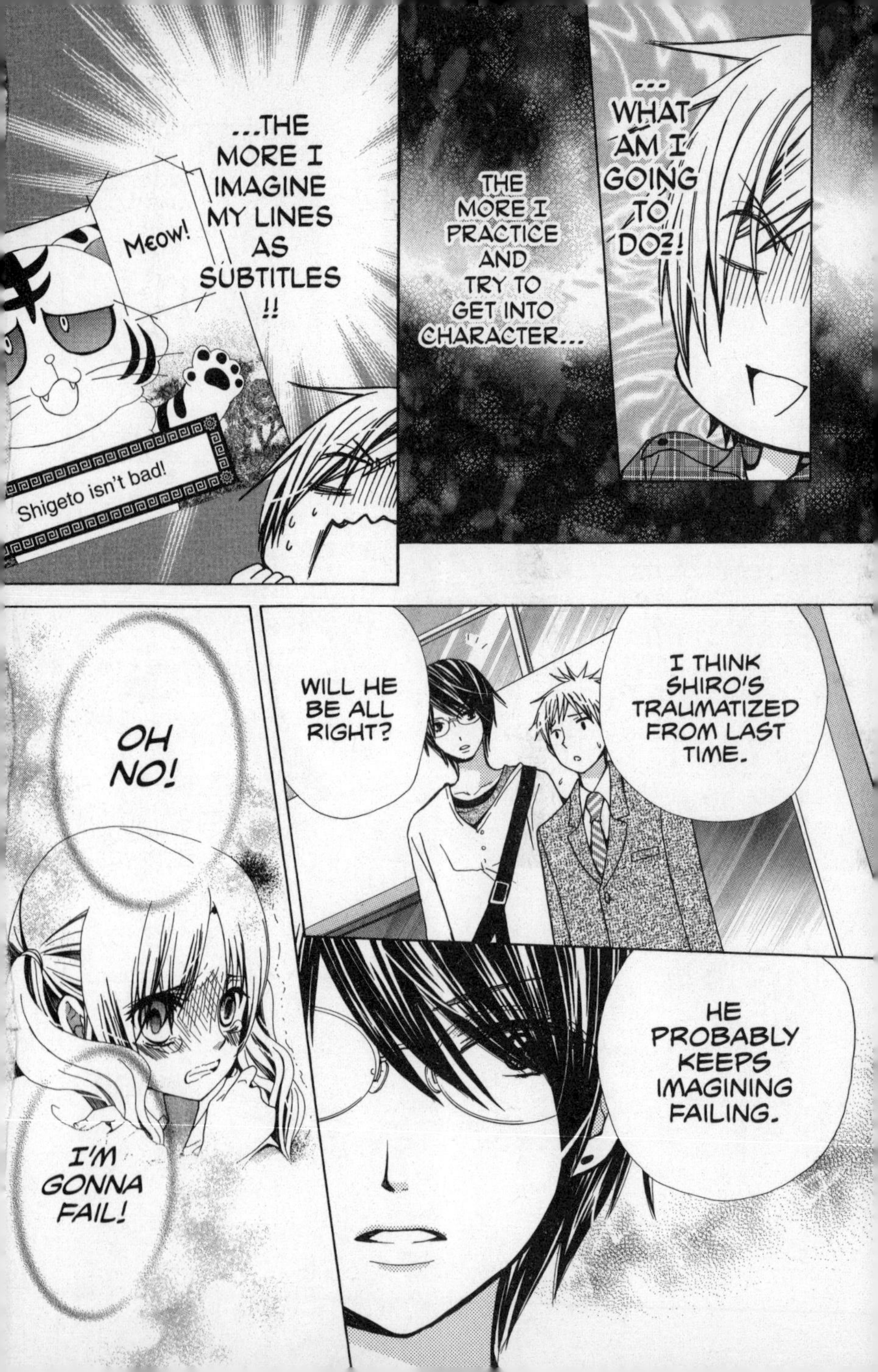

... WHAT AM I GOING TO DO?!
THE MORE I PRACTICE AND TRY TO GET INTO CHARACTER...
...THE MORE I IMAGINE MY LINES AS SUBTITLES!!
Meow!
Shigeto isn't bad!
I THINK SHIRO'S TRAUMATIZED FROM LAST TIME.
WILL HE BE ALL RIGHT?
HE PROBABLY KEEPS IMAGINING FAILING.
OH NO!
I'M GONNA FAIL!

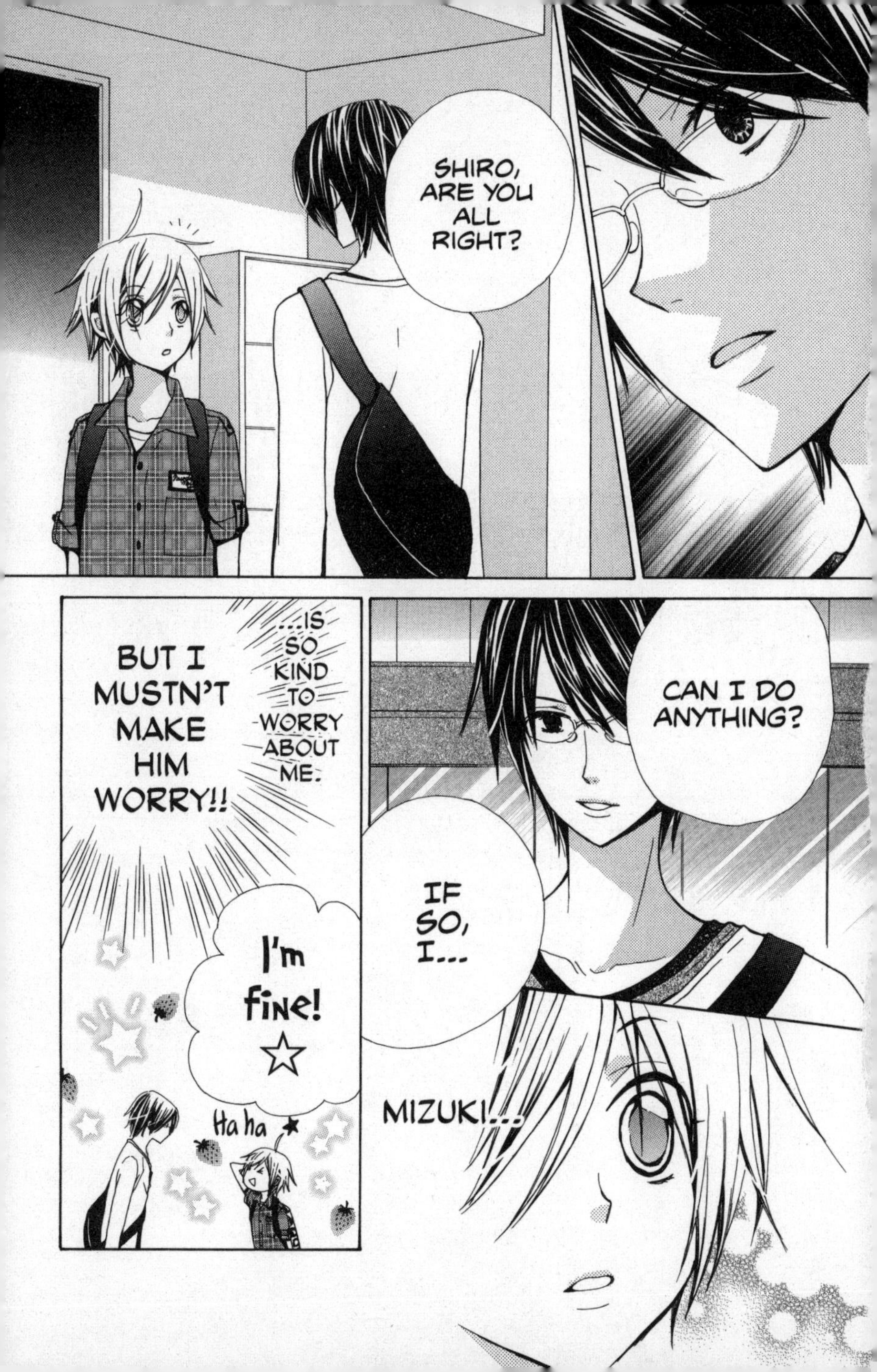
SHIRO, ARE YOU ALL RIGHT?
CAN I DO ANYTHING?
IF SO, I...
MIZUKI...
...IS SO KIND TO WORRY ABOUT ME.
BUT I MUSTN'T MAKE HIM WORRY!!
I'm fine! ☆
Ha ha

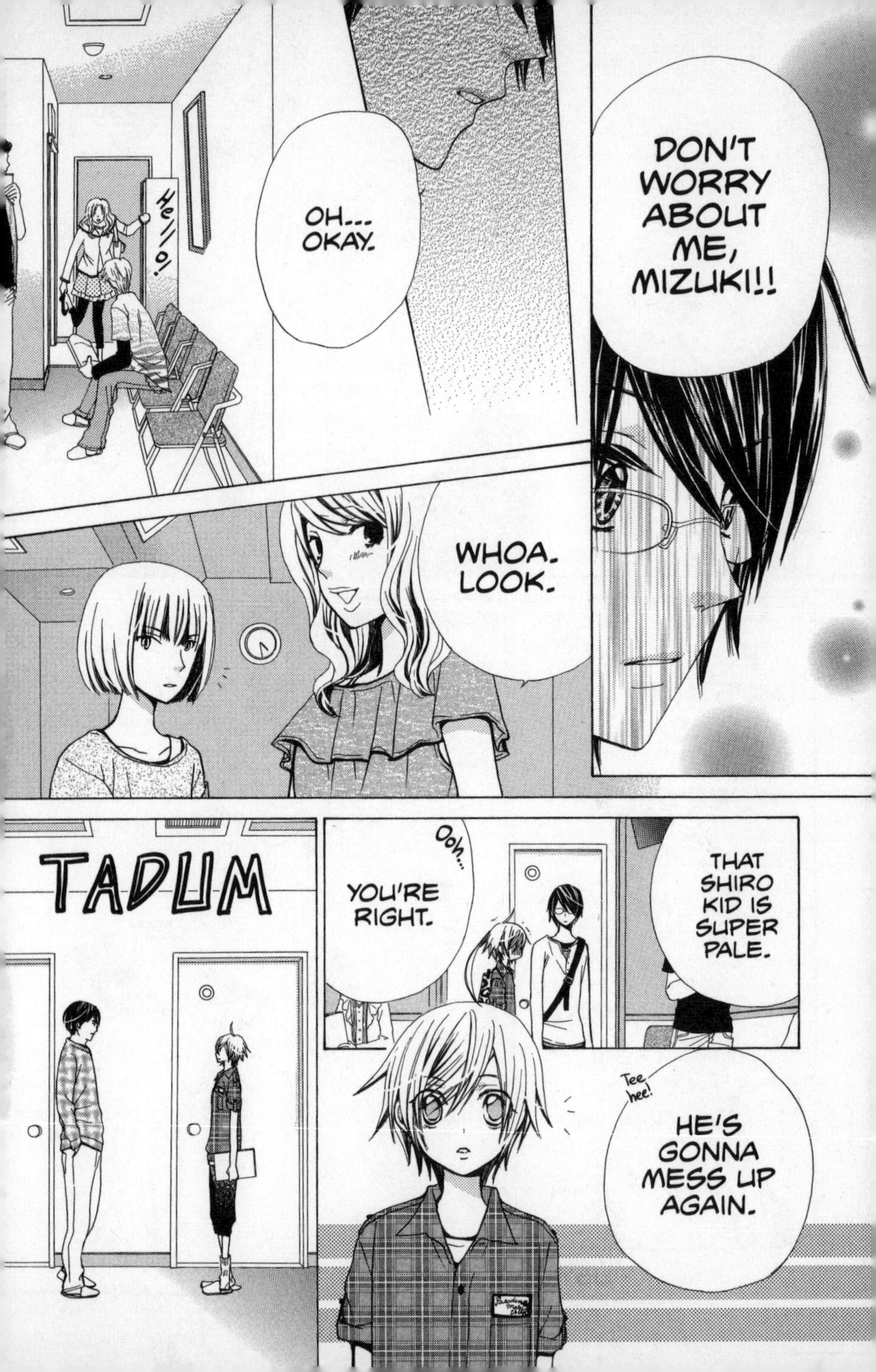
DON'T WORRY ABOUT ME, MIZUKI!!
OH... OKAY.
Hello!
WHOA. LOOK.
THAT SHIRO KID IS SUPER PALE.
Ooh...
YOU'RE RIGHT.
Tee hee!
HE'S GONNA MESS UP AGAIN.
TADUM

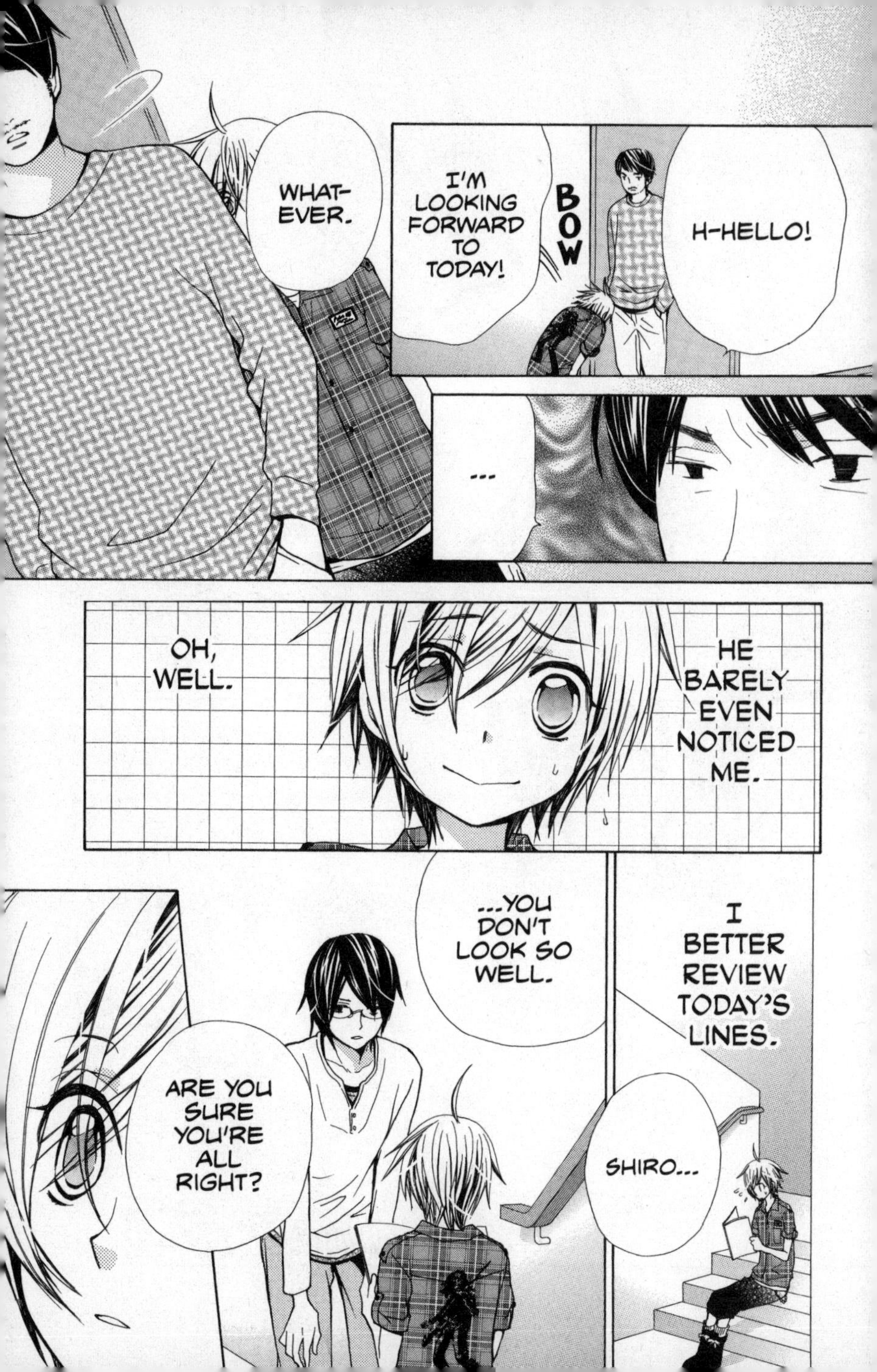
H-HELLO!
I'M LOOKING FORWARD TO TODAY!
BOW
...
WHAT-EVER.
HE BARELY EVEN NOTICED ME.
OH, WELL.
I BETTER REVIEW TODAY'S LINES.
SHIRO...
...YOU DON'T LOOK SO WELL.
ARE YOU SURE YOU'RE ALL RIGHT?

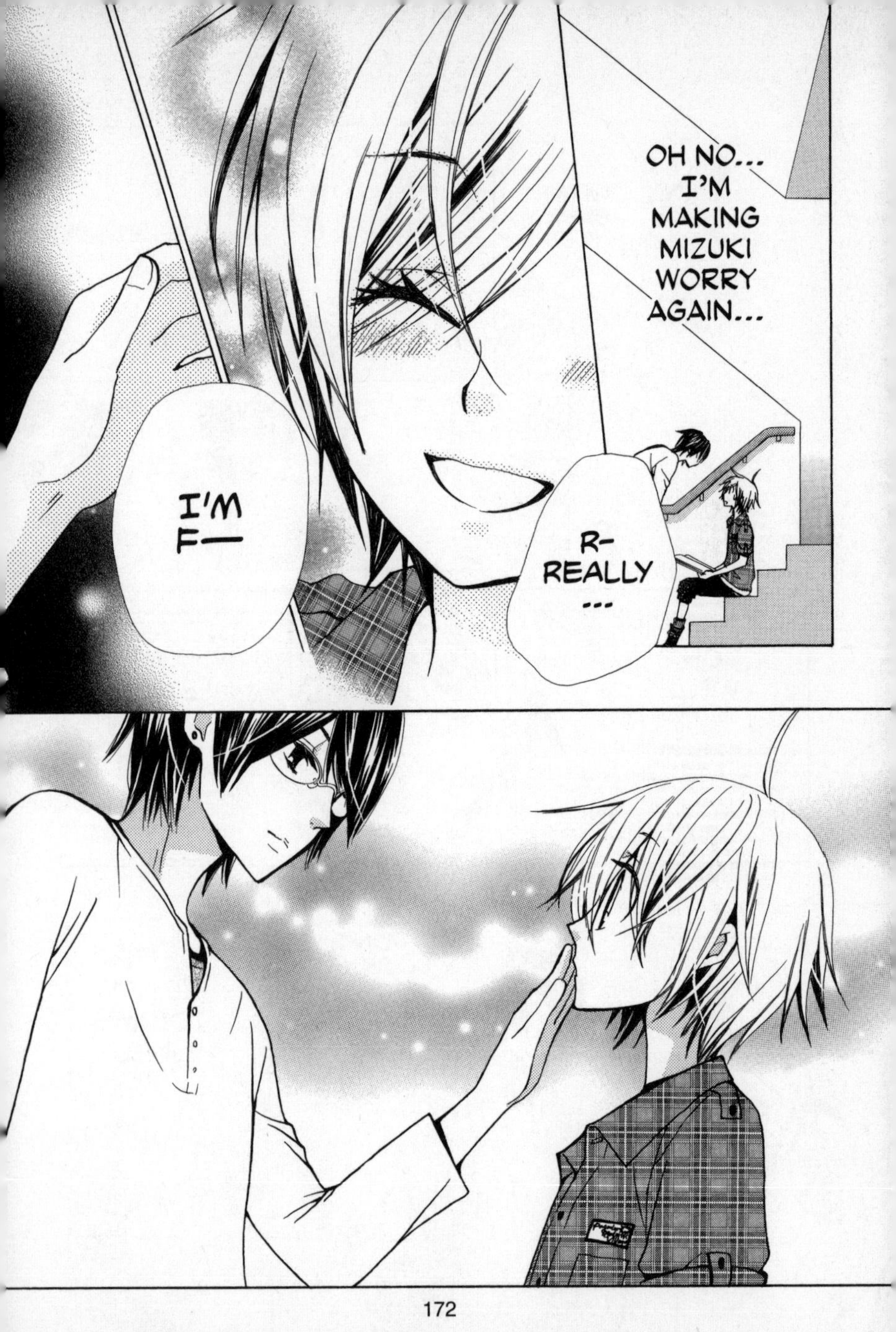
OH NO... I'M MAKING MIZUKI WORRY AGAIN...
R-REALLY ...
I'M F—

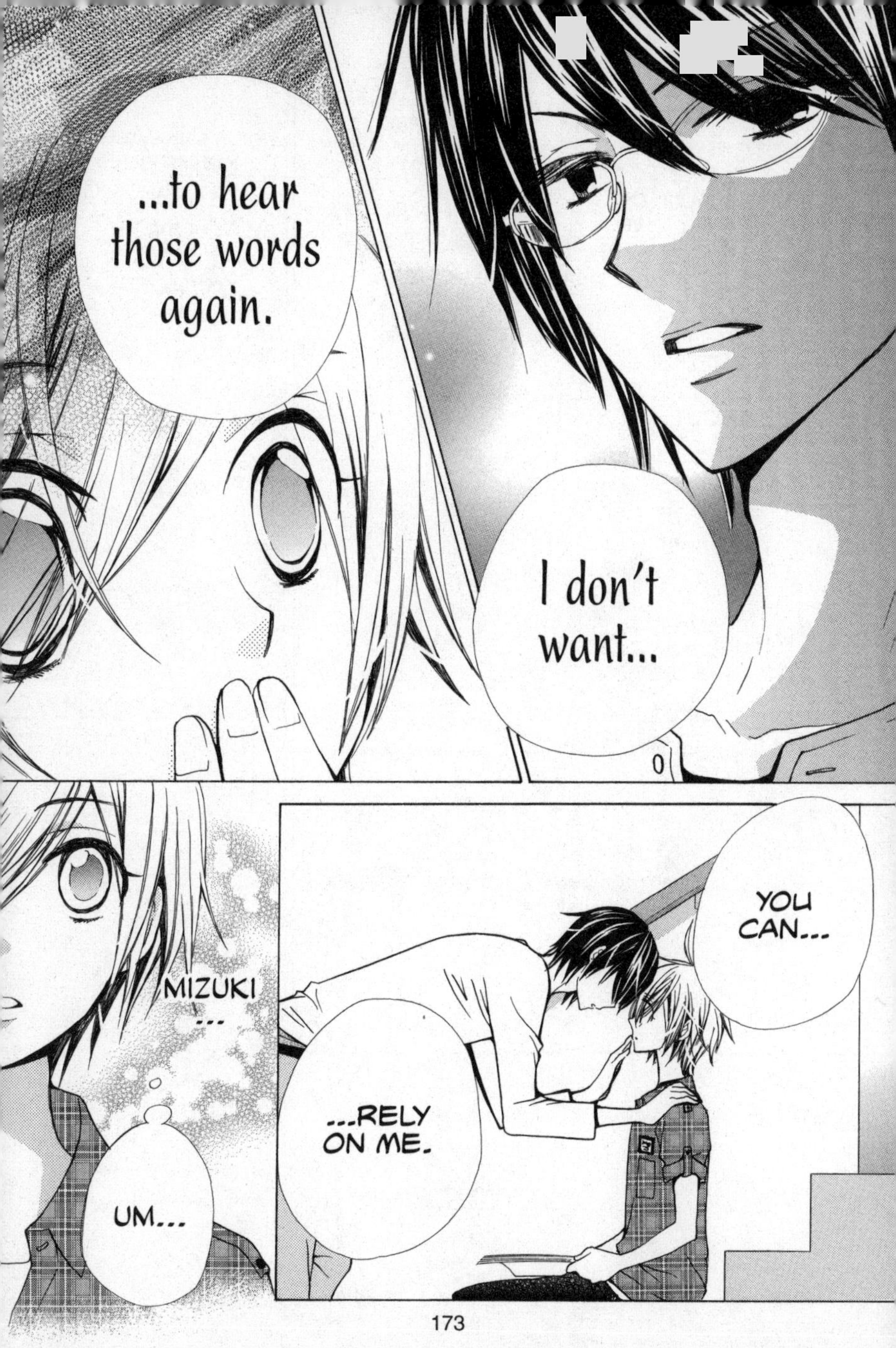
I don't want...
...to hear those words again.
YOU CAN...
...RELY ON ME.
MIZUKI...
UM...

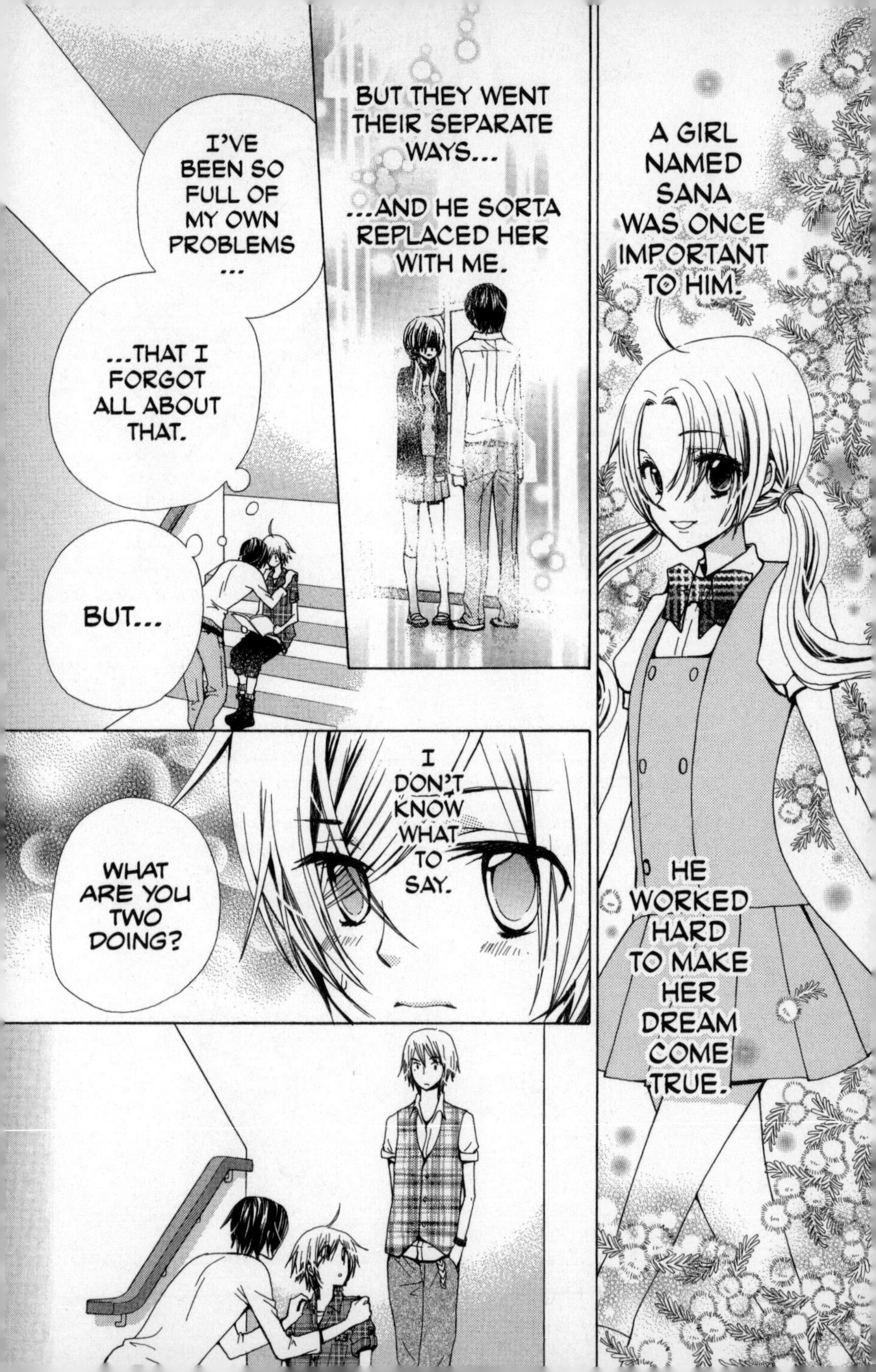
A GIRL NAMED SANA WAS ONCE IMPORTANT TO HIM.
HE WORKED HARD TO MAKE HER DREAM COME TRUE.
BUT THEY WENT THEIR SEPARATE WAYS...
...AND HE SORTA REPLACED HER WITH ME.
I'VE BEEN SO FULL OF MY OWN PROBLEMS...
...THAT I FORGOT ALL ABOUT THAT.
BUT...
I DON'T KNOW WHAT TO SAY.
WHAT ARE YOU TWO DOING?

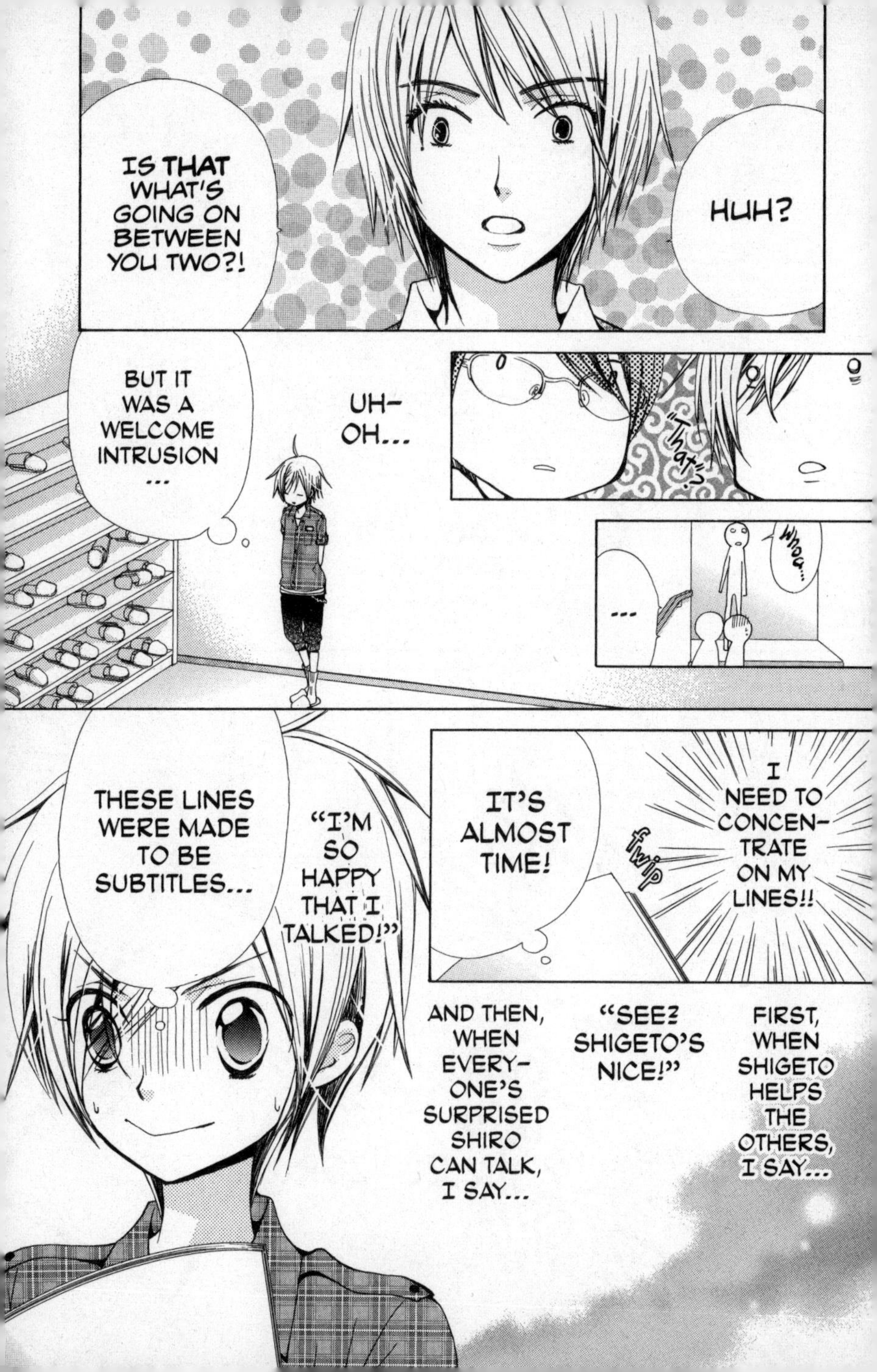
HUH?
IS THAT WHAT'S GOING ON BETWEEN YOU TWO?!
"That"?
whoa...
...
UH-OH...
BUT IT WAS A WELCOME INTRUSION...
I NEED TO CONCENTRATE ON MY LINES!!
fwip
IT'S ALMOST TIME!
FIRST, WHEN SHIGETO HELPS THE OTHERS, I SAY...
"SEE? SHIGETO'S NICE!"
AND THEN, WHEN EVERYONE'S SURPRISED SHIRO CAN TALK, I SAY...
"I'M SO HAPPY THAT I TALKED!"
THESE LINES WERE MADE TO BE SUBTITLES...

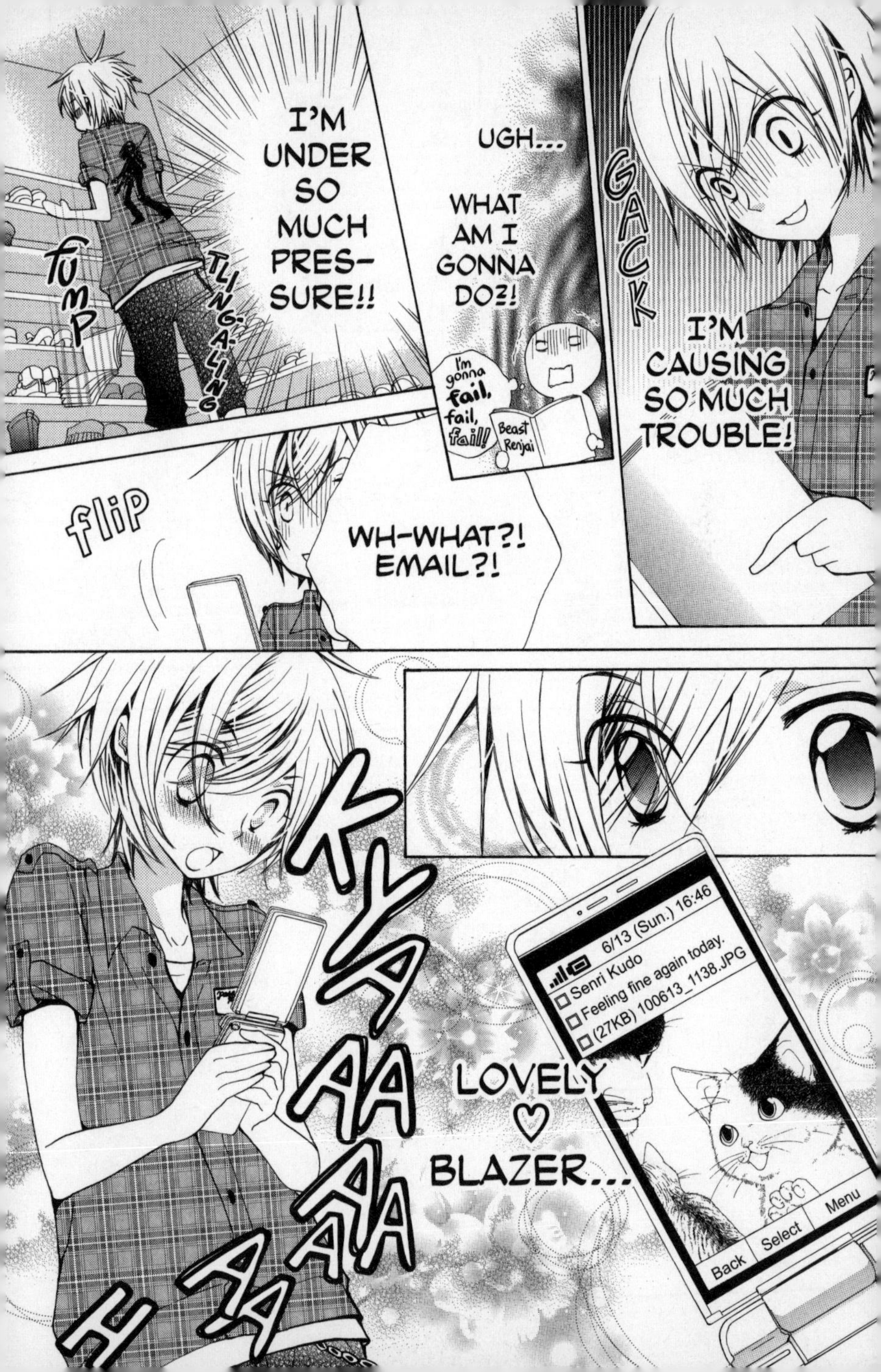
GACK
I'M CAUSING SO MUCH TROUBLE!
UGH...
WHAT AM I GONNA DO?!
I'm gonna fail, fail, fail!
Beast Renjai
I'M UNDER SO MUCH PRESSURE!!
TUMP
TLING-A-LING
WH-WHAT?! EMAIL?!
flip
6/13 (Sun.) 16:46
Senri Kudo
Feeling fine again today.
(27KB) 100613_1138.JPG
Back
Select
Menu
LOVELY ♡ BLAZER...
KYAAAAAAAH

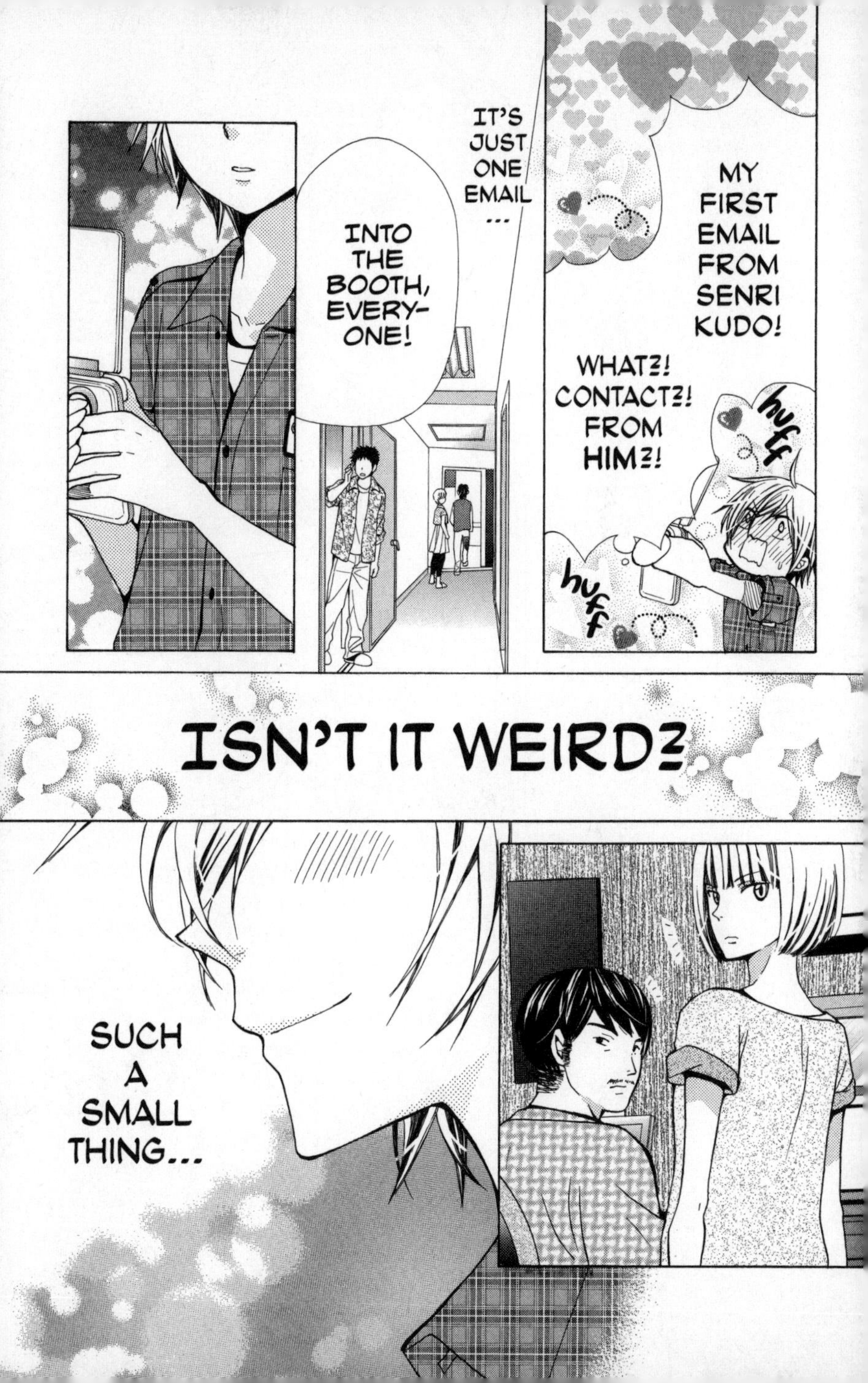
MY FIRST EMAIL FROM SENRI KUDO!
WHAT?! CONTACT?! FROM HIM?!
huff
huff
IT'S JUST ONE EMAIL...
INTO THE BOOTH, EVERYONE!
ISN'T IT WEIRD?
SUCH A SMALL THING...

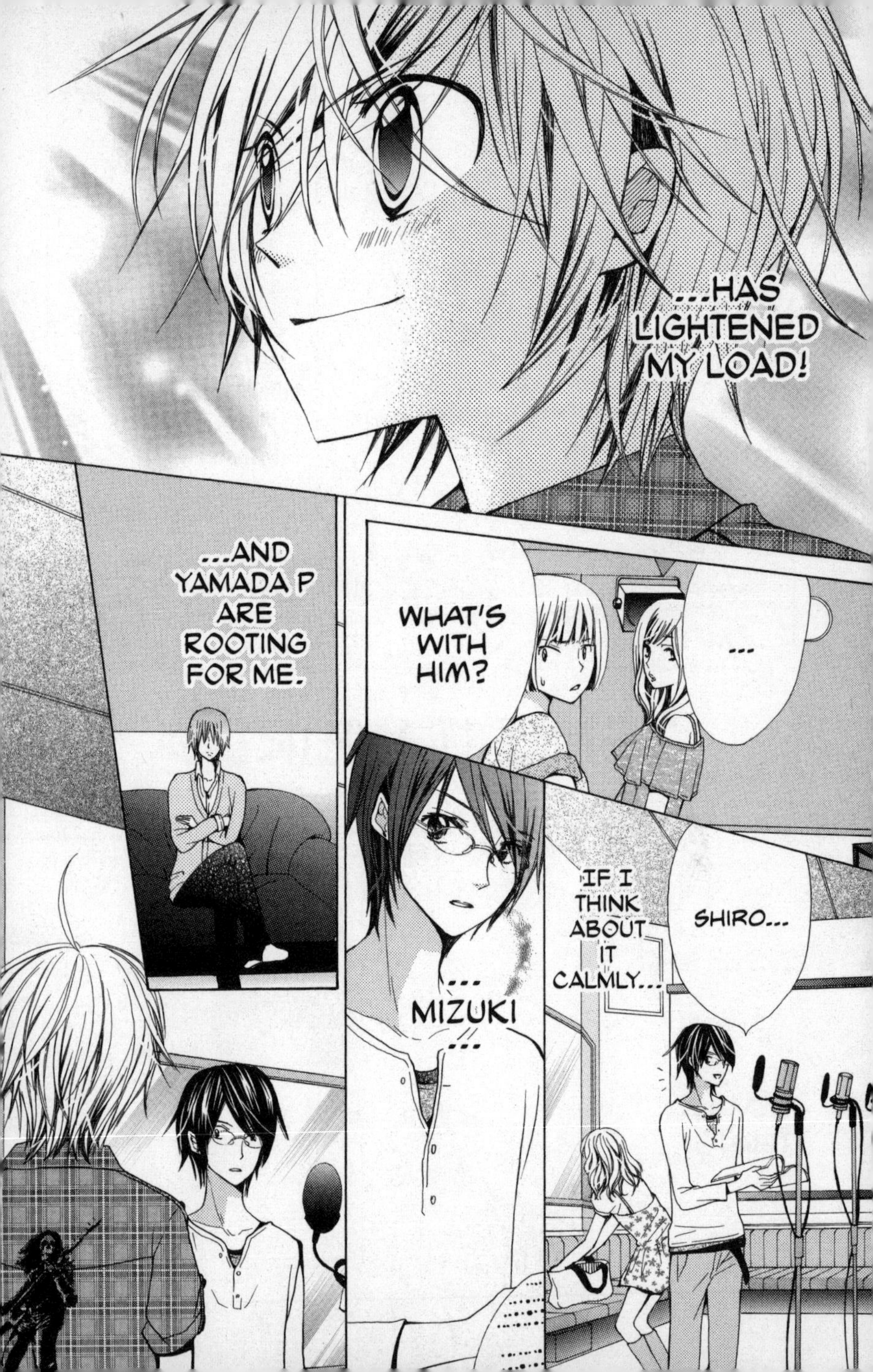
...HAS LIGHTENED MY LOAD!
...
WHAT'S WITH HIM?
...AND YAMADA P ARE ROOTING FOR ME.
SHIRO...
IF I THINK ABOUT IT CALMLY...
...MIZUKI...

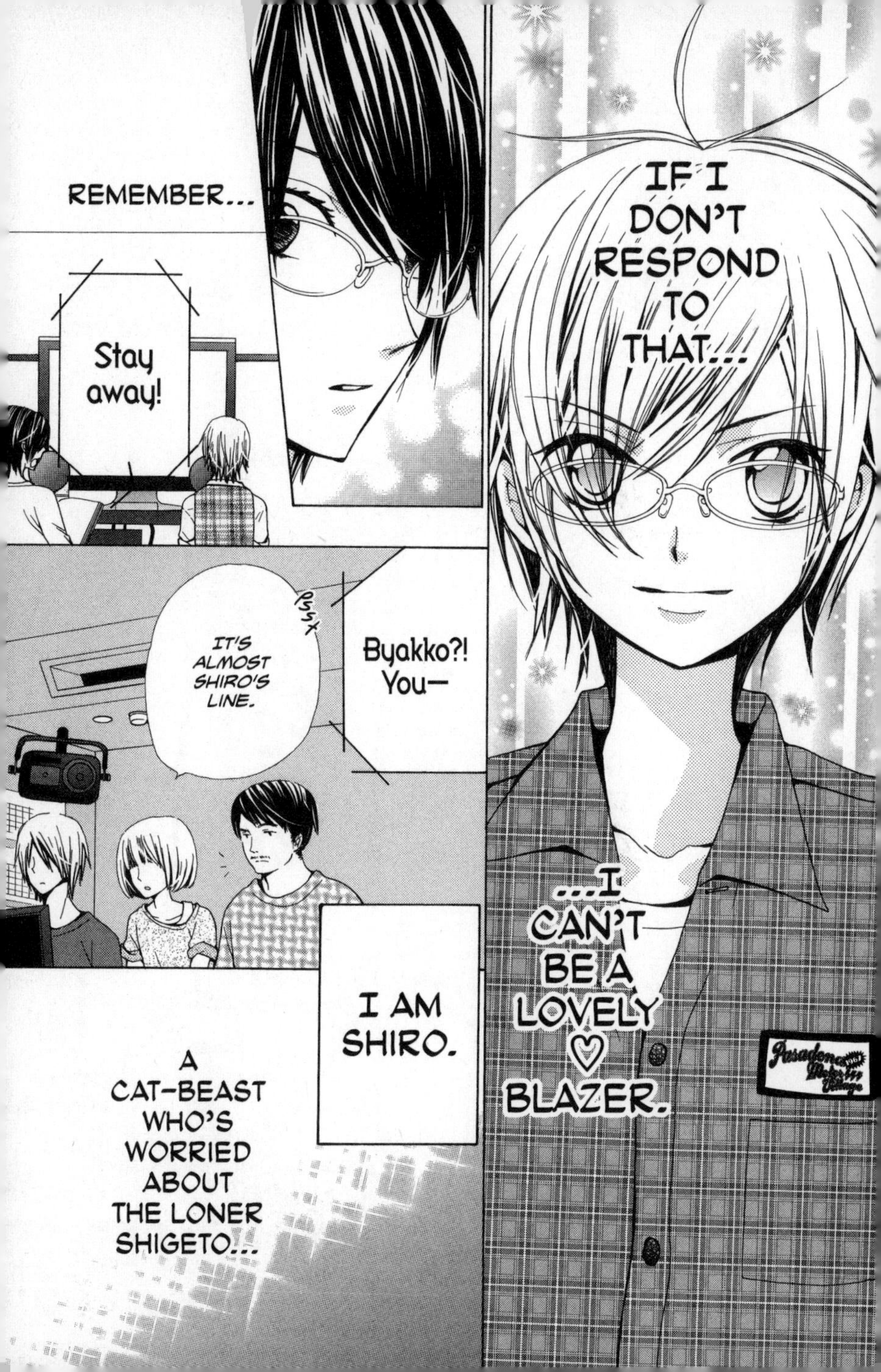
IF I DON'T RESPOND TO THAT...
...I CAN'T BE A LOVELY ♡ BLAZER.
REMEMBER...
Stay away!
Byakko?! You—
Psst
IT'S ALMOST SHIRO'S LINE.
I AM SHIRO.
A CAT-BEAST WHO'S WORRIED ABOUT THE LONER SHIGETO...

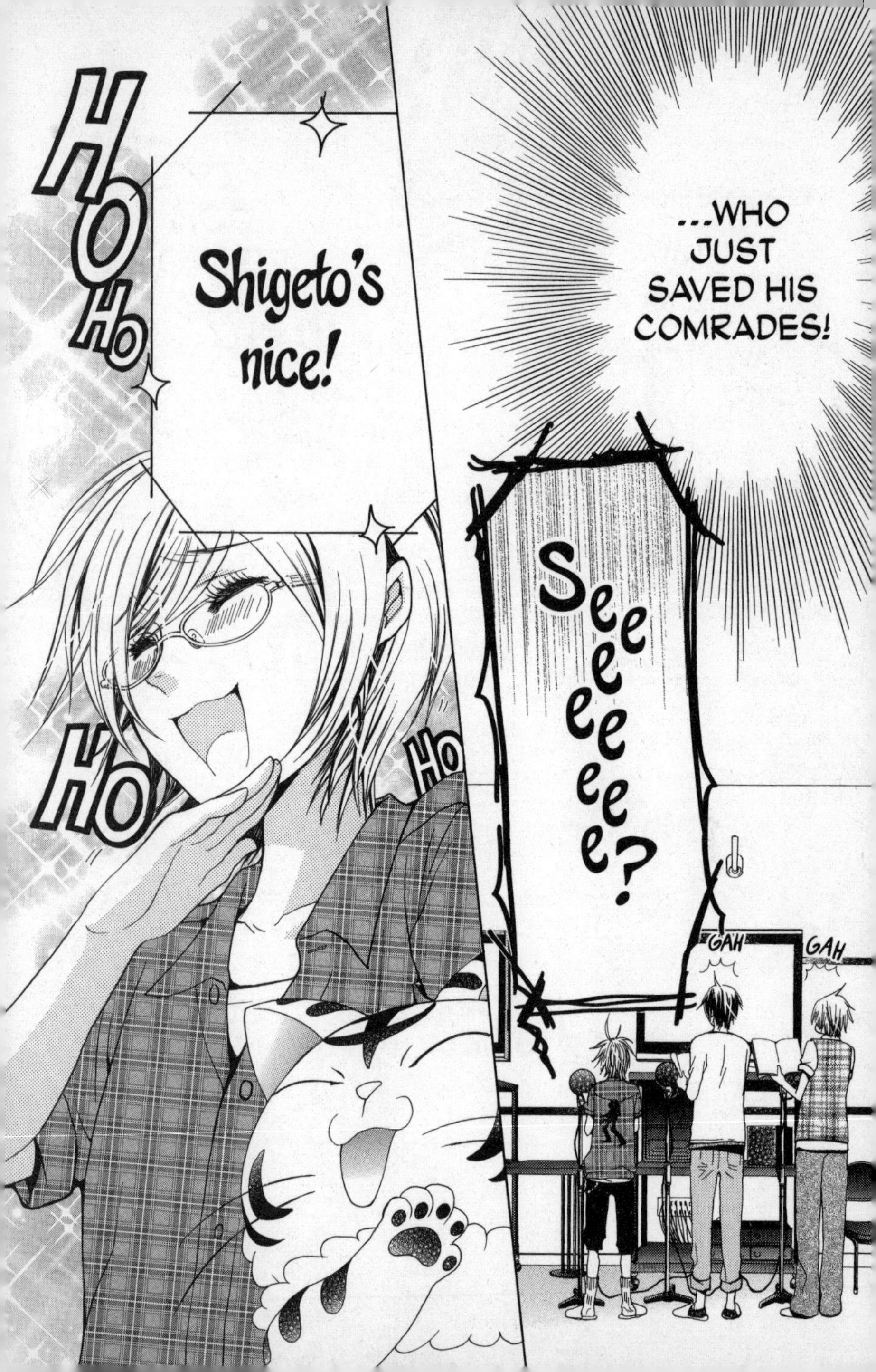
...WHO JUST SAVED HIS COMRADES!
Seeeeeeeee?
GAH
GAH
Shigeto's nice!
HOHOHo
HO
Ho

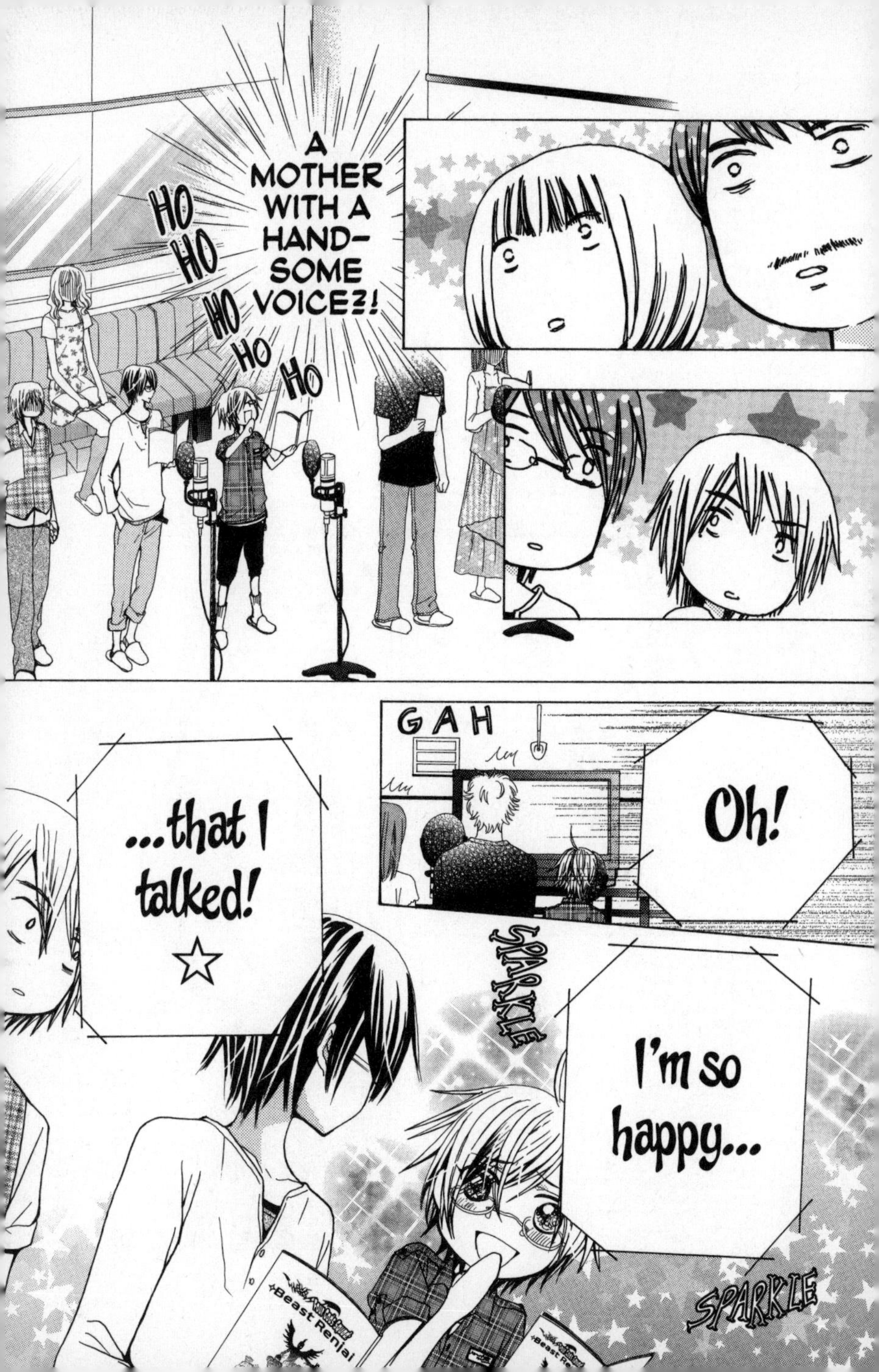
A MOTHER WITH A HAND-SOME VOICE?!
HO HO HO HO HO
GAH
Oh!
SPARKLE
I'm so happy...
SPARKLE
...that I talked! ☆
Beast Renjai

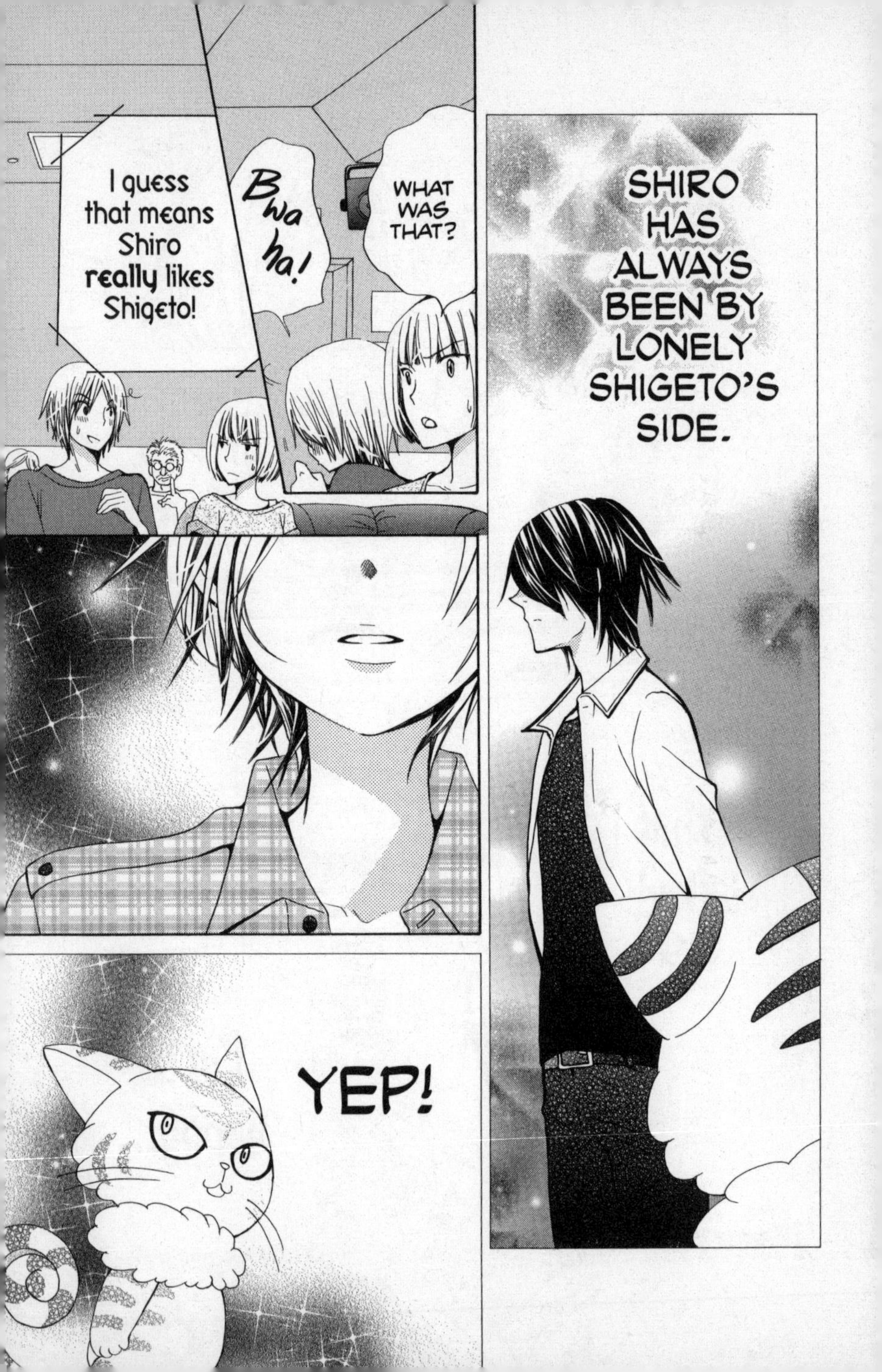
WHAT WAS THAT?
Bwa ha!
I guess that means Shiro really likes Shigeto!
YEP!
SHIRO HAS ALWAYS BEEN BY LONELY SHIGETO'S SIDE.

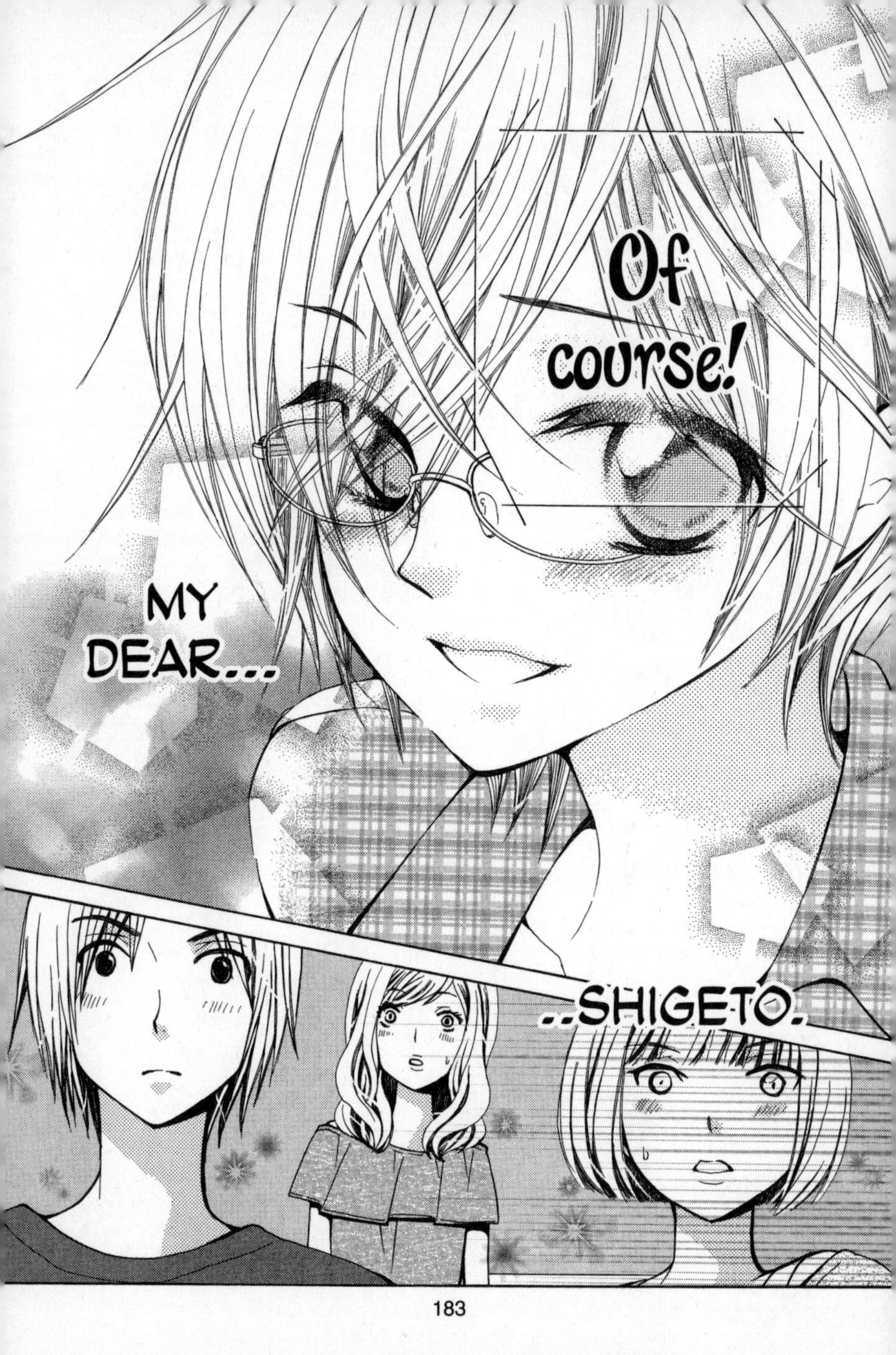
Of course!
MY DEAR...
...SHIGETO.

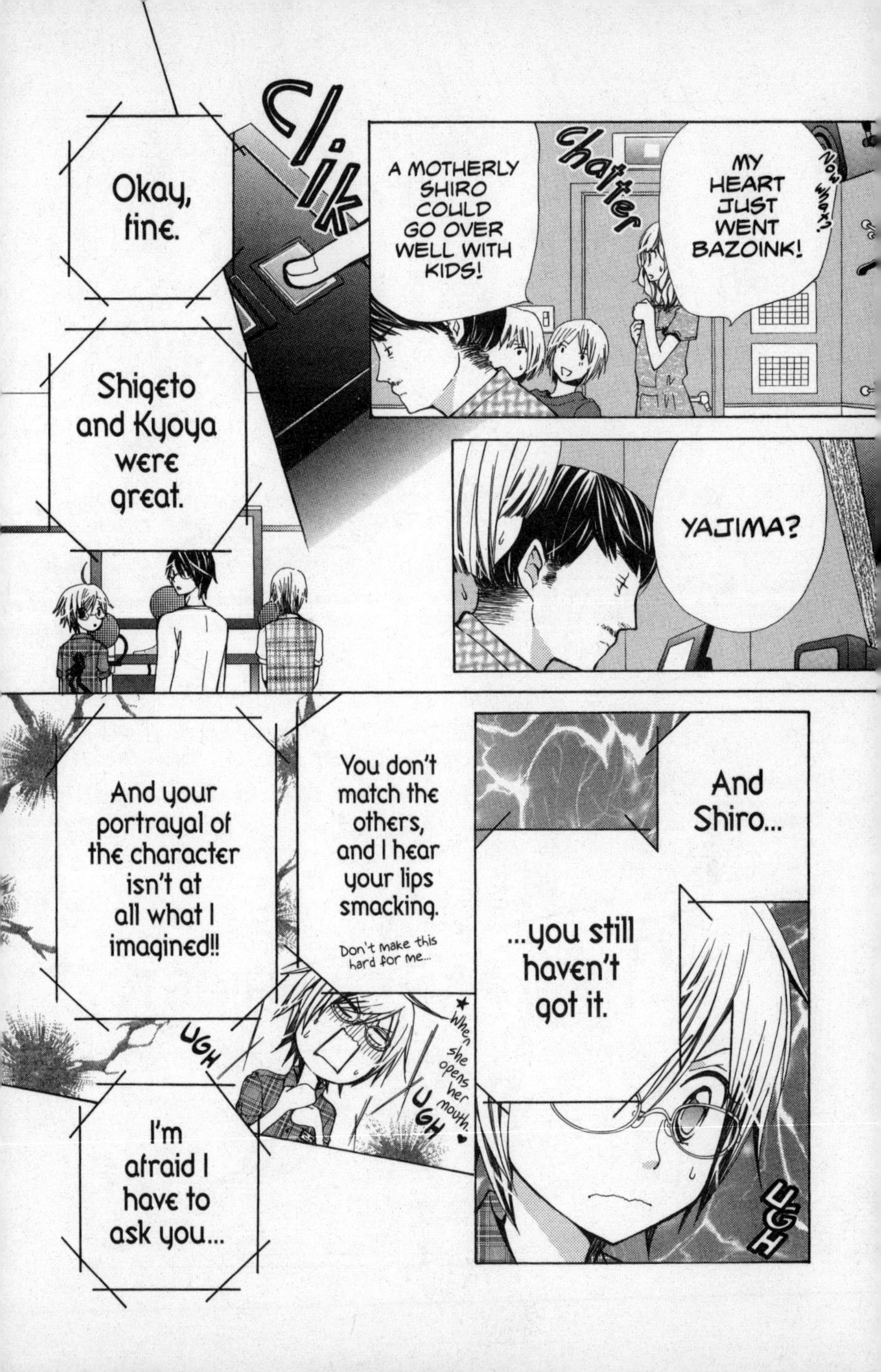
chatter
MY HEART JUST WENT BAZOINK!
Now what?!
A MOTHERLY SHIRO COULD GO OVER WELL WITH KIDS!
YAJIMA?
Click
Okay, fine.
Shigeto and Kyoya were great.
And Shiro...
...you still haven't got it.
UGH
You don't match the others, and I hear your lips smacking.
Don't make this hard for me...
★ When she opens her mouth.♥
UGH
UGH
And your portrayal of the character isn't at all what I imagined!!
I'm afraid I have to ask you...

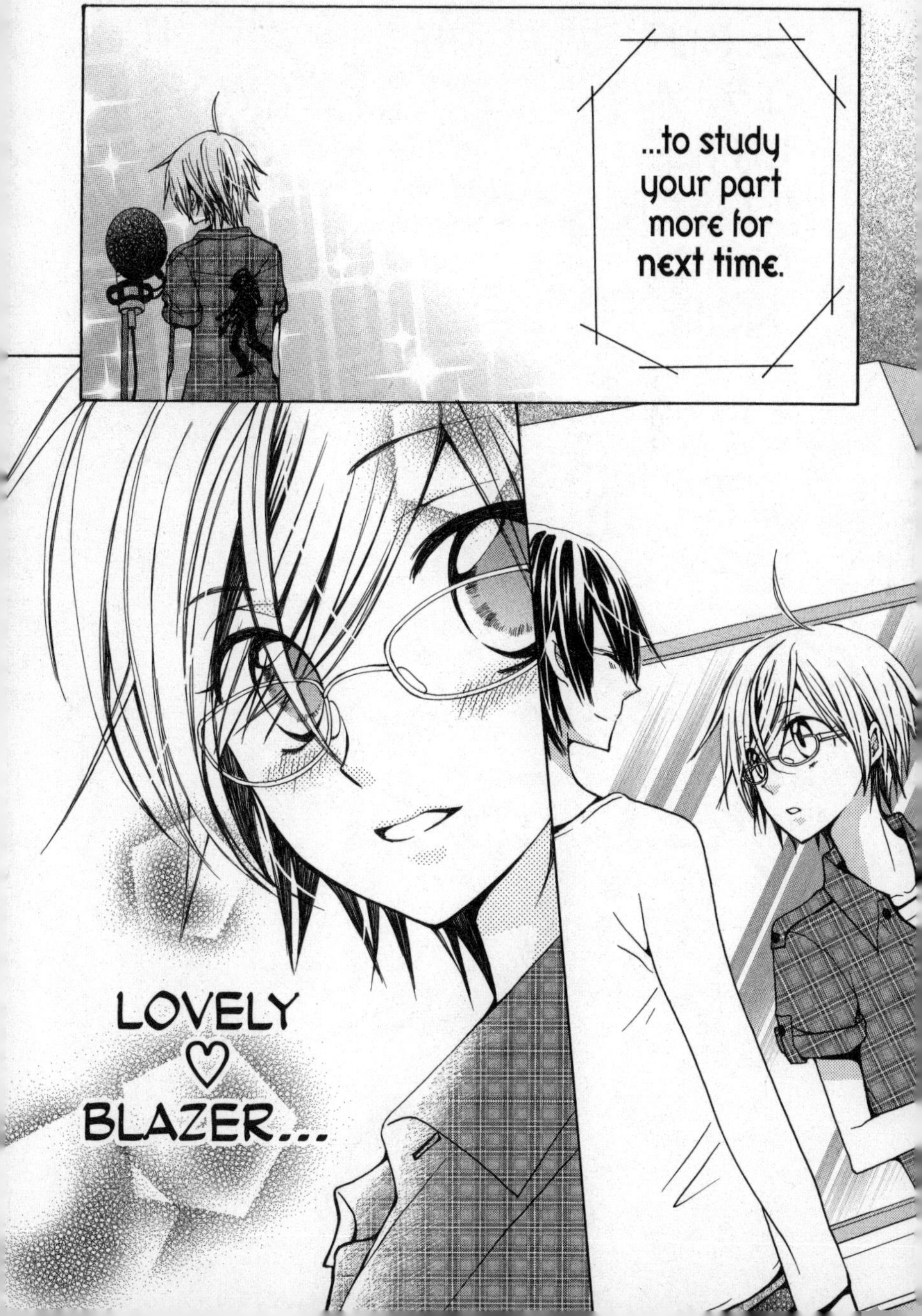
...to study your part more for next time.
LOVELY ♡ BLAZER...

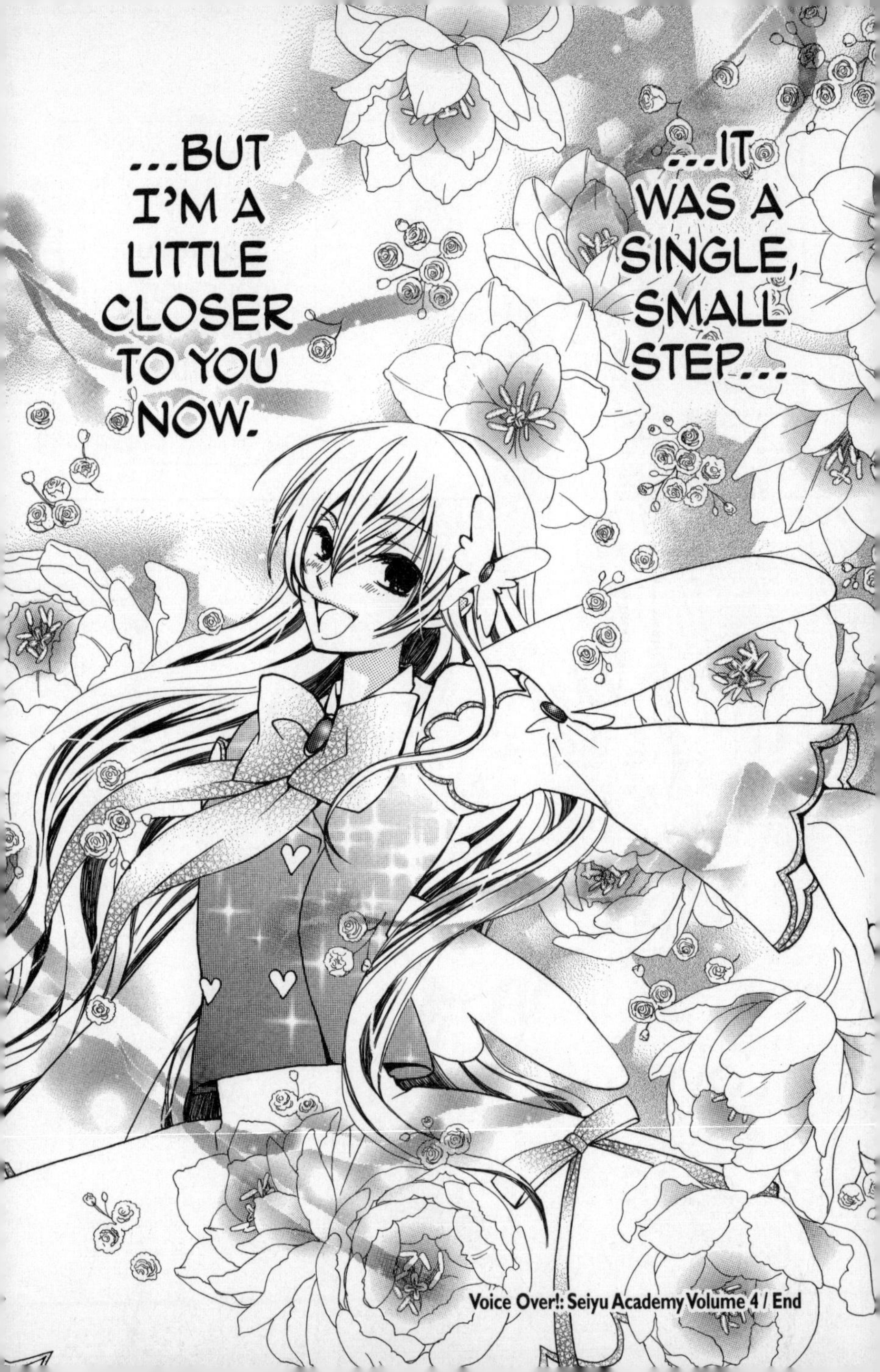
...IT WAS A SINGLE, SMALL STEP...
...BUT I'M A LITTLE CLOSER TO YOU NOW.
Voice Over!: Seiyu Academy Volume 4 / End

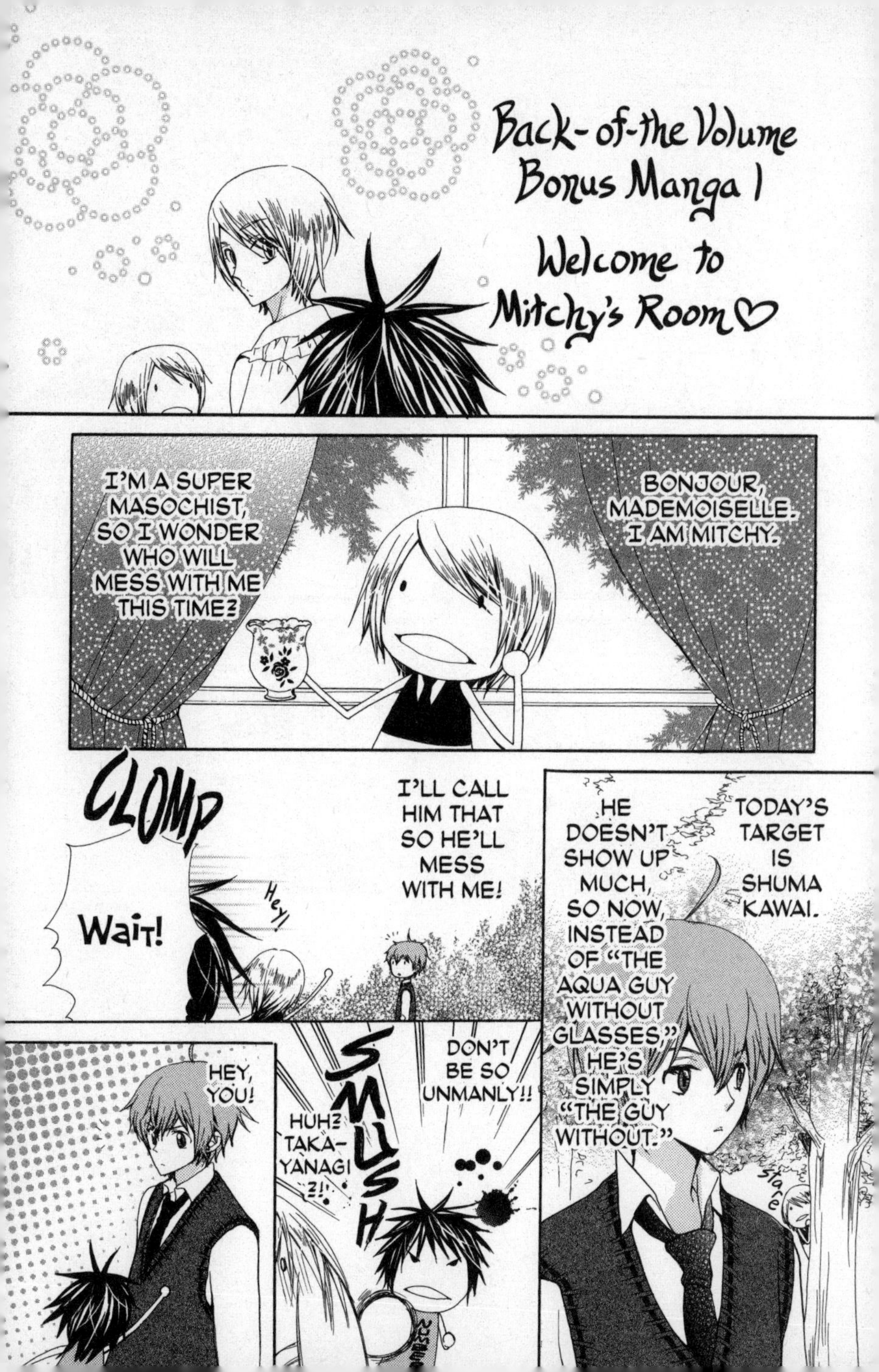
Back-of-the Volume Bonus Manga 1
Welcome to Mitchy's Room ♡
BONJOUR, MADEMOISELLE. I AM MITCHY.
I'M A SUPER MASOCHIST, SO I WONDER WHO WILL MESS WITH ME THIS TIME?
TODAY'S TARGET IS SHUMA KAWAI.
HE DOESN'T SHOW UP MUCH, SO NOW, INSTEAD OF "THE AQUA GUY WITHOUT GLASSES," HE'S SIMPLY "THE GUY WITHOUT."
Stare
I'LL CALL HIM THAT SO HE'LL MESS WITH ME!
Hey!
CLOMP
Wait!
DON'T BE SO UNMANLY!!
SMUSH
HUH? TAKA-YANAGI?!
HEY, YOU!

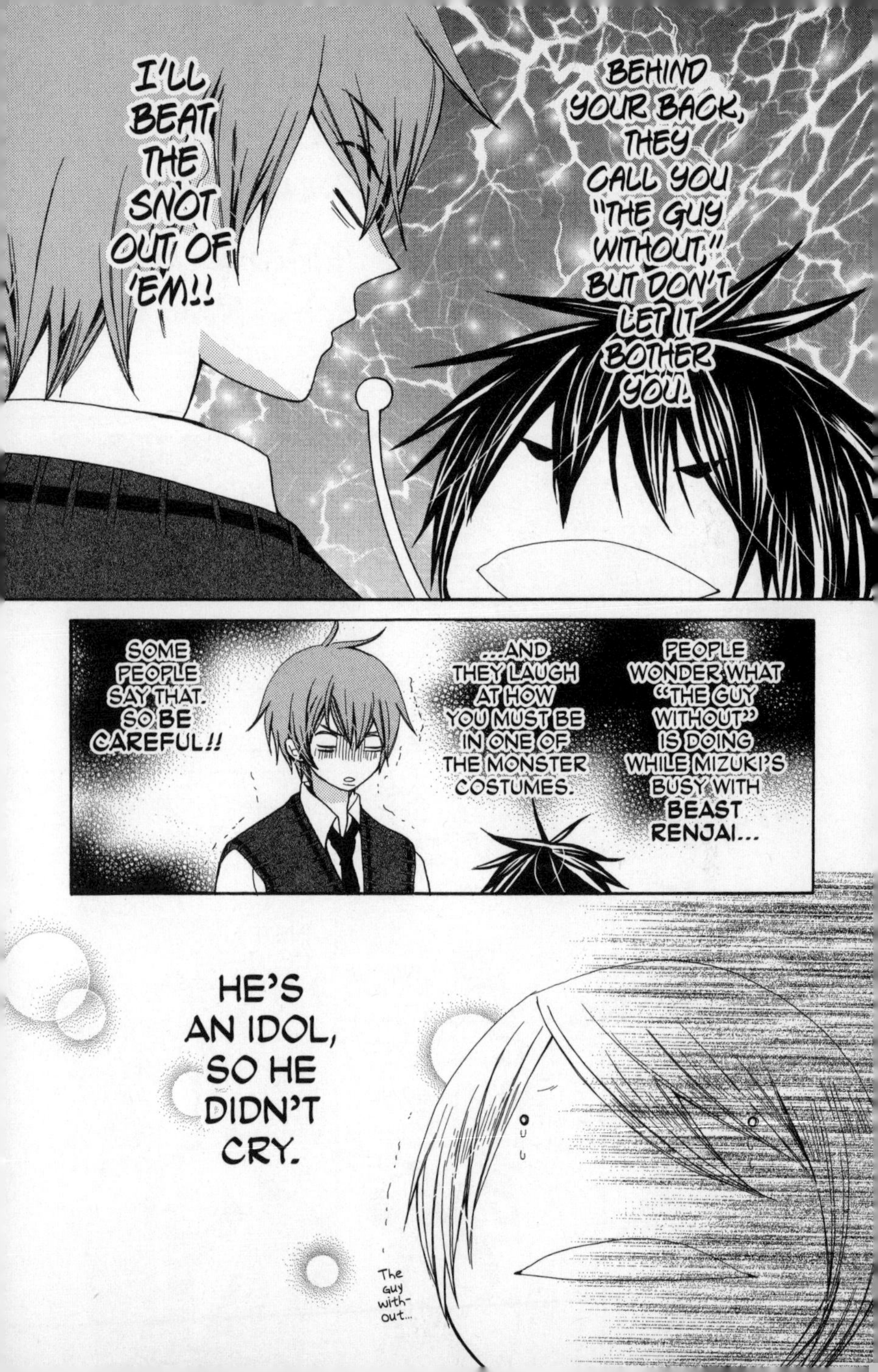
BEHIND YOUR BACK, THEY CALL YOU "THE GUY WITHOUT," BUT DON'T LET IT BOTHER YOU.
I'LL BEAT THE SNOT OUT OF 'EM!!
PEOPLE WONDER WHAT "THE GUY WITHOUT" IS DOING WHILE MIZUKI'S BUSY WITH BEAST RENJAI...
...AND THEY LAUGH AT HOW YOU MUST BE IN ONE OF THE MONSTER COSTUMES.
SOME PEOPLE SAY THAT. SO BE CAREFUL!!
HE'S AN IDOL, SO HE DIDN'T CRY.
The guy with-out...

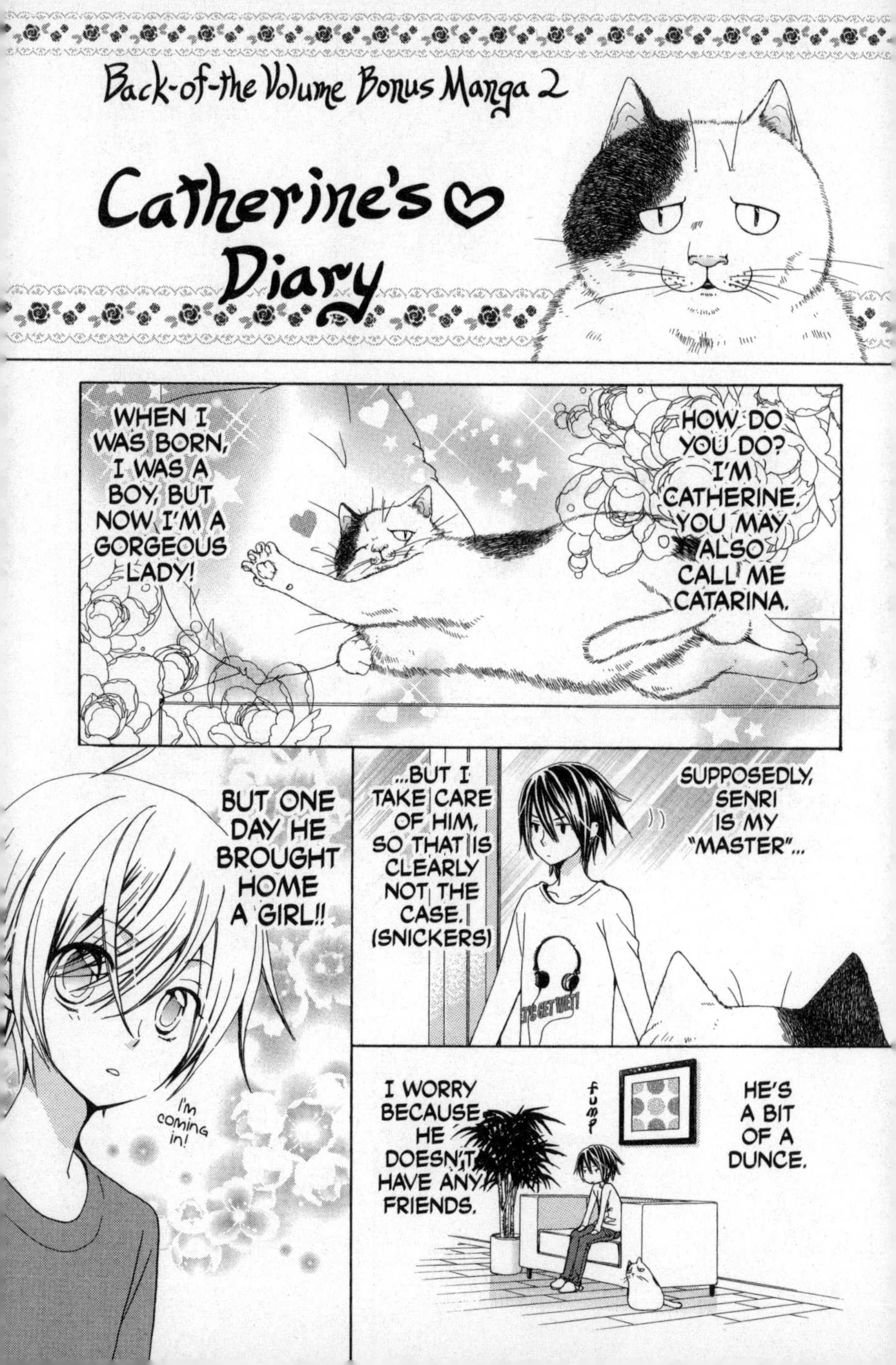
Back-of-the Volume Bonus Manga 2
Catherine's Diary
HOW DO YOU DO? I'M CATHERINE. YOU MAY ALSO CALL ME CATARINA.
WHEN I WAS BORN, I WAS A BOY, BUT NOW I'M A GORGEOUS LADY!
SUPPOSEDLY, SENRI IS MY "MASTER"...
...BUT I TAKE CARE OF HIM, SO THAT IS CLEARLY NOT THE CASE. (SNICKERS)
LET'S GET WET!
HE'S A BIT OF A DUNCE.
FUMP
I WORRY BECAUSE HE DOESN'T HAVE ANY FRIENDS.
BUT ONE DAY HE BROUGHT HOME A GIRL!!
I'm coming in!

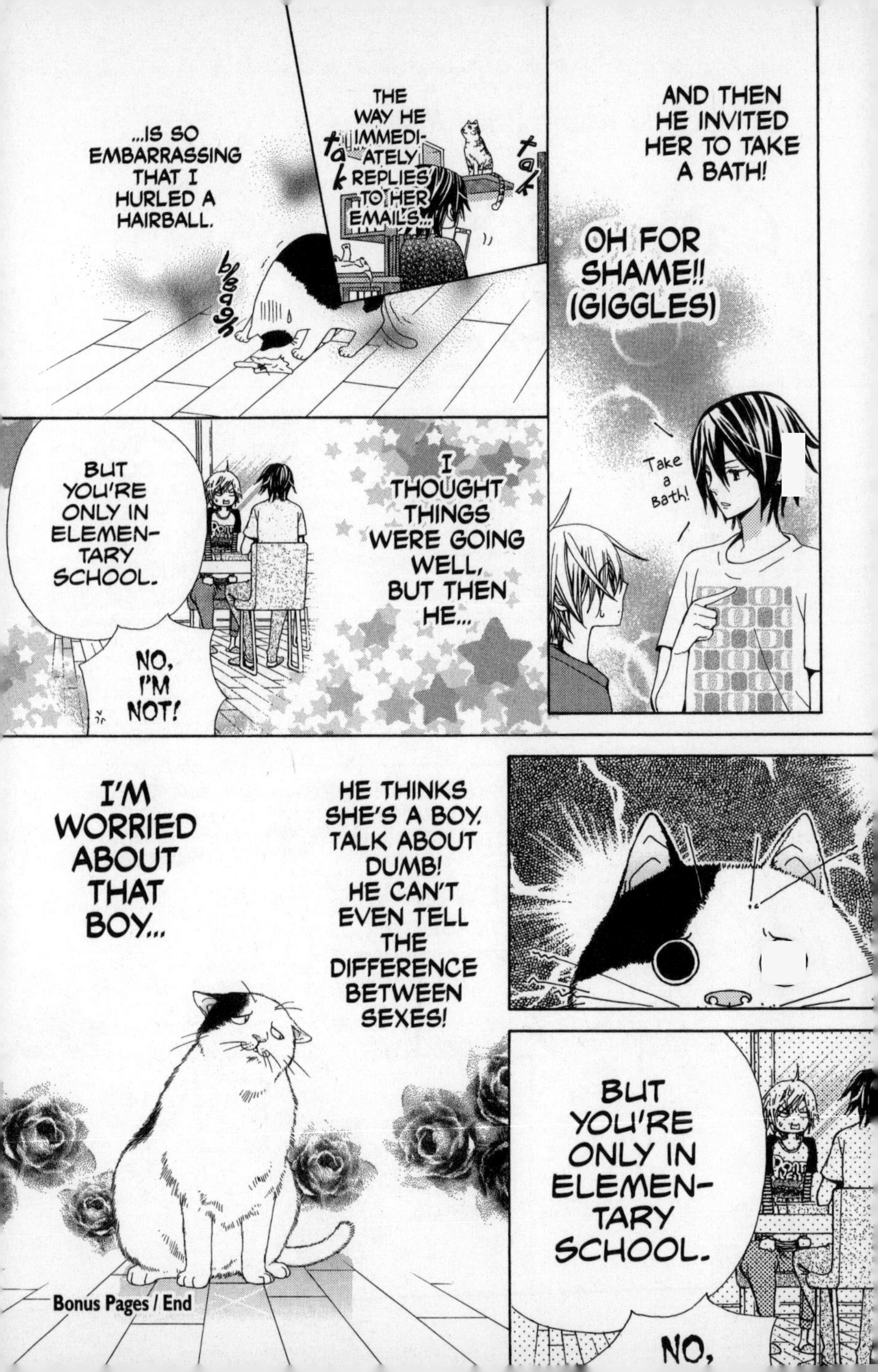
AND THEN HE INVITED HER TO TAKE A BATH!
OH FOR SHAME!! (GIGGLES)
Take a Bath!
THE WAY HE IMMEDI-ATELY REPLIES TO HER EMAILS...
tak
tak
...IS SO EMBARRASSING THAT I HURLED A HAIRBALL.
bleagh
I THOUGHT THINGS WERE GOING WELL, BUT THEN HE...
BUT YOU'RE ONLY IN ELEMEN-TARY SCHOOL.
NO, I'M NOT!
BUT YOU'RE ONLY IN ELEMEN-TARY SCHOOL.
NO,
HE THINKS SHE'S A BOY. TALK ABOUT DUMB! HE CAN'T EVEN TELL THE DIFFERENCE BETWEEN SEXES!
I'M WORRIED ABOUT THAT BOY...

Bonus Pages / End

Voice Over! Seiyu Academy

End Notes

Page 18, panel 5: Divine beasts
Four mythical creatures from Chinese mythology that each represent a cardinal direction and season. They are Seiryu, the Azure Dragon of the East; Suzaku, the Vermillion Bird of the South; Byakko, the White Tiger of the West; and Genbu, the Black Tortoise of the North. They appear in many myths and stories throughout history.

Page 34, side bar: Hamburger steak
Hamburger steaks are ground meat mixed with bread crumbs, egg, sauteed onions and sauce and served on a plate rather than on a bun. Sometimes they are topped with a fried egg.

Page 98, panel 1: Yakiniku
This literally means "grilled meat." At yakiniku restaurants, you cook various meats and vegetables on a small tabletop grill.

Page 131, panel 1: Skytree
A tower in Tokyo, similar to Seattle's Space Needle.

Maki Minami is from Saitama Prefecture in Japan. She debuted in 2001 with *Kanata no Ao* (Faraway Blue). Her other works include *Kimi wa Girlfriend* (You're My Girlfriend), *Mainichi ga Takaramono* (Every Day Is a Treasure), *Yuki Atataka* (Warm Winter) and *S•A*, which was published in English by VIZ Media.

VOICE OVER!
SEIYU ACADEMY
VOL. 4
Shojo Beat Edition

STORY AND ART BY
MAKI MINAMI

TECHNICAL ADVISORS
Yoichi Kato, Kaori Kagami, Ayumi Hashidate,
Ayako Harino and Touko Fujitani

Special Thanks
81produce
Tokyo Animator College
Tokyo Animation College

English Translation & Adaptation/John Werry
Touch-up Art & Lettering/Sabrina Heep
Design/Yukiko Whitley
Editor/Pancha Diaz

SEIYU KA! by Maki Minami
© Maki Minami 2010
All rights reserved.
First published in Japan in 2010 by HAKUSENSHA, Inc., Tokyo.
English language translation rights arranged with
HAKUSENSHA, Inc., Tokyo.

Printed in the U.S.A.

Published by VIZ Media, LLC
P.O. Box 77010
San Francisco, CA 94107

10 9 8 7 6 5 4 3 2 1
First printing, April 2014

www.viz.com   www.shojobeat.com

PARENTAL ADVISORY
VOICE OVER!: SEIYU ACADEMY is rated
T for Teen and is recommended for ages
13 and up.
ratings.viz.com

Kyoko Mogami followed her true love Sho to Tokyo to support him while he made it big as an idol. But he's casting her out now that he's famous enough! Kyoko won't suffer in silence— she's going to get her sweet revenge by beating Sho in show biz!

Vol. 1 ISBN: 978-1-4215-4226-3

Vol. 2 ISBN: 978-1-4215-4227-0

Vol. 3 ISBN: 978-1-4215-4228-7

Only $14.99 for each volume! ($16.99 in Canada)

Show biz is sweet...but revenge is sweeter!

Skip·Beat!

Story and Art by YOSHIKI NAKAMURA

In Stores Now!

www.viz.com

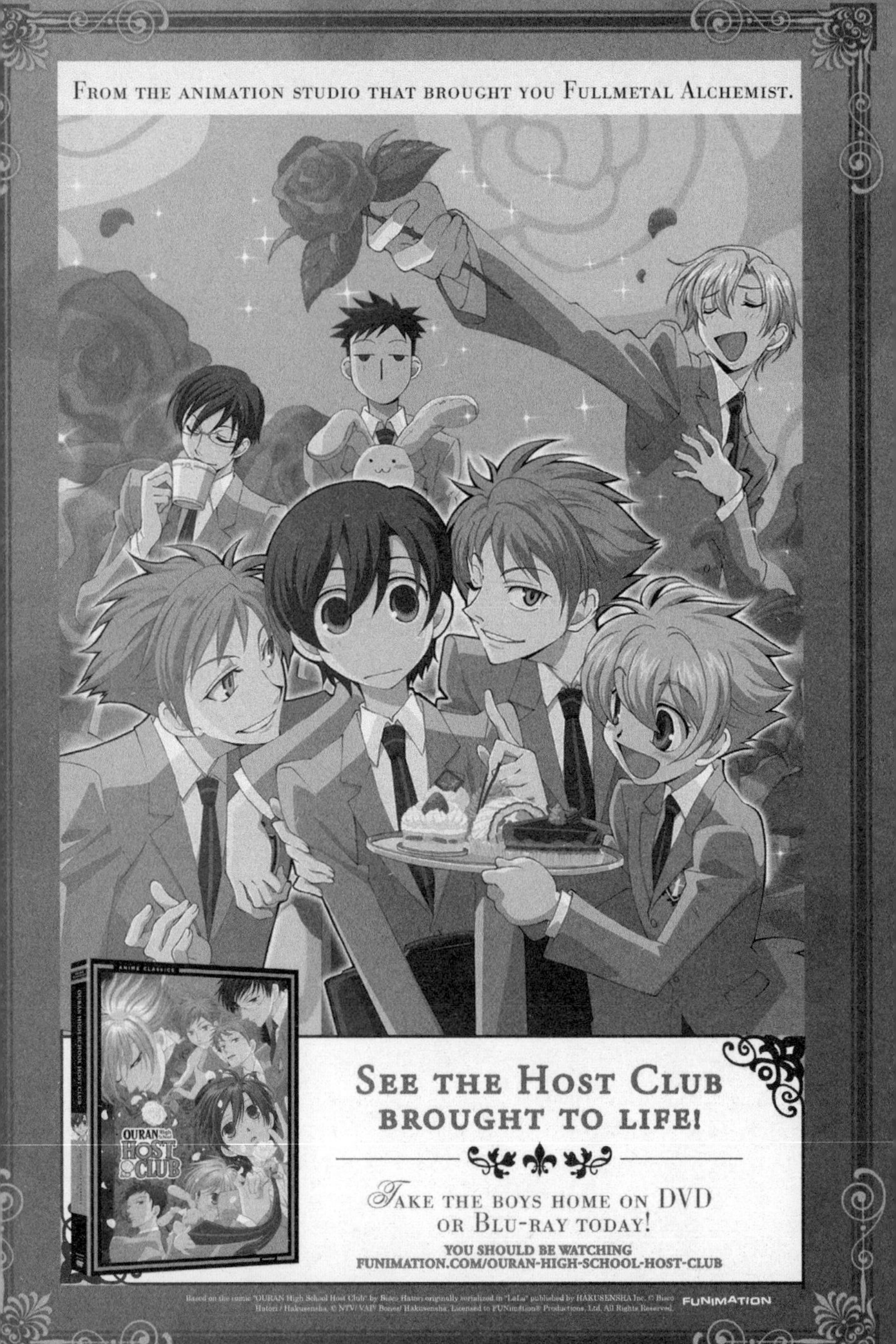

FROM THE ANIMATION STUDIO THAT BROUGHT YOU FULLMETAL ALCHEMIST.
OURAN High School HOST CLUB
SEE THE HOST CLUB BROUGHT TO LIFE!
TAKE THE BOYS HOME ON DVD OR BLU-RAY TODAY!
YOU SHOULD BE WATCHING
FUNIMATION.COM/OURAN-HIGH-SCHOOL-HOST-CLUB
Based on the comic "OURAN High School Host Club" by Bisco Hatori originally serialized in "LaLa" published by HAKUSENSHA Inc. © Bisco Hatori / Hakusensha. © NTV/ VAP/ Bones/ Hakusensha. Licensed to FUNimation® Productions, Ltd. All Rights Reserved.
FUNIMATION